Get the eBook FREE!

(PDF, ePub, Kindle, and liveBook all included)

We believe that once you buy a book from us, you should be able to read it in any format we have available. To get electronic versions of this book at no additional cost to you, purchase and then register this book at the Manning website.

Go to https://www.manning.com/freebook and follow the instructions to complete your pBook registration.

That's it!
Thanks from Manning!

Secret Key Cryptography

CIPHERS, FROM SIMPLE TO UNBREAKABLE

FRANK RUBIN

Foreword by RANDALL K. NICHOLS

MANNING

SHELTER ISLAND

For online information and ordering of this and other Manning books, please visit
www.manning.com. The publisher offers discounts on this book when ordered in quantity.
For more information, please contact

    Special Sales Department
    Manning Publications Co.
    20 Baldwin Road
    PO Box 761
    Shelter Island, NY 11964
    Email: orders@manning.com

 Manning Publications Co.
    20 Baldwin Road
    PO Box 761
    Shelter Island, NY 11964

Development editor: Marina Michaels
Review editors: Aleksandar Dragosavljević
Production editor: Keri Hales
Copy editor: Tiffany Taylor
Typesetter: Dennis Dalinnik
Cover designer: Marija Tudor

ISBN: 9781633439795
Printed and bound by CPI Group (UK) Ltd, Croydon, CR0 4YY

contents

iii

foreword

From secret decoder rings to government policy statements, the challenges of hiding and discovering information within other information have long compelled the intellect. Cryptology is a fascinating subject with which almost every schoolchild has some hands-on familiarity. And yet, for good reasons, it is a discipline that throughout time has been shrouded in the deepest levels of secrecy and used by governments to protect their most sensitive weapons. Cryptography's role in military and diplomatic affairs has always been deadly serious. It is no exaggeration to declare that successes and failures of cryptography have shaped the outcome of wars and the course of history; nor is it an exaggeration to state that the successes and failures of cryptography are setting our current course of history.

Consider the American Civil war battle of Antietam in September of 1862, when George McClellan commanded the Union forces against Robert E. Lee's Confederate forces near Sharpsburg, Maryland. A few days earlier, two Union soldiers had found a piece of paper near their camp, which turned out to be a copy of an order issued by Lee detailing his plans for the invasion of Maryland. The order had not been encrypted. With the information it contained, McClellan precisely knew the location of the commands of Lee's scattered army and was able to destroy Lee's army before they reunited.

Cryptographic successes and failures have shaped more recent history as well. The terrible Russian failure at Tannenberg in August 1914 was the direct result of the German army's intercept of Russian communications. Amazingly, the Russian communications were totally in the clear because the Russians had not equipped their field commanders with ciphers and keys. The Russians were thus unable to securely coordinate the activities of neighboring units within each army.

What was to become 50 years of Cold War following WWII was also set up by a cryptographic failure, this time on the Japanese at the Battle of Midway in 1942. American cryptanalysts broke the Japanese codes and were reading many of the messages of the Combined Fleet. Stories like these are within the purview of classical cryptography. *Secret Key Cryptography* plays in this sandbox.

No one is more capable of enlightening an interested reader in all of the dimensions of recreational classical cryptology, from its mathematical heritage to its sociological implications, than Dr. Frank Rubin. Dr. Rubin's education is in mathematics and computer science. He worked for 30 years at IBM in the Design Automation field and did cryptography for over 50 years. Dr. Rubin served as an editor for Cryptologia and other publications. He has written dozens of mathematics and computer algorithms and has created thousands of mathematical puzzles.

Secret Key Cryptography is more than an update to the classic *Elementary Cryptanalysis* by Helen F. Gaines. It covers the field from ancient times through the era of quantum computers. *Secret Key Cryptography* presents new methods and "cracking" technologies. Lastly, it explains a unique method to measure the strength of a cipher.[1,2]

The book comes at a strategic point in this evolving history. It provides a timely and important contribution to understanding this critical technology. Whether the reader is seeking edification about cryptology itself or is a practitioner of information security, the depth, and breadth of knowledge included in these pages will be a welcome source of useful information and valuable addition to a library.

—Randall K. Nichols, DTM

Randall K. Nichols is a former president, aristocrat, and book review editor for the American Cryptogram Association (ACA); the director of the Unmanned Aircraft Systems Cybersecurity Certificate Program at Kansas State University, Salina; and professor emeritus of Graduate Cybersecurity and Forensics at Utica College.

REFERENCES

Gaines, H. F. (1956). *Cryptanalysis: A Study of Ciphers and their Solution.* NYC: Dover.

LANAKI. (1998). *Classical Cryptography Course Vol. I.* Laguna Hills, CA: Aegean Park Press.

LANAKI. (1999). *Classical Cryptography Course Vol. II.* Laguna Hills, CA: Aegean Park Press.

Nichols, R. K. (1999). *ICSA Guide to Cryptography.* New York City: McGraw Hill.

Rubin, F. (2022). *Secret Key Cryptography.* Shelter Island, New York: Manning Books.

Schneier, B. (1995). *Applied Cryptography: Protocols, Algorithms and Source Code in C.* New York: John Wiley & Sons.

---

[1] Both *ICSA Guide to Cryptography* by R. K. Nichols and *Applied Cryptography* by Bruce Schneier present cipher strength and randomness methods. The former concentrates on classical cryptography, and the latter concentrates on modern ciphers (Nichols, 1999; Schneier, 1995).

[2] *Secret Key Cryptography* is better defined and written than my first two books on classical cryptography, namely, *Classical Cryptography Course Vols. I & II* (LANAKI, 1998; 1999).

preface

There are several threads that led to the writing of this book. Let's begin with my high school friend Charlie Rose. Charlie worked in the school bookstore. One day, while ordering books for the store, he noticed the book *Cryptanalysis* by Helen F. Gaines. Charlie wanted the book, and he also wanted the employee discount. But there was a hitch. The minimum order the store could place was three copies.

Charlie needed to get two other people to buy the book. He promised that we would all read the book together, then make up cryptograms that the others would solve. I bought the book, read it, and made up cryptograms, but Charlie had lost interest.

The back cover of *Cryptanalysis* had a long-outdated street address for the American Cryptogram Association (www.cryptogram.org) but I tracked them down and joined. I started solving the many types of cryptograms they published in their hobbyist newsletter, *The Cryptogram*, and after a few years I became an assistant editor. I remained a member for over 40 years.

In 1977 a more professional journal of cryptography, called *Cryptologia*, began. You can find it at https://www.tandfonline.com/toc/ucry20/current. I started reading the articles, then contributing articles, and then became an editor. Somehow I became the "crackpot handler." Those articles all came to me, and I had to find my way through the illogical logic to see if a good idea was hidden inside. In just one case there was. I turned that into an article for *The Cryptogram*. The author was so grateful he planted a tree in Israel in my honor.

This experience taught me how to separate those articles that were just badly written or where the author had simply overestimated the strength of the cipher from those that were truly off the wall. This is what I learned: the amateur with a weak cipher can describe the cipher and write out the steps. The true crackpots cannot get their vague and grandiose imaginings onto paper. They can write reams about how wonderful their ciphers are, but they cannot write out the steps. They cannot turn their inchoate thoughts into a concrete algorithm.

Starting around 2005, I started taking courses at Marist College CLS, Continuing Life Studies. Soon I was giving lectures on Sudoku, SumSum and other puzzles (I have written three books of Sudoku puzzles); my travels in Tanzania and Mongolia; the construction of the Empire State Building; the life of Alan Turing; and other subjects. I became part of the curriculum committee.

In 2018 I volunteered to give a two-semester course on cryptography. While creating the nearly 450 slides I needed for the course, I realized I had enough material for a book. Fortunately, I discovered that a year earlier I had started writing just such a book. This one.

acknowledgments

The other day I overheard my wife, Miriam, speaking to a friend on the phone, "It is like I am in a *ménage à trois*, me, Frank and the book." Thank you, Miriam, for your forbearance during the 18 months it took to write the book, the year searching for a publisher, the 6 months hunting for a literary agent, the year watching the literary agent get no results, and finally the single month to find a home for this book at Manning. Plus over 18 months of reviewing, revising, editing, revising, typesetting, revising, indexing, writing marketing copy, and more.

I thank all of the people at Manning Publications who helped with this book, especially Michael Stephens who took a chance and offered me a contract, and who helped at every stage of the process; Marina Michaels for her many editorial improvements; Rebecca Rinehart for smoothing the path; Jen Houle and Susan Honeywell for their work on the illustrations; Tiffany Taylor for her many valuable suggestions on: grammar and punctuation; Paul Wells and Keri Hales for their work on the production of the book; Sam Wood for the marketing copy; Dennis Dalinnik for the typesetting; and, of course, Marjan Bace, the publisher.

Special thanks to Prof. Randall K. Nichols for writing the book's foreword and a review in *The Cryptogram* on very short notice. Thanks also to Prof. Thomas Perera of the Enigma Museum for providing the Fialka images.

Thanks to the reviewers who read the manuscript and made numerous suggestions and useful criticisms: Christopher Kardell, Alex Lucas, Gabor Hajba, Michal Rutka, Jason Taylor, Roy Prins, Matthew Harvell, Riccardo Marotti, and Paul Love. Your suggestions helped make this a better book.

Finally, I must acknowledge the unwitting role of Lee Harvey Oswald, whose heinous assassination of Pres. John F. Kennedy prevented me from taking a security interview at FBI headquarters, which prevented me from joining the NSA, which would have made it a felony for me to write this book.

about this book

Who should read this book?

This book is aimed at a broad range of readers: general readers, cryptography hobbyists, history buffs, computer science students, electrical engineers, mathematicians, and professional cryptographers. This makes my job harder, because it is impossible to make every part of the book suitable for every type of reader. Some parts of the book may need too much math for some readers. Some parts may be too elementary for some readers. In this section I attempt to guide readers to what I think is the most appropriate material for them.

- **General readers** can read straight through to the end of chapter 8. Simply skip anything where the math is too hard, or the exposition is too technical. From chapter 9 on it starts to get sticky. They can skim from this point on, and pick out the topics of interest. They may want to read chapter 12 to get the general gist, without getting into the details.
- **Cryptography hobbyists** will probably want to read the entire book, then come back for a more detailed look at sections 4.2 to 5.11, 6.1 to 6.5, 6.7, most of chapter 7, and sections 9.1 to 9.9, plus the Fun Pages and the Challenge page.
- **History buffs** can read the entire book, ignoring the math, to get the timeline of when each method was developed, and by whom.
- **Computer science students** may put special emphasis on sections 5.6 to 5.11, chapter 8, and chapters 11 to 16.

- **Electrical engineers** will be looking for practical methods. They should first read chapters 2 and 4 for a basic grounding, then read sections 7.2 to 7.8, chapter 9, and chapters 11 to 16, with special emphasis on chapter 12.
- **Mathematicians** will be most interested in section 4.5, sections 5.6 to 5.12, sections 10.4 to 10.7, sections 11.7 to 11.10, sections 12.3 to 12.6, chapters 13 to 16, especially section 16.4.6, and chapter 18.
- **Professional cryptographers** will be most interested in sections 7.8, 8.2, 10.5, 10.7, 11.4, 12.3 to 12.6, 13.8, 13.15, 14.2, 14.4, 15.4 to 15.14, 16.4, 16.5, and 18.12.

About the ciphers

I have included a number of Fun Ciphers and Challenge Ciphers for readers who want to try their hand at solving. The Fun Ciphers use standard methods described in the book.

The Challenge Ciphers use methods that I have invented myself. They are simple enough that an amateur hobbyist could both guess the methods, and solve them. I have tried to be fair so that interested readers can solve them. Nothing bizarre or complex. No weird words or distorted letter frequencies. And sufficient material for solving them.

You may notice some sections that begin with a bold * and end with **. These are optional sections that may contain computer algorithms or deeper math. Some readers may choose to skip these.

liveBook discussion forum

Purchase of *Secret Key Cryptography* includes free access to liveBook, Manning's online reading platform. Using liveBook's exclusive discussion features, you can attach comments to the book globally or to specific sections or paragraphs. It's a snap to make notes for yourself, ask and answer technical questions, and receive help from the author and other users. To access the forum, go to https://livebook.manning.com/book/secret-key-cryptography/discussion. You can also learn more about Manning's forums and the rules of conduct at https://livebook.manning.com/discussion.

Manning's commitment to our readers is to provide a venue where a meaningful dialogue between individual readers and between readers and the author can take place. It is not a commitment to any specific amount of participation on the part of the author, whose contribution to the forum remains voluntary (and unpaid). The forum and the archives of previous discussions will be accessible from the publisher's website as long as the book is in print.

Other online resources

You can find the author's cryptographic products at his website, www.mastersoftware.biz.

about the author

FRANK RUBIN holds a BS and MS in mathematics and a PhD in computer science. He worked for 28 years at IBM in the design automation field, where he designed and wrote specialized software that IBM engineers used to design computers and circuits. He is the owner of Master Software Corp. which produces cryptographic software. Frank has been issued four U.S. patents on cryptographic methods. Frank has about 50 papers published in refereed journals on cryptography, computer circuits, graph theory and pure mathematics, plus several books (user manuals and project specifications) published internally at IBM. In cryptography he is best known for solving the Jefferson Cypher Wheel. In computer science Frank is best known for arithmetic coding, now one of the standard methods for text compression, and for his algorithm for finding Hamilton paths. In pure mathematics he is probably best known for introducing the concept of a finite-state recognizer to measure theory. Frank has three published books of Sudoku puzzles and two self-published books of SumSum puzzles. He is the author of more than 3,500 puzzles published in *The Cryptogram, Technology Review,* and *Journal of Recreational Mathematics,* and he is the only person ever honored by having a special issue of *JRM* dedicated entirely to his own puzzles.

about the cover illustration

The figure on the cover of *Secret Key Cryptography* is "Le Garçon de Bureau," or "Office Assistant," taken from a book edited by Louis Curmer, published in 1841. Each illustration is finely drawn and colored by hand.

In those days, it was easy to identify where people lived and what their trade or station in life was just by their dress. Manning celebrates the inventiveness and initiative of today's computer business with book covers based on the rich diversity of regional culture centuries ago, brought back to life by pictures from collections such as this one.

Introduction 1

I have been doing cryptography for more than 50 years. I have learned a great deal in that time. In this book I try to pass along that knowledge to the next generation of cryptographers. Much of this is new discoveries, not found anywhere else in the literature.

I know that there are many cryptography books already available. If I want people to read my book, I need to offer ideas that other books don't have, ideas other authors don't know, or believe are impossible. I need to make the book **SENSATIONAL**. Here goes. I will

- Tell you in simple non-technical language how to construct an unbreakable cipher.
- Provide 140 ciphers that you can use as is. 30 of them are rated Unbreakable.
- Give you a set of tools and techniques so you can combine and strengthen them.
- Describe a computation that can precisely measure the strength of your cipher, and guarantee that it is unbreakable.
- Show how to construct and incorporate data-compression codes.
- Reveal a practical method to achieve the unbreakable One-Time Pad cipher.
- Tell how to generate true random numbers in bulk.
- Show how to construct huge primes and safe primes.
- Teach you how to add an undetectable backdoor to a cipher.
- Expose a possibly fatal flaw in quantum cryptography.
- Explain ways to defeat hypothetical ultracomputers that could be developed decades from now. (Or, that may already exist, but are classified.)

I use a conversational tone throughout the book, as though you and I were speaking face-to-face. When I say "us" or "we," that means you, the reader, and me, the author, working together, cooperating to solve a problem or to guard a secret.

This is not intended to be a scholarly work. I give credit for the methods and ideas when I know the sources, and dates as close as I can remember them, but much of what I have learned was acquired informally. There is little in the way of references, footnotes or erudite exegesis. This is written to be a practical book. Follow its recommendations, and you will produce a secure cipher. Guaranteed.

I also throw in an occasional historical tidbit, partly to lighten the mood, and partly to set the historic record straight. I know a heavy subject like cryptography can be hard going. I hope the use of first person, the little anecdotes and a bit of humor make it easier to absorb.

Much of the material in this book is new. It has methods for constructing ciphers and methods for cracking ciphers that have never been published before. There are even a few of my own mathematical discoveries. You can find them only in this book. There are lots of practical tips on how to do stuff, and a few computer methods to do things faster or using less storage.

The emphasis in this book is on high-security cryptography. You have information that you need to keep secret against opponents who could have supercomputers, or even quantum computers. This book tells you how. I provide a toolbox of methods, both new and historical, that can be combined in myriad ways to make arbitrarily strong ciphers. Cryptography students and developers will find the broadest possible range of practical methods that can be used to develop new cryptographic products and services.

That said, I want to make this material accessible to both professionals and hobbyists alike. There are plenty of methods that can be done by hand using only paper and pencil. You can find such a method at the end of section 9.6.1. These methods are suitable for field use, when electricity and electronic devices may be unavailable. There are even a few ciphers that children can use.

Anybody can create an unbreakable cipher.

You can create an unbreakable cipher. All you need is the right knowledge. If you can read and understand this book, or even half of it, then you can create an unbreakable cipher. The book teaches anyone who has the desire how to construct a cipher that will stand up to a serious attack by trained cryptographers with supercomputers. No other book does that. In fact, you can develop your own secure cipher using only paper-and-pencil methods. I build up a large inventory of methods and concepts starting with historical ciphers from the 15th century onward, and teach you what combinations reinforce your ciphers, and which are merely wasted effort. I am going to give you an armory of tried-and-true techniques plus fresh-and-new techniques that you can use to build an impregnable fortress.

Fair warning: I am a mathematician by training, and a computer scientist by occupation, so I tend to use mathematical notation and mathematical concepts liberally. This book is intended for a broader audience, not just engineers and scientists. I will try to explain all of the needed math so that the book is self-contained. If you understand subscripts and exponents, and you can read expressions containing parentheses, that is about as much math background as you will need. I explain all of the math beyond that, such as prime numbers, modular arithmetic, and, for the more advanced chapters, matrix arithmetic and mathematical rings.

If you don't understand a particular mathematical concept, you have three choices: (1) take my word for it, (2) skip that section entirely, or (3) don't use the related cryptographic method. There are still plenty of methods. Some are sure to fit your needs.

Or, just plunge in and read the math sections anyway. You may surprise yourself with how much you learn. Don't be discouraged if you don't understand some topic. You may find the next one easy. Even professional mathematicians don't understand every topic.

What is cryptography?

This chapter covers
- Basic terms used in cryptography
- What is an unbreakable cipher?
- What are the different types of cryptography?

Cryptography is often called "The Art of Secret Writing." It is more than that. It encompasses everything from invisible inks to transmitting messages by quantum entanglement of photons. In particular, cryptography includes the making and breaking of codes and ciphers.

Different authors use cryptographic terminology in inconsistent ways, so let us begin by agreeing on some basic terms.

Plaintext or *cleartext* is the message or document that you wish to keep secret. In traditional cryptography, the message was text written in some language known to both sender and receiver. In a computer setting, this could be any type of file such as a PDF (text), JPG (image), MP3 (audio), or AVI (multimedia).

A *cipher* is a method, or *algorithm*, for garbling a message to make it unreadable: for example, by changing the order of the characters or by replacing some characters with different characters. In general, ciphers operate on individual characters or groups of characters in the text without regard for their meaning.

A *key* is a secret piece of information known only to the sender and the legitimate receiver(s) that selects which transformation is used for each message. For example, if the cipher (method) is to change the order of the letters in a message, the key might specify which order to use for that day's messages. A key can be a letter, a word or phrase, a number, or a sequence of letters, words and numbers. The strength of a cipher is highly dependent on the total size of the keys it uses.

A *keyword* or *keyphrase* is a word or phrase used as a key.

Encryption or *encipherment* is the process of changing the plaintext into an unreadable garble by the legitimate sender who knows the key.

Ciphertext is the resulting garbled unreadable message or document, which will be transmitted or stored.

Decryption or *decipherment* is the process that the legitimate receiver, who knows the method and the key, uses to turn the garbled ciphertext back into the original plaintext message.

A *code* is also a method for garbling a message to make it unreadable. By contrast to a cipher, a code normally operates on words or phrases in a message. A typical code replaces words or phrases with groups of digits or letters. (Confusingly, the word *code* is also used to mean a standardized representation for letters, such as Morse code. Hopefully the meaning will be clear from the context.)

Cryptology is the formal study of cryptography, the mathematics and methodologies used for constructing and solving ciphers. Scholars study cryptology; code-breakers study cryptanalysis.

Cryptanalysis is the study of codes and ciphers for the specific purpose of identifying weaknesses and finding ways to break them or, conversely, ways to strengthen them.

Code-breaking is the process of solving encrypted messages by third parties (enemies or opponents) who do not have the key and may not even know the method. This can be done by mathematical methods or by the patient amassing and collating of intercepts, but in practice often comes down to the three B's: bribery, blackmail and break-ins.

2.1   Unbreakable ciphers

Now that we have some common language, let me address the main issue. What exactly do I mean by "unbreakable"? First, I mean that a cipher cannot be broken by cryptographic means. This excludes break-ins, bribery, coercion, defections, extortion, honeytraps and similar means. Those lie outside our scope. Second, I mean that the cipher cannot be broken in a practical sense. Any opponent has finite resources and finite time to devote to the code-breaking task. When choosing a cipher, you need to have some idea of how much manpower and computer power your potential opponent(s) may expend on breaking your cipher. Make a conservative guess, allow for improvements in computers, add a margin of safety, and pick a number. Then, when you choose a cipher, you have a target to aim for. Reach that target and your cipher is effectively unbreakable.

Remember that many messages have a limited lifespan. If your message is ATTACK AT DAWN, and your enemy reads your message at noon, it's too late. You have already attacked. A cipher that can be broken in 12 hours is effectively unbreakable when your opponent does not have 12 hours.

Just to make this concept doubly clear, when I say that a cipher has been *broken,* I mean that an opponent can read messages sent using that cipher. Even if the opponent can read only 1% or .01% of the messages, the cipher is broken. But there is a cutoff somewhere. If the opponent can read a message only if they have intercepted many messages of the same length enciphered with the same key, or where 63 out of 64 key bits are zero, then the cipher is still unbroken. The opponent has no *a priori* way of telling which messages used which key, or which keys are nearly all-zero. It may never happen that you send two messages with the same length and same key, or where 63 key bits out of 64 are zero.

If your cipher uses a 256-bit key, and an enemy cryptanalyst finds a mathematical or computational method to reduce this to 200 bits or even 150 bits, that cipher may be weakened, but it is still unbroken if your chosen level of security is 128 bits. Using a 256-bit key to achieve a security level of 128 bits provides a huge margin of safety.

When the government decided that the old Data Encryption Standard was no longer safe, it held an international competition for a new cipher. Proposals were solicited worldwide. Dozens of ciphers were submitted. Hundreds of cryptographers evaluated these candidate ciphers for security, speed and ease of implementation. There were three rounds of winnowing lasting from 1997 to April 2000 until a winner was chosen. That's what you need to do when your cipher is going to be a worldwide standard for governments, banking, industry and the military. If you decide to enter the next competition, this book will help prepare you.

Most readers, however, will not attempt that. Their ciphers will have more limited scope. They may trust their own judgment, or whatever verification process they devise, for evaluating their ciphers. The principles in chapter 12 will help guide them to a sound and confident decision.

2.2 *Types of cryptography*

There are many different types of cryptography. Some types used in the past were

- *Hidden message:* for example, the messenger could swallow the message, or hide it in their boot heel or saddle, or simply memorize it. It was common in ancient times to have a messenger memorize a message phonetically in a language they did not understand.
- *Secret method,* such as the *Caesar Cipher,* where each letter of the alphabet is replaced by the letter 3 places later. That is, A becomes D, B becomes E, C becomes F, and so forth.
- *Disguised message,* where the message is made to look like something else, such as a design in the messenger's garments.

- *Invisible message*, such as microdots, or invisible inks that become visible when heated or exposed to acid.
- *Misdirection*: for example, where the signature or the shape and color of the paper are the true messages, and everything else is distraction or disinformation.

Collectively, all methods for hiding a message are called *steganography*, first described in the 1499 book *Steganographia* by Benedictine abbot Johannes Trithemius, born Johannes Heidenberg. Trithemius's book is itself a form of steganography, since it is disguised as a book of magic.

Some of these steganographic methods have modern counterparts. For example, a message can be concealed in a JPEG image file by using only the low-order bits of each pixel. Another example is to use a random number generator to pick certain bits in each byte of a file. The chosen bits contain the message, and the remaining bits can be random gibberish.

Before describing modern ciphers, let me introduce a useful shorthand. A message is sent from a sender to a receiver, and the purpose of encryption is to keep some enemy from reading the message. For brevity, I call the sender Sandra, the intended receiver Riva, and the enemy Emily. That is more natural than Alice, Bob and Carol, isn't it?

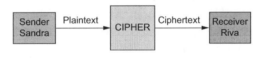

Usually Sandra enciphers the message at her location before sending it to Riva. The message may be sent by any means: letter, telephone, internet, shortwave radio, Aldis lamp, microburst, telegraph, fiber-optic cable, semaphore, quantum entanglement, or even smoke signals if there is a direct line of sight. To make this picture more complete, the cipher may require a key as well as the plaintext, and there may be an enemy listening in. Here is a fuller image.

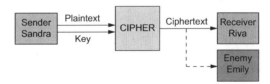

Modern ciphers generally fall into three broad categories: Secret Key, Public Key and Personal Key. Their main distinguishing features are as follows.

Secret Key: Sandra has a secret key, which she uses to encipher messages. Riva has a corresponding secret key, which she uses to decipher those messages. This may be the same key or an *inverse* key. Usually Sandra controls the key. When Sandra changes the key, she must send the new key, or its inverse, to Riva. This is the standard paradigm of classical cryptography.

Public Key: Riva has a public encryption key, which she makes known to everyone. Whenever Sandra wants to send Riva a message, she enciphers it using Riva's public key. Riva also has a secret decryption key, known only to herself, which she can use to decipher the messages that she receives. To make this scheme work, it is essential that nobody else can compute this secret key from the public information. The dominant Public Key method is the RSA algorithm invented by Ronald Rivest, Adi Shamir and Len Adelman in about 1975.

Personal Key: Sandra and Riva each have a personal key they share with nobody, not even one another. Since no keys are ever transmitted or shared, Personal Key cryptography is sometimes called *keyless* cryptography. Here is how it works: (Pass 1) Sandra enciphers the message with her personal key and sends the enciphered message to Riva. (Pass 2) Riva enciphers that message with her personal key and sends this doubly enciphered message back to Sandra. (Pass 3) Sandra deciphers that message using her personal key and sends this back to Riva. The message is now enciphered only with Riva's key, which she uses to read the message.

The tricky part here is that Sandra's encryption and Riva's encryption need to *commute*. That is, they must produce the same result regardless of whether Sandra encrypts first or Riva encrypts first. Symbolically, we express this as SRM=RSM, where M is the message and S and R are Sandra's and Riva's encryptions. The advantage of Personal Key cryptography is that anybody can communicate securely with anybody else without having to prearrange any keys or transmit any keys, so there is no possibility of a key being intercepted.

Personal Key cryptography is also called the *Three Pass Protocol*. A *protocol* is just a sequence of steps used for some purpose such as transmitting a message. In other words, a protocol is an algorithm. The basic idea for the Three Pass Protocol was invented by Adi Shamir in about 1975, and the specific method I present in this book is my own.

2.3   Symmetric vs. asymmetric cryptography

Many books state that cryptography can be divided into two types: *symmetric* and *asymmetric* ciphers. The idea is that in Secret Key cryptography, Sandra and Riva use the same key to both encrypt and decrypt the message, while in Public Key cryptography, Sandra uses one key while Riva uses its inverse. This dichotomy overlooks Personal Key cryptography, which is neither symmetric nor asymmetric, as well as the various classical methods described at the start of section 2.2. Moreover, the symmetric/asymmetric classification is not always accurate. In section 15.1 I describe the *Hill Cipher*, a Secret Key method where encryption consists of multiplying the message by the key, and decryption consists of multiplying by an inverse key — just like Public Key cryptography.

Categorizing a cipher as either symmetric or asymmetric is not particularly useful. It fails to capture the essential difference between Secret Key and Public Key cryptography, namely that in Secret Key cryptography, all of the keys are kept secret, while in Public Key cryptography, each party keeps one key secret and makes one key public and available to everyone.

Public Key cryptography and Personal Key cryptography both came out around 1975. Public Key cryptography fired the imagination, so Secret Key and Personal Key methods have received scant attention since that time. Public Key cryptography is fully covered in many books. This book focuses primarily on Secret Key cryptography, the mainstay and bedrock of cryptography.

2.4 Block ciphers vs. stream ciphers

Another classification is to divide ciphers into block ciphers and stream ciphers. Block ciphers operate on blocks of characters in the message, say blocks of 5 characters. Usually all of the blocks are the same size, and the same key is used for every block.

Stream ciphers operate on one character of the message at a time. Each character has its own key, called the *character key*, typically taken from a larger key called the *message key*. In older stream ciphers the message key was repeated. For example, if the message key size was 10 characters, then the first key character would be used to encipher message characters 1, 11, 21, 31, ... of the message, the second key character would encipher message characters 2, 12, 22, 32, ..., and so forth. Ciphers using regularly repeating keys are called *periodic*. In newer stream ciphers the message key is usually as long as the message itself and is called the *key stream*. This *aperiodic*, or non-periodic, style of enciphering is called the *one-time pad*. In chapter 13, there are discussions of how key streams can be generated.

The block/stream classification is not exclusive. There are hybrid ciphers where the message is broken up into blocks, but different blocks are enciphered with different keys, so the cipher operates on a stream of blocks rather than a stream of characters.

2.5 Mechanical vs. digital

Ciphers can also be classified according to the means used to produce them. The earliest ciphers were done entirely by hand. Not using pencil and paper, but rather stylus and parchment, or stylus and clay tablet.

The first mechanical means of encipherment was the *skytale* or *scytale* (pronounced SKIT-a-lee) used by the ancient Greeks and Spartans, probably as early as 700 BCE. This consisted of a rod with a narrow strip of leather or parchment wound around it so the edges of each turn carefully matched the edges of the adjacent turns. In other words, there were no gaps and no overlaps. The letters of the message were written across two or more turns of the strip. When the strip was unwound, only disconnected pieces of the letters were visible so that an enemy would not recognize that it contained a message. Additional squiggles or patches of color could be added to make it look like a decoration.

The sender kept the staff for reading and writing future messages. Messengers could wear the strip as a belt or use it to tie up their hair or cinch their saddles. The recipient needed a rod of identical diameter to reconstitute the message. Messengers, of course, were not told the purpose of the ribbon or thong. It might even be sewn into their garments without their knowledge.

There is an image of a skytale in the 1593 edition of *De Occultis Literarum Notis* by Giovanni Battista Porta. It shows how each Greek letter spans several turns of the leather strip. Here is a modern version.

The Greeks kept the secret of the skytale for about 700 years. The Romans, however, were not so successful. Eventually their enemies in northern Europe learned the meaning and use of these rods. So, the Romans invented a special measuring tool consisting of a hollow brass or bronze dodecahedron, a solid shape with 12 identical pentagonal faces, with a circular hole on each face. These holes allowed them to make wooden rods of precisely the correct diameter. When a governor (satrap), ambassador, or spy was sent to a post that required travel through hostile territory, it was safer to carry this tool than to carry an actual skytale that could be captured. The 12 holes had different diameters to allow for secure communications with other governors, ambassadors and spies: for example, small for Londinium (now London), medium for Lugdunum (now Lyon), and large for Tarraco (now Tarragona in Catalonia).

So far as is known, the purpose of these dodecahedrons was never discovered by the northern Europeans or, for that matter, by modern archeologists. Archeologists have proposed a plethora of preposterous purposes for these artifacts, such as children's toys, saddle ornaments, practice pieces for blacksmiths, candleholders, range-finders for artillery, or, the answer of last resort, religious objects.

This is a bronze Roman dodecahedron found near Tongeren, the oldest town in Belgium, and displayed in the Gallo-Romeins Museum.

Here is an interesting side note: If you look up *skytale* in Wikipedia and other websites, it says that the skytale was used to produce a transposition cipher by writing each letter within one turn of the strip. This is wrong. Such a strip would easily be recognized as a cipher message. Whether or not the enemy could read the message, they would certainly not let the messenger deliver it. A thorough examination of the whole letter versus broken letter issue can be found at cryptiana.web.fc2.com/code/scytale.htm. In 1841, Edgar Allan Poe, who was a talented cryptographer, wrote an essay, "A Few Words on Secret Writing," which gives a good description of the skytale and his method for decrypting these messages by matching up the broken fragments of letters.

To compound this error, if you look up "transposition cipher" in Wikipedia, it says that the skytale was used to produce a "rail fence cipher," also called a "zigzag cipher." A rail fence cipher has columns that alternate up and down. Writing a message either along or around a rod does not involve any changes of direction. So, if a skytale were used to produce a transposition cipher, the result could be a columnar transposition, never a rail fence. (I corrected these errors in Wikipedia, but my corrections were deleted. I have given up trying to be the Wikipedia Police.)

A 1960s version of the skytale was to sort a deck of computer punch cards, write the message in pencil on an outer surface of the deck, and then thoroughly shuffle the deck, leaving just scattered dots. When the deck was run through a card sorting machine, the cards would be restored to the original order, and the message could be read. This idea was widely discussed by programmers, but I do not know if it was ever put into practice. Another modern equivalent is to write the message on the blank back of a jigsaw puzzle and then scramble the pieces. The receiver needs to solve the puzzle and then flip it over to read the message.

Another mechanical cipher was the Jefferson Wheel Cypher invented by Thomas Jefferson some time between 1790 and 1793. It consisted of 36 same-sized wooden disks threaded on an iron rod to form a wooden cylinder. Around the exposed edge of each disk, the 26 letters of the alphabet were written in some scrambled order. The disks could be rotated independently to spell any message. Versions of the Jefferson cipher using disks or paper strips were used as recently as the 1960s.

Many types of disk ciphers were developed from the 15th through the 19th centuries. The most common type used several thin flat concentric disks that could be rotated around a center pivot. Each disk had the alphabet or some set of numbers or symbols written in some order around the rim of its upper face. The disks got progressively smaller so that all of the alphabets could be seen at the same time. The disks were aligned in some position, and encipherment consisted of finding the plaintext letter on one of the disks, then using the corresponding letter or symbol on one of the other disks as the ciphertext letter. Later types of disk ciphers advanced the inner disk after each letter was enciphered, either manually or through a clockwork mechanism.

This is a picture of the Leon Battista Alberti cipher disk drawn by Augusto Buonafalce, from his 1467 book, *De compendis cifri*. (Image distributed by Wikimedia Commons.)

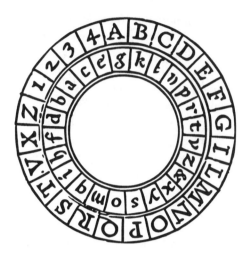

Starting in 1915, a long series of electromechanical rotor ciphers were invented. The most famous is the Enigma machine developed in the 1920s by German engineer Arthur Scherbius. Dozens of types were marketed up through the start of the computer era. They all produced stream ciphers. The basic idea was that the substitute for a letter was determined by the path that the electric current took through the series of turning rotors. After each letter was enciphered, some of the rotors turned, controlled by various cams, gears, lugs and pawls to change the substitutions in myriad ways. So, if the word INFANTRY came out as PMRNQGFW, that might not happen again for billions of turns.

Since the 1960s, cryptography has become increasingly computerized and digital. The Data Encryption Standard (DES) was developed by IBM in 1975 and certified by the National Bureau of Standards in 1977. This touched off a series of block ciphers with names like Serpent and Twofish, culminating in the Advanced Encryption Standard (AES) adopted by the National Institute of Standards and Technology (NIST) in 2001. This class of ciphers is covered in chapter 11.

The progression has been from manual → mechanical → electromechanical → digital.

2.6   *Why choose Secret Key?*

In this era of Public Key cryptography, the question naturally arises, why would anyone choose Secret Key cryptography? There are several reasons.

Secret Key cryptography is much faster. Even the strongest, most complex Secret Key methods tend to be hundreds or even thousands of times faster than the leading Public Key methods. In fact, the main use of Public Key cryptography is to encrypt keys for Secret Key cryptography. The keys are sent using Public Key methods, but the messages themselves are sent using Secret Key methods.

Public Key cryptography (PKC) requires a Public Key Infrastructure. There must be Public Key servers to distribute public keys to potential correspondents. PKC is subject to a variety of man-in-the-middle and spoofing attacks, where an opponent poses as the sender, and/or the receiver, and/or the key server, so PKC requires a great deal of authentication and verification. The person requesting a public key must prove membership in the same network as the recipient. The message containing the public key must be verified to assure it came from the server. The receiver must be authenticated when the public key is first posted on the server and every time it is changed. When a new party is added to the network, the person authorizing that new party must be authenticated. When a new network is added to a server, every party involved must be authenticated. The receiver must verify that the received message has not been altered or replaced by some third party. This all makes for a profusion of messages.

Secret Key cryptography can operate without any of that administrative overload. Two individual people can exchange secret key messages without involving anyone else or any intermediating system. When several people are exchanging Secret Key messages, the only authorization required is that each party has the current key. An unauthorized person won't have the keys and can't read the messages.

Exchanging messages is not the only use for cryptography. An equally important role is securing the secrecy of data files stored on a computer, on an external device such as a flash drive, or in cloud storage, often for a long time. PKC cannot be used for this purpose. Only Secret Key methods are suited for keeping data files secret.

When a message needs to be broadcast to many receivers at the same time, this can easily be done with Secret Key methods. All that is needed is for each party to have the key. They could use a special broadcast key separate from their personal keys. Or, each party could be sent the message key by using a separate key-transmission key. With Public Key methods, you would need to get the individual public keys of all of the recipients, with all of the attendant authorization and verification. This cannot be prearranged because the participants are free to change their public keys at any time.

The most common Public Key method is the RSA method. The strength of this method depends on the fact that it is currently very difficult to factor large numbers (see section 3.4). Given a 200-digit decimal number with no small prime factors, there is currently no feasible way of factoring it. However, when quantum computers become available, this will all change. MIT professor Peter Shor developed a quantum algorithm that can easily factor a number that size. When that happens, all of the RSA messages stored on computers will be able to be read.

There is, so far, no known way to use quantum computers for cracking secret key ciphers. If quantum computers are a concern, Secret Key cryptography is the only choice.

2.7   *Why build your own?*

If you are a cipher hobbyist, it is obvious why you want to build your own ciphers. You build your own ciphers because that's your hobby. Model train hobbyists design, build, and run model trains. Model plane fans design, build and fly model planes. Cipher hobbyists design, build and solve ciphers.

If you are a cryptography student, building your own cipher is good training. It is the best way to learn how to build and how to evaluate ciphers. The current standard cipher, AES (section 11.5), will not last forever, and somebody will need to design its replacement. If you want to be part of that effort, this book may be your best starting point.

If you are a serious cryptographer with responsibilities for protecting high-value data and communications, you might build your own ciphers out of a healthy skepticism that the government-approved ciphers are as safe and secure as your government claims. Let me give you one story that will support your doubts.

Circa 1975, IBM proposed the cipher now called DES, the Data Encryption Standard. It became a worldwide standard for secret key encryption. As IBM originally designed it, DES had a 64-bit key. The National Security Agency (NSA) required that the key be reduced from 64 bits to 56 bits, with the other 8 bits used as a checksum.

This made no sense. If a checksum were really needed, then the key could be increased from 64 to 72 bits. It was widely believed that the real reason the NSA made this demand was that it knew how to crack messages using a 56-bit key, but not messages using a 64-bit key. This proved to be true.

You could reasonably conclude that the NSA would never approve any encryption standard that it could not crack. In that case, you could infer that the NSA can crack all of the different forms of AES. And if the NSA can crack AES, then it is likely that its Russian and Chinese counterparts can crack AES as well.

There are just a handful of experts who construct the candidate ciphers from which the worldwide standard ciphers are selected. It is well-known that these experts receive briefings at NSA headquarters in Fort Meade, Maryland. During these meetings, NSA personnel advise them of techniques that might either strengthen or weaken the ciphers. It is possible that hidden among the recommended methods is some backdoor that lets the NSA, and only the NSA, solve these ciphers easily. It is also plausible that the NSA could offer jobs, contracts and research grants that might induce the experts to adopt those vulnerable methods.

There is a good bit of speculation here, but cryptographers tend to be very conservative. If you can imagine a plausible weakness or vulnerability, whether or not your opponent can realistically exploit it, it is best to guard against it whenever you can.

Finally, you might just be after speed, simpler implementation, or cheaper hardware. You might want to construct your own ciphers to achieve these goals without giving up security. You will find methods in this book that can help you do that.

That said, remember that there are plenty of pitfalls. Don't just create a cipher and assume it is "strong enough." Lots of ciphers turn out to have unexpected weaknesses.

Even the strongest cipher can be defeated by operator errors, such as starting every message with a standard header, frequently reusing keys, or sending the identical message using different keys. For example, many German messages were solved during WW II because they all began, "Heil Hitler."

This book contains all the information you need to construct an unbreakable cipher, but remember that reading only one book about cryptography will not make you an expert overnight. Be sure to check the strength of your cipher using the principles detailed in chapter 12.

Preliminary concepts

This chapter covers

- Bits and bytes
- Functions and Boolean operators
- Prime numbers and modular arithmetic

Before we get into the meat of the subject, let's look at some preliminary concepts. I go through these topics fairly quickly because nowadays many of these ideas are taught in schools, even in the lower grades. More of these basic ideas are given later in the book, as needed.

3.1 Bits and bytes

Data is stored in computers in the form of *bits*, which is shorthand for *binary digits*. A bit is just a number that can have the value either 0 or 1. A bit can be stored in a computer in several ways. A switch can be either open or closed. A magnet can be oriented with its north pole either up or down. Light can be polarized either clockwise or counterclockwise. An electrical pulse can have either a small amplitude or a large amplitude.

These binary digits can be used to form binary numbers. Here are the 3-bit binary numbers and their decimal equivalents. These 3-bit numbers are called *octal* numbers, meaning that they are numbers in the base 8:

```
000 = 0        100 = 4
001 = 1        101 = 5
010 = 2        110 = 6
011 = 3        111 = 7
```

Bits are also used to represent *logic values* or *truth values* in computer logic. 0 represents the logic value *false*, and 1 represents the logic value *true*.

A character, such as a letter or a digit, can be represented by an 8-bit binary number, which is called a *byte*. The term *byte* was coined in 1954 by Werner Buchholz of IBM. Since each bit has 2 possible values, 8 bits can represent 2^8 different characters: that is, 2 to the eighth power, which is 256. This is enough for the 26 lowercase letters, 26 uppercase letters, 10 decimal digits, 33 punctuation marks such as = and $ plus some control characters such as tab and line feed.

There are several schemes that allow for representing additional characters, such as Cyrillic Ж, Arabic س, and even Chinese 是, by using up to 4 bytes for each logogram. None of this is relevant for us. Ciphers can work on strings of characters without regard for their meaning. It is irrelevant that the byte being enciphered might be the third of 4 bytes representing some Chinese logogram.

For our purposes a byte has 3 identities: (1) it is a string of 8 logical true/false values; (2) it is an 8-bit binary number, and hence an integer between 0 and 255, inclusive, and (3) it is a representation of some character, such as a letter, digit, punctuation mark, or part of a logogram.

3.2 Functions and operators

Mathematical functions are now taught in the elementary grades in school, so I am sure I do not need to explain the concept, but it is helpful to establish some notation and terminology. A function takes one or more values and produces another value as the result. The values that are taken are called the *inputs* or the *arguments* of the function, and the value that is returned is called the *output* or *result*. We say that you *apply* the function to the arguments to produce the result.

A function may be denoted by a symbol such as + or by a letter. When a symbol is used, it is called an *operator*, so + and × are operators, and the arguments are called the *operands*. When the function has one argument the symbol may be placed in front of the argument, like −5 or √9, or after the argument, like 5! (5 factorial, which is $1 \times 2 \times 3 \times 4 \times 5 = 120$). If there are two arguments, the symbol is placed between them, like 3+4 or 6×7. When the symbol is a letter, the arguments are enclosed in parentheses, like f(x). The function is denoted by f, and the argument is denoted by x. If there are multiple arguments they are separated by commas, like f(a,b,c). Some books on computer languages distinguish between arguments and parameters, but that is not important here.

3.3   *Boolean operators*

Just as addition, subtraction, multiplication, and similar functions, operate on numbers, there are several functions that operate on bits when they represent truth values. These functions are called *logical operators*, or *Boolean operators* in honor of English mathematician George Boole.

If A and B are truth values, then the logical functions **not**, **and**, **or** and **xor** are defined as follows:

> **not** A is true if A is false, and false if A is true.
> A **and** B is true if A and B are both true, and otherwise it is false.
> A **or** B is true if either A or B or both are true, and otherwise it is false.
> A **xor** B is true if exactly one of A or B is true, and otherwise it is false.

In other words, A **xor** B is true either if A is true and B is false, or if B is true and A is false. **xor** is called the *exclusive-OR* operator. It is commonly denoted by the symbol $\oplus$, a circle with a + inside. The **and** and **or** operators are often represented by the symbols $\wedge$ and $\vee$. It is easy to remember which is which because the symbol $\wedge$ for **and** looks like a capital A without the crossbar.

Here are the values of the four Boolean functions in table form:

```
and        or        xor        not
00  0      00  0      00  0      0  1
01  0      01  1      01  1      1  0
10  0      10  1      10  1
11  1      11  1      11  0
```

These four operators can be extended from single bits to strings of bits by operating on the corresponding pairs of bits. If A is 0011, a string of four bits representing the logic values false,false,true,true, and if B is 0101 representing the logic values false,true,false,true, then applying the four Boolean operators gives

```
      and     or      xor     not      Operator
A     0011    0011    0011    0011     First operand
B     0101    0101    0101    ____     Second operand
      0001    0111    0110    1100     Result
```

The exclusive-OR operator is used extensively in cryptography. For example, a simple implementation of a one-time pad (see chapter 14) is to exclusive-OR the bytes of the message with bytes of a key stream, like this:

```
      H          E          L          P          Plaintext
Msg   01001000   01000101   01001100   01010000   Plaintext in UTF-8 code
Key   10101100   10001011   11000010   00111001   
      11100100   11001110   10001110   01101001   Ciphertext
```

3.4 Number bases

In ordinary arithmetic, numbers are represented in decimal notation. This notation was invented by the Hindus and the Arabs some time between the 5th and 7th centuries. Thus decimal digits are also called *Arabic numerals*. The system was introduced in Europe by Leonardo of Pisa (Leonardo Pisano), popularly known in his time as Fibonacci.

Historical tidbit

In Leonardo's time, roughly 1175–1250, sliding block puzzles were all the rage. (Some people believe this puzzle was the same as the Fifteen Puzzle supposedly invented by Noyes Chapman in 1874.) Public competitions with cash prizes were commonplace. Leonardo was a wizard at this puzzle. He won every time. His competitors gave him the jesting name "Fibonacci," meaning "bonehead," and Leonardo embraced it. Fibonacci became famous throughout Italy. When Fibonacci wrote his *Liber Abaci* (Book of Calculations) in 1202, he wanted people to know that its author was the famous Fibonacci. It would be boastful and undignified to say so directly, so on the title page he put *Filius Bonacci*, which could mean "Lucky Son" or "Son of Bonacci."

Later authors did not grasp this intent, and rejected the thought that the great Leonardo Pisano should be called "bonehead." They surmised that Leonardo's family name might have been Bonacci. For the same reason, to remind his readers that he was the famous Fibonacci, in his private writings Leonardo sometimes slyly referred to himself as Leonardo Bonacci (Lucky Leonardo).

Over time people forgot the name and reputation of Fibonacci the puzzle genius, until 1836 when bibliophile, and notorious book thief, Guglielmo Libri put the pieces together and grasped that *Filius + Bonacci = Fibonacci*. The terms *Fibonacci number* and *Fibonacci sequence* were coined by French mathematician Edouard Lucas circa 1870.

Okay, back to work. To explain decimal numbers we use *exponential notation*. An exponential means that a number is multiplied by itself a specified number of times. For example, 5^3 means that 5 is multiplied by itself 3 times, namely 5×5×5, which is 125. In the exponential expression B^E, which is read "B to the E power," or simply "B to the E," B is called the *base* and E is called the *exponent*. If N is any number, then N^1 is N itself. By convention N^0 is 1 for any number N except 0. The term 0^0 has no defined value because different ways of evaluating 0^0 lead to different results.

When we write a decimal, or base-10, number like 3456, it means 3×1000+4×100+5×10+6×1. Using exponential notation this is the same as $3{\times}10^3{+}4{\times}10^2{+}5{\times}10^1{+}6{\times}10^0$. Starting from the right, the low-order digit, in this case 6, is multiplied by 1, the next digit, namely 5, is multiplied by 10, the next digit by 10^2, then 10^3, and so forth. If there were 50 digits, the high-order digit, on the left, would be multiplied by 10^{49}.

It works the same way in other number bases. For example, the binary system uses base 2. The binary number 11001 is evaluated as $1 \times 2^4 + 1 \times 2^3 + 0 \times 2^2 + 0 \times 2^1 + 1 \times 2^0$, or $16 + 8 + 0 + 0 + 1$, which is 25. A number base commonly used in computer work is *hexadecimal,* or base 16. The digits used in base 16 are 0123456789ABCDEF, or 0123456789abcdef. I prefer to use the capital letters ABCDEF for this purpose, because it makes all of the hexadecimal digits the same height, which is easier to read. The hexadecimal number 9AB would be evaluated as $9 \times 16^2 + 10 \times 16^1 + 11 \times 16^0$, or $9 \times 256 + 10 \times 16 + 11$, which is 2475 in decimal notation.

One use of number bases in cryptography is to convert text into numbers. It is natural to associate the 26 letters of the alphabet with numbers in base 26 like this:

```
A  B  C  D  E  F  G  H  I  J  K  L  M  N  O  P  Q  R  S  T  U  V  W  X  Y  Z
0  1  2  3  4  5  6  7  8  9 10 11 12 13 14 15 16 17 18 19 20 21 22 23 24 25
```

The word WORK could be expressed as a number $22 \times 26^3 + 14 \times 26^2 + 17 \times 26 + 10$, or 396,588. This value can be manipulated like any number, for example by addition, subtraction or multiplication.

Large numbers can be expressed in exponential notation, also called *scientific* notation, like this: 1.23×10^7. This is the product of 1.23 with 10^7, which is 10,000,000, so 1.23×10^7 is 12,300,000. This is the same as taking 1.23 and moving the decimal point 7 positions to the right.

3.5   *Prime numbers*

Numbers, specifically integers greater than 1, are classed as either *prime* numbers or *composite* numbers. If the number is the product of two smaller positive integers, then it is called composite; otherwise it is prime. The first few composite numbers are $4 = 2 \times 2$, $6 = 2 \times 3$, $8 = 2 \times 4$ and $9 = 3 \times 3$. The first few prime numbers are 2, 3, 5, 7 and 11. The number 1 is neither prime nor composite.

An important property of prime numbers is that any number can be written as the product of prime numbers in only one way (aside from the order of the factors). For example, since $30 = 2 \times 3 \times 5$, no prime other than 2, 3 or 5 can evenly divide 30. Here 2, 3 and 5 are called the *prime factors* of 30. The set of prime factors of any integer is unique. Determining the prime factors of an integer is called *factoring* or *factorization*.

If two integers A and B have no prime factors in common, then they are called *coprime* or *mutually prime*. For example, 20 and 27 are coprime. If N is an integer, then N and 1 are always coprime, while N and 0 are coprime only when N=1. N and N+1 are always coprime.

Using positive integers, when any number A is divided by another number B, called the *divisor*, the result is a *quotient* and a *remainder*. Call the quotient Q and the remainder R. Then Q is defined as the largest integer such that QB does not exceed A. The remainder indicates how much is left over, that is, R=A−QB. Note that $0 \leq R < N$. For example, suppose A is 40 and B is 11. The largest multiple of 11 that does not exceed 40 is 33, so the quotient is 3 since 3×11=33. The remainder is 7 since 40–33 is 7.

3.6 *Modular arithmetic*

The study of remainders is called *modular arithmetic*. Modular arithmetic was introduced by the mathematician Carl Friedrich Gauss of the University of Göttingen in 1801. In modular arithmetic the quotient is ignored, the divisor is called the *modulus*, and the remainder is called the *residue*. In the preceding example, the modulus is 11 and the residue is 7. If the modulus is N and two numbers X and Y have the same residue, we say that X and Y are *congruent modulo N*, or, equivalently, that X and Y are in the same *residue class* modulo N. This is written X≡Y (mod N). For example, 40≡7 (mod 11), so 40 and 7 are in the same residue class modulo 11. X and Y will be congruent modulo N whenever X–Y is a multiple of N, or, equivalently, whenever X=Y+aN for some integer a.

Residue classes follow the same rules of arithmetic as ordinary integers, such as

$$a+b \equiv b+a \text{ (mod N) and } ab \equiv ba \text{ (mod N)},$$
$$a+0 \equiv a \text{ (mod N)}, a-a \equiv 0 \text{ (mod N) and } a\times1 \equiv a \text{ (mod N)},$$
$$(a+b)+c \equiv a+(b+c) \text{ (mod N) and } a(bc) \equiv (ab)c \text{ (mod N)},$$
$$a(b+c) \equiv ab+ac \text{ (mod N) and } (a+b)c \equiv ac+bc \text{ (mod N)}.$$

We call –a the *additive inverse* of a. The notation a–b can be considered shorthand for a+(–b).

The situation for the *multiplicative inverse* is more complex. The congruence ax≡b (mod N) has 3 cases to consider: (1) when a and N are coprime, (2) when a and N have a common factor d that does not divide b, and (3) when a, b and N are all divisible by the common factor d.

1   Suppose that a and N are mutually prime. Then there is a unique residue a' that is the multiplicative inverse of a modulo N, so that aa'≡1 (mod N) and a'a≡1 (mod N). If a' exists, then the congruence ax≡b (mod N) can easily be solved as x≡a'b (mod N). In section 15.3.2 I present efficient ways of computing a' when N is large.

2   If a and N have a common factor d>1, then a has no multiplicative inverse modulo N. There can be no a' such that aa'≡1 (mod N). If b is not divisible by d, then ax≡b (mod N) has no solutions. For example, 4x≡5 (mod 12) has no solutions.

3   Suppose d is the greatest common divisor of a and N, denoted gcd(a,N). That is, d is the largest integer that evenly divides both a and N. If a, b and N are all divisible by d, then you can reduce the congruence by dividing a, b and N by d, namely (a/d)x≡(b/d) (mod N/d).

Let's look at an example. Consider the congruence $8x \equiv 4 \pmod{12}$. Dividing through by 4 gives the reduced congruence $2x \equiv 1 \pmod 3$. The solution to this congruence is $x \equiv 2 \pmod 3$, meaning that x can be any integer of the form $3n+2$. Going back to the original congruence, x is a residue modulo 12, so x must lie in the range 0 to 11, inclusive. The numbers of the form $3n+2$ that fall in this range are 2, 5, 8 and 11. This means x can have any of the values 2, 5, 8 or 11. So the congruence $8x \equiv 4 \pmod{12}$ has 4 solutions.

Later in this book, **mod** is used as an arithmetic operator. The expression x mod y, where x is an integer and y is a positive integer, means the remainder when x is divided by y. Thus 27 mod 3 is 0, 27 mod 4 is 3, and 27 mod 5 is 2.

Cryptographer's toolbox 4

This chapter covers

- The rating system used for ciphers
- Substitution ciphers
- Transposition ciphers
- Fractionation, breaking letters into smaller units
- Pseudorandom number generators

Secret Key ciphers are built from a few basic elements. You can think of these as the tools of the trade. To build a strong cipher you want all of these tools in your toolbox. That does not mean you should use every element in every cipher. That could lead to excess complexity without any improvement in security. Your cipher would be slower, with no added benefit. This chapter covers substitution, transposition, fractionation and random numbers. I introduce other tools such as text compression in chapter 10 and block chaining in chapter 11.

Before discussing the elements, let's talk about strength. The strength of a cipher is measured in bits. Each bit represents one binary choice. If there were a cipher where each ciphertext could represent just one of two possible plaintexts, then that cipher would have a strength of 1 bit. For example,

0 = We lost.
1 = We won.

The size of the key is a limiting factor in determining the strength of a cipher. If a cipher uses 64-bit keys, then its strength can be no more than 64 bits, but the strength can be less if the cipher is weak.

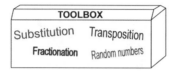

4.1   Rating system

In order to give you a general feel for the strengths of the ciphers described in this book, I rate ciphers on a One to Ten scale. These are my personal ratings, based on my experience and my analysis of how much effort is required to break the cipher using the best techniques I know, and how the ciphers compare to one another and to historical ciphers that were or were not broken in practice. I give much of the analysis in the section preceding each rating:

- One indicates a cipher that can be broken by a beginner with no training using only paper and pencil and moderate effort.
- Two indicates a cipher that can be broken by an experienced amateur or hobbyist using only paper and pencil.
- Three is a cipher that a skilled amateur cryptographer can breach with hand methods.
- Four or Five means that a computer, a trained cryptographer, or both are needed.
- From Six to Nine indicates how much computing power an expert opponent would need.
- Ten denotes a cipher that will stand up against a national cryptographic agency with legions of trained cryptographers using today's largest supercomputers.

Sometimes I go outside the scale. Zero means that the cipher can be understood without needing paper or pencil, such as Pig Latin or **GNITIRW EHT SDROW SDRAWKCAB**. An Eleven rating means that the cipher will stand up to potential future ultracomputers far stronger than quantum computers or supercomputers as we currently conceive them.

By seeing how I rate different ciphers, you can get the gist of how to rate ciphers that you see elsewhere, or that you may invent yourself. Each rating is only an estimate, not a guarantee of strength. The guarantee comes from performing the analyses described in chapter 12.

4.2 Substitution

The first tool in the cryptographer's toolbox is substitution. One unit is substituted for another unit in a text. The plaintext units can be single letters, pairs of letters or longer blocks. The ciphertext units can be letters, blocks of letters, blocks of digits or letter-digit combinations. When all units are single letters, the cipher is called *simple substitution* or *monoalphabetic*. In computer cryptography the units can be bits, bytes, or blocks of bits or bytes of any length. This section gives a quick glimpse. There is a full discussion in chapters 5 and 6.

One of the oldest known substitution ciphers is the *Caesar Cipher*, used and possibly invented by Julius Caesar, where each letter of the alphabet is replaced by the letter 3 positions later. In modern use, this may be any fixed number of positions earlier or later. The Caesar cipher is rated One.

There is no requirement that all plaintext units have the same length. Suppose that the cipher takes letters of the alphabet and substitutes 2-digit pairs. There are only 26 letters of the alphabet, but 100 possible digit pairs. This means there are 74 extra pairs the cryptographer can use for some other purpose. One approach, which has been used for hundreds of years, is to provide substitutes for common letter pairs, such as TH, ER, ON, AS and NT, and possibly short words like THE and AND, in addition to the single letters. The plaintext units would then be 1, 2 or 3 letters long. This makes the frequencies of the digit pairs more uniform. Since differences in letter frequencies can be used for solving ciphers, making the frequencies more uniform makes the cipher stronger.

Another approach is to use the extra pairs to provide additional substitutes for some common letters. This is called *homophonic* substitution. For example, you might provide 10 substitutes for E, 8 substitutes for T, and so forth. The multiple substitutes for a given letter are called *homophones*. This is analogous to the way the homophones F and PH both represent the same sound in English. Providing multiple substitutes makes the frequencies of the 100 digit pairs more even. Naturally, both approaches, letter pairs and homophonic substitution, can be combined to get even more uniform frequencies for the digit pairs. In other words, these methods prevent an opponent from using frequency analysis.

4.2.1 Huffman codes

In a computer context the ciphertext units can be strings of bits. A good example is *Huffman Coding*, developed by David A. Huffman in 1952 when he was a student at MIT. I won't cover the method for optimizing the set of codes, I will just give the general concept as an example of a variable-length binary code. In Huffman coding, the most frequent letters get short codes, while rarer letters get long codes, based on an underlying letter frequency table. Consequently, fewer bits are required to express the message. This is called *text compression*. There are even stronger methods for text compression in section 10.7.

The most frequent letters in English are E and T, which each occur about 1/8 of the time. Since $8 = 2^3$ we use 3 bits to represent E and T. We can arbitrarily choose any 3-bit values, say E = 100 and T = 111. I call this method *Mixed Huffman*. The next most frequent are A, O, I, N, S, R, H. These each occur roughly 1/16 of the time, so we use 4 bits for each of them. We can use any 4-bit codes, except codes starting with 100 or 111, which have already been used. The next group of letters are D, L, U, C, M, F, Y, which each occur about 1/32 of the time, so 5-bit codes are needed. And so forth.

Here is a set of mixed Huffman codes I created based on counts of 150,000 letters of English text. Other languages vary. Huffman codes have the *prefix property*, namely no code is a prefix of any longer code. For instance, if ABCD is a code, then ABCDE could not also be a code for any choice of binary digits A,B,C,D,E. The prefix property was first described by mathematician Emil Leon Post in 1920.

E	100	D	00000	P	010010
T	111	L	01000	B	010011
A	0001	U	10110	V	110101
O	0010	C	10111	K	1101000
I	0011	M	11000	X	11010011
N	0101	F	11001	Q	110100101
S	0110	Y	11011	J	1101001000
R	0111	W	000010	Z	1101001001
H	1010	G	000011		

Using these code groups, the word STYLE would be encoded as **0110 111 11011 01000 100**. Rewriting this in groups of 4 bits gives **0110 1111 1011 0100 0100**, which is hexadecimal **6FB44**.

Although it is nearly impossible for Emily, Sandra's enemy, to identify the code groups for individual letters in a ciphertext, Emily can search for longer repeated strings of bits. These will represent common letter pairs, called *bigrams*, letter triples, called *trigrams*, or words. For example, any given 10-bit string should appear about once every 2^{10}, or 1024, times. If a 10-bit string appears 20 or more times out of 1024 strings, then it almost certainly represents the word THE, which is by far the most common word in English. If you have identified the word THE in a text, then you can look for extensions like THERE or THESE, which are easy to spot because of the repeated E. Mixed Huffman is rated Three.

4.3　*Transposition*

The second major cryptographic tool is transposition, changing the order of the characters in a message. The simplest method is *route transposition*. The letters of the message are written into a grid in one order, and read out in a different order. This section gives a quick look. The full discussion is in chapter 7.

For example, the message THERE IS NO LOVE AMONG THIEVES, which has 25 letters, is written into this 5×5 grid from left to right across the rows, and read out from top to bottom down the columns. The leftmost column in this grid is `TIOOI` when read from top to bottom.

```
T H E R E      Plaintext:    THERE IS NO LOVE AMONG THIEVES
I S N O L
O V E A M      Ciphertext:   TIOOI HSVNE ENEGV ROATE ELMHS
O N G T H
I E V E S
```

Common routes for writing the letters into the grid, and for reading the letters out of the grid, include going straight across the rows, either left or right, straight up or down the columns, alternating left and right across the rows, alternating up and down the columns, diagonally starting at any corner, diagonally in alternating directions, or spiral clockwise or counterclockwise, either inward or outward. Route transposition ciphers are rated One.

4.4 *Fractionation*

Fractionation is the division of characters into smaller units. We have already seen one way, representing a character as a binary number. Each bit of that binary number can be manipulated as a separate unit, substituted or transposed. This section introduces fractionation. There is a detailed discussion in chapters 9 and 10.

A classical way of representing a letter as two digits is the *Polybius Square*, invented in the second century BCE by the Greek historian Polybius. Here is a 5×5 square using a mixed alphabet with the keyword SAMPLE. Notice that the letters I and J share one cell in order to make the 26-letter alphabet fit into the 25-cell grid.

	1	2	3	4	5
1	U	V	W	X	Y
2	Z	S	A	M	P
3	L	E	B	C	D
4	F	G	H	IJ	K
5	N	O	Q	R	T

A mixed Polybius square using the keyword **SAMPLE**

Since A is on row 2 in cell 3, it is represented by 23. B is 33, C is 34, and so on, through Z represented by 21. I and J are both represented by 44. These digits can then be substituted, transposed and regrouped in various ways. Pairs of digits can be turned back into letters using this grid, or another Polybius square arranged in a different mixed order.

A modern version would replace each character with its hexadecimal representation in ASCII or UTF-8 code. Thus A = 41, B = 42, C = 43, through Z = 5A. These hexadecimal digits can similarly be substituted, transposed, regrouped and turned back into bytes.

A fun example is *Fractionated Morse*, invented by M. E. Ohaver in 1910. Ohaver always went by M. E. because he disliked his first name, which was Merle.

Historical note

A footnote on page 241 of Craig Bauer's *Secret History: The Story of Cryptology* states that M. E. Ohaver was one of the pseudonyms of prolific pulp fiction writer Kendell Foster Crossen. This is not true. Crossen sometimes used the pseudonym M. E. Chaber from the Hebrew *mechaber*, מחבר, meaning *author*.

In fractionated Morse, the letters are taken in groups of a fixed size, say 7, and replaced by their Morse code equivalents, using / as a letter separator. Then the lengths of the code groups are reversed, and the resized groups are turned back into letters.

```
E X   A   M   P   L   E      Plaintext
·/-···/·-/--/·---/·-··/·      Morse equivalents
1 4   2   2   4   4   1       Code group lengths
1 4   4   2   2   4   1       Lengths in reverse order
·/-···/·---/·-/·-/·-··/·      Regrouped Morse
E X   J   A   N   L   E       Equivalent letters
```

Morse code was invented by Alfred Vail in 1840 and named for his employer, Samuel F. B. Morse.

This cipher has several obvious weaknesses. Since it uses the standard Morse alphabet, the only key is the length of the letter groups, which can be guessed in just a few tries. Plaintext letters are often replaced by themselves. There are 30 different Morse code groups, but only 26 letters, so 4 extra characters are needed. Ohaver used Germanic ä, ë, ö and ü. Fractionated Morse is rated One.

These problems can be partially fixed with two changes: (1) Use only the Morse groups of lengths 1, 3 and 4. There are 26 such groups, perfectly fitting the 26-letter alphabet. (2) Scramble the order of the alphabet, or, equivalently, scramble the order of the Morse code groups. I call this enhanced version *FR-Actionated Morse*. For example, using the keyword MIXEDALPHBT to mix the alphabet, with the Morse groups in standard order, you get

```
M  ·        P  --·      Y  ·-··     N  -·--
I  -        H  --·      Z  ·--·     O  ----·
X  ···      B  ---      C  ·---     Q  ----·
E  ··-      T  ·---     F  ·----    R  ---·
D  ··-      U  ·-··     G  -···     S  ----
A  ·--      V  ·-··     J  -····
L  -··      W  ·----    K  -····
```

Even with these improvements, FR-Actionated Morse is rated only Two.

4.5   *Random number generators*

A random number generator can be anything that produces a sequence of numbers in some given range. The numbers might be single bits, 8-bit bytes, decimal digits, or numbers in any other desired range. For example, numbers in the range 0 to 25, corresponding to the 26 letters of the alphabet, are useful for some cryptographic purposes. This section introduces the topic. The complete discussion is in chapter 13.

It is important to recognize that there is no such thing as "a random number." You cannot say that 51 is a random number, while 52 is not, or vice versa. You can, however, say that the sequence 51, 52, 53, 54, ... is not random. That sequence is completely predictable. Randomness is a property of the sequence, or of the generator, not of the individual numbers in the sequence. It is more accurate to say "a random sequence of numbers" than "a sequence of random numbers."

The generator might be a physical process, such as cosmic rays, the pinging of a Geiger counter, precise timing of computer keystrokes, a flag fluttering in a stiff breeze, spray from crashing waves or people rushing to catch trains. Most physical sources are not fast enough for cryptographic purposes, but the sequence of numbers might be stored in a computer file for later use.

The generator could also be a mathematical function or computer program that produces a number each time it is called. Random numbers produced by mathematical algorithms are called *pseudorandom* numbers to distinguish them from *true random* numbers. They are considered weaker than true random numbers because an opponent who determines a portion of the random sequence may be able to calculate the preceding and following numbers and thus read the message. True random numbers can never be produced by a mathematical function. In section 13.8 I show methods for generating cryptographically secure pseudorandom number sequences designed to prevent an opponent from extending a segment of the sequence.

One key difference between pseudorandom sequences and true random sequences is that pseudorandom sequences eventually repeat, while true random sequences never repeat. The number of terms before the sequence repeats is called its *period*. The sequence <u>3,1,9,2,4</u>, 3,1,9,2,4, 3,1,9,2,4, 3, ... for example, has a period of 5, shown underlined. In general, the longer the period, the stronger the cipher.

Simply because a sequence of numbers is random does not mean that the numbers are equally probable. For example, suppose you are observing the colors of cars crossing a busy bridge. The colors are random, but certain colors are much more common than others. White, black, silver and red are far more common than orange, fuchsia or chartreuse. Similarly, in the game of craps, if the dice are fair, then each throw is random, yet throwing a 7 is six times as likely as throwing a 12.

In sections 13.14.1 and 13.14.2 I discuss how to "harvest" the randomness in such sequences to obtain sequences where the numbers have essentially equal probabilities. I will henceforth assume that any random number generator produces numbers with equal probabilities. This is called a *uniform distribution,* or an *equiprobable distribution.*

With a good random number generator, pairs and triples, and so on, of generated numbers will also have uniform probabilities, perhaps going as far as octuples or beyond.

4.5.1　Chained digit generator

Let me end this section with a sample pseudorandom number generator that can easily be done using paper and pencil. No computer required. Let's call it the *Chained Digit Generator*. Begin by writing any 7-digit decimal number. These 7 digits are called the *seed*, or *initial value*, or *initialization vector*. They can be considered the key, or a part of the key, for any cipher that incorporates this generator. To get the first pseudorandom digit you simply add the first and last digits. You append this new digit to the sequence, and black out the first digit. So, starting with 3920516 we add 3+6 to get 9.

$$3920516$$
$$39205169$$

Any time the sum exceeds 9 we drop the tens digit. That is, the addition is done modulo 10. This is sometimes called *non-carrying addition*. To get the second pseudorandom digit we repeat the process. Here 9+9 gives 18. We drop the tens digit to get 8.

$$39205169$$
$$392051698$$

This process can be repeated to get as many pseudorandom decimal digits as desired.

$$3920516980056219\ 9940232\cdots$$

The resulting pseudorandom sequence is **9800562199940232....**

Notice that if all of the digits in the seed are even, then all of the generated digits will be even. Likewise, if all of the digits are divisible by 5, namely 0 or 5, then all of the generated digits will be divisible by 5. In that case the period could be no more than 128 since there are 7 digits in the seed, and there are only $2^7 = 128$ possible combinations of 0s and 5s. Since such seeds cannot produce long periods they are called *unqualified*. For the chained digit generator a *qualified* seed must contain at least one odd digit and one digit that is not a multiple of 5. For example, 2222225 is a qualified seed, but 2222222 and 5555555 are not qualified. With a qualified 7-digit seed the period will always be 2,480,437.

This generator has behavior typical of homemade pseudorandom number generators. There are 10^7 possible 7-digit seeds. If you start with any seed, the generator will cycle through some sequence of numbers until it produces that seed again, so the set of 7-digit numbers is partitioned into several discrete cycles, each with its own period. If you choose a qualified seed, then the cycle will always have the maximum possible period of 2,480,437 numbers. There are 4 separate cycles of this length, plus several much shorter cycles produced by the unqualified seeds.

The behavior is similar for seeds of other sizes. Even when the maximal cycle is very short there is often a high probability of getting a maximal cycle because there can be many maximal cycles. This table shows the probability of getting a cycle of a given length using a qualified seed:

Digits	Period	Probability
4	1,560	100%
5	168	86.7%
6	196,812	99.974%
7	2,480,437	100%
8	15,624	98.817%
9	28,515,260	79.999%
9	at least 2,851,526	99.9988%
10	1,736,327,236	86.9%
10	at least 248,046,748	99.31%
10	at least 13,671,868	100%

The table shows that seed lengths of 5 and 8 digits are not safe. They produce a large percentage of very short cycles. Seed lengths of 7 and 10 digits are best because you are always guaranteed a long period.

This random number generator is strictly a demo model, just to show what can be achieved using simple hand methods. It is not suitable for high-security work.

4.6 Useful combinations, wasteful combinations

The 4 basic techniques of this chapter can be used in myriad combinations, which I explore throughout the remainder of this book. However, it is important to recognize right at the outset that not every combination is beneficial. Some combinations add work without adding strength.

Consider an idea that some beginners try. They perform a simple substitution on a message, then a second simple substitution on the resulting text, then a third, and so forth, for 5, 10, even 100 rounds. This is a waste of effort. Performing two simple substitutions is the same as performing one, but with a different mixed alphabet, so performing many simple substitutions does not add any strength. Here is an illustration. The two substitutions are mixed with the keys FIRST and SECOND. The third substitution is equivalent to performing the first followed by the second.

```
ABCDEFGHIJKLMNOPQRSTUVWXYZ        First substitution
XYZFIRSTABCDEGHJKLMONPQUVW

ABCDEFGHIJKLMNOPQRSTUVWXYZ        Second substitution
UVWXYZSECONDABFGHIJKLMPQRT

ABCDEFGHIJKLMNOPQRSTUVWXYZ        Equivalent
QRTZCIJKUVWXYSEONDAFBGHLMP
```

Let's try an example. If we encipher the word **EXAMPLE** using the first substitution, the result is **IUXEJDI**. If **IUXEJDI** is enciphered with the second substitution, the result is **CLQYOXC**. You can verify for yourself that enciphering **EXAMPLE** with the equivalent substitution yields **CLQYOXC**.

Performing one encipherment and then a second encipherment is called *composing* the two encipherments. The previous example shows that composing two simple substitutions just produces another simple substitution. If the first encryption uses a code, then following the code with a cipher is called *superencipherment*. The most common form of superencipherment is non-carrying addition, or addition modulo 10, which works like this:

```
12155  12155  12155  12155     Superencipherment key
61587  02954  70069  53028     Plaintext code groups
73632  14009  82114  65173     Superenciphered code groups
```

4.6.1   *Bazeries type 4 cipher*

Let's look at the opposite case. Let's look at a cipher where using a substitution step followed by a very simple transposition produces a cipher that is much stronger.

The cipher was proposed by the brilliant, irascible and vituperative French cryptographer Étienne Bazeries in 1898. I do not know what Bazeries named this cipher. I call it *Bazeries Type 4* because it was the last of 4 ciphers that he proposed to the diplomatic Bureau de Chiffre during the 1890s. It can easily be done by hand.

The Bazeries type 4 consists of a simple substitution followed by a simple transposition, which I call a *piecewise reversal*. The transposition reverses short pieces of the text according to a key that is a sequence of small integers. Here is an example using the keyword BAZERIS to mix the substitution alphabet, and the key 4,2,3 for the transposition.

```
ABCDEFGHIJKLMNOPQRSTUVWXYZ      Plaintext alphabet
HGFDCBAZERISYXWVUTQPONMLKJ      Ciphertext alphabet
```

```
THEQUICKBROWNFOXJUMPSOVERTHELAZYDOG      Message plaintext
PZCUOEFIGTWMXBWLROYVQWNCTPZCSHJKDWA      After substitution
```

4		2	3	4		2	3	4		2	3	Transposition key
PZCU		OE	FIG	TWMX		BW	LRO	YVQW		NC	TPZ	CSHJ KD WA
UCZP		EO	GIF	XMWT		WB	ORL	WQVY		CN	ZPT	JHSC DK AW · Final ciphertext

```
UCZPE OGIFX MWTWB ORLWQ VYCNZ PTJHS CDKAW      Ciphertext grouped by fives
```

This type of transposition can be used to strengthen many different types of ciphers, so it deserves a name of its own. Let's call it *Piecewise Reversal*. You can strengthen this transposition by mixing in a few segments of text in normal order, perhaps by using negative numbers in the numeric key. Here is an example using the numeric key 3, 4, –3, 2. Note that this key is equivalent to 3, 4, 1, 1, 1, 2.

3	4	-3	2	3	4	-3	2	3	4	-3	2	
THE	QUIC	KBR	OW	NFO	XJUM	PSO	VE	RTH	ELAZ	YDO	GS	Plaintext
EHT	CIUQ	KBR	WO	OFN	MUJX	PSO	EV	HTR	ZALE	YDO	SG	Transposed

The cryptographers at the Bureau de Chiffre were unable to solve any of the sample messages that Bazeries provided. Despite considerable effort, the messages remained unsolved for 40 years until renowned architect, and amateur cryptographer, Rosario Candela solved them and wrote a book about how he did it (*The Military Cipher of Commandant Bazeries*, Cardanus Press: New York, 1938).

Candela, however, was unable to decrypt the messages directly. Instead, he identified and exploited a weakness in the way Bazeries generated the substitution alphabet from a key. If Bazeries had used a stronger method for mixing the cipher alphabet, Candela could not have deciphered the messages. Consequently, Bazeries type 4 with a well-mixed alphabet is rated Five. Pretty good for combining two methods that are each rated One.

Historical tidbit

Candela was a graduate of Columbia School of Architecture, so he planned to publish his book at Columbia University Press. William F. Friedman, then the dean of American cryptologists, got wind of this, and secretly blocked the publication. This again attests to the strength of the Bazeries Type 4 cipher.

Substitution ciphers 5

This chapter covers
- Simple substitution and polyalphabetic substitution ciphers
- Solving polyalphabetic ciphers using the Kasiski test and the index of coincidence
- Autokey and running key ciphers, and methods for solving them
- Simulating rotor-based cipher machines

We are now ready to explore the basic tools described in the preceding chapter in greater depth. Before I begin describing all the various ciphers, let me explicitly state the goals that these ciphers are trying to achieve. The Dutch linguist and polymath Auguste Kerckhoffs first expressed these principles in a pair of articles in *Journal des Sciences Militaires* in 1883:

1 The cipher should be unbreakable in practice, even if not in theory.
2 This should be true even if the enemy learns the system.
3 The key should be easy to remember (without notes) and easy to change.
4 It should be possible to transmit the enciphered messages by telegraph.

5 The apparatus and documents should be easily carried and operated by one person.

6 The cipher should be easy to use; there should be no complex rules or computations.

Rule 4 might be updated to read "transmit the enciphered messages digitally." Otherwise these precepts remain as valid today as in 1883.

One corollary of the second principle is that the strength of the cipher should reside solely in the key. Kerckhoffs also believed that *only cryptographers are qualified to judge the security of a cipher.* Too often the decision of which cipher to use is made by government officials who lack cryptographic expertise, sometimes with disastrous consequences.

5.1 Simple substitution

Simple substitution, also called *monoalphabetic substitution,* is the familiar type of cipher you see in the puzzle sections of newspapers and magazines. In simple substitution, each letter of the alphabet in the message is replaced by another letter of the alphabet consistently and uniformly. So, if the letter M has been replaced by T in one place, then every M in the message will be replaced by T, and every T in the ciphertext will represent an M.

Since most people are familiar with the techniques for solving simple substitution ciphers, I will merely mention them: letter frequency, initial letter frequency, final letter frequency, double letter frequency, letter pair frequency, short words, common prefixes and suffixes, distribution of vowels and consonants, pattern words, and exploiting the punctuation.

For the easy cryptograms in newspapers, often all that is needed is to look at the short words. If you find AB and CBA the words are probably TO and NOT, while AB and BAC are most often OF and FOR. The pattern ABCA is likely THAT, ABCDC suggests THERE, and ABCDB could be WHICH. If you search the internet you may be able to find lists of pattern words for sale, or websites that will find words matching a pattern you supply.

For the more difficult cryptograms, with texts like **FOXY PIXY MANX AXED TOXIC LUXURY ONYX SPHINX**, a more organized approach is needed.

I demonstrate the procedure using the following sample cryptogram. The language is known to be English. The text has 73 letters and 11 words for an average word length of 6.64 letters, versus 5.0 letters for normal English. The absence of short words of fewer than 5 letters and the absence of pattern words suggests that this cryptogram has been deliberately constructed to be difficult.

```
RULEYS YLCRS KLEYXDO GVLEBDVS BWLEKVMC IVQOR KIGXGQLOWUS
KSYIWZ, ZLORUS LOBZQC SQXMV
```

The first phase is to identify vowels and consonants. Begin by counting the number of occurrences of each letter of the alphabet to get the *frequency count*. In the sample cryptogram the letter count for A is 0, for B is 3, for C is 3, and so forth. The full frequency count follows:

A-0	B-3	C-3	D-2	E-4	F-0	G-3	H-0	I-3
J-0	K-4	L-8	M-2	N-0	O-5	P-0	Q-4	R-4
S-7	T-0	U-3	V-5	W-3	X-3	Y-4	Z-3	

Notice that there are only two high-frequency letters here, **L** and **S**, with frequencies of 8 and 7. In normal English text there are 40% vowels. This percentage is robust, and usually holds even when the letter frequencies have been deliberately manipulated. With 73 letters in the cryptogram there should be 29 vowels. That pretty much requires that both **L** and **S** represent vowels, unless the frequency has been severely skewed.

Next you make a contact chart by listing the letters of the alphabet vertically down the center of the page. Each different letter that appears in the cryptogram gets its own row. On each row, each letter that appears before the central letter is listed to its left, and each letter that appears after the central letter is listed to its right. For example, the first row of the chart, **EO B DWZ**, means that in the cryptogram the letter **B** is preceded by **E** and **O** once each, and followed by **D**, **W** and **Z** once each. Here is the full contact chart for this cryptogram (shown in 3 columns to save space).

```
  EO B DWZ        UYKVWQZ L ECEEEOOO      GDKIM V LSMQ
 LMQ C R                VX M CV            BOI W LUZ
  XB D OV          DQLLL O RWRB            YGQ X DGM
LLLL E YYBK        VGZS Q OLCX             EES Y SLXI
  IX G VXQ          COO R USU               WB Z LQ
  KY I VGW        YRVUKU S YQ
   E K LVIS         RWR U LSS
```

The contact chart is used to identify vowels and consonants. In general, vowels contact a wide variety of letters on both the left and the right, while consonants tend to have a limited number of distinct contacts. From the contact chart we can identify 4 probable vowels, **L**, **Q**, **S** and **V**, and 4 probable consonants, **E**, **O**, **R** and **U**. Let's mark these letters ∘ for vowels and × for consonants and see if the distribution seems plausible.

```
RULEYS YLCRS KLEYXDO GVLEBDVS BWLEKVMC IVQOR KIGXGQLOWUS
××o×-o -o-×o -o×---× -oo×--oo --o×-o-- -oo×× -----oo×-×o

KSYIWZ, ZLORUS LOBZQC SQXMV
-o----- -o××o o×--o- oo--o
```

There are 3 long stretches with no vowels, in word 3 **EYXDO**, in word 7 **KIGXG** and in word 8 **YIWZ**. This suggests that **I** and/or **X** might be a vowel. Both have lots of different contacts, but it is extremely unlikely that **X** represents a vowel because then word 11 would start with 3 vowels and end with a vowel. This is rare in English. The only example I could find is OUIJA. (**SQXMV** cannot be AIOLI because of the repeated I.) So, **I** is probably a vowel, and **X** is a consonant.

Let's take a second pass at distinguishing vowels from consonants. In the ciphertext there are 5 pairs of tentative vowels, **VL**, **VS**, **VQ**, **QL** and **SQ**. Pairs of vowels are not common in English, so it is likely that either **V** or **Q** is really a consonant. It is probably not **Q** because then word 10 would end with 5 consonants. The only such 6-letter word I know is ANGSTS.

Let's make **I** a vowel, make **V** and **X** consonants, and see where we stand.

```
RULEYS YLCRS KLEYXDO GVLEBDVS BWLEKVMC IVQOR KIGXGQLOWUS
xxox-o -o-xo -ox-x-x -xox--xo --ox-x-- oxoxx -o-x-oox-xo

KSYIWZ, ZLORUS LOBZQC SQXMV
-o-o--, -oxxxo ox--o- oox-x
```

This looks right. From word 3 we can now identify **D** as a vowel, and from word 11 it is probable that **M** is a vowel. All 6 of the vowels have now been found, so every other letter must be a consonant. Here is the complete breakdown of consonants and vowels.

```
RULEYS YLCRS KLEYXDO GVLEBDVS BWLEKVMC IVQOR KIGXGQLOWUS
xxoxxo xoxxo xoxxxox xxoxxoxo xxoxxox oxoxx xoxxxooxxxo

KSYIWZ, ZLORUS LOBZQC SQXMV
xoxoxx, xoxxxo oxxxox ooxox
```

```
xx  B  oxx        xxxxxox  L  xxxxxxxx        xoxoo  V  oooo
ooo C  x               xx  M  xx                xxo  W  oxx
xx  D  xx           ooooo  O  xxxx              xxo  X  oxo
oooo E  xxxx        xxxo  Q  xoxx               xxo  Y  ooxo
ox  G  xxo          xxx  R  xox                 xx  Z  oo
xx  I  xxx       xxxxxx  S  xo
x  K  oxoo          xxx  U  ooo
```

The second phase is identifying individual letters. The following Letter Contact Table shows the contact characteristics for the letters of the English alphabet. A different language would have different characteristics. For example, the letters M, V and Z are most often both preceded and followed by vowels, while the letter N is usually preceded by a vowel, but followed by a consonant. I compiled this table using the English language corpus of the Gutenberg Project.

Letter contact table

Before \ After	Vowels	Mixed	Consonants
Vowels	MVZ	RX	N
Mixed	BJQW	CDFGLPST	
Consonants	H	Y	AEIOU

There is one good candidate for plaintext H in the cryptogram, namely ciphertext **U**. However, **U** appears twice in the bigram **US** at the end of words, so that is unlikely.

There are two strong candidates for N in the cryptogram, namely ciphertext **E** and **O**. Both **E** and **O** represent consonants that are always preceded by vowels and followed by consonants. However, **O** is the stronger choice because it has higher frequency, and because it precedes two known consonants in the word **ZLORUS**. In English 3-consonant combinations often begin with N, such as **NST** and **NTH**. It is more likely that **O** represents N. This yields

```
RULEYS YLCRS KLEYXDO GVLEBDVS BWLEKVMC IVQOR KIGXGQLOWUS
××o××o ×o×××o ×o×××oN ××o××o×o ××o×××o× o×oN× ×o××××ooN×××o

KSYIWZ, ZLORUS LOBZQC SQXMV
×o×o××,  ×oN××o oN××o× oo×o×
```

It is now feasible to try to find possible words matching some of these patterns. I found 67 words matching **ZLORUS** ×o**N**××o. Of these, 32 ended in E, and 27 ended in Y. I found 37 words matching **SQXMV** oo×o× and not containing N. Of these, 15 began with Y, but only 1 began with E. It is therefore most likely that ciphertext **S** represents plaintext Y. This gives us

```
RULEYS YLCRS KLEYXDO GVLEBDVS BWLEKVMC IVQOR KIGXGQLOWUS
××o××Y ×o×××Y ×o×××oN ××o××o×Y ××o×××o× o×oN× ×o××××ooN××Y

KSYIWZ, ZLORUS LOBZQC SQXMV
×Y×o××,  ×oN××Y oN××o× Yo×o×
```

The ciphertext words **IVQOR** and **ZLORUS** both contain the bigram **OR**. Let's try to identify that. Knowing that **IVQOR** o×o**N**× does not contain a Y leaves only 24 likely words. Of these, 12 end in G and 8 end in S, hence ciphertext **OR** is probably either NG or NS. The number of likely plaintext words for **ZLORUS** ×o**N**××Y is now down to 26. Among these, the fourth letter is G 8 times, T 6 times, but S only 1 time. The most likely choice for ciphertext **OR** is thus plaintext NG. We now have

```
RULEYS YLCRS KLEYXDO GVLEBDVS BWLEKVMC IVQOR KIGXGQLOWUS
G×o××Y ×o×GY ×o×××oN ××o××o×Y ××o×××o× o×oNG ×o××××ooN××Y

KSYIWZ, ZLORUS LOBZQC SQXMV
×Y×o××,  ×oNG×Y oN××o× Yo×o×
```

There are 8 possibilities for the first word, **RULEYS**. These contain only 6 possibilities for the bigram **UL**. For each of these choices, let's look at the possibilities for the word **ZLORUS**.

UL	RULEYS	ZLORUS
HO	GHOSTY	none
LU	GLUMPY	JUNGLY
NA	GNARLY	none
RI	GRIMLY	none
	GRISLY	none
RO	GROSZY	none
	GROWLY	none
RU	GRUMPY	HUNGRY

The choice **ZLORUS** = JUNGLY can be ruled out immediately because **KSYIWZ** would then have the form ×**Y**×∘×**J**. There is no such word in English. This means that **RULEYS** represents GRUMPY and **ZLORUS** represents HUNGRY. Filling in these new letters gives

```
RULEYS YLCRS KLEYXDO GVLEBDVS BWLEKVMC IVQOR KIGXGQLOWUS
GRUMPY PU×GY ×UMP×∘N ××UM×∘×Y ××UM××∘× ∘×∘NG ×∘××××∘UN×RY

KSYIWZ, ZLORUS LOBZQC SQXMV
×YP∘×H, HUNGRY UN×H∘× Y∘×∘×
```

The rest of the letters can be filled in by sight. It is now obvious that the second word is PUDGY and the third word is BUMPKIN, which makes the eighth word BYPATH, and so forth.

The completed cryptogram reads GRUMPY PUDGY BUMPKIN CLUMSILY STUMBLED ALONG BACKCOUNTRY BYPATH, HUNGRY UNSHOD YOKEL.

Simple substitution is rated One. When the letter frequencies and contact frequencies have been intentionally distorted, as in this example, the rating can go up to Two or possibly Three. This makes a good puzzle, but is useless for general communications.

5.2   Mixing the alphabet

Simple substitution requires a mixed alphabet. There are several traditional paper-and-pencil methods for this. One way to obtain a mixed alphabet is to use a keyword. In the simplest case, you just write the keyword starting at some position, and then fill in the rest of the alphabet behind it, wrapping around as needed. The remaining letters can be filled in forward or backward. Here are three examples:

```
ABCDEFGHIJKLMNOPQRSTUVWXYZ        Plaintext
UVWXYZSAMPLEBCDFGHIJKNOQRT        Ciphertext

ABCDEFGHIJKLMNOPQRSTUVWXYZ        Plaintext
HGFDCBSAMPLEZYXWVUTRQONKJI        Ciphertext

ABCDEFGHIJKLMNOPQRSTUVWXYZ        Plaintext
XYZBCDSAMPLEFGHIJKNOQRTUVW        Ciphertext
```

This method was first used by the Argenti family, who were cipher secretaries to several popes and bishops circa 1600. These alphabets are not well mixed. A somewhat better method is to use two keywords, like this:

KLMNOPQUVWXYZFIRSTABCDEGHJ   Plaintext
HGFBASECONDZYXWVUTRQPMLKJI   Ciphertext

COLUMNAR MIXING

Write the alphabet into a block. Write the keyword on the top row, and the rest of the alphabet in as many rows as needed. Longer keywords give better mixing. Then read the letters out of the block, going down the columns. In this example the keyword SAMPLE has been written on the top row. The first column reading downward is **SBIRY**, the second column is **ACJTZ**, and so forth. If you like, you can alternate reading up and down the columns or use other routes.

SAMPLE	Reading down:	SBIRY ACJTZ MDKU PFNV LGOW EHQX
BCDFGH		
IJKNOQ	Alternating:	SBIRY ZTJCA MDKU VNFP LGOW XQHE
RTUVWX		
YZ	Diagonally:	Y RZ IT BJU SCKV ADNW MFOX PGQ LH E

SKIPMIX

When I was in high school, I invented another method suitable for paper and pencil cryptography, which I call *SkipMix*. It uses a string of small numbers called *skips* as a key for mixing the alphabet, for example 3, 1, 4. Begin with the standard alphabet. Skip 3 letters and take the next letter, which is D.

ABC<u>D</u>EFGHIJKLMNOPQRSTUVWXYZ

Delete that letter, then skip 1 letter and take the next letter, which is F.

ABCDEFGH IJKLMNOPQRSTUVWXYZ   D

Delete that letter, then skip 4 letters and take the next letter, which is K.

ABCEFGHIJKLMNOP QRSTUVWXYZ   DF

Then repeat the 3,1,4 cycle. Skip 3 letters and take the next letter, which is O.

ABCEGHIJKLMNOPQRSTUVWXYZ   DFK

Continue to repeat the cycle of key numbers until all 26 letters have been chosen. The resulting mixed alphabet is

DFKOQVZBINRXEHSYCPAJWTGML

SkipMix can be used with a keyword. Suppose the keyword is SAMPLE. Replace each letter by its position in the alphabet, in this case 19,1,13,16,12,5. Optionally, replace any 2-digit number by its individual digits, in this case 1,9,1,1,3,1,6,1,2,5. Use this string of skips as the mixing key. Note that 0 is a valid value to use.

SkipMix is well-suited for computer use. In this case the alphabet is the 256 different 8-bit character codes. The skips can be any integers from 0 to 255. The numeric key still can be derived from a keyword. The advantage of using a keyword rather than just a string of integers is that it is easier for a person to remember and to type accurately. Suppose, again, that the keyword is SAMPLE. The numerical equivalents of these letters in ASCII code are 83, 65, 77, 80, 76 and 69. These values fall in a narrow range from 65 to 90, which gives less-thorough mixing. To spread the letter codes over a wider range, they can be multiplied by some constant value modulo 256. The multiplier can be any odd number between 7 and 39, inclusive. For example, the ASCII codes for the keyword SAMPLE multiplied by 17 modulo 256 are 131, 81, 29, 80, 12 and 149. This covers a range of 149−12 = 137, much wider than the original range of 83−65 = 18.

There are still only 26 possible values for the skips. One way to obtain a larger set of values is to multiply adjacent numbers modulo 256. The sequence of skips would then be 83×65, 65×77, 77×80, 80×76, 76×69 and 69×83, all taken modulo 256. So 83×65 = 5395≡19 (mod 256). The numeric key becomes 19, 141, 16, 192, 124, 95, covering a range of 192−16 = 176.

Another way to produce a larger set of values for the skips is to multiply the first letter of the keyword by 7, the second letter by 9, the third letter by 11, and so forth, with all multiplications done modulo 256.

Since the conversion of the keyword into the numeric key would be done by the computer, not the human operator, an arbitrarily complex calculation could be used. I recommend a quadratic function rather than a linear function to make it harder for opponents to deduce the keyword if they obtain the plaintext of some messages. For example, if N_i are the terms of the numeric key, and K_i are the numeric values of the characters in the keyword, then a suitable function might be

$$N_i = (K_i K_{i+1} + K_{i+2} K_{i+4}) \bmod 256,$$

where the subscripts wrap around when they exceed the length of the keyword. For example, if the keyword had 10 characters, then K_{11} would wrap around to K_1, K_{12} would wrap around to K_2, and so forth.

*The function $K_i K_{i+1} + K_{i+2} K_{i+3}$ would not be as strong. If the length of the keyword was L, then there would be only L distinct quadratic terms. Emily could treat these as L variables and solve the set of L linear equations to find the values of the L products $K_1 K_2$, $K_2 K_3$, $K_3 K_4$, ... $K_L K_1$. It is then easy to find the values of the individual K_i.**

Throughout this book I show alphabets mixed with simple keywords so that you can see at a glance how they are formed, for example, the alphabet

```
SAMPLEBCDFGHIJKNOQRTUVWXYZ
```

This is very weak. *Do not do this in practice.* I have done it here to aid the reader. Since you do not wish to aid your opponent, always use well-mixed alphabets using columnar mixing, SkipMix or some other strong mixing function. See section 12.3.8 for other methods.

5.3   *Nomenclators*

From the 15th through the 18th century, the King of substitution ciphers was the *Nomenclator*, used by kings, popes, diplomats and spies alike. Each nomenclator had a list of hundreds, sometimes thousands, of items, single letters, numbers, bigrams, syllables, words and names, providing up to 25 substitutes for each. Nomenclators are more like codes than like ciphers, so they fall outside the scope of this book.

5.4   *Polyalphabetic substitution*

The techniques for solving simple substitutions involve letter frequencies and letter contacts. If you want to design a cipher to defeat this type of attack, a good place to start is by disrupting the letter frequencies and letter contacts.

Suppose that instead of using the same alphabet for enciphering every letter you use two different alphabets. Use the first alphabet to encipher the letters in odd-numbered positions, and use the second alphabet to encipher the letters in even-numbered positions. That is, the first alphabet will encipher the first, third, fifth, ... letters in the message, while the second alphabet is used to encipher the second, fourth, sixth, ... letters.

The frequencies of the ciphertext letters now come half from the first alphabet, half from the second alphabet. They are the average of the two sets of frequencies. A ciphertext letter will have high frequency only when it represents high-frequency letters in both alphabets. For example, ciphertext K could represent E in the first alphabet and A in the second alphabet so its frequency would be halfway between the frequency of E and the frequency of A in normal text.

Conversely, a ciphertext letter will have low frequency only when it represents low-frequency letters in both alphabets, say K in the first alphabet and V in the second alphabet. So the ciphertext will have fewer high-frequency letters and fewer low-frequency letters than normal text. If you made a bar graph, or *histogram*, of the letter frequencies, the peaks would be lower and the valleys would be shallower. So using two alphabets tends to flatten the frequency counts.

The same happens with contact frequencies. Any common bigram such as TH will start at an odd position in the message about half the time, and at an even position about half the time. Half the time the T is enciphered with the first alphabet and the H is enciphered with the second alphabet, and half the time it is vice versa. So the contact frequencies also get flattened.

The more alphabets that are used, the flatter the frequencies become. In practice, from roughly the US Civil War until World War I using about 20 alphabets was typical. There is a statistical test that measures the flatness of the letter frequencies and uses that to estimate the number of alphabets, but it is not very accurate, particularly with more than 10 alphabets. Better methods are described in sections 5.6 and 5.7.

Let's look at the historical development of polyalphabetic ciphers. Early forms of polyalphabetic ciphers were developed by Leon Battista Alberti in 1467 and by Johannes Trithemius in 1499 (but not published until 1606). Polyalphabetic ciphers begin to take their modern form with the publication of *La cifra del Sig. Giovan Battista Belaso* in 1553.

5.5   *The Belaso cipher*

The *Belaso Cipher*, invented by Giovan Battista Belaso in 1553, used 26 different alphabets, each of which was simply the standard alphabet shifted a number of places. The 26 cipher alphabets can be displayed as a tableau, where each horizontal row contains one shifted alphabet, like this:

```
ABCDEFGHIJKLMNOPQRSTUVWXYZ
BCDEFGHIJKLMNOPQRSTUVWXYZA
CDEFGHIJKLMNOPQRSTUVWXYZAB
          .  .  .
ZABCDEFGHIJKLMNOPQRSTUVWXY
```

The first letter on each row identifies the alphabet, so the top row is the A alphabet, the second row is the B alphabet, and so forth. Belaso was the first to use a key to select which alphabet to use for which letter in the message. (By contrast, the Argenti family used a keyword to mix the alphabet.) Belaso would write the message horizontally. Above the plaintext letters he would write the key, repeated as many times as needed. To encipher a letter, he would find that letter on the top row of the tableau, use the key letter to select the row in the tableau, and replace the plaintext letter by the ciphertext letter directly below it in the selected row. Here is how the plaintext letter S would be enciphered by the key letter C:

```
ABCDEFGHIJKLMNOPQRSTUVWXYZ     Plaintext S (top row) is enciphered
BCDEFGHIJKLMNOPQRSTUVWXYZA     with key letter C (third row)
CDEFGHIJKLMNOPQRSTUVWXYZAB     to yield ciphertext U
```

We find the letter S on the top row of the tableau. Its key is C, so it is enciphered using the third row of the tableau. On the third row, directly below S, we find the letter U. So S gets replaced by U.

To encipher the word SAMPLE with the key CAB using the previous tableau, S is replaced by **U**.

```
CAB CAB    Key
sam ple    Plaintext
UAN RLF    Ciphertext
```

The next letter in the message is A with the key A, so A is enciphered with the top row. It is enciphered as **A**. The M of SAMPLE has the key B. It gets enciphered using the second row and becomes **N**, and so forth. The resulting ciphertext is **UANRLF**.

Instead of using a tableau, the encipherment can be done using a *St. Cyr slide*, named for the French Saint-Cyr military academy. The slide is shown here in the M position.

```
ABCDEFGHIJKLMNOPQRSTUVWXYZABCDEFGHIJKLMNOPQRSTUVWXYZ
       ABCDEFGHIJKLMNOPQRSTUVWXYZ
```

You can make your own slide from wood, cardboard or plastic. The top double-width row is fixed in place, while the single-width bottom row slides. Rubber bands can hold it taut and in the correct position. Either or both of the alphabets can be mixed.

The Belaso cipher is *symmetric* because enciphering a letter X with a key K is exactly the same as enciphering the letter K with the key X. Ciphers based on adding the key to the plaintext or exclusive-ORing the key and the plaintext tend to be symmetric in this sense.

For reasons beyond my ken, the Belaso cipher is now known as the *Vigenère Cipher*, and the cipher invented by Blaise de Vigenère, which is described in section 5.8.2, is now called an *Autokey* cipher. To give credit where due, I will continue to call the cipher invented by Belaso using the standard alphabet the Belaso cipher. With a mixed alphabet I will call it the Vigenère cipher. I will call the autokey cipher invented by Vigenère the *Vigenère Autokey*.

Attributing the Belaso cipher to Vigenère is an example of Stigler's law of eponymy, for Stephen M. Stigler, that no important scientific discovery is named for its discoverer. Some cryptographic examples are the Playfair cipher, invented by Charles Wheatstone, and Morse code, invented by Alfred Vail. Stigler's law itself was proposed by Robert K. Merton, who named it the *Matthew Effect* for St. Matthew.

5.6   The Kasiski method

For over 300 years the Belaso cipher was considered unbreakable. The French called it *Le Chiffre Indéchiffrable*, the *Undecipherable Cipher*. The turning point came in 1863 when Major Friedrich W. Kasiski, a Prussian infantry officer, published a book detailing how the period of a polyalphabetic cipher could be determined. This is now called the *Kasiski Method* or the *Kasiski Test*. There is some evidence that Charles

Babbage may have used the method in 1846, but did not publish it. Ole Immanuel Franksen of the Technical University of Denmark, who has written extensively about Babbage and his Difference Engine, wrote a book, *Mr. Babbage's Secret,* which makes this claim.

The idea is to look for repeated letter sequences in the ciphertext. Some of these sequences may occur by accident, especially bigrams, but most of the repeated sequences will result from the same letters in the plaintext being enciphered by the same part of the key. The longer the repeated sequence, the lower the probability that it happened by chance. If the same part of the key is used to encipher two repeated letter sequences, then the distance between them must be a multiple of the key length. Distance is measured from the first character of one occurrence to the first character of the other occurrence. Consider this cipher fragment using the keyword EXAMPLE.

```
EXAMPLE EXAMPLE EXAMPLE EXAMPLE EXAMPLE    Key
therain inspain staysma inlyint heplain   Plaintext
XEEDPTR MKSBPTR WQAKHXE MKLKXYX LBPXPTR    Ciphertext
----+-- --1---- +----2- ---+--- -3----+   Position
```

The ciphertext trigram **PTR** occurs 3 times, at positions 5, 12 and 33. All three occurrences result from plaintext AIN enciphered with key characters PLE. That is, they result from the same plaintext trigram enciphered with the same part of the key.

The plaintext trigram AIN, which starts at position 21, produces a different ciphertext trigram, **EMK**, because it is enciphered by a different part of the key, namely EEX. Likewise, the plaintext trigram THE, which occurs at positions 1 and 29, and the plaintext trigram INS, which occurs at positions 8 and 13, do not produce repeated ciphertext trigrams because they are enciphered with different parts of the key.

In this fragment, the distances between the repeated trigrams are $12-5 = 7$, $33-5 = 28$ and $33-12 = 21$. These distances, 7, 21 and 28, are all multiples of 7, which is the length of the keyword EXAMPLE. Kasiski showed how these repetitions can be exploited to reveal the period of the encipherment.

Let's look at another example, a cryptogram.

```
ZVZPV TOGGE KHXSN LRYRP ZHZIO RZHZA ZCOAF PNOHF
VEYHC ILCVS MGRYR SYXYR YSIEK RGBYX YRRCR IIVYH
CIYBA GZSWE KDMIJ RTHVX ZIKG
```

This is a Belaso encipherment of a text in normal English. Searching for repeated letter sequences, we find **EK** at positions 10, 64 and 90, **RYR** at positions 17 and 53, and so forth. The full list of repeated letter sequences is

1	EK	10	64	90	
2	RYR	17	53		
3	RY	17	60		
4	YR	18	54	59	71
5	ZHZ	21	27		
6	HZ	22	28		
7	ZI	23	101		
8	YHCI	43	79		
9	HCI	44	80		
10	CI	45	81		
11	YXYR	57	69		
12	XYR	58	70		

We immediately notice two repeated tetragrams, **YHCI** and **YXYR**. Repeated tetra-grams almost never occur accidentally. The distance between the two occurrences of **YHCI** is 79–43 = 36, and the distance between the two occurrences of **YXYR** is 69–57 = 12. The distances 12 and 36 suggest a key length of 4, 6 or 12. We can narrow that down by looking at some of the other repeated sequences.

RYR has a distance of 36, and **ZHZ** has a distance of 6. The other repeated trigrams **HCI** and **XYR** are just parts of the two repeated tetragrams **YHCI** and **YXYR**, so they yield no additional information. The most likely period for this cryptogram is 6.

Okay, that was a bit too easy. Let's look at what happens in harder cases. One method recommended in other books is to take all of the distances between repeated sequences, and find all of their factors. The most frequent factor, they claim, will be the period. For example, if the distance is 36, then the factors are 1, 2, 3, 4. 6, 9, 12, 18 and 36. This could mislead you in several ways.

First, you might falsely conclude that the period is twice its actual value. This is because about half of the distances will be even just by chance. Half of the valid distances, those caused by repeated sequences of plaintext, will be even multiples of the period. For some messages these even multiples of the period will outnumber those distances that are odd multiples of the period. Likewise, half of the accidental repeated ciphertext sequences will have even distances. There can be lots of even distances simply by chance. Similarly, 1/3 of the distances will be multiples of 3 by chance.

When you count the number of divisors of the distances, you should reduce the number of times the factor 2 occurs by 1/2, reduce the number of times the factor 3 occurs by 1/3, and so forth. That will give you a more accurate comparison. For example, if a distance of 3 occurs 6 times, reduce that by 1/3 to 4 times, because 2 of the 6 occurrences are likely to be pure chance.

Second, when a repeated sequence occurs multiple times, the distances between pairs of these repeats may be misleading. If there are N repeats, then the number of pairs is N(N–1)/2. In the example ciphertext there are 4 occurrences of **YR**, so there are 6 pairs, that is 4×3/2 pairs. Hence there are 6 distances between pairs, 54–18 = 36, 59–18 = 41, 71–18 = 53, 59–54 = 5, 71–54 = 17 and 71–59 = 12. Which of these, if any, is a multiple of the period? Suppose that ciphertext **XYZ** appears 5 times, and that 3 of those repeats are due to the same plaintext. There will be 10 distances, of which only 3 result from the repeated plaintext, while the other 7 are spurious.

You don't want to throw out the valid repeats just because you cannot distinguish them from the accidental repeats. Here is what you can do. Suppose that you have a candidate for the period. For example, suppose you suspect that the period is 6. Reduce the locations where the repeated sequence occurs modulo 6. (Remember modular arithmetic? If not, look at section 3.5 again.)

Let's try the *modulo method*. Look at the 4 occurrences of **YR** again, and reduce their positions modulo 5, modulo 6 and modulo 7 to see what happens.

18	54	59	71	Positions of **YR** in the ciphertext
3	4	4	1	Positions reduced modulo 5
0	0	5	5	Positions reduced modulo 6
4	5	3	1	Positions reduced modulo 7

All 4 residues modulo 7 are different. If the period is 7, then all of the repeats of **YR** are accidental. There are only 2 equal residues modulo 5. If the period is 5, then only 2 out of 4 occurrences come from repeated plaintext. But if the period is 6 we hit paydirt. We now see that the 4 occurrences of **YR** come from 2 different repeated bigrams in the plaintext, one bigram at positions 18 and 54 in the plaintext, with a distance of 36, and the other bigram at positions 59 and 71 in the plaintext, with a distance of 12.

How did that happen? Look back at the list of repeated sequences. You can see that the bigram **YR** occurs in the repeated trigram **RYR** and in the repeated tetragram **YXYR**. Each of these contributed one repetition.

Let's look at a second method for determining the period of a polyalphabetic cipher. If the evidence from the repeated sequences is inconclusive, it is good to have a backup plan.

5.7   *Index of Coincidence*

The *Index of Coincidence* was invented by American cryptanalyst William F. Friedman in 1922. The idea is very simple, but its importance is profound. Imagine two messages enciphered using a polyalphabetic cipher, but with different keys, and possibly with different periods. If you compare the two ciphertexts letter by letter, the chance that two corresponding letters are the same is 1 in 26, or about .0385. If both messages are 52 characters long you would expect 52/26 = 2 corresponding pairs of letters to be equal. Here I have enciphered the 52-letter plaintext ON THE FIRST DAY OF SPRING A YOUNG MANS FANCY TURNED TO BASEBALL with a Belaso cipher using the keys MARS and VENUS, respectively. The two equal letters are highlighted. (It is accidental that both pairs of equal letters are F.)

```
ANKZQ FZJET USKOW KBRZF SAPGG NXEMN JXMNT QFUIF QDKGN AJWNA CD
JRGBW AMEML YELIX NTECF BELIM IKZUF NJNHU TXHLF ZHGIT VWRVS GP
```

Now imagine two messages enciphered by the same key. Each pair of corresponding letters is enciphered by the same key character, so if the plaintext letters are the same, then the ciphertext letters will be the same. The frequency of A is about .08, so the chance that both plaintext letters are A is $.08^2$, or about .0064. The chance that they are both B is about $.015^2 = .000225$, and so forth through the alphabet. The total for all 26 letters comes to .0645 to .0675, about 1/15, depending on which letter frequency table you use. The chance of two corresponding ciphertext letters being equal when the same key is used is roughly 1/15, which is 73% higher than the 1/26 chance when the keys are different.

This fact can be exploited to determine the key length for a polyalphabetic cipher. Let's number the characters in the ciphertext C_1, C_2, C_3, ... and let the length of the key be L. We can compare the characters in the ciphertext with those same characters shifted by some number of positions, say S positions. That is, we compare C_1 with C_{1+S}, C_2 with C_{2+S}, C_3 with C_{3+S} and so forth.

When the shift S is a multiple of L, then C_i is enciphered with the same alphabet as C_{i+S} for every position i, so the chance that two corresponding ciphertext characters are equal is 1/15. If the shift is not a multiple of L, then corresponding characters will not be enciphered with the same alphabet, and the chance that they are equal is only 1/26. The number of equal characters should be largest when S = L, S = 2L, and so forth. Trying several different shifts should make this pattern clear. The shifts producing the most matches will usually be multiples of the period.

Trying many different shifts sounds like a job for a computer, but it actually can be done by hand without too much effort. Write the cryptogram onto two long strips of paper. Then just slide one strip against the other and count the number of equal characters for each shift. You need to space the letters evenly so they align correctly. This is easily managed by using graph paper, or by holding a ruler next to each strip while you write the letters.

```
ZVZPVTOGGEKHXSNLRYRPZHZIORZHZAZCOAFPNOHFVEYHCILCVS···
  ZVZPVTOGGEKHXSNLRYRPZHZIORZHZAZCOAFPNOHFVEYHCILCVS···
```

The Index of Coincidence has another use that has proved of immense value for cryptanalysts. It can detect when two messages have been enciphered using the same key. Imagine that Emily is using a machine cipher that produces a polyalphabetic cipher with a very long period, say 100,000. For comparison, the Enigma machine used by the German army in WW II had a period of $26 \times 25 \times 26 = 16,900$. Suppose you have thousands of intercepted messages. Each message is enciphered using some segment of this long key. Sliding each message against the others, and employing both Index of Coincidence and repeated ciphertext sequences, you can detect sections of different messages that have been enciphered by the same part of the key.

When you have found enough of these overlapping segments of the key you can begin splicing the segments together to get longer segments. Once enough messages are found that are enciphered with the same key segment you can begin to solve the messages by the usual means, letter frequency, contact frequency, identifying common words, and so forth.

5.8   Index of Coincidence, again

There is another method for estimating the period of a polyalphabetic cipher, also called the Index of Coincidence, and also due to William F. Friedman. This method calculates the probability that two letters are equal when there are 2 alphabets, 3 alphabets, and so on. This is calculated ahead of time and kept in a table. The idea is to calculate this same statistic for a given message, and compare that number to the table. The closest match is supposed to be the period of the cipher. In practice this often comes close, but it is frequently off by 1, 2 or even 3. When the period is more than 10, the method is useless. This method is not much better than random guessing, so it is not worthwhile to explain the details.

The Belaso and Vigenère ciphers continued to be widely used through the 1880s. As the knowledge of the Kasiski method began to spread, their use diminished, and they largely disappeared after the Index of Coincidence was published. Still, today, it remains one of the most popular hobbyist ciphers. Several times, when I told people that I was writing a book on cryptography, they would tell me that they knew an unbreakable cipher. This always turned out to be the Belaso cipher, which they would call the Vigenère. Then I had to prove it was breakable, by solving a cipher they would make up. These were so badly mangled, that I had to create a webpage *mastersoftware.biz/vigenere.htm* to make sure that the ciphers were done correctly.

5.9   Solving a polyalphabetic cipher

Once you have found the period using either the Kasiski method or the Index of Coincidence, the next step is to solve the individual alphabets. Let's look at the easiest case first, the Belaso cipher.

5.9.1   Solving a Belaso cipher

With the Belaso cipher all of the substitution alphabets are simply the standard alphabet shifted by some amount. Determine the amount and you have solved the cipher. The first step is to separate the characters that have been enciphered with each letter of the key. Let's look again at the example from section 5.5. Since we have determined that the period is 6, let's write the ciphertext in groups of 6.

```
ZVZPVT OGGEKH XSNLRY RPZHZI ORZHZA ZCOAFP NOHFVE YHCILC VSMGRY
RSYXYR YSIEKR GBYXYR RCRIIV YHCIYB AGZSWE KDMIJR THVXZI KG
```

The first letter in each of these groups has been enciphered with the first letter of the key, the second letter in each group by the second letter of the key, and so forth. If we wrote the ciphertext vertically in 6 columns, like this

```
123456
ZVZPVT
OGGEKH
XSNLRY
 . . .
```

then the first column of letters would be enciphered with the first letter of the key, the second column of letters would be enciphered with the second key letter, and so on.

Consider each letter column separately. Each column will have normal English letter frequencies, but shifted according to its key letter. If we can determine the shifts, then we have solved the cipher. I will describe two methods, one for hand solution and one for computer solution. Let's look at the paper-and-pencil method first.

For each column, we can make a frequency count. That will give us 26 numbers. For paper-and-pencil solving, it is better to display the frequencies as a histogram (bar graph). The histogram for the first column of the ciphertext would be

```
                              R                 Y        Frequency
                K       O     R               Y Z        histogram
A - - - - - G - - - K - - N O - - R - T - V - X Y Z      for column 1
```

With only 18 letters this is rather sparse, but it is enough. Let's compare this to a histogram of standard English letter frequencies, shown next, and try to figure out the shift.

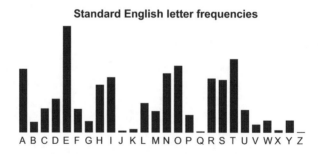

Standard English letter frequencies

A B C D E F G H I J K L M N O P Q R S T U V W X Y Z

Some of the visual characteristics of this frequency distribution are (1) E is by far the tallest peak; (2) there are three peaks evenly spaced 4 columns apart, namely A,E,I, where I has the companion H; (3) there is a double peak at N,O; and (4) there is a triple peak at R,S,T.

Let's try to match this histogram to the ciphertext histogram. We start by looking for a tall peak that could represent E. There are two tall peaks, **R** and **Y**, corresponding to key letters N and U. That is, if E is enciphered by N the result is **R**, and if E is enciphered by U the result is **Y**.

Next, let's look for 3 peaks 4 spaces apart. There are two candidates, `G,K,O` and `N,R,V`, corresponding to key letters G and N. How about a double peak? Likely candidates are `N,O` and `Y,Z`, corresponding to key letters A and L. What about a triple peak? There is only one choice, the triple peak at `X,Y,Z`. This corresponds to the key letter G.

The most likely key for the first column is G, which produces the `A,E,I` peaks and the `R,S,T` triple peak. The second most likely key is N, which gives E as the most frequent letter, and the `N,O` double peak.

Let's turn our attention to the second column of the ciphertext. The letter frequency histogram is

```
                                       S                    Frequency
              G H                      S                    histogram
     C        G H                      S                    for column 2
 - B C D - - G H - - - - - - O P - R S - - V - - - -
```

This time the ciphertext letter S catches our attention. If S represents plaintext E, then the key must be O. Let's check this out by comparing the ciphertext histogram against the shifted alphabet.

```
                                       S
              G H                      S                    Ciphertext
     C        G H                      S                    histogram
 - B C D - - G H - - - - - - O P - R S - - V - - - -        Try key=O
 M N O P Q R S T U V W X Y Z A B C D E F G H I J K L        Alphabet O
```

You can see that all of the high-frequency letters in the ciphertext, namely C, G, H and S, correspond to high-frequency plaintext letters, namely O, S, T and E, respectively. This is an excellent fit, and the second key letter is very probably O. The keyword starts GO.

The other 4 key letters are determined in the same way. The keyword is GOVERN, and the plaintext is THE LEGISLATURE SHALL BE DIVIDED INTO TWO CHAMBERS THE UPPER CALLED THE SENATE AND THE LOWER IS THE HOUSE OF REPRESENTATIVES.

That is the hand method: make the frequency distribution visual by using histograms and then match the distributions by eye. For computer solution we need a numerical method for eyeballing the distributions to find a match. The standard method found in every book that discusses polyalphabetic ciphers is to use the correlation coefficient, specifically the Pearson product-moment correlation coefficient, named for Karl Pearson, a founder of modern statistics.

If you know statistics, this will be familiar to you. You no doubt already have a statistics package with this function ready-made. Use it in good health. For everyone else, I will show you a method that is both simpler and faster—and exactly as accurate.

When we match up two frequency distributions by eye, we are trying to match the tallest peaks in one histogram with the tallest peaks in the other histogram. If we multiply their heights, we are trying to get the biggest product. If you go down the alphabet and add the 26 products, then the sum will be highest when the tall peaks line up with one another, and lowest when the highest peaks line up with the lowest valleys.

That's the idea. Try each of the 26 possible shifts. Line up the letter frequencies of the ciphertext with the shifted frequencies for standard English, and add up the 26 products. The highest sum will indicate the most likely shift. This tells you the most likely key letter. The second-highest sum is the second most likely shift, and so forth. I call this technique the *Tall Peaks* method.

The Belaso cipher is rated Two.

5.9.2   *Solving a Vigenère cipher*

About 30 years after Belaso, Blaise de Vigenère made two improvements over the Belaso cipher. The first was to add guides along the outside of the tableau. This had the effect of producing a mixed alphabet without the work of mixing the tableau. Here is an example, using the keyphrase FIRST LOVE in the horizontal guides, and the keyword YOUTH in the vertical guides. You will find the second improvement, autokey, in section 5.10.

```
    FIRSTLOVEABCDGHJKMNPQUWXYZ      Top guide
  Y ABCDEFGHIJKLMNOPQRSTUVWXYZA  Y
  O BCDEFGHIJKLMNOPQRSTUVWXYZA   O
  U CDEFGHIJKLMNOPQRSTUVWXYZAB   U
  T DEFGHIJKLMNOPQRSTUVWXYZABC   T
  H EFGHIJKLMNOPQRSTUVWXYZABCD   H
  A FGHIJKLMNOPQRSTUVWXYZABCDE   A
  B GHIJKLMNOPQRSTUVWXYZABCDEF   B
                . . .
  Z ZABCDEFGHIJKLMNOPQRSTUVWXY   Z
    FIRSTLOVEABCDGHJKMNPQUWXYZ      Bottom guide
```

To encipher the letter B using the key letter U, find the key letter U in the *key guide* to the left or right of the row, and the plaintext letter B in the *letter guide* at the top or bottom of the column. The ciphertext letter is the letter in the U row and B column, namely **M**. To decipher, use the key letter to find the row, find the ciphertext letter on that row, and take the plaintext from the letter guide at the top or bottom.

If you are enciphering by hand, I suggest drawing horizontal and vertical rules every 4 or 5 rows and columns. Or, use a clear plastic L-square to find the intersections accurately.

Here is a sample message enciphered using this form of Vigenère cipher. It has a period of 5.

```
SLMDQ BXSLM XIHSQ NHJEQ SVJGW LBJSJ BFEII CBHVN RUTGW RPHEN
VXPIL RPPIW SAJHQ SVTKU ACFQQ ACFDT MCTOM XZEKE XZPLP RLHG
```

This cipher has a serious weakness. Since each row in the tableau is the standard alphabet shifted by a number of positions, each cipher alphabet will be the same as all of the other cipher alphabets shifted by some number of positions. You cannot usefully compare the cipher alphabets to the standard alphabet because they are in mixed order, however, you can determine the shifts by comparing the cipher alphabets to one another, either by eye or by using the Tall Peaks method.

The following figure shows the histograms for the 5 cipher alphabets, shifted to match up their peaks and valleys. All of the ciphertext letters in the first column (shaded) represent the same plaintext letter. This means S in the first alphabet, C in the second alphabet and L in the fourth alphabet all represent the same letter. Replace all of these by A. There are no letters in the second column. In the third column, M in the third alphabet and T in the fifth alphabet represent the same plaintext letter. Replace all of these by C, and so forth. The ciphertext letters in the 26th column would all be replaced by Z.

Histograms for the shifted cipher alphabets

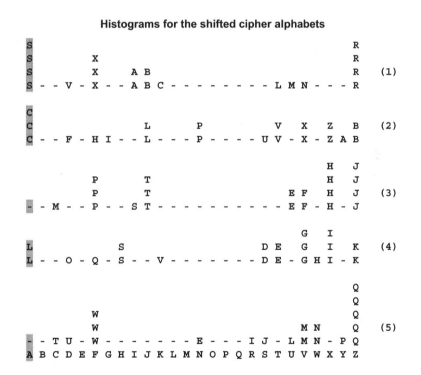

This converts the ciphertext into a simple substitution which can now be solved using the methods of section 5.1. The Vigenère cipher is rated Two.

5.9.3   *Solving a general polyalphabetic cipher*

A general polyalphabetic cipher can also be done using a tableau. The rows of the tableau can be mixed according to any scheme, independently of one another. It is worth noting that the number of rows need not be the same as the number of columns. For computer ciphers it can be valuable to make the tableau 256 characters wide and 512 rows deep so that each ciphertext character appears twice in each column. That will make it difficult for an opponent who has obtained a ciphertext and its corresponding plaintext to determine the key. Here is a partial example of a 100-row tableau:

```
00  IBVMRUCNJYSAWEPZODXGQKTHLF
01  LOEIBQXJTMFRWAPUCZNVGKYHSD
02  GTAOKYSFUJPERHXLBVQDIZMWCN
03  DPNETHVBJZSGMWAXIQOFYRCUKL
          ·  ·  ·
99  BRXIZPYLVJCNQHTKESUAMGWDOF
```

This tableau would be used with a numeric key where 2 decimal digits would be used to select the row for enciphering. A 20-digit key would produce a polyalphabetic cipher whose period is 10.

Solving a general polyalphabetic cipher is very like solving a monoalphabetic cipher. You begin by taking a frequency count and making a contact table for each column. In this case the contacts for column C will be in columns C−1 and C+1, wrapping around from the rightmost column to the first column, as needed. There will be fewer occurrences of each letter in one column, so you need to make inferences from less data. This takes a lot of inspired guessing, which comes from experience.

Let's begin with this polyalphabetic ciphertext.

```
OHOYO RKKDF JKYSU ZONSO OKGSC LHKDK FKHWU ZGGSN ZYYZK JPHZO
RKKDP KCHUK LHYYF BGBSC FKKFK CZIUX VOZRU TZWSN UZYSU ZONSO
OPHCO RPNDZ ZPIHK OGDHN UWOSN ZYYZK XOQDX BNMUO R
```

A quick examination of this ciphertext shows two long repeated sequences, **YSUZONSOO** at positions 13 and 93, and **SNZYYZK** at positions 39 and 124. In both cases the distance between the two occurrences is a multiple of 5, confirming that the period is 5. These long repeats probably represent common words or phrases, or words specific to the subject of the message.

The contact charts for each of the 5 key letters follow. To make it easier to explain the deductions, I will tag each ciphertext letter with a digit specifying its alphabet number. So **C1** would mean the ciphertext letter **C** in alphabet 1 (that is, enciphered with the first letter of the key), **H3** would mean ciphertext letter **H** in alphabet 3 (using the third letter of the key), and so forth.

Recall that letters with many different contacts on both sides tend to be vowels, while letters with fewer distinct contacts tend to be consonants.

```
        (1)                    (2)                    (3)
    FX  B  GN              K  C  H              G  B  S
     K  C  Z            ZBO  G  GBD             G  D  H
    KC  F  KK            OLL  H  OKY           KG  G  SS
    FK  J  KP          RJOFRF K  KYGHKK       KPCP H  WZUC
     P  K  C              B  N  M              ZP  I  UH
    CK  L  HH           ZVZX  O  NZNQ        KHKK  K  DDDF
   OOK  O  HKPG         JORZ  P  HHNI           N  M  U
  OOOO  R  KKP             U  W  O             OOP  N  SSD
     U  T  Z             ZZ  Y  YY             HW  O  YS
    NN  U  ZW           CTU  Z  IWY             O  Q  D
     X  V  O                                     Z  W  S
     K  X  O                                  KYHZY Y  SZYSZ
UUNUZN  Z  OGYOPY                               O  Z  R

        (4)                    (5)
     H  C  O               SS  C  LF
  KKKNQ  D  FKPZX          DY  F  JB
     K  F  K             DZUFHZ K  FJLCOX
    ID  H  KN             SSHS  N  ZUUZ
     Z  R  U            YSZSCU  O  RORORR
YNGGBWYNO S  UOCNCNUON      D  P  K
   HIM  U  KXO            SWRS  U  ZZTZ
     H  W  U                UD  X  VB
    OY  Y  OF                D  Z  Z
   YHY  Z  KOK
```

Based on these contacts we can tentatively identify as vowels G2, K2, O2, P2, H3, K5 and as consonants R1, Z1, K3, N3, D4, S4, O5, U5. Based on its high frequency, S4 probably represents plaintext T.

You proceed exactly as you did for simple substitution. You update the contact charts to show those letters that have been identified as vowels and consonants, and you also write the ciphertext with the vowels and consonants marked. You use this to refine and repair the vowel/consonant identifications, and to identify individual letters.

I will not repeat all the steps taken in section 5.1. It is the same logic, but the incremental steps are smaller and more numerous, with more back-tracking. The general polyalphabetic cipher is rated Three.

5.10 Autokey

You may recall that I said in section 5.9.2 that Vigenère made two improvements to the Belaso cipher. The first improvement was placing the guides around the edges of the tableau to produce a mixed alphabet. The second improvement was the *autokey*.

The autokey uses the plaintext of the message as a key to encipher the rest of the message. An early version was invented by Italian physician/mathematician/astrologer

Girolamo Cardano. In Cardano's system each letter was enciphered using itself as the key. This only works if you have an alphabet with an odd number of letters. Using the English alphabet of 26 letters, an A would produce an **A**, and an N would also produce an **A**, so the intended recipient would have to figure out which was meant. Even with an odd-sized alphabet, the Cardano autokey merely produces a simple substitution.

Vigenère improved upon the Cardano method by using a lag. Vigenère used a 1-letter key to encipher the first letter, used the first plaintext letter to encipher the second letter, used the second plaintext letter to encipher the third letter, and so forth. In modern practice a keyword is used to encipher the first group of letters, then that group of plaintext letters is used to encipher the second group, and so on. This example uses the key SAMPLE with the Belaso tableau, that is, unmixed alphabets.

```
SAMPLE  THEDEL  EGATIO  NMUSTP  RESENT  AUNITE    Key
THEDEL  EGATIO  NMUSTP  RESENT  AUNITE  DFRONT    Plaintext
LHQSPP  XNEWMZ  RSULBD  EQMWGI  RYFMGX  DZEWGX    Ciphertext
```

With unmixed alphabets, decryption is straightforward. The Index of Coincidence described in section 5.7 can be used to determine the length of the keyword. The index is often dramatically higher when the ciphertext is offset by a multiple of the key length, like this:

```
LHQSPP  XNEWMZ  RSULBD  EQMWGI  RYFMGX  DZEWGX
   LHQSPP  XNEWMZ  RSULBD  EQMWGI  RYFMGX  DZEWGX
```

Suppose you have found that the keyword has 6 letters. Try each letter of the alphabet for the first letter of the key. Start with A. Since the first ciphertext letter is L, the first plaintext letter must also be L. This will also be the key for the 7th letter of the message. Since the 7th ciphertext letter is X, the 7th plaintext letter would have to be M.

Proceeding this way, each guess for the first key letter gives you the corresponding 1st, 7th, 13th, 19th, 25th and 31st characters of the plaintext. That is, it gives you every 6th plaintext letter. There are 26 sets of letters, one for each possible key letter. Some of these sets of 6 letters will have normal English letter frequencies, some will be implausible. Repeat this for the second key letter. Each guess for the second key letter gives you the corresponding 2nd, 8th, 14th, 20th, 26th and 32nd plaintext letters.

Now, take the 5 most probable choices for letters 1, 7, 13, ... and pair them up with the 5 most probable choices for letters 2, 8, 14, ... This will give you 25 sets of bigrams. Some of these will be highly likely, some will be implausible. Take the 10 most plausible of these and pair them up with the 5 most likely choices for the third key letter. This will give you 50 sets of trigrams. Choose the 10 most reasonable of these and pair them up with the 5 best choices for the fourth key letter. By this point some plaintext words will start to appear, and the correct choice of key letters will become obvious.

If you are doing this by computer, skip the bigrams. Simply try all 26^3 combinations for the first 3 key letters and go straight for the trigrams. Then repeat this for the second 3 key letters, that is, key letters 2, 3 and 4. The most likely choices for the first 3 key letters and the second 3 key letters will overlap. The same will happen with the third and fourth sets of key letters. This will rapidly narrow in on the correct keyword.

Vigenère autokey using standard alphabets is rated Three.

5.11 *Running key*

Running key is similar to autokey, but instead of a short keyword or keyphrase, running key uses a *keytext* that may be as long as the message itself. Running key has never been widely used in practice because it requires both parties to get the keytext exactly letter perfect. If one party remembers or copies the key as <u>MINE</u> EYES HAVE SEEN THE GLORY OF THE COMING OF THE LORD, but the other party remembers the key as <u>MY</u> EYES HAVE SEEN THE GLORY OF THE COMING OF THE LORD, then they will be unable to communicate. One way to deal with this problem is to use a keytext from a printed book that both parties have, although they must carry the book with them. This is not a problem for computer communication, because a computer can store thousands of books.

Again, assuming the Belaso tableau with the standard English alphabet, running key is straightforward, albeit laborious, to decrypt. One technique, which works for both autokey and running key, is to guess a likely word that may appear in the text. The word could occur in either the keytext or the plaintext. The cryptographer will need to untangle this later. The probable word, or *crib*, could be a common English word, like THE or AND, or it might be a word related to the suspected subject matter. For example, if the message pertains to trade negotiations, then likely words might be TARIFF, SHIPPING, REPRESENTATIVE, BARGAINING, and similar.

The idea is to try the probable word in all possible positions in the message. This is called *word dragging*. Knowing the plaintext word and the corresponding ciphertext gives you a snippet of the key. If the word is correctly placed, then this fragment will look like normal English. The longer the probable word, the more confident you can be that it is correct. Once you have found a word, you try to guess the letters, then the words that precede or follow it in the text to widen the breach.

There is a second technique, one which is suitable for computer solution. This requires a new mathematical concept called *conditional probability*. This is the probability that an event A will occur if event B also occurs. The probability of a single event A is denoted P(A), and the conditional probability of the event A given the event B is denoted P(A|B). If AB denotes the event "A and B," then the conditional probability of A given B is P(A|B) = P(AB)/P(B). That means P(AB) = P(A|B)P(B).

An example may help to clarify this. If you are throwing two standard dice, the probability of throwing a 12 is 1/36. However, if you throw the first die and the result is 6, then the chance of throwing 12 becomes 1/6. Let A mean "throwing 12" and B mean "the first throw is 6." Then P(A) = 1/36, and P(B) = 1/6. P(AB) means throwing a 12 with the first throw being 6. P(AB) is also 1/36 because if you throw a 12 the first throw has to be 6. Using the notation for conditional probability, P(A|B) = P(AB)/P(B) = (1/36)/(1/6) = 1/6. So the conditional probability of throwing 12 when the first throw is 6 is 1/6.

Let's use conditional probability to solve a running key cipher. The tools that are needed are tables of single-letter, bigram and trigram probabilities. These can be compiled by counting the letters, bigrams and trigrams in a large body of text. You can find many such bodies at the Project Gutenberg website, www.gutenberg.org. Select the plaintext option. You can also find some tabulations on the internet.

You will need to assign a probability for every possible bigram and trigram, not just those found in that body. For bigrams this is obvious. If AB is a bigram that did not appear in the count, you could set P(AB) = P(A)P(B), however, I suggest setting it lower simply because AB was never found. I use P(AB) = P(A)P(B)/3. Once you have a complete set of bigram probabilities, you can extend this to trigrams by setting P(ABC) to the greater of P(A)P(BC) and P(AB)P(C). Again, I suggest setting them lower because the trigram ABC never appeared. For example, set P(ABC) to the greater of P(A)P(BC)/3 and P(AB)P(C)/3. These artificial probabilities mean that the total probabilities for all bigrams and all trigrams are greater than 1. Mathematically this is nonsense, but it has no practical effect.

Now that we have the necessary tools, we can tackle a running key cipher. Choose a starting position in the message, say, s, and try all possible key trigrams in positions s, s+1, s+2. See what the corresponding plaintext trigrams are. Multiply the probabilities of the key trigram and the text trigram to get the probability for that placement. Keep the top 10,000 of these placements, and discard the rest. For each of the chosen trigrams, try all possible key letters in position s+3, and see what the corresponding plaintext letter is. Suppose the key trigram is JKL, the next key letter is M, and the corresponding plaintext tetragram is ABCD. You can estimate the probability of the key tetragram JKLM by using the conditional probability P(KLM|KL), which is the probability that an M will follow the bigram KL. This is calculated from the trigram probabilities as P(KLM)/P(KL), which is the probability of the trigram KLM divided by the probability of the bigram KL. The probability of the tetragram is thus estimated as P(JKL)P(KLM|KL). This is done for both the key tetragram and the plaintext tetragram ABCD.

Estimate the probability of this placement by multiplying the probabilities of the key tetragram and the plaintext tetragram. Again, keep the top 10,000 and toss out the rest. Keep going until the solution becomes obvious. This can all be done by computer, without any human supervision.

Vigenère running key using standard alphabets is rated Four.

*5.12 Simulated rotor machines

The *sine qua non* of polyalphabetic ciphers are the electro-mechanical rotor machines used from the 1920s on. These machines can have periods in the billions or trillions, or no period at all if the movement of the rotors depends on the plaintext or ciphertext characters. At least 70 different types of machines were produced from about 1915 until after World War II. There are several websites that have pictures and descriptions of these machines.

Each machine has one or more rotors, usually 3 to 6, but sometimes as many as 10. Each rotor performs a simple substitution. After each letter is enciphered, some of the rotors turn so that a different substitution is used for the next letter. Various systems of gears, lugs, cams, levers and pawls make the rotors turn in unpredictable ways. That is, unpredictable for your opponent.

It is easier to describe the rotor machines if we replace the letters of the alphabet with numbers. For mechanical rotor machines, where each rotor has 26 positions corresponding to the 26 letters of the alphabet, we replace A by 0, B by 1, C by 2, through Z, which is replaced by 25. In other words, we use the classical numbering system minus 1. For the computer simulation, we use 8-bit bytes and replace characters by their numeric codes in some standardized system such as UTF-8 code. In this system A is 65, B is 66, C is 67, through Z, which is 90. Other characters such as lower-case letters, digits and punctuation are also replaced by their UTF-8 character codes.

Now that we are dealing with numbers, we can do arithmetic on them, such as adding to them and taking residues modulo 26 or 256, as appropriate. If you wish to review modular arithmetic, refer back to section 3.6.

Cipher machines with as many as 16 rotors have been produced. This is the 10-rotor assembly of the Russian-made Fialka machine, which was used by the Warsaw Pact nations from 1956 until the 1990s. Photo courtesy of Paul Hudson and licensed under CC BY 2.0.

5.12.1 *Single-rotor machine*

Let's start with a single mechanical rotor. The rotor performs a simple substitution, so it can be simulated by a substitution table S. The table S is just a scrambled alphabet, like one row of a tableau. The entries in the list are numbered from 0 to 25, corresponding to the 26 letters of the alphabet. The Nth entry in the substitution table, denoted S(N), is the substitute for the Nth letter of the alphabet. So S(0) is the substitute for A, S(1) is the substitute for B, and so forth.

As the rotors turn, they change position. The position can be represented by a number P, which can range from 0 to 25. When a rotor has turned 26 positions it will be back to its starting position, namely position 0. The substitute for the Nth letter when the rotor is in position P is S(N+P). So when the rotor is in position 5, S(5) is the substitute for A, S(6) is the substitute for B, and so on. It is understood that N+P wraps around, so S(26) is the same as S(0), S(27) is the same as S(1), and so on. In other words, N+P is really shorthand for (N+P) mod 26.

In a mechanical rotor machine, the rotors turn by different amounts after enciphering each letter. This irregular motion can be simulated by using a sequence of *step numbers*, say (a,b,c,d,e). On the first cycle the rotor steps (advances, rotates) a positions. On the second cycle it steps b positions, and so forth. On the sixth cycle the sequence repeats. So, if the rotor starts at position P, after one cycle it will be at position P+a. After two cycles it will be at position P+a+b. After 5 cycles it will be at position P+a+b+c+d+e. After 6 cycles the rotor will be at position P+2a+b+c+d+e. In mechanical devices each rotor usually turns only a few positions, often either 0 or 1 position per cycle depending upon whether a particular lug is up or down. In a computer simulation we have no such constraints. The steps can be any amount from 0 to 25 positions when simulating a mechanical rotor, or from 0 to 255 when using 8-bit bytes to represent the characters.

Since we chose a key with 5 steps, this single-rotor machine will repeat after $5\times26 = 130$ cycles. When a+b+c+d+e is even, the machine will repeat after 65 cycles, and if a+b+c+d+e is a multiple of 13, the machine will repeat after only 10 cycles. Obviously one rotor does not give much security. The one-rotor machine cipher is rated Three.

5.12.2 *Three-rotor machine*

Let's look at simulating a more practical kind of rotor machine. This machine has 3 rotors and uses the 8-bit UTF-8 code. Three rotors need 3 substitution tables, S_1, S_2 and S_3. When the rotors are in positions P_1, P_2 and P_3, the Nth letter of the alphabet gets enciphered as $S_3(S_2(S_1(N+P_1)+P_2)+P_3)$.

Each of the 3 substitution tables has its own list of steps: say S_1 has steps $(a_1,a_2,a_3,...,a_i)$, S_2 has steps $(b_1,b_2,b_3,...,b_j)$ and S_3 has steps $(c_1,c_2,c_3,...,c_k)$. If the sum of the steps for each rotor is an odd number, and i, j and k are coprime, then the period of this machine is 256ijk. For example, if i = 10, j = 11 and k = 13, then ijk is 1430, and the period is $1430\times256 = 366,080$. The effect is like having a polyalphabetic cipher whose tableau has 366,080 rows, with each row used only once per cycle.

Suppose the 3 substitution tables and the sequences of steps are known, for example, suppose they have been standardized over a large network. One might imagine that Emily needs to try only the $256^3 = 1.67\times10^7$ initial rotor settings to crack each message. This might take a few seconds on a current-day personal computer. This is misleading.

Consider two different states of the machine. Both states have the rotors in the same positions, but they are in different parts of the stepping sequence. Starting to encipher from those two states will give different sequences of the cipher alphabets, so the same message will be enciphered differently. Cracking this cipher by an exhaustive search would require trying all possible rotor settings and all possible places in the step sequence for a total of $256^3\times1430$, or 2.40×10^{10} cases. This is still feasible using a personal computer, but would take several hours, not a few seconds.

With known rotors and known step sequences, this 3-rotor cipher is rated Four.

If the rotors and step sequences are secret, then Emily must fall back on the techniques for a general polyalphabetic cipher, namely gathering large numbers of intercepts and matching them up to find sections that are enciphered with the same settings. To separate true matches from accidental matches, the Index of Coincidence test (section 5.7) needs to be done on long overlaps. I suggest at least 200 characters. Matching should be attempted only for messages longer than 200 characters. For a message of length L characters, with $L \geq 200$, the number of matchable positions is L-199. When the combined total, M, of matchable positions for all intercepted messages exceeds $\sqrt{2.40 \times 10^{10}} = 1.55 \times 10^5$, matching sections of text could begin to be detected.

This does not seem like much, but the work to detect these overlaps is on the order of M^2. Moreover, a single overlap is nowhere near sufficient. You need enough overlaps that you can start to distinguish high-frequency letters and separate vowels from consonants. This will require a mainframe computer and some talented cryptanalysts. The 3-rotor machine with unknown rotors and unknown step sequences is rated Six.

5.12.3 *Eight-rotor machine*

Three rotors is a good start. To really ratchet up the strength of the simulated rotor machine, let's increase the number of rotors from 3 to 8. Let the number of steps for the rotors be 11, 13, 17, 19, 23, 25, 27 and 31, in some order, and make the sum of the steps odd for each rotor. The period of this machine is about 5.69×10^{12}.

If this is a hardware device, the internal wiring of the rotors and the sequences of steps might be built in. Even if this is the case, it still would not be feasible to match up messages the way we did with the 3-rotor version. This is because there are now $256^8 = 1.84 \times 10^{19}$ possible initial positions for the 8 rotors. Since the period is 5.69×10^{12}, the total number of states for the machine becomes $(1.84 \times 10^{19}) \times (5.69 \times 10^{12}) = 1.05 \times 10^{32}$. When the rotors and stepping sequences cannot be changed, this 8-rotor machine is rated Nine.

Let's take this further. Instead of 8 rotors, suppose we have a supply of 16 possible rotors. For each message we select 8 out of the 16 rotors in some order. There are 5.19×10^8 such permutations. For each such permutation there are 1.84×10^{19} possible initial rotor positions and 5.69×10^{12} positions for the step sequences for a total of 5.43×10^{40} states.

Even if Emily somehow knows the substitution tables and the stepping sequences for all 16 rotors, it is not feasible to crack a message enciphered with this machine, even using the largest and fastest supercomputer in the world. (At this writing the fastest supercomputer in the world is the Summit computer, capable of up to 200 petaflops.) This 8-rotor cipher is rated Ten.

If the contents of the substitution tables and the stepping sequences are kept secret, or are changed frequently, this rotor cipher with 8 interchangeable rotors should remain far beyond the reach of the largest supercomputers for 10, 20, or perhaps even 30 years to come.

Since this is a software simulation of a rotor machine, the rotors can be changed at will. Instead of a fixed set of 16 rotors, the rotors could be changed for every message by using a key to mix each of the 8 rotor alphabets. This would greatly increase the security at the cost of requiring a separate setup phase for each message. An intermediate level of security is to use 7 standard rotors from the set of 16, and 1 rotor whose alphabet is generated independently for each message. This reduces the setup time by 87%.

Even though this cipher has already earned a rating of Ten, you may still wish to strengthen it. You might not trust my rating, or you believe your opponent has stupendous computing power available. One way is to use the output of some of the rotors to modify the operation. I suggest taking the output of the fourth rotor, halfway through the encipherment, and use that character to advance the first rotor. Either use the character directly, or perform a simple substitution on the character to get the number of positions to advance the first rotor. Except for the first character in the message, the first rotor is stepped twice, once from its stepping sequence, and once using the feedback from the fourth rotor.

This double-stepping does not affect the encipherment of the current character. It is the next message character that is enciphered using this modified setting. Double-stepping might be difficult to accomplish with a hardware rotor machine, but it can be done easily with the simulated machine since the rotors are simulated one at a time.

BTW, it might seem like it would be stronger to use the output of the eighth rotor, but this is not true. The output of the eighth rotor is the ciphertext character, which would be known to an eavesdropper. The outputs of the two middle rotors, that is, the fourth and fifth rotors, are the least accessible to an eavesdropper and hence the safest.

This feedback from the fourth rotor makes the simulated 8-rotor machine aperiodic. No matter how many messages are sent, Emily can never find two messages with the same sequence of rotor settings.**

Countermeasures 6

To recap section 5.9, polyalphabetic ciphers can be solved by a two-step process. First, the period or the key length is determined using the Kasiski Method or the Index of Coincidence. This separates the ciphertext into several smaller texts, each enciphered by just one letter of the key. Second, these individual texts are deciphered using the standard methods for simple substitution ciphers, frequency and contacts.

Let's turn it around. What can the cryptologist do to prevent a polyalphabetic cipher from being cracked by this two-step process? We will look at a few countermeasures.

6.1 Double encipherment

If a message is enciphered with one polyalphabetic cipher whose period is P, and the resulting intermediate text is enciphered with a second polyalphabetic cipher whose period is Q, the result is equivalent to a polyalphabetic cipher whose period is the least common multiple of P and Q, denoted *lcm(P,Q)*. That is, the period is the smallest integer that is a multiple of both P and Q. For example, if P is 10 and Q is 11, then the double encipherment will have a period of 110, but if P is 10 and Q is 12, then the double encipherment will have a period of 60 because 60 is a multiple of both 10 and 12.

Each of the individual alphabets in the double encipherment is the composition of the two alphabets from the first and second encipherments, as described in section 11.7.4. If these are shifted standard alphabets, the result is also a shifted standard alphabet. If these are mixed alphabets, the result is likely an alphabet that is more thoroughly mixed.

Even though the double encipherment is still polyalphabetic, it can be stronger than a single polyalphabetic encipherment because the period is longer, and there will be fewer letters enciphered by each character of the key. This type of double encipherment is rated Three.

If the two polyalphabetic encipherments are autokey, running key, or one of each, the double encipherment will be a running key encipherment. However, the key will not be English text, so that the word dragging technique of section 5.11 cannot be used. The probabilistic technique in that section, though, can be adapted for use with two running keys.

If the encipherment is done with straight alphabets, that is, with the Belaso tableau, then the order of the encipherments does not matter. Enciphering a message M with the running key R and then reenciphering with running key S is the same as enciphering the running key R with the running key S to get a new composite running key C, then enciphering the message M with that composite running key C.

Keys derived this way, by enciphering one running key with another running key, are not random. They have their own characteristic letter frequencies and contact frequencies. There are common sequences, such as THE enciphered by THE, or AND enciphered by THE. All of this can be tabulated. If a long phrase such as UNITED STATES OF AMERICA or NEGOTIATING STRATEGY is dragged through a text you can look for sections of the running key that adhere to this distribution. Thus double running key encipherment can be solved by computer.

With unmixed alphabets, the composition of two autokey and/or running key encipherments is rated Four. With well-mixed keyed alphabets, the composition is rated Six.

6.2 Null characters

Nulls are a time-honored way of thwarting enemy code-breakers. They have been used at least as far back as the Argenti family in the 15th century. Nulls are meaningless characters that are inserted into a message to confound enemy cryptanalysts. They are most commonly used with codes. With polyalphabetic ciphers they can pollute the frequency counts and disrupt a Kasiski or Index of Coincidence analysis.

There are several ways that nulls can be used. The most direct way is to add a null character to the alphabet. This is commonly represented as an * asterisk. This character could then be sprinkled into the plaintext. It should be used sparingly, so as not to stand out and be obvious. About 3% to 6% nulls would be reasonable. A useful way to use nulls is to insert them into high-frequency words to confound a Kasiski attack. This should be done randomly. If you change *every* THE to T*HE you are assisting Emily by providing 4-character repeats. It is better to use THE about half of the time, T*HE one-quarter of the time and TH*E one-quarter of the time. It is not beneficial to use *THE or THE* because the THE trigram remains intact.

The enciphering tableau would then be 27 columns wide, and asterisks would appear in the ciphertext. You might think that this would be a giveaway that nulls are being used, but there is a cipher called a trifid cipher, described in section 9.9, which utilizes a 27-character alphabet. Emily might think your polyalphabetic cipher is a trifid (not to be confused with the 3-legged monster plants from John Wyndham's 1951 novel *The Day of the Triffids*).

Using nulls this way is fairly weak. It does not change the letter frequencies much, and does not affect the Kasiski or Index of Coincidence badly. The method is rated Three.

A second way to use nulls is to have some specific null letter sequences that are inserted into a plaintext. These need to be easily recognizable. I suggest forming the null sequences from a small number of medium-frequency letters such as C, D and P. The bigrams CC, DD and PP could be used to represent letters C, D and P, and the other 6 bigram combinations of these letters would be nulls. This method is also rated Three.

6.3   *Interrupted key*

A stronger way of using nulls is to insert the nulls into the ciphertext so that they break up the repeating period. A simple way of doing this is first to encipher the message using the polyalphabetic cipher in the normal way. Then each time some *trigger* event, such as some chosen letter or bigram, occurs in the ciphertext, insert a null after it. The null can be any letter or even a bigram. It is the presence of the trigger that marks it as a null.

This type of null insertion can be fairly elaborate. You could insert a null

- 4 characters after each W in the ciphertext, for example ciphertext `NPGWSOVKLEWPIDF` could become `NPGWSOVTKLEWPIDCF`,
- After every second H in the ciphertext,
- After the first A that follows each Q in the ciphertext,
- 1 position after the first V, then 2 positions after the next B, 3 positions after the next L, then repeat V, B, L, V, B, L, ... ,

- After each double letter in the ciphertext, or after 3 consecutive vowels, or after 4 letters in a row in either ascending or descending alphabetic order,

or some combination of these. The only limit is your imagination. Just don't make it so complex that Sandra and Riva can't encipher and decipher quickly and accurately. If Sandra is supposed to insert a null after every second K, and every third M, and she misses one, or puts the null after the fourth M, then Riva may be unable to decipher the message.

This method of inserting nulls is rated Four with standard alphabets, and Five with well-mixed alphabets, assuming, as always, that the mixed alphabets are kept secret.

There are several other methods for interrupting the periodic repetition of the key. One way is to restart the key whenever some trigger occurs in the plaintext. This is more secure than the preceding method where the trigger is in the ciphertext because Emily can see the ciphertext, but not the plaintext. On the other hand, it is harder for the legitimate receiver. When the triggers are in the ciphertext, Riva can just scan through and delete the nulls by eye. When the triggers are in the plaintext, Riva must decipher one character at a time, watching for the triggers.

The triggers can be similar to the ciphertext triggers just mentioned, except in the plaintext, not in the ciphertext. The action that is taken after the trigger occurs could be

- Skip a specific number of characters in the key, or
- Repeat a specific number of characters in the key, or
- Restart the key from the first character, or
- Switch directions, go backward through the key.

Here are examples of these 4 types of key interruption using the key SAMPLE and the trigger letter A:

Skip 2	Repeat 1	Restart	Reverse	
SAMPLE	SAMPLE	SAMPLE	SAMPLE	Key
MA··RY	MA····	MA····	MA····	Plaintext
HA··DA	·RYHA·	RYHA··	YR····	
··LITT	····DA	DA····	····AH	
LELA··	·····L	LITTLE	····DA	
MBITSF	ITTLEL	LA····	ELTTIL	

This form of key interruption is rated Five with straight alphabets, and Six when using well-mixed alphabets. The key should not be restarted too often, otherwise the first character of the key will be overused while the last character of the key could be neglected.

A stronger form of key interruption is to use two separate keys of different lengths. This cipher is strongest when the key lengths are mutually prime. When the trigger occurs, you switch from one key to the other. This method is rated Six when well-mixed alphabets are used. Here is an example using the keys FIRST and SECOND and the trigger A:

```
FIRST    SECOND      Two keywords
MA···    RYHA··      Plaintext showing which key letter is used
··DA·    ····LI      The ciphertext is not shown.
·····    TTLELA
····M    ······
BITSF    ······
LEECE    ······
WA····   SWHITE
```

This cipher keeps track of which letter of the key was last used. When you switch to the other alphabet encipherment continues with the next letter of the key. For example, plaintext MA is enciphered with the key letters FI, so the next key letter is R. After enciphering RYHA with the key letters SECO in the second key, encipherment resumes in the first key with the key letters RS.

This way, all of the letters in each key are used about the same number of times.

6.4 *Homophonic substitution*

Homophonic substitution, introduced in section 4.2, provides several substitutes for each plaintext letter in order to flatten the letter frequencies. The most common method is to enlarge the ciphertext alphabet to provide extra substitutes. Since classical polyalphabetic ciphers employ a fixed 26-letter alphabet, at least for English, they normally do not use homophonic substitution.

For a computer implementation using 8-bit bytes, homophonic substitution is easy to accomplish. There are 256 possible values for a byte. The 26 uppercase letters, 26 lowercase letters, 10 digits and perhaps 32 punctuation marks use up only 94 of the 256 values. Call it 98 if you include the control characters tab, backspace, line feed and carriage return. That leaves 158 characters that can be used for nulls, bigrams and trigrams, and key interruption.

Let's look at how homophonic substitution could be achieved using paper and pencil with a normal 26×26 mixed tableau. If you reserve one letter as a trigger letter, that letter will have such a high frequency that it can be spotted easily. The same is likely true with 2 trigger letters. I suggest using 3 trigger letters, each with a frequency of under 4%. Let's call this cipher *Trig3*. The letters BCDFGJKLMPQUVWXYZ are suitable. Suppose you have chosen B, C and D. There are 78 bigrams starting with these 3 letters, that is 3×26. You would not use bigrams containing the high-frequency letters AEINORST because that would increase their frequency, which works against the goal of flattening the letter frequencies. That leaves 54 bigrams that can be used as nulls, homophones and key interrupters. Here is one possible set:

BB O	BM T	CB +2	CM O	DB N	DM B
BC RE	BP A	CC -	CP S	DC -	DP IN
BD -	BQ +3	CD C	CQ E	DD T	DQ R
BF N	BU E	CF I	CU +2	DF +1	DU -
BG R	BV ON	CG D	CV I	DG +2	DV S
BH E	BW E	CH A	CW ER	DH AN	DW -
BJ +1	BX R	CJ -	CX +3	DJ -	DX I
BK O	BY +1	CK +3	CY -	DK S	DY T
BL -	BZ T	CL E	CZ A	DL TH	DZ N

Here - represents a null character, so plaintext BD, BL, CC, and so on, are nulls. Codes +1, +2 and +3 are key-interrupters meaning skip 1, skip 2 and skip 3 key letters, respectively. The set of homophones includes 6 bigrams, AN, ER, IN, ON, RE and TH as well as single letters.

It is important to maintain balance. If you overuse these substitutes, then the letters B, C and D will have too-high frequencies and will be easily spotted as the triggers. If you use them too sparely, then they won't have any useful impact. About 10% is right, using the B, C and D bigrams roughly equally often, so about 3% each. Remember, with this cipher you cannot use the letters B, C and D by themselves, you must use their substitutes, DM, CD and CG.

Used properly, with well-mixed keyed alphabets, the Trig3 cipher is rated Five.

6.4.1 *Cipher 5858*

Let me present one more cipher before moving on to bigram substitution. I call it *Cipher 5858*. This is a computer cipher using 5-bit characters. Five bits gives an alphabet of 32 characters, enough for 26 letters, 3 nulls and 3 homophones. (1) The plaintext is written out as a sequence of 5-bit characters using a mixed alphabet. (2) The nulls and homophones are inserted, using about 3% of each for a total of 18% of the plaintext. It is best to use them in a haphazard way rather than a systematic way. (3) The plaintext is padded to make its length an even multiple of 8 by adding a null character, if needed, and up to 4 random bits. (4) The padded message is treated as a string of 8-bit bytes and a well-mixed substitution is performed. For example, if the message contained eighty 5-bit characters, the 400 bits would be taken, in order, as fifty 8-bit bytes. (5) The message is again regarded as a string of 5-bit characters. Three of these characters are chosen as key interrupters +1, +2 and +3, as in the Trig3 cipher. (6) The message is enciphered using a general polyalphabetic cipher and a well-mixed 32×32 tableau of 5-bit characters. (7) The string of 5-bit characters is then regrouped into 8-bit bytes, and a second 8-bit substitution is done.

To recap, Cipher 5858 uses 4 substitution steps, an initial 5-bit substitution, an 8-bit substitution, a 5-bit general polyalphabetic substitution with key interruption, and a final 8-bit substitution. This cipher is rated Seven.

6.5   *Bigram and trigram substitution*

Another way to prevent Emily from using letter and contact frequencies to break your cipher is to perform substitution on bigrams or even trigrams. The simplest way to do this is with a tableau. For bigrams you would use a 26×26 tableau where each entry would be a bigram. Here is the start of such a tableau:

```
      A    B    C    D    E    F    G   ...
A     BL   TC   UB   NK   RA   KS   BW  ...
B     CA   CS   FN   GX   OD   MH   YL  ...
C     PS   DE   YO   UJ   BK   GC   NZ  ...
      ...
```

The substitute for AA would be **BL**, the substitute for AB would be **TC**, and so forth. For trigram substitution you might use a booklet with 26 such tableaus, one for each first letter of the trigram.

This type of substitution can be used by itself, or it could be combined with another method, such as polyalphabetic substitution. Used alone, bigram substitution is rated Three, and trigram substitution is rated Four. Bigram substitution followed by polyalphabetic substitution with secret well-mixed alphabets is rated Five, and trigram substitution followed by polyalphabetic substitution with secret well-mixed alphabets is rated Six.

*6.6   *Hiding messages in images*

An interesting idea, dating back to about 1999, is hiding messages inside various types of data files on a computer. This is a modern version of steganography (section 2.2). Let's look at one such method, hiding messages inside a bitmap, or BMP file. Bitmaps are images that are stored pixel by pixel. The most common bitmap format represents each pixel by 3 bytes that specify how much blue, green and red color depth is in that single dot on the image. (This is the device-independent order in the Microsoft standard for bitmap images. If you have trouble remembering the order, notice that Blue, Green and Red are in alphabetic order.) For example, 0,0,0 has no color so it is pure black, 255,255,255 has maximum depth for all 3 colors so it is white, and 255,0,0 would be a pure blue.

Pixels are commonly represented in hexadecimal, so pure blue would be FF0000. In some computer languages this is written $FF0000 or X'FF0000' or even 0xFF0000 since 255 in decimal is FF in hexadecimal. In some languages the order of the color components is reversed. For example, in HTML pure blue would be #0000FF.

The entire image may contain hundreds or thousands of rows of pixels, each row containing hundreds or thousands of pixels. It is not unusual for a bitmap to contain 3000 rows of 4000 pixels each. Such an image would have 12,000,000 pixels, and would require 36,000,000 bytes of storage, plus 54 bytes of header information. That's why having many high-resolution images can fill up a computer's memory so quickly.

The trick is to use the low-order bit in each component of the pixel to carry one bit of the message. This could go undetected because the difference between FF0000 and

FE0000 or even FE0101 is barely perceptible to the eye. In a single pixel of a large image it would be visually undetectable. Besides, half of the bits would not change value. When hiding a message in an image it is essential that the file containing the image is transmitted exactly. The image must not be enlarged, reduced, cropped, rotated, skewed, compressed or converted into another image format.

The message can be enciphered with any method. However, if Emily suspects you are hiding the message this way, then it would not add any extra security. You would be paying the price of transmitting 8 bits of data for every bit of the message with no corresponding benefit. If you simply took every low-order bit from each pixel in turn, the rating would be the same as whatever method of encipherment you chose.

One way of gaining some extra security from this scheme is not to use all of the bits, but to select certain bits from each pixel in some cyclic order. To do this you use a string of octal digits (see the table in section 3.1) such as 1,3,7,4,6 as a key for selecting the message bits. This can be called a *selection key*. It has 5 octal digits, hence 15 selection bits. Start with the first pixel of the image and the first digit of the selection key. If the first bit of this digit is 1, put one bit of the message into the low-order bit of the blue component of the pixel, otherwise set the low-order bit to 0 or 1 at random. If the second key bit is 1, do the same for the green component, and if the third bit is 1 do this for the red component. Then repeat this for the second pixel and the second digit of the selection key. And so forth.

Someone might think that when the key bit is 0 it is better to leave the corresponding bit of the image unchanged. This would result in less distortion of the image and make it harder for Emily to detect that it contained a hidden message. True, but if Emily suspects that you are using this method then it will make it possible to determine the selection key.

Suppose this is the case. Emily has intercepted your message containing a bitmap image. Further suppose Emily has done an image search on the internet and found the original image. Emily can match up the two images, pixel by pixel and color component by color component. This enables Emily to make a map of where the two versions of the image differ. Everywhere the low-order bits match, Emily can mark an X in the map, and everywhere they do not match Emily can mark a |. Emily can then try each possible length for the selection key. When the correct length L has been chosen, and the marks are lined up at intervals of L pixels, then every column where the selection bit is 0 will contain all X's, while the columns where the selection bit is 1 will contain half X's and half |'s. For example, again using the selection key 1,3,7,4,6 you might see

```
001  011  111  100  110     Selection key
XXX  X|X  XX|  XXX  X|X     Difference map
XXX  XX|  |XX  XXX  X|X
XX|  X||  XX|  XXX  |XX
XXX  XXX  ||X  |XX  XXX
XX|  XX|  X|X  |XX  X|X
```

For every column that contains a | the corresponding bit of the selection key must be 1. All other bits of the selection key are probably 0. With more rows in the difference map, the probability gets higher.

For this reason, wherever the selection bit is 0 the low-order bit of the color component should be set randomly. Using a cyclic selection key, this method of hiding the message adds 2 if the rating of the underlying cipher is One to Four, or 1 if the rating is Five to Eight.

The selection key could also be generated using the Chained Digit pseudorandom generator from section 4.5 using a qualified seed of 7, 9 or 10 digits. Use generated digits from 0 to 7 as selection digits. If the generated digit is 8 or 9, discard it and generate the next digit. It is not important here whether the pseudorandom digits are statistically random. The essential property is that the sequence of generated digits is longer than the message, measured in bits, so that Emily cannot match up sections of the ciphertext that have the same selection key.

Using a Chained Digit selection key, this method of hiding the message adds 3 if the rating of the underlying cipher is One to Four, 2 if the rating is Five to Seven, and 1 if the rating is Eight.**

6.7   Adding null bits

This idea of mixing bits of the message with null bits can also be done without embedding the message in an image or other file, and it can be done by hand. First encipher the message using simple substitution, or any method of your choice. Write this preliminary ciphertext in binary, say 5-bit binary. The simple substitution and conversion to binary can be done in one step. You could just substitute 5-bit numbers for the 26 letters of the alphabet in some mixed order, like this:

A 00011	G 10011	M 11011	S 01001	Y 11000	3 00110
B 11110	H 01101	N 00001	T 10111	Z 01010	4 01111
C 01000	I 10100	O 11111	U 01110		6 11100
D 00000	J 10000	P 00101	V 10010		7 00010
E 10110	K 11001	Q 11101	W 11010		8 01100
F 01011	L 00100	R 10001	X 00111		9 10101

Notice that there are 6 decimal digits in addition to the 26 letters of the alphabet. The digits 0, 1, 2 and 5 are omitted to prevent confusion with the letters O, I, Z and S when handwritten. This gives you the 32 characters necessary to convert the 5-bit numbers back into symbols for transmission.

Now that the message is in the form of a bit string, the null bits can be added. A selection key is used to specify where the null bits are inserted. The selection key has the form m1,n1,m2,n2,m3,n3,..., which means take m_1 bits of the message and insert n1 null bits, take m2 more bits of the message and add n2 more null bits, take another m3 bits of the message and add n3 more null bits, and so on. Here is an example using the selection key 2,1,3,1,4,2,3,2.

```
M     E     S     S     A     G     E                          Plaintext
11011 10110 01001 01001 00011 10011 10110                      5-bit groups
2 13  14    2 3   2 2 13 14   2 3   2 2 13  14    2 3           Selection key
11-011-1011--001--00-101-0010--001--11-001-1101--10            Regrouped
111011010110000101000101100101100110111001011010110           Add the null bits
11101 10101 10000 10100 01011 00101 10011 01110 01011 01011 01011   Regroup
Q     9     J     I     F     P     G     U     F     F     F
```

With this scheme MESSAGE is enciphered as `Q9JIF PGUFF F`. Four null bits (the shaded bits) are appended to complete the last group of 5 bits. This is called *padding* or *null-padding*.

The selection key could also be given in binary form, say 110111011110011100. Each 1 bit in the key means take the next message bit, while each 0 bit means insert a null bit.

This scheme is stronger when two different alphabets are used for changing the letters to bits and for changing the bits back to letters. The strength is also improved by using variable-length substitutes like the Huffman codes described in section 10.4. For this purpose, the lengths of the codes need not correspond to the frequencies of the letters, but they still must have the prefix property so that Riva can decipher the message.

You can avoid the need for adding extra characters for the second substitution, which goes from bits back to letters, in two ways. (1) You could take the bits in groups of 4 and use only 16 letters of the alphabet, or use the 16 hexadecimal digits, or (2) you could use a variable-length code with six 4-bit code groups and twenty 5-bit code groups. Again, these code groups must have the prefix property. Here is an example:

E	0101	S	00010	C	01000	P	01111	J	01110	A 4-bit / 5-bit
T	1011	H	11011	M	11010	B	11110	Z	00001	substitution
A	1110	R	10000	F	10010	V	10001		
O	0011	D	00011	Y	00101	K	11001		
I	0110	L	11000	W	11111	X	00000		
N	1010	U	01001	G	00100	Q	10011		

Notice that I used 4-bit substitutes for the 6 highest-frequency letters. This will make those 6 letters have about twice the frequency in the ciphertext as the other 20 letters. This could make an unwary opponent believe this is an entirely different type of cipher.

Adding null bits is applicable to many types of encipherment. Since a null bit is indistinguishable from any other bit, adding null bits is stronger than adding null characters. It can increase the rating of a cipher by as much as Three.

Let's look at a specific example. Call it *Cipher Null5*. As earlier, there are 3 steps, convert from letters to bits, add null bits, and convert back from bits to letters. Letters are converted to bits using a homophonic substitution from letters to 5-bit groups. Two substitutes are provided for each of the letters E,T,A,O,I,N. Null bits are inserted using a selection key, as in section 6.6. Bits are converted back to letters using a 4-bit/5-bit substitution like the previous table.

Cipher Null5 is rated Six.

6.8   *Merging multiple messages*

The binary form of key can also be used as a merge key to merge two messages. That is, the bits of two messages are interleaved to form a single message. A merge key in base 3 or base 4 could be used to merge 3 or 4 messages. A base-4 merge key could likewise merge 3 messages plus null bits.

Two advantages of merging multiple messages are that you don't add as much extra length as using null bits, and you can use simpler, faster encryption. If you interleave 4 messages with a long merge key, and you use a different simple substitution for each message, that alone gets a rating of Five. If you perform an additional simple substitution on the merged message, the rating increases to Eight.

The keys for merging messages can take two forms, a bit count form or a selection form. In the bit count form, the messages are taken in rotation. Each digit of the key specifies how many bits are taken from each successive message. In the selection form the messages may be taken in any order, but only one bit is taken each time. Each digit of the key specifies which message to take the next bit from. These examples show how the messages **010101111010001101011** and **11101010011011100110** are merged by the bit count method using the key 123123, and by the selection method using the key 12122112.

```
12 3   12 3   12 3   12 3   12 3   12 3   12 3      Bit count key
0   101 01    1   110 10    0   011 01    0   1      Message 1
  11    1   010 10    0   110 11    1   001 10       Message 2
011101101010110110010110011011101001010 1           Ciphertext

12122112 12122112 12122112 12122112 12122112         Selection key
0 1   01 0 1   11 1 0   10 0 0   11 0 1   01          Message 1
  1 11   0 1 01   0 0 11   0 1 11   0 0 11   0        Message 2
011110100110111010011100010111100011010              Ciphertext
```

Merging multiple messages may be messy when the messages have different lengths. You need to have an end-of-message marker on all but the longest message. Another way of dealing with non-matching lengths is to balance the merge. Begin by writing all of the messages end to end, separated by some reserved character or character sequence. Then simply divide this long string into equal parts. For example, if the messages have lengths of 50, 60, 70 and 80 characters, that is a combined length of 260 characters, plus 3 separators for a total of 263 characters. You could divide that into 4 strands of 66, 66, 66 and 65 characters. If you are using 8-bit bytes, you could divide the 263×8 = 2104 bits into 4 strands of 526 bits each. It is not necessary to split the bit string on even byte boundaries, but you should choose keys that take an equal number of bits from each strand.

Incidentally, the number of messages and the number of strands are independent. There can be one message or many, and any number of strands from 2 up. For example, one message could be divided into 3 strands, and 3 messages could be divided into 2 strands.

Balancing is half the solution. The other half comes when you get near the end of the merging process. Eventually you will have merged all the bits from one of the strings, while the other strings have bits left. If the merge key specifies another bit from a string that has no bits left, just skip to the next bit selection.

Let's pull all of this together into one cipher, which can be called *Merge8*. The Merge8 cipher operates on one or more messages concatenated end to end. In the base-26 version, the 26 letters are converted to binary using a 4-bit/5-bit code like the 4-bit/5-bit substitution in section 6.7. The message divider can be a letter sequence such as XXX or END. In the base-256 version a well-mixed keyed simple substitution is applied to the ASCII code. The resulting bit string is divided into 8 equal-length strands of bits. A key of 32 octal digits is used to merge the 8 strands. Each of the 8 octal values appears 4 times in the key, so there are $32!/(4!)^8 = 2.39 \times 10^{24}$ possible merge keys. A second simple substitution is performed on the resulting string. An 8-bit substitution is used for both the base-26 and base-256 versions. Merge8 is rated Six.

6.9 Embedding a message in a file

When a message is hidden in a picture file, there are at least 7 bits of the image for every bit of the message. That's mighty inefficient. You can hide a lot more message bits in a file if you don't try to make it look like something else. It's a ciphertext, so let it look like a ciphertext. There are dozens of ways to hide a plaintext message inside a file. I will simply list some of the options. As in section 6.6, for each byte of the file a certain number of plaintext bits are hidden among the 8 bits.

- A fixed number of plaintext bits or a variable number of plaintext bits are taken each time.
- The bits are placed in fixed bit locations or variable bit locations within each byte.
- The bits are placed in order, or rearranged.
- The plaintext bits are inserted as is, or lightly enciphered, for example by simple substitution.
- The ciphertext bits are left as is, or lightly enciphered, for example by simple substitution.

The number of bits, the locations of the bits and the order of the bits can be controlled by either a periodic key or some random sequence. Depending on which options are chosen, ciphers in this class may be rated anywhere from One to Ten.

Here is an example of such a cipher. (1) Perform a well-mixed keyed simple substitution on the message. (2) Using a pseudorandom number generator with a large internal state, choose 2 to 6 bit positions in each byte. Place the next 2 to 6 bits of the message, in order, into these 2 to 6 bit positions. Set the remaining bit positions to random values. (3) Perform a second well-mixed keyed simple substitution.

This method, called *EmbedBits*, is extremely fast and simple. The downside is that the ciphertext is about twice as long as the plaintext. EmbedBits is rated Eight. To bump the rating up to Ten, replace the simple substitution with a bigram substitution such as Two Square.

Transposition 7

In chapters 5 and 6 we looked at substitution ciphers. The second major category of Secret Key encryption methods is transposition. Transposition means changing the order of elements in the message. These elements may be words, syllables, letters or the individual digits or bits that represent the letters. In this chapter we will deal primarily with letter transposition, but keep in mind that you can use the same methods for other elements, such as the word transposition in section 7.2.2. This chapter will cover many different types of transposition ciphers. You can do most of these transposition ciphers using only pencil and paper.

7.1 Route transposition

Route transposition is the simplest, and oldest, form of transposition cipher. There is no key involved. The secrecy comes from the choice of routes or paths.

Route transposition is a great way to get children interested in cryptography. It makes a great activity for classrooms, scout troops or other clubs. The main caveat is that the children must write the letters uniformly in straight columns, otherwise the message gets garbled. This can be avoided by using graph paper with wide spacing.

The basic idea is that the message is written into a rectangle using one route, and read out using a different route. For example, if the message has 30 characters, then a 5×6 rectangle is best. If the message has 29 characters, just add a null. Pad the message with nulls until it fits into a rectangle of suitable size. It is helpful to draw the outline of the rectangle before you start to fill it in. If the message is long, break it into blocks of a convenient size. For example, a message of 1000 characters might be broken into twenty 5×10 blocks.

We have already seen one example of a route transposition in section 4.3. The message was written into the 5×5 grid horizontally from left to right across the rows and read out vertically top to bottom down the columns. Horizontal and vertical are two types of routes. Here is a fuller list.

- Horizontally, left to right, right to left, or alternating left and right
- Vertically, top to bottom, bottom to top, or alternating up and down
- Diagonally, upper left to lower right, lower left to upper right, and so forth, or alternating
- Spiral, from any corner inward or from the center outward, clockwise or counterclockwise

You can start in any corner of the rectangle, use any route to write the message in, and use any other route to read the message out. Here is an example of a fancy route:

1	2	3	4	5	26	27	28	29
36	6	7	8	9	10	30	31	32
37	38	11	12	13	14	15	33	34
39	40	41	16	17	18	19	20	35
42	43	44	45	21	22	23	24	25

The message would be written into the grid in the order indicated by the numbers, and read out by columns, that is, 1, 36, 37, 39, 42, 2, 6, 38, ...

For a route transposition Emily only needs to guess the route you used to read the message out. After Emily has filled the message into the rectangle, it can be read by inspection. Note that it does not matter to Emily whether you wrote the message horizontally into a 5×6 rectangle or vertically into a 6×5 rectangle. Neither does it matter whether you started at the top row and worked down or the bottom row and worked up. Emily cannot tell the difference.

Route transposition is rated One.

7.2 Columnar transposition

Columnar transposition is the workhorse of transposition ciphers. It has been used by armies, diplomats and spies since the 17th century. The method is first described in a 1685 book by John Falconer, *Cryptomenysis Patefacta* (Secret Communication Revealed). After the Glorious Revolution of 1688, John Falconer followed James II into exile in France, where he died before the second edition of the book was published in 1692 under the new title *Rules for Explaining and Decyphering all Manner of Secret Writing*.

Columnar transposition uses a key that may be a string of consecutive numbers in mixed order, or a keyword or keyphrase that gets turned into a numeric string by numbering the letters in alphabetic order. Consider the keyword SAMPLE. The letter A comes earliest in alphabetic order, so it gets numbered 1. Next in alphabetic order is E, which gets numbered 2. Then L, M, P and S. So SAMPLE gets converted into the string 6,1,4,5,3,2. If the same letter appears more than once, the occurrences are numbered from left to right. For example, ANACONDA becomes 1,6,2,4,8,7,5,3.

```
SAMPLE    ANACONDA   M  I  S  S  I  S   S   I  P  P  I
614532    16248753   5  1  8  9  2  10  11  3  6  7  4
```

Write the message into a grid horizontally from left to right. The number of columns is the size of the key. If the key is SAMPLE there are 6 columns. If the key is ANACONDA there are 8 columns. Write the numeric key above the grid, like this:

```
ANACONDA    Keyword
16248753    Numeric key
ENEMYTAN    Plaintext
KSSECTOR
FORTYTWO
HEADINGW
EST
```

```
EKFHE ESRAT NROW METD AOWG NSOES TTTN YCYI   Ciphertext
EKFHE ESRAT NROWM ETDAO WGNSO ESTTT NYCYI    Ciphertext groups of 5
```

Read the message out vertically top to bottom, according to the numeric key, starting with the column numbered 1, EKFHE, then column 2, ESRAT, column 3, NROW, through column 8, YCYI, as shown.

Riva, the legitimate receiver, needs to do a little arithmetic to read this message. The key length is 8 letters, and the message length is 35 letters. 35 divided by 8 is 4 with a remainder of 3. That means that the array will contain 4 complete rows of 8 letters, plus a short row of 3 letters. Riva should draw the outline of this array before she starts filling in the columns so that she places the correct number of characters in each.

The task for Emily, the enemy, is a little harder. The technique is to write the letters from each column vertically onto a strip of paper, and then match up those strips to determine the order of the columns. She looks for pairs of strips where the matching letters form common bigrams. When she gets a good match, she tries to add a third strip either before or after those two strips. Once 3 or 4 strips are correctly matched, short words begin to appear and the task becomes easy.

Emily does not know the length of the keyword, so she needs to guess it. She might start at 5 and work up. Let's suppose she has gotten up to 8, the correct length. Like Riva she divides 35 by 8. She knows that there are 5 short columns of 4 letters each, and 3 long columns of 5 letters each. Emily's problem is where to start and end each strip so that it contains at least one full column.

The first strip starts at the first character of the ciphertext, and must be 5 letters long in case the first column read out of the array was a long one. The second strip starts at the fifth letter of the ciphertext in case the first column was short, and ends at the tenth letter in case both the first and second columns were short. Similarly for the third and fourth strips. Then Emily will do the opposite for the other 4 strips, working from the last letter of the ciphertext backward toward the center.

Emily will then match up the strips, sliding them against one another to determine the correct alignments. All of this is done by eye, so Emily must know the frequencies of the most common bigrams and trigrams by heart. This can also be done by computer in a simple, straightforward way.

The most common countermeasure to this type of matching procedure is for Sandra, the sender, to read out some of the columns from top to bottom, and some of them from bottom to top. This means that Emily will need a second set of strips reading backward. She will then have twice as many strips to attempt to match up.

With all columns reading down, columnar transposition is rated Two if the array is a rectangle, and Three if it is not. With columns reading in alternating directions, columnar transposition is rated Three if the grid is a rectangle, or if the columns are long, and Four otherwise.

Columnar transposition is a tried-and-true method for adding strength to any type of substitution cipher. Columnar transposition combined with a well-mixed keyed simple substitution is rated Five. When combined with a well-mixed general poly-alphabetic cipher it is rated Seven. The combination is strongest if the lengths of the two keys are coprime.

The most common technique for strengthening a columnar transposition is to make some of the rows different lengths. This makes it harder for Emily to know where the strips should begin and end. Four such ideas are shown. Of these, number (4) is the strongest since it disrupts the strips at an unpredictable point in the middle, rather than at the ends. More elaborate patterns of blanks could have 2 or more blanks in some columns.

Columnar transposition with these variations is rated Four, provided that Emily does not know the pattern. The rating goes up to Five for variant (4) if the key is long and there are a variable number of blanks in the columns. The French used a system like this toward the end of World War I. It is believed that the Germans were able to read at least some of those messages, largely because the French reused their keys many times.

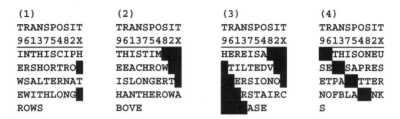

```
(1)              (2)              (3)              (4)
TRANSPOSIT       TRANSPOSIT       TRANSPOSIT       TRANSPOSIT
961375482X       961375482X       961375482X       961375482X
INTHISCIPH       THISTIM          HEREISA           THISONEU
ERSHORTRO        EEACHROW          TILTEDV         SE  SAPRES
WSALTERNAT       ISLONGERT         ERSIONO         ETPA  TTER
EWITHLONG        HANTHEROWA        RSTAIRC         NOFBLA  NK
ROWS             BOVE              ASE            S
```

```
(1)  TSAIW  POAGH  HLTSC  TROSR  ELNRS  WOIOT  HIRNN  IEWER  HT
(2)  IALNV  TWSCO  TEMOE  RIRGE  HESAO  THNHW  ROTEI  HBA
(3)  RIEOR  ELRRA  DOAES  EITSE  TITSS  AVNIH  C
(4)  TPF  EEEN  HAB  OPT  SAA  ETO  ISL  NRT  SENS  USRK
```

Two further variations on number (3), the staircase, are (5) start from column 1 when you reach the right edge, making a skew pattern, and (6) reverse direction when you reach the right edge, creating a chevron or zigzag pattern. The advantage of these patterns is that the number of characters is the same on every row except possibly the last, making it very easy for Riva to calculate the number of rows. Here are examples of these two variations.

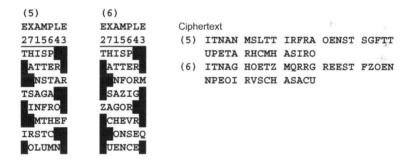

```
(5)              (6)
EXAMPLE          EXAMPLE          Ciphertext
2715643          2715643          (5)  ITNAN  MSLTT  IRFRA  OENST  SGFTT
THISP            THISP                 UPETA  RHCMH  ASIRO
 ATTER            ATTER           (6)  ITNAG  HOETZ  MQRRG  REEST  FZOEN
  NSTAR            NFORM               NPEOI  RVSCH  ASACU
TSAGA            SAZIG
 INFRO           ZAGOR
  MTHEF          CHEVR
IRSTC            ONSEQ
 OLUMN           UENCE
```

You can also have two or more separate staircases of different widths, or have staircases in both the diagonal and anti-diagonal directions \ and /.

When you are deciphering a message sent with any of these columnar transposition variants, if you have any difficulty calculating how many rows are needed, or how long the last row is, here's a trick. Count the letters in the message, and fill in the array left to right with that number of little dots, following the same pattern that Sandra used to write in the letters. Then fill in the letters over the dots.

For example, in variant (2), suppose you have agreed that you will always start with 7 letters on the first row. Ciphertext (2) has 38 letters, so you put 7 dots on the first row, 8 dots on the second row, ... until you have placed a total of 38 dots. Then you start filling in the letters in their proper columns, replacing the dots like this:

```
961375482X       961375482X       961375482X       961375482X
· · · · · · ·    · · I · · · ·    · · IS · · M     · HIS · IM
· · · · · · · ·  · · A · · · · ·  · · AC · · O ·   · EAC · RO ·
· · · · · · · · · · · L · · · · · T · · LO · · E · T · SLO · GE · T
· · · · · · · · · · · · N · · · · · W · · · NT · · R · W · · ANT · ER · W ·
· · · ·          · · V ·          · · VE           · OVE
```

Another way to use blacked-out squares is to fill them with nulls. The nulls should be chosen so they form uncommon letter pairs on both sides to make matching the columns harder for Emily. It is better to use common letters rather than rare letters, which might easily be recognized as nulls. Here is an example.

```
961375482X       961375482X       Ciphertext
· WHEN · ANEE    FWHENAANEE        HBGAC  NMEYW  ITTEI  HEADO  AIDIT  HUAEN
L · BITE · SYO   LWBITEISYO        ANNAW  WRHUA  ONTAP  HTRNS  PNSAY  FLUTO
UR · HAND · WI   URGHANDPWI        AAEOI  YGS
THA · PAIN · Y   THAEPAINIY
OUCA · NTST ·    OUCAHNTSTG
· ANDT · HATS    AANDTNHATS
A · MORA · Y     AOMORAUY
```

Columnar transposition with nulls is rated Three. With a fixed pattern of blacked-out spaces, the rating is Four.

7.2.1 Cysquare

Historical tidbit: During World War II the British used a variant of this idea, called *Cysquare*, invented by Brigadier John H. Tiltman in 1941. Cysquare was a columnar transposition cipher with lots of blackouts. The British issued pads of 26×26 grids with about 60% of the squares blacked out in a random pattern. Each page had a different pattern. The message was written into the white squares going across the rows, and then read out vertically in some order. The grid was square, so it could be used in any orientation.

The key was the page number in the pad, the orientation, and the starting and ending positions within the grid. The cipher clerk would draw lines on the page to mark the message area. Using different areas allowed pages to be used for multiple messages.

The drawback was the need to distribute so many pads. To minimize the number of pads, the British used each page for a full day, for perhaps as many as 50 messages. This meant writing faintly and erasing many times. The pages became unreadable, and eventually the cipher clerks refused to use them. Cysquare was abandoned in 1944.

After the Germans captured some of these pads, along with the instructions, they started using the system themselves, from 1944 until the end of the war. They called it

Rasterschlüssel, meaning *Grid Key*. The Germans, however, did a poor job of selecting the black and white squares. They used too many adjacent white squares, so the British could identify bigrams and trigrams when they matched up the strips. These messages became a valuable source of intelligence for the British. Cysquare is rated Seven. Rasterschlüssel is rated Four.

It should be noted that in the computer era, the black and white squares could be transmitted as a pattern of bits, the grid could be any size, and the grid could be changed for every message. I suggest 65% to 75% black squares. Done this way, cysquare would be rated Eight.

There is a simplified version of cysquare for hand use that does not require printed grids, and that allows you to use a numeric key to specify which squares are blacked out. Here are two variations of the *Blackout* transposition cipher, a left-right alternating version and a stairstep version. Both use the numeric key 3174255 for the blackouts. The blackout key can be a repeating key, or it could be generated by a pseudorandom number generator. You would use a separate key to specify the order for reading out the columns.

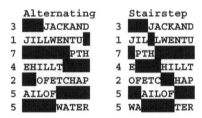

Another method for strengthening columnar transposition is to break the text into blocks of irregular size. For instance, if the message length is 150 you could break it into blocks of 37, 71 and 42 letters. This method is rated Four. If you use a different key for each block, the rating increases to Five.

Combining a columnar transposition with any type of substitution cipher greatly enhances its security. Even combined with a simple substitution the rating increases to Five because matching the strips is much harder. It makes no difference which one is done first. Combining a general polyalphabetic cipher with a columnar transposition of at least 12 columns increases the rating to Seven, even if the period of the polyalphabetic is as little as 3. This is because you have essentially removed the possibility of matching the strips.

7.2.2 *Word transposition*

Word transposition is a historically important columnar transposition based on words rather than letters. It is the main method used by the Union Army during the American Civil War. The idea came from Anson Stager, a Union telegrapher who later founded the Western Union telegraph company. Union Army communications were hampered by a high rate of transmission errors. In many cases commanding officers would forego the telegraph and simply send a messenger on foot or horseback. Stager realized that sending words instead of individual letters would cut the rate of errors, and reduce the need for retransmitting the messages.

Union cipher clerks wrote the messages word by word from left to right in a rectangular array, and then read them out using a variety of routes, such as alternately going up and down the columns, or alternately taking columns from the left and right halves of the array. Null words were used liberally. Here is an example. Notice that the third row is nulls. The columns are read out in the order 1,3,5,2,4.

```
BRING    CANNON  BRIGADE  SIX     FIVE        Plaintext
SOUTH    WEST    TO       ATTACK  ENEMY
SHOULD   RECENT  ABOUT    HORSE   NORTH
LEFT     FLANK   MOUNT    CHARGE  FROM
EAST     TO      DRIVE    ENEMY   TOWARD
OUR      GUNS
```

```
BRING SOUTH SHOULD LEFT EAST OUR BRIGADE TO ABOUT MOUNT DRIVE
FIVE ENEMY NORTH FROM TOWARD CANNON WEST RECENT FLANK TO GUNS
SIX ATTACK HORSE CHARGE ENEMY
```

7.3   *Double columnar transposition*

As the name implies, *double columnar transposition* means doing two columnar transpositions in succession, preferably with two different keys. This eliminates the possibility of matching strips. Remarkably, a general solution was found in 1934 by Solomon Kullback and published by the Signals Intelligence Service. The 31-page book was declassified in 1980 and published by Aegean Park Press. Aegean Park Press was for many years an invaluable resource for books on cryptography. It went out of business some time after 2001 when Wayne G. Barker, its founder, died, and the books became unavailable. I am happy to say that www.openlibrary.org now has these books (accessed July 2019).

I will not repeat Kullback's analysis here, except to say that it is based on determining where each plaintext letter will occur in the ciphertext. Instead, I will discuss 3 methods for defeating Kullback's solution. (BTW, Kullback went to the same high school as my father, but 6 years earlier.)

One simple method is to change the shape of the grid by blacking out a few squares. These squares could form a rectangle, or some other shape, in one of the corners, or even in the middle of the grid. Here are some examples:

2×2 Rectangle   3×1 Rectangle   Staircase   Triangle

The blacked-out sections can have different sizes, shapes or locations for each of the two transposition steps. The size, shape and location of the blacked-out section(s) can be appended to the key, so that a different blackout is used for each message. Double columnar transposition is rated Four. Double columnar transposition with blackouts is rated Five.

The opposite method, called *NullBlock*, is also effective. You can insert a block of null characters into the intermediate ciphertext or the final ciphertext, or both. It is not helpful to add the null block to the plaintext. The size and location of the block can be specified by a numeric key. These should be varied from message to message.

Combining any transposition cipher with any substitution cipher strengthens both. Double columnar transposition combined with simple substitution is rated Six. Double columnar transposition combined with a general polyalphabetic substitution is rated Eight.

7.4 *Cycling columnar transposition*

Another variation on columnar transposition is *Cycling Columnar Transposition.* It comes in two flavors, horizontal cycling and vertical cycling. Horizontal cycling requires two keys, one for cycling the rows, and one to determine the column order. Begin by writing the message into a rectangular block left to right across the rows. Next write the cycling key vertically to the left of the rows. If there are more rows than the length of this key, repeat the key as many times as needed. If the cycling key is a word or phrase, convert it to numbers in the usual way using alphabetic order.

Once the cycling key is in numeric form, cycle each row left by the number of positions indicated. Then read out the letters vertically in the order specified by the column key. Here is an example using the cycling key CYCLES and the column key PAULREVERE.

```
Cycle key          PAULREVERE    Column key
                   619572x384
C 1 ONEIFBYLAN     NEIFBYLANO    Ciphertext
Y 6 DANDTWOIFB     OIFBDANDTW     EIAPR LYAIT AADNH EOWSO HFBNS SNOEP
C 2 YSEAANDION     EAANDIONYS     OEBDD IHNTY ESIFA OEBLN OTL
L 4 THEOPPOSIT     PPOSITTHEO
E 3 ESHORESHAL     ORESHALESH
S 5 LBE            ELB
```

The same method of matching up paper strips that was used to solve the columnar transposition still works for the cycling columnar transposition. It is only slightly harder because the last letter on each row is adjacent to the first letter, potentially forming a low-frequency bigram. This is at most a minor impediment to Emily. Columnar transposition with horizontal cycling is rated Three.

Vertical cycling is similar. Instead of cycling the rows of the block left, you cycle the columns of the block upward. Here is an example using the keyword CYCLE for cycling the columns and the keyphrase PAULREVERE for selecting the order in which the columns are read out.

```
CYCLECYCLE        PAULREVERE        Keyphrase
1524315243        619572x384        Numeric key
ONEIFBYLAN        DBEOPWYIAT        Plaintext
DANDTWOIFB        YNEIRNOSAL
YSEAANDION        TAHDFPDHFN
THEOPPOSIT        ESEATEOLOB
ESHORESHAL        LHEOABSIIN
LBE               OSN
```

```
BNASH SWNPE BISHL ITLNB NOIDA ODYTE        Ciphertext
LOPRF TAAAF OIEEH EENYO DOS
```

This cipher can still be solved by matching up paper strips, the same as a regular columnar transposition, but Emily will need two strips for each column, one for the top section and one for the bottom. When each column is cycled, some of the characters from the top of the column are moved to the bottom, and become the new bottom section. The remaining letters move upward and become the new top section. In the example, the left column **ODYTEL** moves up 1 position, so **DYTEL** becomes the new top section, and **O** becomes the new bottom section. These sections need to be on separate strips because Emily does not know whether these letters came from a long column or a short column. This makes the matching process considerably harder. Columnar transposition with vertical cycling is rated Four.

It is feasible to perform both vertical and horizontal cycling on the block. This is comparable in strength to double columnar transposition. Remember, though, that the more complex you make your cipher the more time it takes, and the more difficult it is both to encipher and to decipher accurately. *Double cycling columnar transposition* is rated Five.

7.5   *Random number transposition*

Let's look at an entirely different type of transposition. This transposition does not involve any sort of array or grid. Instead, it simply numbers the letters in the message randomly.

You can use any random number generator. There are several presented in chapter 13. The only random number generator I have described so far is the chained digit generator in section 4.5.1, so let's use that generator to illustrate. Generate one random digit for each letter of the message, like this:

```
43193274865927830145989650864375219 6
INCREASEBIDTOTWELVEPOINTSEVENMILLION
```

First take all of the letters numbered 1, going left to right. These are C, V and I.

```
43193274865927830145989650864375 2 196
IN-REASEBIDTOTWEL-EPOINTSEVENMILL-O N    CVI
```

Next take all of the letters numbered 2. These are A, O and L.

```
43193274865927830145989650864 3752196
IN-RE-SEBIDT-TWEL-EPOINTSEVENMIL--ON    CVIAOL
```

Then take all of the letters numbered 3, namely N, E, E and M.

```
43193274865927830145989650864375 2196
I--R--SEBIDT-TW-L-EPOINTSEVEN-IL--ON    CVIAOLNEEM
```

Continue this way until all of the letters have been taken.

To decipher this message, Riva would first generate the random digits. There are three 1's, so she would write the first 3 letters of the ciphertext, **CVI**, under the three 1's, like this:

```
43193274865927830145989650864375219 6
--C--------------V--------------I--
```

Riva would write the next 3 letters of the ciphertext, **AOL**, under the 2's, like this:

```
43193 27486592 78301459896508643752 196
--C--A------O----V-------------LI--
```

and so forth.

Random number transposition is rated Four. It can be broken by trying all possible seeds for the random number generator.

The cipher can be strengthened by using a longer seed, or by selecting letters from the plaintext using the 10 digits in an order other than 1, 2, 3, ... This is equivalent to applying a simple substitution to the outputs of the random number generator. For example, if you wanted to start with the letters marked 4, then you would change all the 4's into 1's. If you next wanted to take all of the letters marked 7, you would change all 7's into 2's, and so forth. Then you proceed as described. This increases the number of possible keys by a factor of 10!, or 3,628,800.

With this improvement, chained digit transposition is rated Five. For a computer version, where the random number generator produces random bytes, the method is rated Seven because there are so many possible orders for rearranging the 256 different bytes.

7.6   Selector transposition

Since we are looking at random numbers, let's look at a different transposition cipher based on random numbers, namely a *Selector Transposition*. The idea is to break the message into roughly equal pieces, and then to merge those pieces using the random number sequence.

Suppose the plaintext has 100 characters, and you want to split it into 3 parts. Assume you have a random number generator that produces the digits 0, 1 and 2 with equal probability, and that you have chosen a seed, which acts as the key for the transposition. You need to know how big to make each part of the message. This is easily done. Just generate the first 100 random digits, and count how many of each digit are produced. Say there are 36 zeros, 25 ones and 39 twos. You would slice the message into 3 pieces, P0 with 36 letters, P1 with 25 letters and P2 with 39 letters.

Enciphering is easy. Each time the generator produces a 0, take the next letter from P0. Each time the generator produces a 1, take the next letter from P1. Each time the generator produces a 2, take the next letter from P2. Deciphering is even easier, because Riva does not need to know how large each piece had been. Each time she gets a 0, she puts the next letter into P0. Each time she gets a 1, she puts the next letter into P1. Each time she gets a 2, she puts the next letter into P2. Then she concatenates the 3 pieces, or she simply reads the message ignoring the line breaks.

When this is done with only 2 pieces, it is trivial for Emily to reconstruct the message. The rating is One. With 3 pieces it is a bit harder, and the rating is Two. With 20 or more pieces, the rating is Five.

7.7   Key transposition

Sometimes it is preferable to transpose a message one block at a time. The best choice for transposing blocks is a *key transposition*. Write the numerical key above the characters of the message, then move each character to the position indicated by its key number. In this example, the block size is 8, and the numeric key is 41278563. The key number for the first letter, <u>R</u>, is 4, so move the <u>R</u> to the fourth position in the block. The key number for the second letter, <u>U</u>, is 1, so move the <u>U</u> to the first position in the block, and so forth.

```
41278563 41278563 41278563 41278563 41278563 4127
RUSSIANT RADEDELE GATIONEX PECTEDTO ARRIVELO NDON
USTRANSI ADTRELED ATXRNEIO ECOPDTTE RROAELIV DONN
```

The key transposition may be used on the plaintext, the ciphertext or both. A key transposition by itself is weak. Key transposition is rated One to Three depending on the block size.

*Let's take a deeper look at transpositions. In mathematics, transpositions are called *permutations*. Here is an example. I have used the hexadecimal digits A, B and C to denote the numbers 10, 11 and 12. In a cipher, these numbers will represent the bits, letters or other units that are being permuted.

`123456789ABC`	Original order
`4A1729C5B683`	Permuted order

The top line is standard. It represents the original order, before the permutation. The second line is the permuted order. Later in this section, the second line will be used to describe permutations.

In this permutation, the number in position 1 moves to position 4, the number in position 4 moves to position 7, the number in position 7 moves to position 12, the number in position 12 moves to position 3, and the number in position 3 moves to position 1, completing the cycle **1→4→7→C→3→1**. The cycle can be represented as (1,4,7,12,3).

The first number that is not in this cycle is 2. Starting from position 2 we find the cycle **2→A→6→9→B→8→5→2**, which can be represented as (2,10,6,9,11,8,5). The whole permutation can then be expressed as (1,4,7,12,3) (2,10,6,9,11,8,5).

These two cycles have periods of 5 and 7, respectively, so this permutation has a period of 35. That is, if you kept applying this transposition to a block of 12 letters, it would produce 35 different permutations of the letters, and the 36th permutation would be the same as the original plaintext.

Suppose that you wanted to produce a strong block transposition cipher, one where every block has a different transposition. Applying the previous transposition a different number of times for each block would not be adequate because it repeats every 35 cycles. This problem can be overcome by using two different permutations and alternating.

Let the two transpositions be A and B. If A and B are suitably chosen, then you can generate a huge number of transpositions A, B, AA, AB, BA, BB, AAA, AAB, ABA, ... that are all different.

This is where understanding the cycle structure of the permutations becomes important. Suppose that you chose the permutations (1,4,7,12,3) (2,10,6,9,11,8,5) and (1,4,3,12,7) (2,10,9,6,5,11,8). These two permutations partition the block of 12 units the same way, namely [1,3,4,7,12] and [2,5,6,8,9,10,11]. When you alternate the two permutations repeatedly, the [1,3,4,7,12] partition will get permuted separately from the [2,5,6,8,9,10,11] partition. That is, there is no interaction between the two sets of numbers. To get a long period, each cycle of the second permutation should overlap each cycle of the first permutation as much as possible. Here is a suitable set of permutations.

$$(1,4,7,12,3) \ (2,10,6,9,11,8,5)$$
$$(1,10,8) \ (4,6,5,12) \ (2,11,9,7,3)$$

This transposition cipher is rated Three. It can be solved simply by trying all of the 12! possible permutations for the first block. This is only 4.79×10^8. For each permutation that produces reasonable text for the first block, Emily can try each of the 12! permutations for the second block. In practice this takes far fewer than $(12!)^2 = 2.29 \times 10^{17}$ tries because just looking at the first 3 or 4 characters of the block can eliminate many implausible combinations. In fact, it is feasible to solve this cipher by hand methods. The difficulty increases slowly with larger block sizes.**

There are several ways to increase the security of a key transposition. One way is to overlap the blocks. If the block size is 16, for example, instead of starting the blocks at positions 1, 17, 33, ... in the message, start the blocks at positions 1, 9, 17, 25, 33, ... That way, each block overlaps 8 units with the block before, and 8 units with the block after. The last 8 units of the message may be combined with the first 8 units to form a wraparound block. This cipher is rated Four.

The amount of overlap can be variable. If the current block starts at position P, and the block length is L, the next block can begin anywhere from position P+1 to position P+L. This cipher is rated Five. If two different transpositions are used, and chosen randomly, the rating increases to Seven.

*A second way to strengthen a block transposition cipher is by composing the permutations. If T and U are transpositions, then the composition of T and U, denoted TU, is formed by first performing transposition U and then performing T. The resulting transposition is the same as using T to transpose U and then transposing the text using the resulting transposition. Let's try an example. Suppose T is **419628573** and U is **385917462**. Since U is a block of 10 characters, you can use T to transpose U the same way you would use T to transpose a 10-letter word. Write T on the top line to use as the transposition key, and write U on the second line as the text being transposed. The first digit of the result is the number below the digit 1 in the key, namely <u>8</u> (see shading). The second digit of the result is the digit below 2 in the key, namely <u>1</u>, and so forth. Using T to permute U gives **812349675**.

```
419628573    T
385917462    U
812349675    TU
```

Composing transpositions this way lets you generate a sequence of transpositions, U, TU, TTU, TTTU, ... The period of this sequence is the same as the period of T. For a block size of 12, the longest possible period occurs when the lengths of the cycles are 3, 4 and 5, namely $3 \times 4 \times 5 = 60$. If your messages are longer than 60 blocks, you may want a longer period. This can be done by permuting the transposition with either U or T in some repeating or random pattern, say U, TU, TTU, UTTU, UUTTU, ... This can generate a very large set of distinct transpositions, provided that T and U individually have long periods, and the cycles of T overlap the cycles of U, as described earlier.

You can test whether the cycles overlap sufficiently by using the *accretion test*. Start with any one of the cycles of T or U. This forms a set containing just that one cycle.

Add to this set any other cycle of T or U that has elements in common with it. Now add to this larger set any other cycle of T or U that has elements in common with the cycles you have already chosen. Continue this way until there are no more elements in common. If the set of cycles now contains all of the cycles of both T and U, then you have good overlap. If you decide to use more than two transpositions, say T, U and V, then T and U should overlap, T and V should overlap, and U and V should also overlap.

Here is an example using some transpositions from earlier in this section, T = (1,4,7,12,3) (2,10,6,9,11,8,5) and U = (1,10,8) (4,6,5,12) (2,11,9,7,3). Start with the cycle (1,4,7,12,3).

$$(1,4,7,12,3)$$

This has the element 1 in common with the cycle (1,10,8) of U, so add that cycle to the set.

$$(1,4,7,12,3) \ (1,10,8)$$

This has the element 4 in common with the cycle (4,6,5,12) of U, so add that cycle to the set.

$$(1,4,7,12,3) \ (1,10,8) \ (4,6,5,12)$$

And so forth. Since this will include all of the cycles of T and U, they are a good overlapping pair of transpositions, and will generate a very large family of transpositions when they are composed.**

7.8 Halving transposition

Halving transposition is a computer technique I invented that uses a binary key to swap units that may be either bits or bytes, or possibly hex digits. IBM published this in the company's Invention Disclosure Bulletin, and it was considered for possible inclusion in the Data Encryption Standard (DES). Halving transposition operates on a block whose size is some power of 2, typically 32 or 64 units. For a block of n units, the key will have n−1 bits.

Let's use a block size of 16 characters as an example. The plaintext is GEORGE WASHINGTON. The transposition will use a 15-bit key. The first bit of the key determines whether the left and right 8-unit halves of the block are swapped. A 0 means no swap, a 1 means swap the halves. The next 2 key bits determine whether the 4-unit halves of those halves are swapped. If bit 2 of the key is 1 then the first quarter of the block is swapped with the second quarter. If bit 3 of the key is 1 then the third quarter of the block is swapped with the fourth quarter. The next 4 bits of the key determine whether the halves of those quarters get swapped. For example, if the fourth bit of the key is 1 then the first eighth of the block is swapped with the second eighth. The final 8 bits control whether the sixteenths of the block get swapped. For example, if the last bit of the key is 1 then the last 2 units, the 15th and 16th units of the block, letters O and N, are swapped.

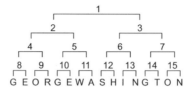

To decipher this transposition the steps must be done in the reverse order. That is, the individual units should be swapped first, then the pairs, foursomes, and so forth.

7.9   *Multiple anagramming*

A general technique for solving transposition ciphers, one that works with many types of transpositions, even when the type is unknown, is *multiple anagramming*. To use the technique, you need to intercept several messages of the same length. If these messages have been transposed with the same key, then the first letters of each message will end up in the same position in all of the ciphertexts, the second letters will end up in the same position in all of the ciphertexts, and so forth.

We can exploit this fact. Make paper strip 1 with all of the first letters in the ciphertexts. Make paper strip 2 with all of the second letters in the ciphertexts, and so forth. Make as many strips as the length of each ciphertext. These strips can be matched up just the way we did when we solved a columnar transposition. The more messages that are available, the longer the strips will be, and the greater the chance of success. It is generally felt that a minimum of 3 messages are required.

Let's look at an example. Suppose we have these 3 cipher messages:

		1	2	3	4	5	6	7	8	9	10	11	12
(1)	TTWACNAATKAD	T	T	W	A	C	N	A	A	T	K	A	D
(2)	NEMSMORMEODA	N	E	M	S	M	O	R	M	E	O	D	A
(3)	ETCMMEANEETO	E	T	C	M	M	E	A	N	E	E	T	O

The message length is 12. The 12 strips are shown to the right.

Message (1) contains a K. Some likely letters to precede that K are C and N. Message (1) contains one of each. Message (2) contains a D. A likely letter to precede the D is N. Message (2) contains one N. Let's check that these are plausible choices. We have

5	10		6	10		1	11
C	K		N	K		T	A
M	O		O	O		N	D
M	E		E	E		E	T

In message (2) the most likely letter to precede **ND** is **A** or **E**. This gives 3 possibilities:

```
2  1 11      9  1 11      12  1 11
T  T  A      T  T  A       D  T  A
E  N  D      E  N  D       A  N  D
T  E  T      E  E  T       O  E  T
```

Matching each of these 3 choices with the remaining 9 strips, the best match is with strip 4.

```
4  9  1 11
A  T  T  A
S  E  N  D
M  E  E  T
```

This matches up well with columns 5 and 10, which we had already combined previously.

```
4  9  1 11
A  T  T  A
S  E  N  D
M  E  E  T
```

The 3 messages are now easily completed, (1) ATTACK AT DAWN, (2) SEND MORE AMMO, and (3) MEET ME AT ONCE.

Jefferson Wheel Cypher

This chapter covers

- Thomas Jefferson's wheel cypher
- Solving a wheel cypher using a known word
- Solving a wheel cypher when no words are known

Thomas Jefferson invented the *Jefferson Wheel Cypher* sometime between 1790 and 1793, while he was serving as secretary of state to George Washington. The device consists of an iron rod or spindle 1/8 to 1/4 inch in diameter and 6 to 8 inches long with 36 wooden disks about 2 inches in diameter and 1/6 inch thick. Each disk has a hole drilled through its center the same size as the rod so that all of the disks can be placed snugly onto the rod, forming a wooden cylinder. The flat faces of the disks touch one another, with the outside rounded edges visible. One end of the rod has a head, like a nail head. The other end has screw threads so that a nut can be screwed onto the rod, holding the disks firmly in place.

The disks are numbered from 1 to 36 on their flat sides. The round outer edge is divided into 26 equal sections. The 26 letters of the alphabet are written or incised into these 26 sections in some scrambled order, which is different for each disk. The order of the disks on the spindle is the key for the cipher, which is nowadays called a *multiplex cipher*.

Here is a reproduction of a 26-disk Jefferson Cypher Wheel displayed at the National Cryptologic Museum in Fort Meade, Maryland. (Photo courtesy of Daderot under the Creative Commons CC0 1.0 license.)

A message is enciphered with this device by first placing the disks on the spindle in the order specified by the key. The nut is screwed on loosely so that the individual disks can be turned. The first letter of the message is found on the first disk, and the second disk is turned so that the second letter of the message is next to the first letter. Then the third disk is turned so the third letter of the message is next to the second letter, and so forth until the first 36 letters of the message are lined up in an even row. The nut is then tightened to keep them in place.

Turning the cylinder, there are 25 other rows of letters, all of which are meaningless jumbles. Sandra may choose any one of these as the ciphertext. Riva repeats this process, setting up the ciphertext on one row of the cylinder. It will be obvious which of the 25 other rows is the intended message.

Jefferson apparently never put this cipher into use. The concept lay dormant until it was reinvented by Étienne Bazeries in the early 1890s. It was adopted by the French in 1901. Bazeries's version had two improvements. It had a stand or cradle so the device could be placed on a desk for two-handed operation, and it had a guide that helped the user line up the letters evenly and select the row for reading out the ciphertext. A version of this cipher using 25 aluminum disks was invented by Col. Parker Hitt in 1914 and adopted by the US Army in 1922 as the M-94, and by the US Navy in 1926 as the CSP-488. Hitt's version was only 4.25" long, small enough to fit in a pocket, and had notches and prongs on the flat faces of the disks that kept them from slipping after they had been aligned.

Here is a photo of a CSP-488 from the National Cryptologic Museum.

A flat version of the cipher was invented by Hitt in 1916 and adopted by the Army in 1935 as the M-138. This version was a flat aluminum board with 25 channels that held paper strips that could slide back and forth to simulate the turning of the disks. Each strip had two copies of the scrambled alphabet. This device was more secure since the paper strips could easily be replaced, and even hand-written in the field if necessary. This was soon replaced by the M138A, or CSP-845 in the Navy, which had slots for 30 paper strips. 100 strips were supplied with the device, designated by 2-digit numbers, so any message used 30 out of 100 possible strips. This allows for $100!/70! = 7.79{\times}10^{57}$ possible keys.

The M-138A had a hinge in the center so that it could be folded for easier carrying. Each half had a separate guide that was used for aligning the strips and reading out 15 letters of the cipher. These improvements considerably strengthened the cipher.

These strip ciphers were dropped by the Army around 1942 or 1943, but they remained in use by the Navy as a standby in case a loss of electrical power makes it impossible to use any of their electronic or electromechanical cipher devices.

It is not feasible to solve a multiplex cipher if Emily does not have a copy of the device and does not know the alphabets. If Emily possesses the device, the cipher is relatively easy to solve if she knows some probable words. When Emily possesses a copy of the device and knows some probable words, the Jefferson Cypher Wheel is rated Four to Five. When no probable words are known, the rating is Six to Seven. The more ciphertext Emily has, the lower the rating. Conversely, if the device has lots of extra disks, the rating goes up. For example, if the device holds 30 disks that the user selects from a supply of 100 disks, the rating can go to Eight. For very short messages, less than two times the number of disks, solution may be impossible unless Emily intercepts multiple messages using the same key. This may happen if the sender changes the order of the disks only once per day.

8.1   *Known-word solution*

You can solve a message enciphered with the Jefferson Cypher Wheel when you have enough text, and you know at least part of the message. Often, just a single known word is sufficient. Suppose you know that Sandra is using the M-94 device, which has 25 disks, and you have intercepted a message:

```
CLPOXFDQBOMTUCESZITNCVGWX
ESIWVILLSCQYRNPFJCNSRWXGK
GAFOEMZTGHJWQZTYMSAXTBILF
UICSBHWHPMBZQRCDH
```

Suppose you also know the plaintext message begins URGENT. This has been transformed into the ciphertext **CLPOXF**. Since URGENT is on one row and **CLPOXF** is on another row, the distance between corresponding pairs of letters must be the same. Let's call the row with URGENT row 1, and suppose the row with **CLPOXF** is row 8.

The first letter of the plaintext, U, and the first letter of the ciphertext, C, are taken from row 1 and row 8 of the first disk. So, on the first disk the distance from U to C must be 7. On the second disk the distance from R to L must be 7. On the third disk the distance from G to P must be 7, as well as E to O, N to X and T to F.

The easiest way to search is to try each possible distance from 1 through 25 in turn. Start with distance 1. Find all of the disks where the distance from U to C is 1. In other words, where the next letter after U is C. If there are no such disks, then you know the distance is not 1. Then find all of the disks where the distance from R to L is 1. Again, if there are none the distance cannot be 1.

Let's suppose that you have found 12 sets of disks where the letter pairs are all at a distance of 1. You now need to test these 12 sets to see if any of them are correct. Let the first set of disks be, say, 18-4-21-9-13-11. Start testing with the second block of the ciphertext, letters 26 through 50. This block starts **ESIWVI**. Set disk 18 to letter **E**, disk 4 to letter **S**, disk 21 to letter **I**, and so on. Now look at the other 25 rows. If they are all gibberish, like **HNSAEI** or **TFPGUW**, then you know 18-4-21-9-13-11 is not the correct sequence of disks. On the other hand, if you see some plausible text like NCONDI, which could be part of the word UNCONDITIONAL, then 18-4-21-9-13-11 might be the correct sequence of disks. Test again using the third block of the ciphertext starting with **GAFOEM**. If the third and fourth blocks all lead to reasonable text segments, then 18-4-21-9-13-11 is probably correct ... but keep searching because you might find better disk sequences.

If you don't see any likely snippets of text, then try the other 11 disk sequences. If none of these work, try distance 2, then distance 3, ... through distance 25. There will probably be a few hundred combinations of disk order and distance to test. This is tedious, but still feasible by hand. If nothing works, go back and look for disk sequences where 2 out of the 3 tests gave plausible text.

Once you have settled on the most probable sequence for the first 6 disks, and the corresponding distances, then you try to extend this to the 7th disk. For each choice of disk you already know the distance from the plaintext to the ciphertext, so the extension process goes fairly quickly.

*8.2 Ciphertext-only solution

It is also possible to solve multiplex ciphers when there are no known words. This is called a ciphertext-only solution. I was the first person to find such a solution ("Computer Methods for Decrypting Multiplex Ciphers." *Cryptologia* 2 (Apr. 1978), pp. 152–160). In the original 1978 paper I used bigram frequencies and worked up to trigrams. Computers today are much faster, and have much more storage, so we can skip the bigram step. The method assumes that you have a table giving the probabilities for each possible trigram in English. You can compile such a table your-self, or just download a trigram table from the internet. Here is the gist of the method.

Let us assume as before that Emily is using the M-94 device with 25 cipher alpha-bets, and that we have intercepted a message of at least 3 blocks, or 75 letters. All that we know about the message is that it is in English. For example, suppose we have intercepted

```
CLPOXFDQBOMTUCESZITNCVGWX
ESIWVILLSCQYRNPFJCNSRWXGK
GAFOEMZTGHJWQZTYMSAXTBILF
```

Start by trying all possible choices for the first 3 disks. There are $25 \times 24 \times 23 = 13,800$ such choices. For each choice, set the disks to the first 3 letters in each block of the ciphertext, namely **CLP**, **ESI** and **GAF**. For each of these trigrams, look at the other 25 rows. These rows contain the possible plaintext trigrams corresponding to the ciphertext trigrams. Since there are 25 choices for each of the 3 rows, the total number of possibilities is $13800 \times 25^3 = 215,625,000$. This can be easily handled by a desktop computer, or even a notebook computer.

For each combination of 3 disks and 3 rows, the probability of that combination is the product of the probabilities for the 3 plaintext trigrams. Equivalently, the logarithm of the probability is the sum of the logarithms of the 3 trigram probabilities. The idea is to keep only the most likely combinations and discard the rest. For example, you could keep only the top 1%, or you could keep a fixed number of good combinations, perhaps the 1,000,000 best. Let's assume that you chose to keep the top 2,000,000.

One way to do that is to generate all 215,625,000 combinations, then sort them on the probability, and throw out the bottom 99%. That would take a lot of storage. There are better ways to do this. Start by allocating a table that is 10% to 25% bigger than the number of combinations you want, let's say 2,500,000 combinations. Begin generating the combinations and putting them in the table. When the table gets full it needs to be trimmed by about 20%.

That could be done by sorting the table and deleting the bottom 20%. That is, you sort by descending probability and then just set the number of table entries to 2,000,000. Sorting 2,500,000 items is a lot faster than sorting 215,625,000 items, but there are far faster ways. Select 10 items from the table at random. (If you don't know how to choose randomly, then choose the items 1/11, 2/11, ..., 10/11 of the way through.) Sort these 10 items from least-probable to most-probable. Call these sorted items a,b,c,d,e,f,g,h,i,j. Let P be the probability of item b. Delete every item in the table whose probability is less than P.

Continue generating combinations, but do not add any item to the table whose probability is P or less. Each time the table fills up, repeat the process of sampling, sorting the samples, and resetting the cutoff probability P.

At the end of all this, you will have about 2,000,000 combinations of 3 disks and 3 rows. The next step is to extend this to 4 disks. Try all 22 possible choices for the 4th disk. This will give you about 44,000,000 combinations. Now look at the trigrams formed by disks 2, 3 and 4. For each combination multiply the probability for the trigram on disks 1,2,3 by the probability of the trigram on disks 2,3,4 to get an approximate probability for the tetragram on all 4 disks. Multiply the probabilities for the plaintext tetragrams corresponding to the 3 ciphertext tetragrams CLPO, ESIW and GAFO.

This will give you probabilities for the 44,000,000 combinations of 4 disks and 3 rows. Again, you can keep the best 1% to give you 440,000 sets of tetragrams. Use the same method as you used for the trigrams.

Continue this way to get the pentagrams, hexagrams, heptagrams, and so forth. Each time you add a disk you can keep fewer combinations than the time before. When you get down below 100, you can just pick out the correct combination by sight and complete the solution by hand.

One problem that may cause this procedure to fail is this: even in normal text, a trigram may appear that has a probability of 0 in your trigram table. If Emily is using nulls, this may occur fairly often. This could cause the legitimate plaintext to get rejected.

One solution is to jigger the trigram probabilities so that a 0 probability never occurs. Let's write $P(x)$ for the probability of a string x. If the probability of a trigram, say XYZ, is zero you can use the greater of $P(X)P(YZ)$ and $P(XY)P(Z)$. I suggest dividing this by 3, say, because XYZ never occurred in your trigram count. If the probability of XYZ is still 0, then use the individual letters. For example, set $P(XYZ)$ to $P(X)P(Y)P(Z)/10$.

A different solution is not to multiply the probabilities, but to use some other function to combine them. For example, you could add the sum of the squares of the probabilities. This will strongly reward common trigrams, while largely ignoring rare trigrams.

If all of this fails, then simply try the procedure again from a different starting point in the ciphertext. For example, start at the fifth disk.**

Fractionation 9

This chapter covers

- The Polybius square
- Splitting a letter into smaller parts, such as bits or hexadecimal digits
- Mixing and recombining those parts

The first two basic tools of cryptography are substitution and transposition, which are covered in chapters 5 through 8. The third fundamental element of cryptography is fractionation. This means breaking the normal units of language, letters, syllables and words into smaller units and operating on those units. The smaller units are commonly bits, decimal digits, hexadecimal digits, or digits in other number bases. This chapter covers fractionation using digits in bases 2, 3, 5, 6, and 16, plus some other forms of fractionation.

9.1   *Polybius square*

Possibly the oldest method for representing letters as smaller units is the *Polybius Square*, which we saw in section 4.4. Here each letter is represented by two base-5 digits, making 25 possible 2-digit combinations. (The Greeks did not have a representation for 0, so their digits started at 1.)

Here is the Polybius square from section 4.4. Each letter is represented by its *coordinates* in the square, that is, by its row and column numbers. For example, the letter P is on row 2 in column 5, so it is represented as 25. When needed for clarity this can also be written as 2,5.

	1	2	3	4	5
1	U	V	W	X	Y
2	Z	S	A	M	P
3	L	E	B	C	D
4	F	G	H	IJ	K
5	N	O	Q	R	T

A mixed polybius square using the keyword **SAMPLE**

A Polybius square by itself can produce a number of different ciphers. For example, it can produce a simple substitution by replacing each letter in a message by the letter to the right in the square (U becomes **V**), or below (U becomes **Z**), or below and to the right (U becomes **S**) or left (U becomes **P**), and so forth. This idea can be extended to a polyalphabetic cipher by changing directions, say right, left, down, right, left, down, etc. You can also go 2 letters away or use knight moves, as in chess.

A Polybius square can also be used to produce a *Polybius Ripple* cipher. Begin by replacing each letter of the message by its coordinates, simply written out in one line. Starting with the second number in this list, add the previous number to the current number. If the sum is more than 5, subtract 5 to keep the numbers in the range 1 to 5. Then turn these numbers back into letters using the Polybius square again.

S E N D H E L P	Plaintext
2232513543323125	Coordinates
2424453325353411	After the ripple operation
M M J B P D C U	Ciphertext

The Polybius ripple cipher is rated Three. The cipher can be strengthened by using a different Polybius square for converting the coordinates back to letters.

Let's look at a few hand ciphers from the 1800s based on the Polybius square in sections 9.2 to 9.7. I cover some additional hand methods in sections 9.8 to 9.11. Then I discuss some computer methods in the rest of the chapter.

9.2 Playfair

The *Playfair* cipher was invented by Charles Wheatstone (pronounced WHIT-stun) in 1854. Wheatstone is well-known among electrical engineers as the inventor of the Wheatstone bridge, which measures electrical resistance. Wheatstone and William Cooke invented the needle telegraph several years before Samuel Morse invented his key telegraph. Cooke commercialized the needle telegraph in England years before Morse began his telegraph company in the US.

Wheatstone's cipher is called the Playfair cipher because it was Wheatstone's look-alike friend Baron Lyon Playfair (both had bright red hair and stood about 5'2") who advocated for its use and convinced the British Foreign Office to use the cipher for diplomatic communications.

Historical aside

Since this cipher was not called the Wheatstone cipher, that left the Wheatstone name available for a second cipher that Wheatstone invented circa 1860 and exhibited at the Paris Exposition Universelle in 1867. The Wheatstone Cryptograph, which resembled a large pocket watch, consisted of two stationary concentric rings made of stiff cardboard and two moveable clock hands connected by a simple clockwork mechanism. The inner ring was erasable, and could be changed for each message. This ring had the 26-letter alphabet in scrambled order, while the outer ring had the standard 26-letter alphabet plus a blank, making 27 positions. You move the long clock hand to indicate the plaintext letter on the outer ring, and the short hand moves to indicate the ciphertext letter on the inner ring. When the long clock hand completes one revolution of 27 positions, the short hand also moves 27 positions, which is 1 complete revolution plus 1 extra letter position. So the short hand starts from a different point on each revolution. An equivalent device with moveable rings and no hands had been produced by Col. Decius Wadsworth, chief of ordnance, in 1817, based on plans made by Thomas Jefferson in 1790, but it is Wheatstone's name that is forever associated with this concept.

Photo provided by Ralph Simpson. The inscription reads

"The Cryptograph. C. Wheatstone Inv^r."

The Playfair cipher is based on the Polybius square, and enciphers two letters at a time. That is, it enciphers bigrams. The square can be prepared by mixing the alphabet using any of the methods of section 5.2. One low-frequency letter of the alphabet such as J, Q or Z is omitted to make the alphabet fit into a 5×5 square. (In French, J, Q and Z are common, so omit W. In German, omit Q, X or Y.) When the omitted letter occurs in the message, some other letter is chosen to replace it. In our case each J is replaced by an I.

The next step is to divide the message into bigrams, for example ME ET ME TO MO RR OW. If a bigram is a double letter, this should be broken up, typically by inserting an X in the middle. (This is a good reason not to omit X from the square.) Also, if the message contains an odd number of letters, an X is added at the end. The message becomes ME ET ME TO MO RX RO WX. Now we are ready to encipher it.

Playfair has 3 rules: (1) if the two letters are on the same row, each letter is replaced by the letter to its right; (2) if the letters are in the same column, each letter is replaced by the letter below it; (3) for all other letters, each letter is replaced by the letter in the same row, but in the column of the other letter of the bigram. It is understood that the square wraps around, so in the square in section 9.1, the letter to the right of Y is U, and the letter below Q is W.

These rules can be restated in terms of the coordinates. Let the bigram we wish to encipher be r1c1 r2c2, so that the first letter is on row r1 in column c1 and the second letter is on row r2 in column c2. Now the 3 rules become

1 If r1 = r2 then substitute r1,c1+1 r2,c2+1.
2 If c1 = c2 then substitute r1+1,c1 r2+1,c2.
3 Otherwise substitute r1,c2 r2,c1.

Let's encipher our sample message ME ET ME TO MO RX RO WX and see how these rules work. The first bigram is ME. M and E are in different rows and different columns so Rule 3 applies. M is in row 2 column 4 and E is in row 3 column 2. So M gets replaced by the letter in the same row, namely row 2, in the same column as the letter E, namely column 2. The letter in row 2 column 2 is S, so M is replaced by **S**. Likewise, E is replaced by the letter in row 3 column 4, namely **C**.

In the same way ET is replaced by **DO**, and the second ME is replaced by **SC**. The letters T and O are in the same row, so Rule 1 applies. They are replaced by the letters to their right. T gets replaced by **N** and O gets replaced by **Q**. So TO is replaced by **NQ**.

MO goes by Rule 3. It is replaced by **SR**. R and X are in the same column so Rule 2 applies. RX is replaced by **XM**. RO and WX both use Rule 1 and are replaced by **TQ** and **XY**. The entire message thus becomes **SC DO SC NQ SR XM TQ XY**, which is **SCDOS CNQSR XMTQX Y** after regrouping.

Here are some diagrams to help you visualize how the bigrams LY, TO and RX are enciphered.

	1	2	3	4	5
1	U	V	W	X	Y
2	Z	S	A	M	P
3	L	E	B	C	D
4	F	G	H	IJ	K
5	N	O	Q	R	T

LY → DU

	1	2	3	4	5
1	U	V	W	X	Y
2	Z	S	A	M	P
3	L	E	B	C	D
4	F	G	H	IJ	K
5	N	O	Q	R	T

TO → NQ

	1	2	3	4	5
1	U	V	W	X	Y
2	Z	S	A	M	P
3	L	E	B	C	D
4	F	G	H	IJ	K
5	N	O	Q	R	T

RX → XM

The Playfair cipher remained in military and diplomatic use until at least 1960. Next, let's take a brief look at how a Playfair cipher can be solved.

9.2.1   *Solving a Playfair cipher*

Notice that each letter can be enciphered by only 5 possible substitutes, namely the 4 other letters on its row and the letter immediately below it. For each letter there are 24 other letters in the grid. Of these, only the 4 letters in its own column will cause the letter to be replaced by the letter below it. So the chance of a letter being replaced by the letter below is 4/24, or 1/6. The chance that it is replaced by another letter on its row is therefore 5/6.

Since there are 5 rows in the square and 9 English letters with frequencies over 5% there must be several rows that contain at least 2 high-frequency letters. If there are fewer than 4 such rows, then there must be at least one row with 3 high-frequency letters. The other letters on these rows will appear more frequently in the ciphertext than any other letters. If you have sufficient ciphertext there is a good chance that the 3 to 5 most frequent letters in the ciphertext appear on the same row in the square.

If we remove all of the bigrams containing these letters, the 3 to 5 most frequent letters in the remaining bigrams are likely to be on the same row of the square. Knowing the high-frequency letters on 2 out of the 5 rows is enough to get started in the reconstruction of the square. The next step would be to try to place some probable words.

The Playfair cipher is rated Three. There are several ways to increase the strength of the Playfair cipher. Let me mention just a few.

9.2.2   *Strengthening a Playfair cipher*

Here are several stronger variants of the Playfair cipher.

NULLFAIR OR NOFAIR

Nulls can be added to the ciphertext at repeating intervals, like this:

```
2   3   2   3   2   3      Null key is 23
BR  CNT FG  IUS MH  RAO L  Playfair ciphertext
BRECNTPFGRIUSUMHMRAOAL     Ciphertext with nulls
```

Nullfair is rated Five.

PLAYFAIR+1

This super-simple enhancement adds a repeating binary key to the Playfair ciphertext. Wherever there is a 1 bit, the next letter of the alphabet is used. Playfair+1 is stronger if the binary key has an odd length.

```
0101101011010110      Binary key is 01011
BRCNTFGIUSMHRAOL      Playfair ciphertext
BSCOUFHIVTMIRBPL      Ciphertext+1
```

   Playfair+1 is rated Five. Playfair+1 can also be done with ternary numbers. The digits in the additive key are kept small so the addition can be done in your head, without needing a tableau.

DOUBLE PLAYFAIR

The Playfair cipher can be strengthened by applying it twice. On the second round, the pairs should straddle the bigrams created in the first round. (1) Encipher the message with a Playfair cipher. (2) Either move the first letter to the end, move the last letter to the beginning, or add a null at both ends. (3) Apply another round of Playfair. This is strongest if a different mixed alphabet is used for the second Playfair cipher. Double Playfair is rated Six.

PLAYFAIR RIPPLE

This is a variant of double Playfair that takes only one pass through the message, and needs only one Polybius square. Let the plaintext be $P_1P_2P_3P_4$ ... Start at the left end and encipher plaintext bigram P_1P_2 using Playfair, producing ciphertext bigram C_1C_2. Then encipher C_2P_3 as the second bigram, getting D_2C_3. Notice that D_2 has been enciphered twice. Next you encipher C_3P_4, to get D_3C_4, and so forth, moving one character to the right at each step. Playfair ripple is rated Six.

   Since the first letter C_1 and the last letter C_n of the ciphertext have been enciphered only once, you may wish to encipher them as a bigram to complete the cycle.

$$P_1\ P_2\ P_3\ P_4\ P_5\ P_6 \qquad \text{Plaintext}$$
$$/\ \ /\ \ /\ \ /\ \ /$$
$$C_1\ C_2\ C_3\ C_4\ C_5\ C_6 \qquad \text{Intermediate text}$$
$$C_1\ D_2\ D_3\ D_4\ D_5\ D_6 \qquad \text{Ciphertext}$$

POLYPLAYFAIR

Use two different Polybius squares and alternate between them by using a repeating key. For example, a key of 11212 means that on each cycle of 5 bigrams the first, second and fourth bigrams would be enciphered with Square 1, while the third and fifth bigrams would be enciphered with Square 2. This can be extended to three or more squares, with a correspondingly longer setup time. Using two squares and a key of not more than 10 digits PolyPlayfair is rated Five. If the key is generated by the Chained Digit algorithm, using the first square when the digit is 0 to 4, and the second square when the digit is 5 to 9, the rating increases to Six. (Note: using the parity of the chained digit sequence has a much shorter period, so it is far weaker.)

TRANSPOSITION

After the plaintext has been enciphered with the Playfair cipher the resulting ciphertext can be transposed. The transposition can be as elaborate as the columnar transposition of section 7.2, or as simple as the piecewise reversal of the Bazeries Type 4 cipher in section 4.6.1. With columnar transposition the Playfair is rated Seven. With piecewise reversal the Playfair is rated Five.

9.3   *Two Square*

The *Two Square* cipher, sometimes called *Double Playfair*, is an improved version of the Playfair cipher. It was invented by French amateur cryptographer Félix-Marie Delastelle and described in his 1902 book *Traité Élémentaire de Cryptographie*. As the name implies, it uses two Polybius squares instead of one, so that there are two mixed alphabets instead of one. The two squares may be placed side-by-side horizontally, or bottom-to-top vertically. The horizontal version is illustrated. In this example the two squares were mixed using the keywords FIRST and SECOND, and the letter Q was omitted to fit the 5×5 grids.

```
F I R S T     M P R T U
A B C D E     V W X Y Z
G H J K L     S E C O N
M N O P U     D A B F G
V W X Y Z     H I J K L
```

Like the Playfair, the message is enciphered 2 letters at a time. That is, Two Square enciphers bigrams. To encipher the bigram SO we find the S in the left square and the O in the right square. The substitute for S is the letter in the right square in the same row as S and the same column as O, namely **T**. The substitute for O is the letter in the left square in the same row as O and the same column as S, namely **K**. Thus the bigram SO becomes **TK**.

Unlike the Playfair, there is no need to break up double letters. The two letters could be on different rows in the two squares. For example, SS becomes **MK**. In most cases, a double letter in the ciphertext will not correspond to a double letter in the plaintext.

Here is the substitution process visually.

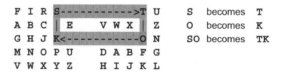

```
F I R S----------->T U     S   becomes   T
A B C  E      V W X  Z      O   becomes   K
G H J  K<----------O N      SO  becomes   TK
M N O P U      D A B F G
V W X Y Z      H I J K L
```

An important weakness of the Two Square cipher is that when the two letters of a bigram fall on the same row in the grid the substitute is simply those letters in reverse. For instance, ST would become **TS**. This weakness, called a *transparency*, sometimes allows an entire word to leak through. For example, SU ND AY would become **US DN YA**.

To prevent this, I propose this *Same Row Rule*: when the two letters are on the same row, they are replaced by the letters immediately below them, wrapping to the top row when necessary. For example, ST would now become **DY**, and VI would become **FP**.

With the Same Row Rule, Two Square is rated Four. Call this variation *Two Square B*.

The Germans took the name Double Playfair literally. They enciphered each bigram using the Two Square cipher, and then enciphered that bigram again, using Two Square with the same two squares. The result is essentially a general bigram substitution (section 6.5).

The same methods that were used to strengthen the Playfair cipher may also be used to strengthen the Two Square cipher, such as *TwoSquare+1* and *Two Square Ripple*, with the same ratings. Here is an additional variant.

PLAYFAIR TWOSQUARE

The Two Square cipher uses two Polybius squares. Either of these squares could be used for a Playfair cipher. This suggests a hybrid method that mixes Playfair and Two Square. Again, we will use a numerical key to control how each successive bigram is enciphered. A 1 means encipher the bigram using Playfair in the left square, a 2 means encipher the bigram using Playfair in the right square, and a 3 means encipher the bigram using Two Square or Two Square B. It is best if the numeric key contains at least one of each digit. Since Two Square is stronger than Playfair, 3 should occur more often than 1 or 2 in the key. About 50% would be suitable. *Playfair TwoSquare* is rated Six.

9.4   Three Square

Three Square is my own idea. Otherwise, it has no special merit. I include it here simply because one of the books I read while researching for this book said that Two Square could not be extended to more than two squares. I love a challenge.

As the name suggests, Three Square uses three Polybius squares. These squares should be well-mixed with independent keys. Three Square enciphers 3 letters at a time, that is, it enciphers trigrams. This makes it stronger than Two Square.

```
F I R S T     U V W X Y     L M N O P
A B C D E     Z S E C O     S U V W X
G H J K L     N D A B F     Y Z T H I
M N O R U     G H I J K     R D A B C
V W X Y Z     L M P R T     E F G J K
```

The basic idea is that each letter is replaced by a letter in the square to its right. The replacement letter is in the same row, but in the column containing the next letter of the trigram.

Suppose we wish to encipher the trigram THE. The first letter is T, the second letter is H, and the third letter is E. We encipher using the T in the first square, the H in the second square and the E in the third square, like this.

```
F I R S T     U V W X Y     L M N O P
A B C D E     Z S E C O     S U V W X
G H J K L     N D A B F     Y Z T H I
M N O R U     G H I J K     R D A B C
V W X Y Z     L M P R T     E F G J K
```

The substitute for T is on the row containing the T, and in the column in the second square containing the H, so T is replaced by **V**. The substitute for H is on the same row as the H in the same column as the E in the third square, so H is replaced by **R**. The substitute for E is on the same row as the E in the column in the first square containing the T, so E is replaced by **Z**. Thus, THE becomes **VRZ**.

This can be seen pictorially as follows:

```
F  I  R  S  T---->V  W  X  Y      L  M  N  O  P      Enciphering
A  B  C  D  E      Z  S  E  C  O   S  U  V  W  X      T  becomes  V
G  H  J  K  L      N  D  A  B  F   Y  Z  T  H  I      H  becomes  R
M  N  O  R  U      G  H-------->R  D  A  B  C         E  becomes  Z
-------->Z         L  M  P  R  T   E-------->         THE  becomes  VRZ
```

The decipherment goes in the opposite direction. Since the first letter of the ciphertext trigram **VRZ** came from the second square, we begin deciphering in the second square, like this:

```
F  I  R  S  T<----V  W  X  Y      L  M  N  O  P      Deciphering
A  B  C  D  E      Z  S  E  C  O   S  U  V  W  X      V  becomes  T
G  H  J  K  L      N  D  A  B  F   Y  Z  T  H  I      R  becomes  H
M  N  O  R  U      G  H<--------R  D  A  B  C         Z  becomes  E
<--------Z         L  M  P  R  T   E<--------         VRZ  becomes  THE
```

Three Square has a worse problem than Two Square with letters falling on the same row. In a trigram such as XYZ, it is possible that X and Y could fall on the same row, Y and Z could fall on the same row, or Z and X could fall on the same row. This requires two extra rules to prevent a transparency where a letter represents itself.

Rule 1: If two consecutive letters in the trigram fall on the same row, the first of these two letters is enciphered as the letter to the right of the second of the letters, wrapping to the left column, if needed. For example, in the trigram SUB the S is on the top row of the first square, and the U is on the top row of the second square. Therefore S is replaced by **V** instead of by **U**. Similarly, in the trigram LET, the T is on the third row of the third square, and the L is on the third row of the first square. So T is replaced by **G** instead of **L**.

This diagram illustrates Rule 1. Without Rule 1, in the trigram SUB the S would be replaced by **U**. Instead, it is replaced by the letter to the right of U in the middle square, namely **V**. Without Rule 1, in the trigram LET the T would be replaced by **L**. Instead, it is replaced by the letter to the right of L in the left square. This wraps from column 5 to column 1, which has the letter **G**.

```
F  I  R  S---->U  V  W  X  Y      L  M  N  O  P      In the trigram SUB
A  B  C  D  E      Z  S  E  C  O   S  U  V  W  X      S  becomes  V, not U
G  H  J  K  L      N  D  A  B  F   Y  Z  T---->
M  N  O  R  U      G  H  I  J  K   R  D  A  B  C      In the trigram LET
V  W  X  Y  Z      L  M  P  R  T   E  F  G  J  K      T  becomes  G, not L
```

Rule 2: If all three letters in the trigram fall on the same row, each letter will be replaced by the letter immediately below it, wrapping to the top row, if needed. Thus FUN would be replaced by `AZV`, and WRE would be replaced by `IXL`.

With these rules Three Square is rated Five.

PLAYFAIR THREESQUARE

The Three Square cipher uses three Polybius squares. Any of these squares could be used for a Playfair cipher. This suggests a hybrid method that mixes the Playfair and Three Square ciphers. You can use a numerical key such as 1,4,1,3,4,2,4 to control how each successive bigram or trigram is enciphered. A 1 means encipher the next 2 letters as a bigram using Playfair in the first square. A 2 means encipher the next 2 letters as a bigram using Playfair in the second square. A 3 means encipher the next 2 letters as a bigram using Playfair in the third square. A 4 means encipher the next 3 letters as a trigram using Three Square. It is best if the numeric key contains at least one of each digit. Since Three Square is much stronger than Playfair, the digit 4 should occur more often than 1, 2 or 3 in the numeric key. About 50% would be suitable. That is, 4 should occur as often as 1, 2 and 3 combined. Equivalently, generate random numbers from 1 to 6, and use Three Square with 4, 5 or 6.

Since Playfair ThreeSquare mixes bigrams and trigrams, about half of the bigrams and two-thirds of the trigrams will not fall on even boundaries. This means the increase in strength is greater than the increase for Playfair TwoSquare. Playfair ThreeSquare is rated Seven.

It is possible to combine Playfair, Two Square and Three Square into an even more complex cipher, no doubt with greater strength, but Playfair ThreeSquare is already pushing the limits of what a human code clerk can do. Both speed and accuracy would suffer.

There is an opposite approach, which I call a *Straddling Three Square*. Group the plaintext into rows containing four blocks of 3 characters each. Encipher each of the blocks using the Three Square cipher. Now take the last letter of block 1 and the first letter of block 2 and encipher that bigram using the Playfair cipher with the first Polybius square. Take the last letter of block 2 and the first letter of block 3 and encipher that bigram using the Playfair cipher with the second Polybius square. Take the last letter of block 3 and the first letter of block 4 and encipher that bigram with the third Polybius square. This improves the strength of the Three Square cipher without adding much complexity, or much time. Use the Same Row Rule throughout.

9.5   *Four Square*

The *Four Square* cipher was invented by Félix-Marie Delastelle circa 1890, and described in his book *Traité Élémentaire de Cryptographie*, published 3 months after his death in 1902. Delastelle invented the Two Square cipher after the Four Square cipher as a simplified and slightly less secure version. However, with the Same Row Rule described in section 9.3 the two ciphers can be considered equal in strength.

As the name implies, the Four Square cipher utilizes four Polybius squares. Two of the squares contain the standard alphabet, and the other two squares contain alphabets mixed using independent keys. The message is enciphered two letters at a time, that is, Four Square enciphers bigrams.

Here is a sample arrangement.

```
a b c d e    M O N K E    Keyword: MONKEY
f g h i j    Y A B C D
k l m n o    F G H I J
p r s t u    L P R S T
v w x y z    U V W X Z

U V W X Y    a b c d e    Keyword: CHIMPANZEE
C H I M P    f g h i j
A N Z E B    k l m n o
D F G J K    p r s t u
L O R S T    v w x y z
```

Enciphering uses the familiar rectangular scheme. You locate the two plaintext letters in the standard alphabets and replace them with the letters at the opposite corners of the rectangle, like this:

```
a b c d e    M O N K E
f g h i j    Y A B C D
k l m n o    F G H I J
p r s t---------->R S T    Plaintext TH is replaced
v w x y z    U V W X Z     by ciphertext RM

U V W X Y    a b c d e
C H I M<---------h i j
A N Z E B    k l m n o
D F G J K    p r s t u
L O R S T    v w x y z
```

Since the two plaintext letters can never be in the same row or the same column of the 10×10 grid there is no need for special rules, or for separating double letters. The only need for a null character is for completing the last bigram. Four Square is rated Five.

CYCLING METHOD

To get a little more strength you can use a simple transposition similar to the piecewise reversal in section 4.6.1. This transposition uses a repeating numeric key such as 1,3,1,4,2,6. Divide the ciphertext into blocks of 7 characters, or any other odd length. Write the successive key digits above each block. Then cycle each block left the number of positions indicated by its key digit. For example, if the key digit is 4 you would move the leftmost 4 digits to the right end of the block. Here is an example:

```
   1        3        1        4        2        6        1        3
BSMTPSZ  LDNTPRB  EXYFHWM  IXRCNIO  OKLPRSC  UBEACZV  NEULHDF  PLECNGU
SMTPSZB  TPRBLDN  XYFHWME  NIOIXRC  LPRSCOK  VUBEACZ  EULHDFN  CNGUPLE
```

Four Square using the cycling method is rated Six.

HALVING METHOD

Another approach to strengthening Four Square is to transpose the message beforehand. Suppose the message is AMBASSADOR WILKINS ASSASSINATED KABUL TODAY. This has 39 letters. Dividing 39 by 2 and rounding up gives 20. Write the message in two rows of 20 letters each, and read off the bigrams reading vertically. Encipher these bigrams using Four Square.

```
AMBASSADORWILKINSASS
ASSINATEDKABULTODAYX
AA MS BS AI SN SA AT DE OD RK WA IB LU KL IT NO SD AA SY SX
```

These bigrams no longer have the normal bigram frequencies, or the normal contact frequencies, for English bigrams. Four Square using the halving method is rated Seven.

9.6 *Bifid*

Let's look at one more historical hand cipher based on the 5×5 Polybius square. This is the *Bifid* cipher, also invented by Félix-Marie Delastelle in the 1890s. Bifid is a 3-step cipher where (1) the letters are converted into their Polybius coordinates, (2) those coordinates are rearranged, and (3) the coordinates are then converted back into letters. Originally, Delastelle wrote out the entire message with the coordinates written vertically under each letter, then he combined the pairs of coordinates reading horizontally, first across the top row and then across the bottom row.

The modern method is to break the message into blocks of a fixed size. The block size should be an odd number, such as 5, 7 or 9. If the block size is an even number, then Emily can separate the blocks into bigrams.

The first step is to convert the letters into their coordinates in the Polybius square. Suppose the block length is 5. The 5 plaintext letters can be represented as $X1$, $X2$, $X3$, $X4$ and $X5$. Their row and column coordinates can be represented as $R1C1$, $R2C2$, $R3C3$, $R4C4$ and $R5C5$. Each of these R and C symbols is a number from 1 to 5, with the row coordinate first and the column coordinate second. These pairs of coordinates are written vertically below each letter in the block, like this:

```
X1 X2 X3 X4 X5
R1 R2 R3 R4 R5
C1 C2 C3 C4 C5
```

Then they are read out going across the rows in the order R1R2, R3R4, R5C1, C2C3, C4C5. Here is an example. The word MAJOR is enciphered using a Polybius square that was mixed using the keyword SAMPLE.

	1	2	3	4	5		M	A	J	O	R			Plaintext
1	S	A	M	P	L		1	1	3	4	4			Coordinates written vertically
2	E	B	C	D	F		3	2	4	2	3			13, 12, 34, 42, 43
3	G	H	I	J	K									
4	N	O	R	T	U		11	34	43	24	23			Coordinates read horizontally
5	V	W	X	Y	Z		S	J	R	D	C			Ciphertext

Notice that the third set of letter coordinates in the ciphertext, **R5C1**, is a row/column pair. This means that the third ciphertext letter will come from the same row, **R5**, in the Polybius square as the fifth plaintext letter, and from the same column, **C1**, as the first plaintext letter. This concurrence of both row coordinate and column coordinate is called a *natural*.

Since there are 5 letters in each row and 5 letters in each column in the square, there is a 1 in 5 chance that the third ciphertext letter is the same as the fifth plaintext letter, and a 1 in 5 chance that the third ciphertext letter is the same as the first plaintext letter. That is, there is a 20% chance that **R5C1** is the same as **R5C5**, and a 20% chance that **R5C1** is the same as **R1C1**. In this example, that is exactly what happened. The fifth plaintext letter is R and the third ciphertext letter is also **R**.

Now look at the first ciphertext letter, **R1R2**. This is a row/row pair, not a row/column pair. Here only the first coordinate, **R1**, is in the correct place for a row/column pair. The other coordinate, **R2**, is a row coordinate in the column position. Such a single placement is called a *half-natural*. It means that the first ciphertext letter comes from the same row in the Polybius square as the first plaintext letter. So there is a 20% chance that the first ciphertext letter is the same as the first plaintext letter.

This also happens with the second, fourth and fifth ciphertext letters. Each one of them falls in either the same row or the same column as one of the plaintext letters. Thus each of them has a 20% chance of being the same as that plaintext letter. This happened in the example, where the second ciphertext letter, **J**, is the same as the third plaintext letter.

This is a serious weakness in the bifid cipher which makes it easy for Emily to guess at and place probable words. On the other hand, if the plaintext and ciphertext letters are different, then you know that they are in the same row or column. In the example, the first plaintext letter **R1C1** is M, and the first ciphertext letter **R1R2** is **S**. This means that M and S must be in the same row of the Polybius square. When Emily deduces or guesses a word, that provides several of these equivalences. This, in turn, makes it easier to place additional words. When enough of these letter pairs have been accumulated, Emily can reconstruct the square.

Due to these weaknesses, the bifid cipher is rated Three.

9.6.1   *Conjugated matrix bifid*

These problems can be eliminated by using a different Polybius square to convert the coordinates back to letters. For example, Square 2 yields the ciphertext **VBJEF**.

```
     Square 1      Plaintext        Square 2      Ciphertext
     1 2 3 4 5     M A J O R        1 2 3 4 5     11 34 43 24 23
  1  S A M P L     1 1 3 4 4     1  V W X Y Z     V  B  J  E  F
  2  E B C D F     3 2 4 2 3     2  D I F E R
  3  G H I J K                   3  N T A B C
  4  N O R T U                   4  G H J K L
  5  V W X Y Z                   5  M O P S U
```

Bifid with two separate Polybius squares is called by the highfalutin name *Conjugated Matrix Bifid*. In this context, a matrix simply means a rectangular array of letters or characters. The conjugated matrix bifid cipher is rated Five.

There are several ways to boost the strength of the bifid cipher. One way is to vary the block length using a repeating numeric key such as 5, 11, 7. The block lengths would be a cyclic repetition of this key, namely 5, 11, 7, 5, 11, 7, 5, ... If you prefer, you can generate the block lengths by using the chained digit generator and translating the digits to odd block lengths. One possibility is

Digit	0	1	2	3	4	5	6	7	8	9
Length	5	7	9	11	13	5	7	9	11	13

So, if the generator produced digits 3, 6, 2, 7, ... , then the block lengths would be 11, 7, 9, 9, ...

Using a short repeating key and conjugated matrices the cipher is rated Six. With a long repeating key or generating the block lengths using a random number generator the cipher is rated Seven.

A similar idea is to read out the coordinates starting from a different point in each block. You could use a numeric key to specify the sequence of starting points. If the block length is L, each number in the key may be anywhere from 1 to 2L. A number from 1 to L would indicate a starting position on the top row of coordinates, while a number from L+1 to 2L would indicate a starting position on the bottom row, like this:

```
     1   2   3   4   5   6   7      Starting positions for reading
     8   9  10  11  12  13  14      out the coordinates
```

The coordinates would be taken out in pairs reading from left to right. Here is the order for reading out the coordinates using the numeric key 4, 9. The starting positions 4 and 9 are shaded.

```
                  4                   9              Numeric key
      12 13 14    1   2   3   4     7   8   9 10 11 12 13    Block 1 position 4
       5  6  7    8   9  10  11    14   1   2   3   4  5  6  Block 2 position 9
```

This method increases the rating to Six.

Another way to strengthen the bifid cipher is to use a stronger transposition to mix the coordinates. The standard bifid using a block of length L takes the 2L coordinates and writes them into a 2×L block. The coordinates are written into the block vertically and read out horizontally. We recognize this as a very simple route transposition, described in section 7.1. There are several stronger transpositions covered in chapter 7, notably columnar transposition. One example of this type of cipher is the *ADFGVX* cipher invented by intelligence officer Lt. Fritz Nebel and used by the Germans in World War I. In the ADFGVX cipher, the coordinates, represented by the letters A,D,F,G,V,X, are mixed using a columnar transposition, and then transmitted as a string of those letters. This cipher is rated Five.

If you used longer blocks, say 20 characters, that would give you 40 coordinates. (With this method the block lengths may be either even or odd.) This is enough to use columnar transposition effectively to mix the coordinates. Or, you could go back to Delastelle's original concept and take the coordinates for the entire message as a single block. Either way, using conjugated matrices this cipher is rated Eight. Using a double columnar transposition the cipher is rated Ten. Assuming four long independent keys and well-mixed alphabets, this is an unbreakable paper and pencil cipher. Call it *Double Columnar Bifid.*

9.7   *Diagonal bifid*

A variation on the bifid cipher is to write the Polybius coordinates vertically under each letter, as usual, but to read them out diagonally, going from lower left to upper right (or southwest to northeast). This is called a *left diagonal* or an *antidiagonal.* (On a heraldic crest it is called *bar sinister*, and indicates out-of-wedlock birth.) For the last letter, you wrap to the first column (the shaded digit 1). The advantage of this is that there are no naturals or half-naturals to help Emily guess words. Here is an example.

```
      1 2 3 4 5     M A J O R      Plaintext
  1   S A M P L     1 1 3 4 4 1    Coordinates written in vertically
  2   E B C D F     / / / / /      13, 12, 34, 42, 43
  3   G H I J K     3 2 4 2 3
  4   N O R T U
  5   V W X Y Z     31  23  44  24  31    Coordinates read out diagonally
                    G   C   T   D   C     Ciphertext
```

Diagonal bifid is rated Four. With conjugated matrices it is rated Five. With conjugated matrices and periodically varying block sizes it is rated Six. Unlike classical bifid, both odd and even block sizes can be used with diagonal bifid.

9.8   *6×6 squares*

If your messages contain a lot of numbers, it may be advantageous to use a 6×6 Polybius square instead of a 5×5 square. A 6×6 square allows you to have the full 26-letter alphabet plus the numerals from 0 to 9. There is no need to omit J or Q from the alphabet. If you are enciphering by hand, this requires taking extra care to distinguish the letters O, I, Z, S and G from the digits 0, 1, 2, 5 and 6. Some people adopt special conventions, such as underlining all digits. I find this cumbersome and error-prone. I usually just exaggerate the characteristics that distinguish each of these characters from its mate, such as writing the letter I with extra-wide serifs.

All of the methods from the preceding 5 sections, namely Playfair, Two Square, Three Square, Four Square and Bifid, can be used with 6×6 squares, along with all of their variations.

9.9   Trifid

If you like squares, how about cubes? Another fractionation method, also invented by Félix-Marie Delastelle in the 1890s, is the *Trifid* cipher. Instead of representing each letter of the alphabet by two digits in base 5 (quinary numbers), each letter is represented by three base-3 digits (ternary numbers). This gives 3×3×3, or 3^3, different 3-digit combinations. This is enough for all 26 letters of the alphabet plus one extra character. Delastelle used a + plus sign for the 27th character.

The extra character + might be used as a form of punctuation, or it might be a signal that the following plaintext letter should be interpreted as a digit. The correspondence +A = 1, +B = 2, ... , +J = 0 could be used. The rest of the alphabet could also be used as special characters. For example, +K could mean period, +L could mean comma, and so forth.

Just as the 2-digit combinations can be displayed as a 5×5 letter square, the 3-digit combinations can be displayed as a 3×3×3 letter cube. The 3 digits in each triple can be interpreted as the coordinates in the cube where that letter is located. These coordinates are commonly called the layer, the row and the column.

Here are the 27 ternary combinations, in order, with letter equivalents weakly mixed by using the keyword EXAMPLE and alternating columns. For instance, the letter N is represented by the triple 102, so it would be located on layer 1, row 0 and column 2 of the 3×3×3 letter cube.

E	000	Q	100	+	200	Example of a trifid
X	001	O	101	R	201	substitution table
A	002	N	102	S	202	
M	010	K	110	T	210	
P	011	J	111	U	211	
L	012	I	112	V	212	
B	020	H	120	W	220	
C	021	G	121	Y	221	
D	022	F	122	Z	222	

The trifid cipher works similarly to the bifid cipher. The plaintext is written in blocks of some fixed size. The size may be any number that is not a multiple of 3. The 3 digits are written vertically beneath each letter of the message, and then read out horizontally in groups of 3. Then they are converted back into letters using the same equivalences. Here is an example with the plaintext SEND HELP and block size 4.

```
S E N D    H E L P    201 000 022 022    Ciphertext REDDQ BKC
2 0 1 0    1 0 0 0    R   E   D   D
0 0 0 2    2 0 1 1    100 020 110 021
2 0 2 2    0 0 2 1    Q   B   K   C
```

The same analysis and techniques that were used for bifid can also be applied to trifid, and they have the same ratings. You can use two separate substitution tables for converting the letters to digits and the digits back to letters. You can vary the block sizes. You can start reading out the digits from different places in each block. You can use a strong transposition to mix the ternary digits.

A natural question is whether there is a diagonal version of the trifid cipher analogous to diagonal bifid. The advantage of diagonal bifid over the original bifid is that the diagonal version does not give rise to the half-naturals that weaken the original version. In the analogous diagonal trifid the middle digit of every group would be a third-natural, so the advantage is lost. The problem of naturals disappears, though, if you use two different mixed alphabets, one for writing in the digits and another for reading them out. Diagonal trifid with two alphabets is rated Five.

9.10 *Three Cube*

As I was typing the preceding paragraph about the trifid cipher, I realized that the 3×3×3 cubic arrangement lends itself to a 3-dimensional analogue to the Two Square cipher described in section 9.3. It is easy to visualize the Two Square cipher in two dimensions, but much harder to visualize a cube in three dimensions, so I am going to describe the new cipher solely in terms of the coordinates. Let's call this cipher *Three Cube*.

Two Square enciphers two letters at a time using two substitution tables, ergo Three Cube will encipher three letters at a time using three substitution tables. Here is a set of three tables well-mixed using the keywords COLUMBIA, STANFORD and HOPKINS. These three substitution tables are designated S, T and U. That's S for Substitution, T for Table, and U for the next letter in the alphabet.

The substitution tables correspond the 26 letters of the alphabet and the character + with the 27 ternary triplets.

Subst table S			Subst table T			Subst table U		
A 000	Y 100	H 200	A 000	U 100	W 200	H 000	D 100	L 200
N 001	I 101	T 201	E 001	N 101	S 201	A 001	Q 101	W 201
X 002	K 102	O 202	P 002	G 102	B 202	J 002	Y 102	P 202
B 010	W 110	E 210	+ 010	Q 110	L 210	V 010	N 110	C 210
J 011	L 111	Q 211	D 011	O 111	Y 211	I 011	F 111	M 211
V 012	F 112	Z 212	K 012	I 112	T 212	E 012	T 112	X 212
C 020	R 120	U 220	X 020	V 120	C 220	R 020	+ 120	S 220
D 021	+ 121	G 221	F 021	R 121	M 221	Z 021	O 121	G 221
P 022	M 122	S 222	H 022	J 122	Z 222	K 022	B 122	U 222

Like trifid, Three Cube begins by writing the 3-digit triplet for each letter vertically beneath it. The 3 digits for the first letter are taken from substitution table S, the 3 digits for the second letter are taken from table T, and the 3 digits for the third letter are taken from U. The pattern is shown here and illustrated by the trigram FLY.

```
                    F L Y        Writing in the triplets
        S1  T1  U1  1 2 1            S1S2S3, T1T2T3 and U1U2U3
        S2  T2  U2  1 1 0        Plaintext is FLY
        S3  T3  U3  2 0 2
```

Then the digits are read out left to right, and these horizontal triplets are converted back to letters. It would seem natural to use table S for converting the top row, table T for the middle row and table U for the bottom row. However, that would lead to a 1 in 9 chance that the top row would be identical to the left column, so that the first plaintext letter would be replaced by itself. That is, there is 1 chance in 9 that S1S2S3 is the same as S1T1U1. The same is true for the middle and bottom rows. Let's call this situation, where one digit is the same, a *part natural.*

For this reason, substitution table S is used for the second row, table T is used for the third row, and table U is used for the top row. This eliminates the naturals. Here is the pattern.

```
                    F L Y        Reading out the triplets
        U   U   U   1 2 1        121  110  202
        S   S   S   1 1 0        O    W    B
        T   T   T   2 0 2        Ciphertext    OWB
```

Since this is hard to keep straight when you are enciphering by hand, I suggest writing the choice of substitution table over each triplet of digits. This is similar to writing the key letter over each plaintext letter when using the Belaso cipher (section 5.5). Here is an example of Three Cube using the plaintext message FLY TO ROME.

```
        STU STU STU    U   S   T   U   S   T   U   S   T
        FLY TOR OME   121 110 202 210 012 110 220 021 212
        121 210 220    O   W   B   C   V   Q   S   D   T
        110 012 021
        202 110 212   Ciphertext  OWBCV QSDT
```

The Three Cube cipher is rated Seven.

There is a simple way to strengthen the Three Cube cipher. Instead of converting the triplets back to letters using the three substitution tables in strict rotation as we just did, use a key to set the order of the read-out tables. The key would consist of the letters S, T and U in some scrambled order, for example SUTUTTUUSTS. The length of this key should not be a multiple of 3. I call this variant *Three Cube Plus*. Here is how FLY TO ROME would be enciphered using this read-out key.

```
STU STU STU     S   U   T   U   T   T   U   U   S   T   S
FLY TOR OME     121 110 202 210 012 110 220 021 212
121 210 220     +   N   B   C   K   Q   S   Z   Z
110 012 021
202 110 212     Ciphertext +NBCK QSZZ
```

Using Three Cube Plus about 1/3 of the letters will have part naturals. That is, one of the 3 write-in digits will be the same as one of the read-out digits. However, Emily will not know which letters have this defect, and will not be able to exploit it.

Three Cube Plus is rated Nine.

So, you might well be saying, is it possible to nudge the rating up to Ten without making the cipher too complex for hand use? Thank you for asking. First off, let's increase the number of substitution tables from 3 to 6. Let's call them S, T, U, V, W and X. Instead of writing in the triplets using a strict rotation STU, STU, STU, ... we will use another letter key consisting of those 6 letters in some scrambled order. The write-in key could be TWXUSTTVWV, and the read-out key could be VWTXXSUSVTU. Ideally, the lengths of these keys would be mutually prime, and neither length would be divisible by 3. Here the lengths are 10 and 11. Let's call this cipher *Three Cube Super*. This is an example of Three Cube Super using the plaintext FLY TO NEW YORK.

```
TWX UST TVW VTW     V   W   T   X   X   S   U   S   V   T   U   V
FLY TON EWY ORK     021 202 121 121 100 221 001 021 111 210 020 012
021 121 001 210     S   P   R   C   V   G   A   D   +   L   R   M
202 100 021 020
121 221 111 012     Ciphertext SPRCV GAD+L RM
```

Three Cube Super is rated Ten. This is another unbreakable hand cipher.

9.11 *Rectangular grids*

Up to now we have discussed only square and cubic arrays of letters. There is no restriction in cryptography that requires all of the dimensions of a letter grid to be the same. It is basically a historical accident that the English alphabet has 26 letters, and 26 is very close to 5×5. If we used the 33-letter Russian alphabet we might choose a 4×8 or 5×7 rectangle.

If we want to have all 26 letters of the alphabet, then a 3×9 or 4×7 rectangle might be preferable. These give you the full 26-letter alphabet plus one or two extra characters. We have discussed the use of such extra characters earlier, for example for switching between letters and numerals. Most of the ciphers based on Polybius squares work just as well with 3×9 or 4×7 rectangles as they do with 5×5 squares, assuming all of the rectangles are oriented in the same direction. These are the Playfair, the Two Square, the Three Square, the Four Square, and the diagonal bifid ciphers.

In fact, these 5 ciphers may be stronger when used with those rectangles because each letter of the alphabet has more possible substitutes. The downside, when using Playfair or Two Square, is that there is a higher probability that the two letters are on the same row, and therefore are replaced with the letters below them or to their right.

Here is an example of a Playfair cipher done with a 3×9 rectangle:

```
    1 2 3 4 5 6 7 8 9    ME ET AT MA IN CA MP US   Plaintext
  1 A J S B K T C L U    VN NK JC XS HO JL VG AB   Ciphertext
  2 X D M V E N W F O
  3 R + G P Y H Q Z I
```

9.12 Hexadecimal fractionation

So far this chapter has focused solely on hand methods. This meant small arrays using only the uppercase alphabet. For computer use you usually want the full alphabet, uppercase and lowercase, numbers, punctuation, special symbols, diacritics, and perhaps multiple alphabets. In short you may want the full text capabilities of the computer. The simplest way to do this is to represent each character by an 8-bit byte using one of the standard computer codes such as UTF-8 or UTF-16.

A natural way to fractionate an 8-bit byte is to split it into two 4-bit hexadecimal digits, or hex digits. All of the fractionation methods that are based on Polybius squares also work for 16×16 squares, namely Playfair, Two Square, Three Square, Four Square, and bifid. If the 16×16 square is well-mixed using a large key, these methods are stronger than the same methods used with 5×5 squares. This is because there are vastly more arrangements of 256 characters than of 25 characters, namely 8.58×10^{506} versus 1.55×10^{25}.

A simple method for using hexadecimal fractionation is to (1) convert the characters of the message to hexadecimal digits by using a well-mixed keyed substitution table, (2) scramble those digits using some transposition cipher, and then (3) convert the pairs of hex digits back to bytes using a second well-mixed keyed substitution table.

The simplest transposition is just moving the first hex digit to the end, so that 12 34 56 78 would become 23 45 67 81. This might be called *Cycle Hex*. It is essentially diagonal bifid (section 9.7) done in base 16 instead of base 5. Cycle hex is rated Five. You could also use the piecewise reversal transposition described in section 4.6.1 to scramble the letter order. This might be called *Piecewise Hex*. It is also rated Five. A stronger method would be to scramble the hex digits using a columnar transposition cipher. This could be called *Columnar Hex*. It is rated Seven. With a double columnar transposition the rating increases to Ten.

These methods can be used to encipher any computer file. However, if the files are pure text, the methods can be further enhanced. Pure text will normally use fewer than 100 of the 256 possible byte values. The remaining character codes can be used for nulls, bigrams, trigrams and other purposes described in section 6.4. If done well, this raises the ratings to cycle hex Six, piecewise hex Six, and columnar hex Eight.

9.13   *Bitwise fractionation*

Fractionation can also be done with the individual bits that represent the characters in a message. The block of N characters would be represented by 8N bits. These can be formed into a rectangle in several ways, such as 2×4N, 4×2N, 8×N and N×8. For example, a block of 5 letters would be represented by 40 bits, which could be written as 2 rows of 20 bits, 4 rows of 10 bits, 8 rows of 5 bits, or 5 rows of 8 bits. This is cumbersome for hand operations, but easily done with a computer.

Here is an example of how 5 characters can be written horizontally into a 5×8 block and then read out vertically. This example uses the standard UTF-8 character codes. For example, uppercase letter A is represented as 01000001. The plaintext is the word DELTA.

```
Writing in     Reading out   Ciphertext
D 01000100     01000100      00000111    (BELL)
E 01000101     01000101      11000000    Ã
L 01001100     01001100      00100010    "
T 01010100     01010100      01111000    x
A 01000001     01000001      00001001    (HTAB)
```

The bits are read out going down the columns. Since each column contains only 5 bits, each byte of the ciphertext must span two or more columns. The 8 bits for the first ciphertext byte are found in columns 1 and 2 with medium highlighting. The first column contains 00000, and the first 3 bits in the second column are 111, so the first byte of the ciphertext is 00000111, or hex 07. This is the control character BELL, dating back to the teletype era, when it used to cause the carriage-return bell to sound. It has no graphic representation anymore. I will use the note ♪ to represent the bell character.

The second ciphertext byte comes from the darker highlighted section spanning columns 2, 3 and 4. The last 2 bits in column 2 are 11, column 3 contains 00000, and the first bit in column 4 is 0. Combining these, the second ciphertext byte is 11000000. This represents the character Ã, which is an uppercase A with a grave accent.

Bytes 3 and 4 of the ciphertext are " and x, that is, double quote and lowercase x. The fifth byte comes from columns 7 and 8, namely 000 and 01001. The byte 00001001 represents the HTAB, or horizontal tab character, which is invisible. I will use the arrowhead ► to represent it. Thus the ciphertext is ♪Ã"x►.

This looks pretty cryptic, but the method is weak because it uses the standard alphabet for both the conversion of the plaintext into bits and the conversion from bits back to characters. It is rated One. If two independent well-mixed keyed alphabets are used for these steps, then this cipher is simply a binary version of the conjugated matrix bifid (section 9.6.1). This method could be called *Hex Rectangle*. It has the same rating as the conjugated matrix bifid cipher, namely Five.

It is natural to form eight 8-bit bytes into an 8×8 bit square. Write the 8 bits for each character vertically into the square using a mixed alphabet, and read them out horizontally using a different mixed alphabet. This is just an 8×8 square version of the hex rectangle, and has the rating Six.

9.13.1   *Cyclic 8×N*

It is easy to improve the strength of this cipher. For any block of N characters, write their 8-bit representations into an 8×N rectangle vertically. Shift each row cyclically to the left by some amount from 0 to N-1 bit positions. For example, abcdefgh cyclically shifted, or *rotated*, left by 2 positions would give cdefghab. Then read each 8-bit column out vertically. Here is an example using an 8×8 bit square. Each row is cycled left by the amount indicated to its left.

```
        AMBUSHED   Shifted        Plaintext AMBUSHED
     2  10101110   10111010
     3  11100100   00100111
     0  01011110   01011110
     5  00001011   01100001
     1  11000010   10000101
     7  00100001   10010000
     2  11011110   01111011
     4  00011101   11010001
                   8%þŸdͺI¦        Ciphertext 8%þŸdͺI¦
```

This cipher is at the limit of what can be done by hand. It requires 3 keys, namely 2 keys for mixing the 2 alphabets, and an 8-digit key for specifying the shift amounts. It can be called *Cyclic 8×N*. When N is 6 or larger it is rated Seven. The cipher gets stronger as the block size, N, increases.

When the rectangle is square you can rotate both the rows and columns to get a *Bicyclic 8×8* cipher. You should alternate directions for this. Write the bits in horizontally, cycle the bits vertically, cycle the bits horizontally, and read out the characters vertically. The Bicyclic 8×8 is rated Eight.

The cyclic 8×N cipher can be repeated to get a *Double Cyclic 8×N* cipher. This requires 5 keys, namely 3 keys to mix the 3 alphabets, and two 8-digit keys to control the 2 rounds of shifting. There are 5 steps. (1) Use the first alphabet to do a simple substitution. The resulting N bytes are written into the 8×N bit rectangle vertically. (2) Cyclically shift the rows using the first shift key. (3) Use the second alphabet to perform a simple substitution on the N columns. (4) Cyclically shift the rows using the second shift key. (5) Use the third alphabet to perform a final simple substitution on the vertical columns. Notice that all the shifts are horizontal and all the substitutions are vertical. The double cyclic 8×N cipher is rated Nine.

This can be continued to *Triple, Quadruple* and beyond, if desired. All of these variations can be further enhanced by varying the block sizes, either periodically or using a random number generator.

9.14 *Other fractionation*

In sections 9.12 and 9.13 we looked at dividing a byte into two hexadecimal digits or into eight individual bits. There are numerous other ways of partitioning 8 bits, such as 3,2,3. If the 3,2,3 bit representation of each character is written vertically, and then the 3 rows are cyclically shifted left by some number of positions, then each column will still have the 3,2,3 bit distribution, so the 8 bits can be converted back into bytes. Here is an example. Each row is cycled left by the number of positions shown at the left, that is, 1 position, 3 positions and 2 positions, respectively.

	R	E	T	R	E	A	T								
1	001	101	110	001	101	010	110		101	110	001	101	010	110	001
3	11	10	10	11	10	00	10		11	10	00	10	11	10	10
2	111	101	010	111	101	011	010		010	111	101	011	010	111	101
									@	w	«	θ	K	_	⌐

Here the plaintext RETREAT has been transformed into the ciphertext @w«θK_⌐. Let's call this a *BitCycle Substitution*. This method is rated Five. Like the cyclic 8×N cipher in section 9.13.1, this can be doubled, tripled, or more, and the block sizes can be varied.

This basic idea can be enhanced in two powerful ways.

First, the bytes can be divided in several different ways, such as 1,3,2,2 or 2,4,2. For example, you could encipher the block first using the 3,2,3 split, then reencipher it using the 1,3,2,2 split, then reencipher that using the 2,4,2 split. This would involve 7 keys and 7 steps. (1) Use the first substitution to produce the 3,2,3 bit representation of the message. (2) Shift the 3 rows using the first shift key. (3) Use the second substitution to produce the 1,3,2,2 bit representation of the bytes. (4) Shift the 4 rows according to the second shift key. (5) Use the third substitution to produce the 2,4,2 bit representation of the bytes. (6) Shift the 3 rows according to the third shift key. (7) Use the fourth substitution to produce the final ciphertext bytes.

Second, the message blocks can be divided in several different ways. Suppose you used long plaintext blocks of, say, 32 characters. For Step 2 in the previous technique you could divide the 32 bytes into groups of 6, 14 and 12 bytes. For Step 4 you could divide the 32 bytes into groups of 11, 8 and 13 bytes. For Step 6 you could divide the 32 bytes into groups of 8, 17 and 7 bytes. Each group would be shifted independently. This division could be different for every message.

Or, you could take a more inclusive approach. For Step 2, divide the entire message into blocks of size X. For Step 4, divide the message into blocks of size Y. For Step 6, divide the message into blocks of size Z. X, Y and Z may be any length from 6 bytes up to the full message length.

I will not rate all of the variations of the BitCycle substitution. Suffice to say that the ratings may range anywhere from Five to Ten. In chapter 12 I will describe how you can verify that a block cipher truly deserves a rating of Ten.

9.15   *Stronger blocks*

Several of the ciphers described in this chapter work on blocks of plaintext. There are several things that you can do to the plaintext blocks to make your cipher just a bit harder for Emily. Here is a short list of ideas:

- Vary the block lengths, periodically or pseudorandomly.
- Reverse the first few letters of each block, periodically or pseudorandomly.
- Reverse the last few letters of each block, periodically or pseudorandomly.
- Cycle each block left or right, periodically or pseudorandomly.
- Swap the last N letters of the block with the first N letters of the next block.

But a word of warning: if you are enciphering and deciphering by hand, use these methods sparingly. If you make your cipher so complex that you cannot encipher and decipher accurately, then it becomes worthless.

10

Variable-length fractionation

This chapter covers

- Ciphers based on Morse code
- Mixed letters and bigrams
- Variable-length binary codewords
- Ciphers based on text compression

This chapter covers a broad range of fractionation ciphers where the plaintext groups and/or the ciphertext groups have variable lengths. These include monombinom (section 10.2), Huffman substitution (section 10.4) and Post tag systems (section 10.5).

In section 4.4 I illustrated the concept of fractionation by describing two versions of M. E. Ohaver's Fractionated Morse cipher. Fractionated Morse is an example of variable-length fractionation because it uses 1-, 3- and 4-symbol Morse groups. Let me begin the broader discussion of variable-length fractionation with a different form of Morse fractionation that resembles the trifid cipher described in section 9.9. Let's call it Morse3.

10.1 Morse3

Morse3 is a cipher that operates in 4 steps. (1) Replace the letters of the messages by Morse code groups. You can use either the standard Morse code, or a mixed Morse alphabet like the one in section 4.4. (2) Separate the Morse groups using a / symbol. Use a double // to separate words and to mark the end of the message. (3) Divide the symbols into groups of 3. Append an extra · or ·· if needed to complete the last group of 3 symbols. The recipient will ignore these extra dots following the last //. (4) Substitute a letter for each group of 3 symbols using a second mixed alphabet.

To illustrate I will use the mixed Morse alphabet from section 4.4 (shown here on the left) to form the Morse groups. This uses only groups of 1, 3 and 4 symbols, but groups of 2 symbols may also be used, perhaps as nulls or homophones. The substitution from Morse symbols back to letters uses a mixed alphabet similar to the trifid cipher, except using the Morse symbols · - / instead of the digits 0 1 2. Notice that /// can never occur, so it is not necessary to provide a letter substitute for it. Thus only 26 substitutes are needed.

Letters to Morse			Morse to Letters		
M ·	B ---	Q ·-··	E ···	Q -··	R /··
I -	T ·---	R ·---	X ··-	O ---	S /·-
X ···	C ·---	S ·---	A ··/	N -·/	T /·/
E ···	F ·-··	U ·---	M ···	K ---	U /-·
D ·-·	G ·---	V ·---	P ·--	J ---	V /--
A ·--	J ·---	W ·---	L ·-/	I --/	W /-/
L ·-·	K ·---	Y ·---	B ·/·	H -/·	Y //·
P ·-·	N ·---	Z ·---	C ·/-	G -/-	Z //-
H --·	O ·---		D ·//	F -//	

Let's encipher the sample message SEND AMMO.

```
S   E   N   D   A   M M O        Plaintext
-··/···/·---/·--//---/·/·/·---//  Convert to Morse
-··  ·/·  ·-/  ·--  ·/·  ··/  /·-  -/·  /·/  ···  -//  Groups of 3
O    B    L    P    B    L    S    H    T    P    F    Letters
```

Ciphertext **OBLPB LSHTP F**

If a well-mixed keyed alphabet is used for both substitution steps this cipher is rated Five. One disadvantage of Morse3 is that the ciphertext is longer than the plaintext. In this example an 8-letter plaintext became an 11-letter ciphertext.

10.2 Monom-Binom

Monom-Binom, or *Monome-Binome*, is a class of ciphers in which each letter is replaced by either a single digit or a pair of digits. The most famous of these ciphers is the *VIC* cipher used by Russian spies from about 1920 to 1960. The name comes from the code name VICTOR given by the FBI to KGB spy Reino Häyhänen. The VIC cipher was never broken until Häyhänen defected to the US in 1957 and divulged its details.

The VIC cipher has two parts, the monom-binom substitution, and the modulo-10 addition of a random sequence of digits. Let's begin with the monom-binom substitution. Each letter of the alphabet is replaced by 1 or 2 decimal digits. In order for Riva, the intended receiver, to read the message, two digits are selected as the first digits for all of the 2-digit pairs. Let's suppose Sandra, the sender, chose 2 and 5. All of the 2-digit substitutes will begin with 2 or 5, and all of the other digits will be 1-digit substitutes. Whenever the next digit in the message is a 2 or a 5 the reader knows it is the start of a 2-digit substitute, otherwise it is a single-digit substitute. The substitutions can be represented in a 3-row diagram called by the peculiar name *straddling checkerboard*. The name is ill-suited because the diagram is not square, is not 8×8, and does not have an alternating pattern of black and white squares. Oh, and it isn't used for playing checkers. Other than that, it's a perfect name. Here is an example:

```
    0 1 2 3 4 5 6 7 8 9
-   N E ▮ A S ▮ I T R O
2   F K C J U V * B P Q
5   Z G X W Y L H # D M
```

The eight 1-digit substitutes are on the top row, and the twenty 2-digit substitutes starting with 2 and 5 are on the second and third rows. The digits 2 and 5 cannot be used as 1-digit substitutes, so these spaces are blacked out on the top row. For example, the substitute for S is 4, the substitute for U is 24 and the substitute for Y is 54.

Since there are 28 boxes and only 26 letters in the English alphabet, there are 2 extra characters that I have denoted by * and #. It is common practice to use the * as an all-purpose punctuation mark, for example . ? , " or whatever else may make the message easier to read. The # is used for switching from letters to digits and back. The message 600 TANKS ARRIVE 1800 TODAY would be sent as #600#TANKSARRIVE#1800#TODAY and would be enciphered as **57600 57730 21438 86251 57180 05779 58354.**

An obvious weakness of this type of substitution is that more than 1/3 of the substitutes (actually 10 out of 28, or 35.7%) begin with 2 and the same percentage start with 5, so the 2 selected digits are far more frequent than any of the other 8 digits. They will stand out like elephants in a waltz competition. To help mitigate this problem, the 8 most frequent letters are placed on the top row. These are ETAONIRS. To help remember them, you can use the mnemonic SERATION, which is SERRATION with the duplicated R removed. Or, you can use my favorite, RAT NOISE. Using 1-digit substitutes for the most-frequent letters also helps reduce the length of the ciphertext.

Used by itself, the straddling checkerboard is rated Three.

However, the VIC cipher adds a second step. (In its most complex form it also transposes the digits.) The result of the monom-binom substitution is treated as an intermediate ciphertext. For each digit in the intermediate text a key digit is added modulo 10, that is, added without the carry. There are two flavors to this. You can simply add a repeated numeric key such as 2793. That would work like this:

```
27932  79327  93279  32793  27932  79327  93279    Repeated key 2793
57600  57730  21438  86251  57180  05779  58354    Intermediate ciphertext
74532  26057  14607  18944  74012  74096  41523    Final, key+intermediate
```

This form of the VIC cipher is rated Five.

*One stronger form of the VIC cipher is to use a non-repeating numeric key produced by a random number generator. For this purpose, the Russians used what is called a *lagged Fibonacci generator*. You may already be familiar with the Fibonacci sequence, which is a sequence of integers where each term is the sum of the two preceding terms. The sequence starts with $x_0 = 0$ and $x_1 = 1$. Additional terms of the sequence are generated by this mathematical formula:

$$x_n = x_{n-1} + x_{n-2} \quad \text{for } n = 2, 3, 4, \ldots$$

That is, term n is the sum of term n–1 and term n–2. For the VIC cipher only the low-order digit is relevant. This can be written as

$$x_n = (x_{n-1} + x_{n-2}) \bmod 10.$$

A lagged Fibonacci generator can generalize this in three different ways. First, it can add terms other than the last two, such as

$$x_n = (x_{n-j} + x_{n-k}) \bmod 10.$$

Notice that the Chained Digit generator described in section 4.5.1 has this form, with j = 1 and k = 7.

Second, the numbers can be generated with a different modulus. The most common modulus is some power p^e of a prime p:

$$x_n = (x_{n-j} + x_{n-k}) \bmod p^e.$$

Third, the two terms can be combined using a binary operator other than addition. Common choices are subtraction, multiplication, and exclusive-OR. This can be written

$$x_n = (x_{n-j} \bullet x_{n-k}) \bmod p^e,$$

where $\bullet$ can represent $+ - \times \oplus$ or some other binary operator. (Division can also be used. It is the same as multiplying by the multiplicative inverse of the second operand. See section 3.6.) In practice, addition is used most often because additive generators produce the longest periods.

Using this form of pseudorandom digit generator, monom-binom is rated Seven.**

10.3   *Periodic lengths*

One easy way to achieve variable-length encryption is to use multiple substitution tables, one table for each desired block length. If these were blocks of letters, the substitution tables would quickly become enormous. Instead, we'll use bits. Let the message be represented as a bit string. The message is enciphered by dividing it into short blocks of bits and substituting a block of the same length using the substitution table for that length. The lengths of the blocks can be periodic using a repeating numeric key, or they can be produced by a random number generator.

Let me demonstrate using a small example. There are 3 substitution tables for blocks of 2, 3 and 4 bits. In a practical cipher I would use blocks of 3, 4, 5 and 6 bits, but you could go up to 16 bits, or possibly longer, if you had the storage.

For this simple demonstration I have used a standard alphabet, filling it out to 32 characters by taking symbols from the top row of the keyboard going straight left to right.

A 00000	I 01000	Q 10000	Y 11000
B 00001	J 01001	R 10001	Z 11001
C 00010	K 01010	S 10010	@ 11010
D 00011	L 01011	T 10011	# 11011
E 00100	M 01100	U 10100	$ 11100
F 00101	N 01101	V 10101	% 11101
G 00110	O 01110	W 10110	& 11110
H 00111	P 01111	X 10111	* 11111

The 3 substitution tables are

2-bit	3-bit	4-bit		
00 11	000 101	0000 1110	1000 1111
01 00	001 010	0001 0100	1001 1001
10 10	010 111	0010 1101	1010 0010
11 01	011 000	0011 0101	1011 1010
	100 011	0100 0000	1100 0001
	101 100	0101 0110	1101 1011
	110 001	0110 0111	1110 0011
	111 110	0111 1000	1111 1100

Here is a sample encipherment using the repeating key 3,2,2,4,2:

```
M     O     S     C     O     W        Plaintext
01100 01110 10010 00010 01110 10110    Plaintext in binary

3   2  2  4    2  3   2  2  4    2  3    Key
011 00 01 1101 00 100 00 10 0111 01 011 0    Binary divided by key
000 11 00 1011 11 011 11 10 1000 00 000 0    After substitution

00011 00101 11101 11110 10000 00000    Blocks of 5 bits
D     F     %     &     Q     A        Ciphertext DF%&QA
```

This version, which I will call *BitBlock SA* for Standard Alphabet, has modest
strength. There is one key for mixing each of the substitution tables, and one additional
key for the sequence of block sizes. When there are just a few substitution tables, the
block sizes are all small, and the sequence of block sizes is small, BitBlock SA is rated
Three. Otherwise it is rated Four.

One way to strengthen this cipher is to use well-mixed keyed alphabets for
converting the letters to bits and the resulting bits back to letters. Let's call the mixed-
alphabet version *BitBlock MA*. It is rated Seven.

10.4 Huffman Substitution

Section 4.2 describes how you can use Huffman codes for text compression. *Huffman
Substitution* is a way that you can use Huffman codes for encryption. Huffman substitution uses two sets of codes. The codes from the second set are substituted for the
codes in the first set. These might be the same set of codes, but in different orders.

The message is represented as a string of bits, for example by using one of the
standard computer representations such as UTF-8 or Unicode. This bit string is
separated into a string of codes from the first set of Huffman codes, then these
codes are replaced by codes from the second set. Huffman substitution does not
compress the message, although the length of the message, measured in bits, can
change if the codes in the first set have different lengths from their substitutes in
the second set.

Recall that a set of Huffman codes must have the prefix property. That is, no
Huffman code in a set can begin with another Huffman code from that same set. For
instance, you could not have both **1101** and **11011** because, if the string you are
decoding started with **11011**, you would not know whether the first code had 4 bits or
5 bits. With the prefix property there is no need to have a separator between the codes
the way that Morse code groups need to be separated.

Let's look at how to construct a set of Huffman codes with the prefix property.
Begin by listing the single bits in either order, namely 0,1 or 1,0. For example,

1
0

For each item on this list, either accept it as a complete code, or extend it to make two longer codes by appending a 0 to one copy and a 1 to the other copy, again in either order. For example, we could accept the code 1 as complete, and extend the code 0 to make two codes, 00 and 01, like this:

```
1
00
01
```

This process can be repeated as often as desired. For example, we could accept the code 01 as complete, but extend the code 00 one more step to make codes 000 and 001.

```
1
001
000
01
```

This process can be continued until you have the desired number of codes, or the desired range of code lengths. However, 4 codes are enough for this example. We will accept both 000 and 001 as complete codes, making a complete set of 4 codes.

*We can estimate how long the average code will be when we encipher a bit string using these codes. There is a 1/2 chance that the string will begin with 1, thus a 1/2 chance that the code will be 1 bit long. There is a 1/8 chance that the string will begin with 000 and a 1/8 chance that it will begin with 001. In either case the code would be 3 bits long. There is a 1/4 chance that the string will begin with 01 and the code will be 2 bits long. This is a complete set of codes so there are no other possibilities. Combining them gives the expected code length $1/2+3/8+3/8+2/4 = 14/8 = 1.75$ bits.

After the first code has been substituted, the probabilities are the same for the next code, so the expected length of all codes is 1.75 bits. This is less than the average length of the codes, which is 2.25 bits.**

Here is an example of Huffman substitution. There are two sets of Huffman codes. The codes in the left column are replaced by the codes in the right column. Both sets of codes have the prefix property. The plaintext is LIBERTY encoded with the standard 5-bit representation A = 00000, B = 000001, C = 00010, . . ., Z = 11001.

Set1	Set2
000	011
001	0100
01	00
100	0101
101	11
11	10

```
   L     I     B     E     R     T     Y                      Plaintext
 01011 01000 00001 00100 10001 10011 11000                    Bit string
 01 01 101 000 000 01 001   001   000 11 001   11 100   01    Huffman codes
 00 00 11   011 011 00 0100 0100 011 10 0100 10 0101 00        Substitutes
 00001 10110 11000 10001 00011 10010 01001 0100               Groups of 5
   B     W     Y     R     D     S     J     I                Ciphertext
```

The first line of 5-bit groups is the word LIBERTY encoded in the standard way, A = 00000, B = 00001, and so on. The second line of binary is the same string of bits, but divided into Huffman codes from Set1. The underlined digit 1 is padding that was needed to fill out the last Huffman code. The third line of binary replaces each code from Set1 with the corresponding code from Set2, that is, the third line is the result of the substitution step. The fourth line of binary is the same bit string as the third line, but divided into groups of 5 bits. Notice that line 4 is 4 bits longer than line 1. The final line is the ciphertext using the same standard 5-bit representation for the alphabet. The last letter of the ciphertext could be either I or J, since the last binary group has only 4 bits.

*If you are doing this by computer it is not necessary to compare the front end of the bit string to each of the Huffman codes in turn. Suppose that the longest code has 6 bits. You can make up a table of all 64 possible 6-bit combinations. Each entry in the table will tell the length of the code, in bits, and give its substitute. Each time you perform a substitution you use the first 6 bits of the string to look directly in the table.

Suppose, for example, that the first Huffman code is 00000 and its substitute is 0110. The possible values for the first 6 bits of a string starting with that code are 000000 and 000001. So entries 000000 and 000001 in the table would both give the code length as 5, and the substitute for that code as 0110. To perform the substitution, you would delete the first 5 bits of the string, and append 0110 to the result string.**

10.5 Post tag systems

Mathematician Emil Leon Post of the Courant Institute of New York University invented *Post Tag Systems* in 1920. The basic idea is very simple. You start with a string of bits. Then you take some bits from the front of the string, replace them with a different set of bits, and put them on the end of the string. You keep doing this. One of three things will happen: either the string shrinks until you can't do this anymore, or you get into an endless repeating cycle, or the string grows forever.

Historical aside

Post did not create his Post tags for use in cryptography. Post proved that the question of whether the string grows, shrinks or repeats cannot be answered within standard mathematics, then he used this fact to construct a proof of Kurt Gödel's famous Incompleteness Theorems. I consider this to be a simpler and more elegant proof than Alan Turing's proof using symbols written onto an infinite tape, although the similarity between Post's bit string and Turing's tape is striking.

This *Post Substitution* is similar to Huffman substitution, except that you move the substitute to the end of the bit string. The advantage of this system is that you can keep right on going after you have substituted for the entire string. That is, you can go through the string more than once. This obliterates the divisions between the Huffman codes.

The pieces that you take from the front of the strings are called the *tags*. The set of tags must be chosen so that there is at most one tag that can be taken at each step. That is, the replacement process is *deterministic*. This requires that the set of tags has the prefix property. This will allow you to use the set of tags to encipher a message represented as a bit string. The prefix property is discussed in section 4.2.1 in connection with Huffman codes. In brief, no tag may begin with any other tag. For instance, you could not have both 1101 and 11011 because if the string started with 11011 you would not know whether to take the first 4 bits or the first 5 bits. With the prefix property there is no need to have a separator between the tags the way that Morse code groups need to be separated. The Huffman codes and Post tags have the same form, but they are used differently. For starters, Huffman codes are used to shorten the bit string, while Post tags are not.

A method for constructing a set of Huffman codes is described in section 10.4.

When you encipher using Post tags, you replace each tag with another tag and move the new tag to the end of the string. Since Riva will have to decipher the message working from the right, the replacement tags will need to have the *suffix property*, that is, the inverse of the prefix property. None of the suffix tags can end with another suffix tag. For example, if 1011 is one of the suffix tags then neither 01011 nor 11011 could be a suffix tag.

You can construct the set of suffix tags the same way that you construct the set of prefix tags, except that you extend each tag on the left rather than on the right. If this is confusing, you can just construct a second set of prefix tags and then reverse the order of the bits in that set to get the suffix tags. There must be at least as many suffix tags as prefix tags. There can be more. The extra tags can be used as homophones. For example, the prefix tag 0111 might be replaced by a choice of suffix tag 110 or 10101.

When the expected length of the suffixes is less than the expected length of the prefixes the string is likely to shrink. That is, it is probable that there are some initial strings that will grow shorter. Conversely if the suffixes are longer than the prefixes it is probable that some initial strings will grow. This is usually true when homophones are used. The greater the difference in expected length, the more the initial strings will shrink or grow. However, "probable" is no guarantee. It is possible to construct prefix/suffix sets that have the opposite behavior.

To use Post tags for encipherment, you first represent the message as a string of bits, then you perform the tag substitutions a few times. If you are enciphering by hand, you turn those bits back into characters. If you are enciphering by computer, this last step may be unnecessary; you simply transmit the resulting bit string.

10.5.1 *Same-length tags*

One problem with the cipher described in the preceding section is that Riva does not know how to divide the message she receives into blocks. You might need to have a separate length field for each block, or else treat the entire message as a single block. This can be unwieldy when the message is long. One solution to this problem is to replace each prefix tag by a suffix tag of the same length. That way, the blocks stay the same length throughout the process and there is no problem in demarcating the ends of the blocks. Block sizes of 32 bits or 64 bits are typical.

I suggest doing a fixed number of substitutions for each block. You can determine the appropriate number from the shortest length and the expected length of the tags. Say the blocks are 32 bits, the shortest tag is 3 bits and the expected tag length is 4.3 bits. Using the shortest length, if you perform at least $32/3 = 10.67$ substitutions, then you are guaranteed that every bit in the block is substituted at least once. Round that up to 11. Using the expected length, on average $32/4.3 = 7.44$ substitutions are needed so that every bit gets substituted.

A good margin of safety is to have each bit substituted twice on average. Double 7.44 and round up to get 15 substitution steps. This is greater than 11, so it is certain that every bit is substituted at least once. On average every bit is substituted twice. About half the time some of the bits are substituted 3 times. Most importantly, Emily will not know how many times any given bit has been substituted.

You may have noticed that I have been saying "every *bit* gets substituted" rather than "every *tag* gets substituted." This may be confusing. The first time through the block, each tag gets replaced with a new tag that has the same length. So, on the first round, it is the tags that get replaced. But when the second round of substitution begins, it might not start on an even tag boundary. That is, the next tag may span two or more of the tags from the first round.

Here is a miniature example to illustrate the point using a 12-bit block. The first bit of the block is shaded, and the prefix tags are underlined.

Set1	Set2		
00	01	101101110100	Original 12- bit block, tag is 10
010	110	1101110100111	Replace 10 by 11, next tag is 110
011	000	1110100111010	Replace 110 by 010, next tag is 111
10	11	010011010100	Replace 111 by 100, next tag is 010
110	010	011010100110	Replace 010 by 110, next tag is 011
111	100	Second round begins	

After four substitutions the first bit is now in the second position, right in the center of the next prefix tag, which is 011.

For hand use I suggest encoding the letters of the alphabet as 5-bit or 6-bit groups, using 20 to 30 pairs of tags of 3 to 6 bits, 32-bit blocks, and 16 substitution steps, that is, about 2 times through the block. Convert the resulting bit strings back to characters using 4-bit groups to represent the letters A through P in some mixed order. Such a cipher would be rated Six.

For computer use I suggest using a standard 8-bit representation such as UTF-8 for the letters, digits and special characters in the message. Use 40 to 80 pairs of tags of 4 to 8 bits, 64-bit blocks, and 32 substitution steps. Using 32 steps is enough for 3 passes through the block. Perform a well-mixed keyed substitution on the characters before doing the Post tag substitutions, and a second independent keyed substitution on the resulting bytes after finishing the Post tag substitutions. This cipher, called *Post64*, would be rated Ten. It would have 4 separate keys used to mix the initial substitution, the final substitution, the Post tags, and their substitutes.

Another way to use Post tag substitution is to use short overlapping blocks. Start with the first 4 bytes of the message and perform 2 Post substitutions. Assuming the tags are 4 to 8 bits each, this is sufficient to assure that all of the bits in the first byte have been substituted. Then move 1 byte right. The next 4-byte block of the message is bytes 2, 3, 4 and 5. Again, perform 2 Post substitutions on this block. Continue this way until the last 4-byte block of the message. The final 3 blocks will wrap around to the front of the message. This method, called *PostOv*, is rated Six.

10.5.2 *Different-length tags*

When the substitute for each tag is not the same length you get into a variety of complexities, the length of each block can change, and the blocks may not end up aligned on byte boundaries. For example, a 32-bit block could become a 35-bit block. This means that Riva will need a means to separate the blocks. The simplest method is to transmit the length of each block.

It might seem feasible simply to perform Post tag substitutions on a block until its length becomes a multiple of 8 bits again. Unfortunately, this potentially could take thousands or even millions of substitution steps — or it might never happen.

The simplest solution is to encipher the entire message as a single block. The length of the message tells Riva the number of bytes in the block. Sandra just needs to add a 3-bit field to tell Riva how many bits are in the last byte, ranging from 1 to 8 bits. This could be placed at the start of the message, or it could be the last 3 bits of the last byte. The length field might require an extra byte.

Here is an example of different-length Post tag encipherment. Each prefix tag and its resulting suffix tag have matching underlines.

```
Prefix   Suffix
00       101      10110100001000111001        Plaintext, bits
010      100        010000100011100111
011      1010         000100011100111100
1000     000           0100011100111100101
1001     001            0011100111100101100
1010     110             11100111100101100101
1011     11               100111100101100101 0010
11       0010               11100101100101 0010 001
```

*It might look like you will need to shift the entire message each time a tag gets removed from the front. These shifts can be eliminated by keeping pointers to the first and last bit of the message. Each pointer will simply be an integer giving the location of each end. The low-order 3 bits of the pointer will give the bit position within the byte, and the high-order bits will give the byte position. Allocate a space 4 times the length of the message. Place the message at the start of this space, and zero-out the rest.

To delete a tag from the front of the string, just increment the front pointer by the length of the prefix tag. To append a tag to the end, just shift the tag to the required bit position and OR it with the last 2 bytes of the string, then increment the end pointer. Continue this process until you reach the end of the space. This means that the number of Post substitution steps depends on the message itself.

That leaves just one shift to perform at the end to get the bit string onto an even byte boundary. However, this long shift can also be eliminated by telling your correspondent both the starting and ending bit positions in the first and last bytes of the message. This requires only 6 bits, which can be packed into a single byte and placed at the start of the message. I recommend enciphering this byte with a simple substitution so as not to give Emily the starting and ending positions. Also, be sure to fill the unused parts of the first and last bytes of the message with random bits.

One question remains: since Riva does not know the original length of the message, and hence does not know the original size of the enciphering space, how can she know when to stop deciphering? Riva does not know how many substitution steps were done, and she cannot simply allocate a space 4 times the length of the received message, because that may not be the same as the length of the sent message.

Here's how. Riva knows three things: the plaintext message started on a byte boundary, the message ended on a byte boundary, and the enciphering space was 4 times the length of the original message. Riva can begin by placing the received message at the end of a space 5 times as long as the ciphertext message. That should be more than ample. Riva works backward until the three conditions are met, in particular until the distance from the start of the partially deciphered message to the end of the deciphering space is exactly 4 times the length of the message. This can happen only once.**

I suggest that you use 50 to 80 pairs of tags, with each tag 4 to 8 bits long. The expected length of the original tags should be close in value to the expected length of the replacement tags. About 1/3 of the replacement tags should be shorter, 1/3 should be the same size, and 1/3 of the replacement tags should be longer than the original tags. Don't insist on making every tag a different length from its substitute. Message characters should be represented as 8-bit bytes in a well-mixed alphabet. If the expected length of the tags is T bits, and the length of the message is L bits, then at least 3L/T substitution steps should be made. That is, you go through the whole message 3 or more times. The final bit string, including the length indicator, should be converted back into characters using a second, independent keyed simple substitution. If all of these suggestions are followed, then this cipher, called *PostDL*, is rated Ten.

When you reach section 12.6, you will see that the PostDL cipher does not meet all of the criteria that guarantee an unbreakable cipher. The reason it gets a Ten rating is that Emily does not know where in the ciphertext any given plaintext bit will end up. The position will differ from block to block. So Emily cannot set up a correspondence between the plaintext bits and the ciphertext bits, and thus cannot set up equations relating the ciphertext bits to the plaintext and key bits.

10.5.3 *Multiple alphabets*

There are several things you can do to strengthen a Post tag cipher, or a Huffman substitution cipher. We have already looked at having multiple rounds of substitution. Another trick is to use multiple alphabets. Each alphabet will consist of a set of tags with the prefix property and the corresponding set of replacement tags, which must have the suffix property. You can simply use the multiple alphabets in rotation, or you can use a keyword to select among them. If you are doing this by hand, you will not want more than 2, or at most 3, such alphabets, so I suggest using a numeric key, like 01101011.

These ciphers, which may be called *PolyPost* and *PolyHuff*, are rated Four to Eight depending on the number of rounds, the number of alphabets and the key length.

10.5.4 *Short and long moves*

So far we have assumed that when a Post tag has B bits, these B bits are moved to the end of the block. However, it is possible to move fewer than B bits, or more than B bits. For example, you could move B-1 bits, leaving 1 bit to be substituted again as part of the next tag. This makes the tags overlap. The advantage is that it conceals the boundaries between the tags. The disadvantage is that it requires more substitution steps per round, making the cipher slower.

Conversely, when a Post tag has B bits you could move B+1 bits to the end of the block. This leaves one bit unchanged, and that bit is always the last bit in the block. This is not a serious problem if the cipher has multiple rounds so the unchanged bit will probably be substituted in some other round. There is still a chance that some bits will pass through this cipher intact. This is not a serious weakness if Emily cannot determine which are the unchanged bits. Bits are anonymous. There is nothing about any bit that says, "This bit came from byte 5, bit position 2 in the plaintext."

Finally, the number of bits that are moved can be made independent of the length of the tag. You could have a table that tells the number of bits to move. This can be less than, more than or the same as the length of the tag. You can have several of each.

When the number of bits moved is different from the length of the tag, the suffix property no longer applies to the set of substitute tags. Instead, the set of bit strings that are actually moved must have the suffix property. For example, if the tag 0110 is replaced by 1101, but 5 bits are moved, then the set of suffix strings must include both **11010** and **11011**.

10.6 Fractionation in other bases

So far, this chapter has discussed monom-binom in base 5, and Huffman and Post substitution in base 2. Variable-length substitution can be done in other bases as well. For hand enciphering, it is easier to do Huffman substitution and Post substitution in base 3 or base 4 than in binary. However, variable-length substitution can be done in any base, even oddball bases like 11 or 13. This can give you extra substitutes, which can be used for homophones or for encoding bigrams.

When you work in base 13, you can use any 13 of the 16 hexadecimal digits for substitution, and leave the other 3 digits as nulls. If done well, so that all 16 digits have roughly equal frequency and distribution, Emily will not be able to tell the valid digits from the nulls.

10.7 Text compression

Section 4.2.1 discusses the use of Huffman codes for compressing text. Several strong encryption schemes can be based on text compression. In this section I present several more-advanced text compression schemes and some encryption schemes based on Huffman codes. The remainder of Chapter 10 is optional. If at any point the math becomes too daunting, just skip directly to the next chapter.

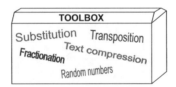

10.7.1 Lempel-Ziv

The *Lempel-Ziv* text compression scheme was developed by Israeli computer scientists Abraham Lempel and Jacob Ziv in 1977, called *LZ77*, with an improved version in 1978, called *LZ78*. It is based on the same underlying concept as Huffman encoding, namely letters and letter combinations are represented by binary codes, that is, by groups of bits. However, Lempel-Ziv takes the opposite approach to this. Huffman uses shorter codes in order to save space. Lempel-Ziv uses codes of roughly the same length, but has some of the codes represent longer letter combinations to save space.

Huffman and Lempel-Ziv are opposite in another sense, too. Huffman bases the length of the codes on a fixed preset table of letter frequencies. Lempel-Ziv determines the most-frequent letter combinations on the fly, while it is encoding the text. This is known as *adaptive coding*. Huffman encoding is good only for text in a single language. A different language would have different letter frequencies. Even changing from uppercase to mixed case text would require a different set of Huffman codes. By contrast, Lempel-Ziv can be used for any type of computer file, text in any language or mixed languages, computer code, images, telemetry, music videos, and so forth.

There are several versions of Lempel-Ziv. The version I present here, called *Lempel-Ziv-Welch*, or *LZW*, was developed by Terry Welch of Sperry Research in 1984. LZW has both fixed-width and variable-width versions. I am presenting the variable-width version, which is easy to adapt for cryptographic use.

All versions of Lempel-Ziv use a list of letters and letter combinations called a *dictionary*. The dictionary is built on the fly as the algorithm progresses through the file. In the LZ77 and LZ78 versions the dictionary starts empty. The code for any given letter combination is its location in the dictionary.

LZW begins by assigning a code to each of the single characters in the file. LZW codes all have the same number of bits. For example, if the file were a message in English, all in uppercase without punctuation or word divisions, then you would need 26 codes, so you could use 5-bit codes. It is more common to start with 256 codes, one for each of the 256 possible values of an 8-bit byte.

As the algorithm progresses through the file it looks for letter combinations that are not already in the dictionary. When it finds one, it adds that combination to the dictionary. For example, suppose that the algorithm has found THE in the file, and that THE is already in the dictionary. Suppose the next letter in the file is M, and that THEM is not in the dictionary. It outputs the code for THE followed by the code for M, and adds THEM to the dictionary. The code for THEM is the next available location in the dictionary, say 248.

Since THE was already in the dictionary, the algorithm will not look at combinations starting with HE or E. It will start at M looking for another combination that is not in the dictionary. If that combination is MOR, then MOR is put in dictionary entry 249 and has the code 249. The next time the algorithm finds THEM in the file it will be coded as 248, and the next occurrence of MOR will be coded as 249.

When the algorithm has filled up all 256 dictionary entries for 8-bit codes, the next assigned code will need to have 9 bits. At that point the algorithm will switch from 8-bit codes to 9-bit codes. THEM will still have the code 248, but it will be the 9-bit code 011111000 instead of the 8-bit code 11111000. When the algorithm fills up all 512 dictionary slots for the 9-bit codes, the code for THEM becomes the 10-bit code 0011111000, which is still 248. Note the order of these operations. The code for the current letter combination is output first at the old size, then the new combination is added to the dictionary and the code size is increased. Both Sandra and Riva must use the same order, or else the message will not be decompressed correctly. Enlarging the codes typically stops at 12 bits. Increasing the code size from 12 bits to 13 bits usually does not improve the compression, and may even worsen it.

Let's look at an example. Let's encode the word TETE-A-TETE using this algorithm. Suppose the dictionary starts off with the single letters A, E and T using 2-bit codes. Let's follow the dictionary as it gets built. At each stage the bit strings to the left show the encoded word, while the letters to the right show the remaining portion of the word.

	Code	Dict	Remainder	
		00	A	
		01	E	
		10	T	**TETEATETE**	Original text
	10	11	TE	**ETEATETE**	Add **TE** to dictionary
	10 01	100	ET	**TEATETE**	Switch to 3-bit codes
	10 01 011	101	TEA	**ATETE**	Add **TEA** to dictionary
	10 01 011 000	110	AT	**TETE**	Add **AT** to dictionary
	10 01 011 000 011	111	TET	**TE**	Add **TET** to dictionary
10 01 011 000 011 011		---	---		Finished, add nothing

When Riva decompresses the message, the dictionary must be built up exactly the same way. Note that the bit string **10 01 011 000 011 011** by itself is not enough for Riva to decompress the message. She also needs to know that the codes **00**, **01** and **10** represent the characters A, E and T.

Okay. That's Lempel-Ziv compression. This is a book about cryptography. How can Lempel-Ziv compression be used for encryption?

In building the dictionary, Lempel-Ziv assigns codes sequentially. The 43rd letter or letter combination will get the code 42 (not 43, since the codes start at 0). To use this scheme for encryption, add a second column to the dictionary. The first column contains the letter combinations, and the second column contains the corresponding codes. Instead of using the position in the dictionary as the code for each letter combination, use the number in the second column of the dictionary.

Suppose that the dictionary starts with the 256 single-byte characters. The first column will contain the characters. In the second column put the numbers from 0 to 255 in some scrambled order. They can be mixed by any of the methods described in section 5.2. Sandra and Riva must use the same order, which could be determined by a keyword or by the seed for a random number generator. When the first 9-bit code is needed, the next 256 dictionary entries will get the codes from 256 to 511 in scrambled order. Likewise, when you move from 9-bit codes to 10-bit codes the next 512 codes will be assigned at one time. Assigning codes in bulk is more efficient than assigning them one at a time.

An alternative to assigning the codes in bulk is to assign only the first 256 codes using a keyword or random number sequence. After that each new code is calculated by adding 256 to the code 256 entries earlier. That is, $X(N) = X(N-256)+256$.

This cipher, which I will call *Lempel-Ziv Substitution*, is rated Three. The rating is so low because the first few characters of the message are essentially enciphered with simple substitution. Each code will represent a single character until the first repeated bigram occurs. This might not happen until 30, 40 or more characters have been encoded. Even after that point most of the 9-bit codes will represent single letters. These codes are easily distinguished because they are the only 9-bit codes starting with

0. Emily will have plenty of opportunities to use both letter frequencies and contact frequencies to crack the message.

To make Lempel-Ziv substitution strong you can add a second substitution step. This substitution should not be on byte boundaries. I suggest using 7-bit groups. These groups will not coincide with the code groups until the codes reach 14 bits. This may never happen because codes are usually limited to 12 bits. Lempel-Ziv substitution followed by 7-bit substitution is rated Six. Both substitutions can be accomplished in a single left-to-right pass.

10.7.2 *Arithmetic coding*

Arithmetic Coding (pronounced "a-rith-MET-ic") is a text compression method that I invented in the 1970s ("Arithmetic Stream Coding Using Fixed Precision Registers," *IEEE Trans. on Info. Theory* vol. 25 (Nov. 1979), pp. 672–675). It is based on a clever idea from Peter Elias of MIT.

Elias's idea was to encode every character string as a fraction. Imagine all the possible fractions from .0 through .999... The ellipsis ... means that this fraction ends with an infinite sequence of 9's. Now divide this range up according to the first character of the string. For simplicity, let's suppose there are 25 characters in the alphabet, like a Polybius square alphabet. Each letter will get 1/25 of the full range. Those strings starting with A get the first 1/25, or 4%, of the range, namely .0 to .04. Strings starting with B get the next 1/25 of the range, namely .04 to .08. Strings starting with Z get the last 1/25 of the range, .96 to .999.... (I am giving this example using decimal notation to make it easier to read. In a computer, binary fractions would be used.)

For the second character you divide this range again. Strings starting with AA would be in the range .0 to .0016. Strings starting with AB would be in the range .0016 to .0032. Strings starting with BA would be in the range .0400 to .0416. And so forth. Strings starting with ZZ would get the range from .9984 to .9999....

To visualize this, let's use a miniature 5-letter alphabet with A being .0 to .2, B from .2 to .4, C from .4 to .6, D from .6 to .8, and E from .8 to .999.... Using this alphabet, let's encode the word BED.

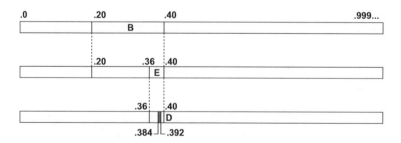

BED could be encoded as any fraction f with $.384 \leq f < .392$. As more characters are added, this interval will continue to shrink.

That's the concept. However, this encoding of strings as fractions does not give any compression. One more idea is needed to get compression. Instead of giving each letter of the alphabet the same fraction of the range, make the fraction proportional to the frequency of that letter. A would get 8.12%, B would get 1.49%, through Z, which would get .07%. The range for A would be .0 to .0812. The range for B would be .0812 to .0961. The range for Z would be .9993 to .9999... .

In theory this would give optimal compression based on the frequencies of the individual letters. Unfortunately, there is a practical problem. The method produces fractions that potentially require thousands or even millions of digits. How can such fractions be represented in the computer? How can you perform arithmetic on them?

So, the method was great in theory, but seemingly infeasible in practice. It appeared to require fractions of unbounded precision. The time needed to add and multiply long fractions, whether decimal or binary, increases with their length, so even if there were a good way to represent these fractions the method would be impractically slow.

The solution I found was to use a moving window where all of the arithmetic would be done. That lets you use ordinary 32-bit integers. No floating-point arithmetic was required. To keep the integers within the 32-bit size, the letter frequencies were approximated by 15-bit integers, that is, by a fraction of the form $N/2^{15}$ or $N/32768$. For example, the frequency for the letter A is 8.12%. This can be expressed as $2660/32768$, or $665/8192$. This approximation was found to cause no detectable reduction in the degree of compression.

Here is a decimal example to show how a letter is encoded and how the moving window works. Suppose the first few characters have been encoded, and the range is now .784627 to .784632. The first 4 digits for the start and end of the range are the same, namely .7846. These 4 digits would be output, and the window would be moved 4 digits to the right to show the range .2700 to .3200.

The width of this range is .0500. Suppose the next character in the message has a frequency of .0300 and its range is .4050 to .4350. This character gets encoded by selecting that fraction of the current range .2700 to .3200. Its width is .0500×.0300, which is .0015. It will run from .2700+.0500×.4050 to .2700+.0500×.4350, which is .29025 to .29175. Notice that the width of this range is .0015, as expected.

Since the start and end of this range both begin with the digits .29, these digits can be output. The digits that have been output are now 784629. The window can now be moved 2 more digits to the right to make the current range .0250 to .1750.

Arithmetic coding is ideally suited for encryption because there are no longer discrete codes for each letter or letter combination. There are no boundaries where the bit stream can be broken into separate codes. Instead, the code for each letter influences how all subsequent letters are represented.

Now that we understand how the arithmetic coding method works, the next step is to see how to use it for encryption. We do not want to change the percentage of the range allotted to each character, because that would lose the compression. Instead, we can change the order of the characters, so that the range for each character falls in an unpredictable part of the full range. That is, unpredictable for Emily. For example, using just the letters A,B,C,D,E the ranges might be:

		Standard Order				Mixed Order
A	8.12%	.0000 - .0812	D	4.32%	.0000 - .0432
B	1.49%	.0812 - .0961	A	8.12%	.0432 - .1244
C	2.71%	.0961 - .1232	B	1.49%	.1244 - .1393
D	4.32%	.1232 - .1664	E	12.02%	.1393 - .2595
E	12.02%	.1664 - .2866	C	2.71%	.2595 - .2866

These intervals can be used to encode the letters of the message. Let's call this method *Arithmetic Encipherment*. Since Emily does not know either the starting point or the ending point of any of the ranges, there is no opening for an attack. It is true that Emily knows that the first range starts at .0 and that the last range ends at .999..., but Emily does not know which characters these ranges represent.

There is one difficulty with arithmetic coding that has not been discussed yet. Using the normal alphabet, Riva does not know where the message ends. The same code that stands for ROTUND could also stand for ROTUNDA, ROTUNDAA, ROTUNDAAA, ad infinitum, assuming that the range for A begins at 0. With conventional arithmetic coding this problem can be solved by using various ways of encoding the length of the message and appending this length code to the ciphertext, or by adding a special end-of-message character to the alphabet. This was not discussed earlier because it is not needed for arithmetic encipherment.

With arithmetic encipherment all you need to do is assign a rare character, or any character that is seldom found at the end of a message, to the first range, that is, to the range starting at .0000. Then when Riva sees ROTUNDVVV... or ROTUND###... it is obvious where the message ends.

As described here, arithmetic encipherment is rated Five using a 26-letter alphabet, or Six using a 256-character alphabet. All the usual tricks can be used here, nulls, homophones and bigrams. Using nulls would reduce or destroy the compression, so I do not recommend that. Using homophones has the effect of splitting the range for a letter into two or more separate ranges. This makes the ranges for the letters more even, which is equivalent to flattening the letter frequencies. This can improve the security without affecting the degree of compression. Using bigrams, or even trigrams, can sometimes increase the level of compression while improving the security. Using homophones and bigrams, arithmetic encipherment is rated Eight.

Since arithmetic encipherment is so strong by itself, it takes very little extra to push it up to a Ten rating. I suggest using a general polyalphabetic cipher of period 4, that is, a substitution with four independent well-mixed alphabets used in rotation. An arithmetic encipherment followed by a general polyalphabetic encipherment with a period of 4 or higher is rated Ten. It leaves an opponent with nothing to go on, no letter frequencies, no contact frequencies, and no way to utilize a probable word.

10.7.3 *Adaptive arithmetic coding*

Lempel-Ziv gives decent compression for any type of file because it is adaptive. Huffman coding and arithmetic coding give better compression, but only for files whose character frequencies match the underlying frequency table. There are several ways to make Huffman coding and arithmetic coding adaptive, and all of them make the corresponding encryption methods stronger. All such methods involve counting the characters in the file as you encode them.

The more closely the character counts match the character frequencies in the file, the better the compression you get. You might think that you could just count all of the characters in the file and then use the actual counts. The problem is that Riva cannot count the characters in the file. Riva must use the same frequencies as Sandra or she cannot decipher the file. The solution to this dilemma is for Sandra to count the characters as she enciphers, and for Riva to count the characters as she deciphers, so they will both have the same counts at all stages.

All the character counts start at 1. If you know the frequencies of the characters beforehand, even if they are only rough estimates, you can increase the counts for the more frequent characters. For example, if you are using a 256-character set and you expect that messages will contain about 1% uppercase E and about 10% lowercase e, then you could increase the character count for E by 2 and the character count for e by 25, that is, about 10% of 256. The initial range for each character is proportional to its initial count. For example, if the 256 character counts total 500, and the initial count for the lowercase e is 25 then e would get a range of 25/500, or .05.

There are two basic methods for adjusting the codes, character mode and batch mode. Character mode is practical only for arithmetic coding. In character mode, each time a character is found in the file its range and the two adjacent ranges are adjusted. (One adjacent range when the character has either the first or last range. For the 26-letter standard alphabet that means A or Z.)

Here is an example. Suppose that the letter T has been encountered, and that the adjacent ranges belong to the letters S and U. (This would probably not be the case for arithmetic encipherment. The mixed alphabet probably would not contain S,T,U consecutively in that order.) Suppose the character counts for S, T and U are 15, 20 and 5, so they total 40. Suppose the ranges for S, T and U are .062, .074 and .024, so they total .160. This combined range is reapportioned in the ratio 15:20:5.

S gets .160×15/40, or .060. T gets .160×20/40, or .080. U gets .160×5/40, or .020. Over time the ranges for the characters will converge to the correct widths.

Character mode works reasonably well with a 26-letter alphabet. It works very poorly with a 256-character alphabet. Most of the 256 characters will not be adjacent to any of the high-frequency characters, so their frequencies will remain static. This is particularly true for the standard ASCII representation where all of the letters are clumped together.

Batch mode works for both arithmetic coding and Huffman coding. In batch mode the entire set of ranges is adjusted at specific points during the encoding. For example, the ranges could be adjusted after encoding 64 characters, after 128 characters, after 256 characters, and so forth. At each of these points the entire range would be reapportioned according to the current character counts. This converges more rapidly than character mode, but between reapportionments you are working with old, unadjusted frequencies.

In batch mode it is possible to count the frequencies for bigrams, and even trigrams. Bigrams or trigrams that occur more than once could be given their own Huffman codes or arithmetic code ranges. With this refinement, arithmetic coding will almost always give better compression than Lempel-Ziv.

There is one problem with counting bigram and trigram frequencies, namely storage. With a 256-character alphabet there are 65,536 different bigrams and 16,777,216 different trigrams. If storage is plentiful this might not be a problem. If storage is limited, one solution is to count only bigrams and trigrams containing the most frequent letters. For example, if bigrams and trigrams were restricted to the 20 most common characters, then there would be only 400 bigrams and 8,000 trigrams to count. To determine the most frequent characters, counting of bigram and trigram frequencies could be postponed until some fixed number of single characters have been encoded, say 256 or 1024 characters.

One way to accomplish these restricted counts is to count only single characters in the first batch to establish the most frequent characters. Count bigrams in the second batch using those high-frequency characters. Count trigrams in the third batch using only a high-frequency bigram plus a high-frequency letter. Once the high-frequency bigrams and trigrams have been chosen, they are given their own Huffman codes or arithmetic ranges. In other words, they are treated just like single characters.

For arithmetic coding, character mode and batch mode are not mutually exclusive. You can balance the ranges for each individual character as soon as it is encountered, and balance the extended set of characters plus bigrams and trigrams, at the end of each batch.

When doing Huffman encipherment or arithmetic encipherment, at the end of each batch the alphabet should be reshuffled before the codes are replaced or the ranges are rebalanced. This is particularly needed if bigrams or trigrams have been added or deleted. This means that Emily will have a limited amount of material to attack before the codes change. For encipherment it may be preferable to use batches of irregular length, say after 217 characters, then after 503 characters, and so forth, so Emily will not know when the codes change.

One further refinement to adaptive coding is to divide all of the counts by 2 after the ranges have been rebalanced. This lets the codes adapt to situations where the character frequencies change. Older frequencies will have less influence on the ranges, and newer frequencies will have more influence. For example, suppose the text is a book of stories by different authors. Each author could have a different vocabulary or different subject matter, or even write in a different language.

Of course Sandra and Riva must agree on all of this beforehand so that Riva will be able to decipher and decompress the message correctly.

Block ciphers 11

This chapter covers

- The DES and AES encryption standards
- Ciphers based on matrix multiplication
- Involutory ciphers, where encryption and decryption are identical
- Ripple ciphers
- Block chaining

We have already seen several ciphers that operate on text that has been divided into blocks of characters. Some operate on small blocks of just 2 or 3 characters, such as Playfair, Two Square, Three Square and Four Square. Some operate on longer blocks, but change only 2 or 3 characters at a time, such as bifid, trifid or FR-Actionated Morse. These ciphers act locally, on just one portion of each block. A change in one character of the plaintext typically changes at most 2 or 3 characters of the ciphertext.

This chapter deals with much stronger types of block ciphers. In these ciphers, changing even a single bit of the plaintext, or a single bit of the key, will change roughly half of the bits of the ciphertext, and nearly all of the bytes of the cipher-text. This indicates that the cipher is highly non-linear (see section 12.3). These ciphers are intended only for computer use, often with special-purpose hardware to speed the encryption.

Most of the remainder of this book is concerned with computer ciphers and methods. If you are not concerned about computer methods, simply skip those sections.

11.1 *Substitution-permutation network*

Many block ciphers take the form of a *substitution-permutation network* (SPN). This idea was first described by Horst Feistel of IBM in 1971. Encipherment consists of several rounds, each of which may consist of one or more substitution steps and/or one or more permutation steps. There is usually a main key that controls the overall operation.

The most common choices for the substitution step are (1) simple substitution, (2) exclusive-ORing part of the block with part of the key, or (3) polyalphabetic substitution under the control of a key. The key may consist of bits taken from the main key and/or bits taken from a part of the block that is not being substituted. For example, the odd-numbered bytes in the block may be used as keys to encipher the even-numbered bytes, or vice versa. A slightly more complex form of substitution takes some bits from the key, exclusive-ORs them with an equal number of bits from the block, and uses that result as a polyalphabetic key to substitute a different part of the block.

The substitution alphabets are usually chosen beforehand and never change. These are called *S-boxes*. They may be simple substitutions, or they may be polyalphabetic substitutions, so the S-box is the computer equivalent of a tableau. They commonly take 4 to 8 key bits to select the row of the tableau and either 4 or 8 bits of the block as input, and the same number of bits as output. Often some sophisticated mathematics goes into the construction of the substitution alphabets. In particular, the alphabets are designed to be non-linear, which is detailed in section 12.3.

The permutations for each round are also usually predetermined and unchanging. The permutations may operate on units that are single bits, 4-bit groups or 8-bit bytes. In most block ciphers there are no keys for the permutations; they are hard-coded in software or hard-wired into the encryption chip.

The earliest of the modern block ciphers was *Lucifer*, designed by Horst Feistel of IBM. The name was changed several times before Feistel settled on Lucifer because he wanted a name that embodied the diabolic nature of the design. Feistel also changed the design of Lucifer repeatedly, from an original 48-bit key working on a 128-bit block to a 128-bit key working on a 128-bit block. You can read more about Lucifer at https://derekbruff.org/blogs/fywscrypto/tag/lucifer (accessed May 2022).

Here is a diagram of a miniature substitution-permutation network cipher. This cipher takes a 16-bit plaintext and produces a 16-bit ciphertext. It has 4 substitution rounds and 3 transposition rounds. The substitutions and transpositions are fixed; they are built into the hardware. There are 4 different substitutions used, S_1, S_2, S_3 and S_4. Each substitution takes 4 input bits plus a key, K_{11} through K_{44}, typically 4, 6 or 8 bits, so the cipher could potentially have 64, 96 or 128 key bits if all of the keys were independent. The transpositions are different for each round.

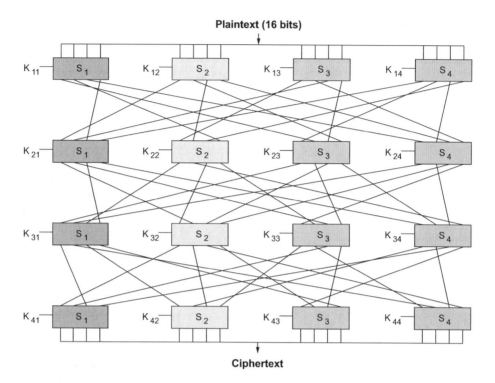

This mini network cipher is rated Three, because it is equivalent to a bigram substitution, but it can be scaled up from 16 bits to 64 bits with 6 substitution rounds, rated Eight, or 128 bits with 8 substitution rounds, rated Ten.

The design of the final version of Lucifer led directly to the *Data Encryption Standard* (DES) which was formally adopted by the National Bureau of Standards (NBS) in 1977. Therefore, let's jump directly to it.

11.2 *Data Encryption Standard (DES)*

The DES was developed at IBM in 1976 by trimming down the then-current version of Lucifer. That version used 128-bit keys and worked on 128-bit blocks of the message. The block size was reduced to 64 bits, which can be justified because that reduced the hardware cost. IBM wanted to use a 64-bit key, but the NSA insisted on reducing the key further, down to 56 bits, on the flimsy rationale that the extra 8 bits could be used as a checksum. It is generally accepted that the actual reason was that the NSA had the ability to solve 56-bit DES, but not 64-bit DES.

IBM originally planned to make DES a 6-round cipher. When the NSA told IBM that it could crack the 6-round version, IBM jumped straight to 16 rounds, the same number of rounds that Feistel had used in his final version of Lucifer.

A new feature of DES, not found in any version of Lucifer, is a bit transposition before the first and after the last substitution steps. These are 8×8 columnar transpositions in which the order of the columns and the order of the rows are both changed. For the initial transposition the 64 bits of the block are written into the grid from left to right. The columns are read out in reverse order, namely 8,7,6,5,4,3,2,1. The rows are read out in the order 2,4,6,8,1,3,5,7. The final transposition is the inverse of this.

These transpositions have no cryptographic value. They add nothing to the strength of DES. They were added because the NSA had told IBM that the encryption should be fast when done in hardware, but slow to simulate in software. The idea was to make it more time-consuming for Emily to crack the cipher by brute force, that is, by trying all possible keys in software. IBM believed that permuting the bits would make any software implementation very slow. IBM probably envisioned a process where the bits were extracted one by one by masking, and then shifted into place.

This turned out to be all wrong. First, enemies wishing to crack DES could simply purchase the encryption chips through proxies. Second, for some legitimate applications DES needed to be embedded in software, so the software had to be fast. Third, bit transpositions can be done quickly, without extracting individual bits or shifting. I will show how in section 11.2.3.

Between the initial and final transpositions, DES has 16 substitution rounds. The 64-bit block is split into two 32-bit halves. In each round the right half serves to encipher the left half. The right half is first expanded from 32 bits to 48 bits, as follows. The 32 bits are treated as eight 4-bit groups. Each of these groups is expanded from 4 bits to 6 bits by appending the bit before and the bit after, taken from the adjacent groups. For example, the third group would consist of bits 9 through 12. This 4-bit group would be expanded from 4 bits to six bits by appending bit 8 to the left and bit 13 to the right. In other words, the 6-bit group would be bits 8,9,10,11,12,13. Eight such 6-bit groups form a 48-bit block.

This 48-bit block is then exclusive-ORed with 48 bits taken from the 56-bit key. Which 48 bits are used for each round is determined by a *key schedule*, which is basically shifting the full 56-bit key a few positions after each round. The resulting eight 6-bit groups are then fed into eight fixed S-boxes, that is, substitutions. Each S-box gives a 4-bit result, so the eight 4-bit results taken together form a 32-bit block. This block is then exclusive-ORed with the left half of the whole 64-bit block.

Historic aside

IBM did not design DES to have a key schedule. The original idea was to cycle the 64-bit key by 4 bit positions after each of the 16 rounds. That left the key in its original position, ready for enciphering the next block. IBM was forced to introduce the key schedule when the NSA made IBM reduce the key size to 56 bits. Four-bit shifts no longer worked. Of course IBM called the key schedule a "feature."

Another way to look at each S-box is to picture it as a 4×16 tableau. Like a Belaso or Vigenère tableau, each row is a substitution table for 4-bit groups. The two extra bits that were appended to the 4-bit groups are used to select which one of the 4 rows of the tableau is used.

Each S-box was carefully designed so that there would be as little correlation as possible between the 6 input bits and the 4 output bits. The NSA had found a top-secret way of designing the S-boxes to give the lowest possible correlation. Because DES was so important, the NSA decided to share this secret with the IBM designers of DES. However, after examining the IBM design, the NSA realized that IBM had also discovered this method and had used it in its design.

After each round, except the last, the left and right halves of the 64-bit block are swapped.

11.2.1 Double DES

It was understood from the outset that a 56-bit key was too small for strong security. Only 4 months after DES was adopted, Electronic Frontier Foundation built a $250,000 special-purpose computer called Deep Crack that solved a DES message in only 56 hours.

The first proposed solution to this apparent weakness was to encipher a message twice with DES using two different keys. This idea was rejected because it was theoretically possible to mount a meet-in-the-middle attack that would crack DES. That is, you work forward from the plaintext and backward from the ciphertext and meet in the middle. You do this by taking a block of ciphertext whose plaintext is known. You encipher the plaintext with all 2^{56} possible keys, and you decipher the ciphertext with all 2^{56} possible keys. You compare these results, and wherever you find a match you have a possible pair of keys.

This attack was only theoretical. You would need to store 2 sets of 2^{56} solutions, meaning 2^{60} bytes, to make all of the comparisons. No computer in the 1970s approached that level of storage. Further, you would expect about 2^{48} matches. These would all need to be checked out. That is a daunting task. But IBM and the NSA were hoping that DES could last 20 to 30 years, and it was plausible that this attack would become practical in that timespan. Double DES may be used, but it has never been accepted as a standard.

11.2.2 Triple DES

Triple DES, or *3DES*, was another attempt to compensate for the small 56-bit key size of DES. It consists of taking a 64-bit block and encrypting it with one DES key, decrypting it with a second DES key, then encrypting it with a third DES key. Obviously this takes 3 times as long as ordinary DES. It is not widely used because this makes it so slow.

There is a much faster way of increasing the security of DES. Simply exclusive-OR the 64-bit block with a 64-bit key before the DES step, and with a different 64-bit key after the DES step. There would be 3 independent keys, the two 64-bit exclusive-OR keys and the 56-bit DES key, for a total of 184 bits. This method takes only marginally longer than a single DES encipherment.

Even if the second exclusive-OR key could be determined by looking at the waveforms, this is still far stronger than single DES. You can eliminate the danger of the waveforms undoing the exclusive-OR by performing keyed simple substitutions before and after the DES step.

*11.2.3 Fast bit transposition

DES starts and ends with a bit transposition. The naive way of doing this would be to unpack the bits one by one, shift them into the desired position, and OR them into place. There is a much faster method, invented independently by me and by David Stevenson of IBM Research in Yorktown, NY circa 1975. I will demonstrate this technique using a transposition of a 32-bit block. Suppose that the plaintext, expressed in bit form, is

$$\texttt{abcdefgh ijklmnop qrstuvwx yz}\alpha\beta\gamma\delta\varepsilon\zeta$$

where each Latin or Greek letter represents the value of one bit, that is, it can be either 0 or 1. Let's see how this can be transposed so that a moves to the third position, b moves to the sixth position, c moves to the ninth position, and so forth.

The transposition can be accomplished by using 4 special tables, each with 256 entries. Each entry is a 32-bit block or computer word. The first table shows the transposed positions of the 8 bits in the first byte of the 32-bit block, like this:

$$\texttt{..a..b.. c..d..e. .f..g..h ....}$$

The second table shows the positions of the 8 bits in the second byte of the 32-bit block:

$$\texttt{k..l..m. .n..o..p ....i..j..}$$

The third table shows the positions of the 8 bits in the third byte of the 32-bit block:

$$\texttt{.v..w..x ....q..r.. s..t..u.}$$

The fourth table shows the positions of the 8 bits in the fourth byte of the 32-bit block:

$$\texttt{........ ..y..z.. }\alpha\texttt{..}\beta\texttt{..}\gamma\texttt{. .}\delta\texttt{..}\varepsilon\texttt{..}\zeta$$

The dots are there to make it easy for you to see where the 32 bits are placed. They represent zeros in the computer word. The transposition can now be accomplished by looking up the 4 bytes in these special tables and ORing the four resulting 32-bit blocks together, like this:

```
..a..b..  c..d..e.  .f..g..h  ........
k..l..m.  .n..o..p  ........  ..i..j..
.v..w..x  ........  ..q..r..  s..t..u.
........  ..y..z..  α..β..γ.  .δ..ε..ζ
kvalwbmx  cnydozep  αfqβgrγh  sδitεjuζ
```

This requires no shifts and no masking. The entire 32-bit transposition uses only 4 table look-ups and 3 OR operations. One use of this technique is to flip an 8×8 block of bits. This can be done using 8 tables of 256 entries, or just a single table, shifting the bits into the correct positions within each byte, like this:

```
No shift    a.......  b.......  c.......  d.......  e.......  f.......  g.......  h.......
Shift of 2  ..a.....  ..b.....  ..c.....  ..d.....  ..e.....  ..f.....  ..g.....  ..h.....
```

⁂

11.2.4 Short blocks

An issue that comes up with DES, and other block ciphers, is what to do with short blocks. With DES, all of the blocks must have exactly 8 characters. Suppose your message has 803 characters, 100 blocks of 8 characters plus 3 over. How do you handle those last 3 characters?

The traditional solution is to pad the last block with nulls. With paper-and-pencil cryptography, some favorite techniques were to append XXXXX or NULLS as the last 5 characters. Unfortunately, this gives Emily 5 letters of known plaintext. Some better solutions for manual ciphers are to use a marker such as XX or JQ, then make the rest of the remaining padding characters random, like XXESV, or simply to pad with any combination of low-frequency characters, like ZPGWV. Deciphering depends on Riva's ability to recognize where the real message ends and the padding begins.

In the computer, there are two issues that padding must address. First, Riva must be able to tell where the message ends, or, equivalently, how many bytes of padding there are. Second, Sandra wants to give Emily as little known plaintext as possible. Some of the proposed schemes fail on both scores. For example, one scheme proposed padding a message on the end with one of the following:

```
01
02 02
03 03 03
 ·  ·  ·
```

This can give Emily up to 31 bytes of known plaintext when the block size is 32. In a general file the last block could be a full block ending in 01, or even 02 02, which could be mistaken for padding.

A better solution is to place a length field somewhere in the plaintext file. This need not be the number of bytes in the file, which could require a 4-byte length field, it can be the number of padding bytes in the last block. For DES this is a number from 0 to 7, so it would require only 3 bits. The length field can be anywhere in the file. The most common places are the first byte, the last byte, and the first byte of the last block. The padding bytes themselves can be chosen at random.

To avoid giving Emily even one byte of known plaintext, the length can be coded in either the low-order or the high-order bits of the length indicator, and the remaining unused bits can be random. This lets the length indicator take any value from 0 to 255.

By the way, there is no law that you have to pad at the end of the file. If you want to pad at the front, at the start of the last block, or in the middle of 13th block, go ahead. As long as Sandra and Riva agree, they can do whatever they feel will hinder Emily the most. One possibility is to spread the padding bytes around. For example, if the file requires 4 padding bytes, you could put them at the end of the second, fourth, sixth and eighth blocks of the file, as long as Riva can tell how many padding bytes were added.

The *overlap method* is an alternative to padding. Suppose, again, that the block size B is 8 and the message has 803 characters, and you encipher the first 800 characters as 100 blocks of 8 characters. Then you encipher characters 796 through 803 as the 101st block. This way, the length of the message does not change, but Riva must decipher block 101 before deciphering block 100.

11.3 *Matrix multiplication*

The next block cipher we will look at is the *Advanced Encryption Standard* (AES). However, AES uses a mathematical operation called matrix multiplication, which has not yet been covered in this book. I promised in the introduction that I would present each mathematical concept that was needed, so in that spirit I will cover matrix multiplication here. This concept is needed in several later chapters. Unless you already know matrix multiplication well, it is best not to skip this.

A *matrix* is simply a rectangular array of elements called *scalars*. A sequence of scalars forms a *vector*, so each row and each column of a matrix is a vector. These are called *row vectors* and *column vectors*, respectively. A matrix with m rows and n columns is called an m×n matrix. If m = n, the matrix is called a *square matrix*. Here is an example of a matrix M with 3 rows and 5 columns, called a 3×5 matrix. It has 15 scalar elements denoted here by the letters a through o.

$$
\begin{pmatrix}
a & b & c & d & e \\
f & g & h & i & j \\
k & l & m & n & o
\end{pmatrix}
$$

In this matrix the 3 row vectors are [a,b,c,d,e], [f,g,h,i,j] and [k,l,m,n,o], and the 5 column vectors are [a,f,k], [b,g,l], [c,h,m], [d,i,n] and [e,j,o]. The rows of a matrix are numbered from top to bottom, and the columns are numbered from left to right. The element of M found on row i in column j is denoted M_{ij}, so M_{11} is a, M_{15} is e, and M_{31} is k.

Types of scalars include numbers such as integers, integers modulo N, rational numbers, real numbers, complex numbers and other types that are described later. Matrix multiplication works the same for every type of number.

The product of two matrices X and Y, denoted XY, is formed by multiplying the rows of X by the columns of Y. Let's look at how this works in detail. The rows of a matrix are vectors, and the columns of a matrix are vectors. Two vectors that have the same length can be multiplied by what is called an *inner product*, also called a *dot product* since vector multiplication is sometimes denoted by a • dot. This operation takes the elements of one vector, multiplies them pairwise by the corresponding elements of the second vector, and then takes the sum of those products.

Suppose the first vector is [a,b,c,d] and the second vector is [e,f,g,h]. They have the same length, 4 elements, so they can be multiplied. Their inner product is

$$[a, b, c, d] \bullet [e, f, g, h] = ae + bf + cg + dh.$$

Let X and Y be 4×4 matrices, and let P be their product. That is, P = XY. Suppose [a,b,c,d] is row i of X and [e,f,g,h] is column j of Y. Their product is denoted P_{ij}. In other words, the element at row i, column j is the product of row i of X and column j of Y. This can be written using subscripts as

$$P_{ij} = [X_{i1}, X_{i2}, X_{i3}, X_{i4}] \bullet [Y_{1j}, Y_{2j}, Y_{3j}, Y_{4j}] = X_{i1}Y_{1j} + X_{i2}Y_{2j} + X_{i3}Y_{3j} + X_{i4}Y_{4j}$$

A similar expression is used for other matrix sizes. Two matrices of sizes a×b and c×d can be multiplied whenever b = c.

11.4 *Matrix multiplication*

No, this duplicate section title is not a mistake. There are many other objects in mathematics besides numbers that can be added and multiplied. Some examples are vectors, matrices, polynomials, quaternions and, more generally, elements of a ring. You can even have vectors of matrices, matrices of polynomials, and so forth. There is more about rings in sections 15.6 to 15.8. Matrix multiplication can be based on these types of elements and their rules for multiplication and addition. The process is the same. You take the inner product of row i of X with row j of Y to get the element at row i column j of the product matrix.

Matrix multiplication is not commutative, meaning that you usually get a different result when you multiply a given square matrix X by a second square matrix A on the left or on the right. AX ≠ XA. These are called *left-multiplication* and *right-multiplication* of X by A.

For AES we are concerned with multiplication and addition of polynomials. We all learned how to add and multiply polynomials in high school algebra. People who went on to careers in science and engineering probably still remember how it's done. Polynomials can also be divided. This division can leave a remainder, so there is the same notion of modulus for polynomials as there is for integers. (Refer back to section 3.6 if you wish to review this.)

The scalar multiplication used in AES is not integer multiplication, but polynomial multiplication modulo another polynomial. This is probably as deep as we can go in this book, which is aimed at a general audience.

11.5 Advanced Encryption Standard (AES)

The *Advanced Encryption Standard* is a newer block cipher that replaced DES in 2001. It was initially called *Rijndael* after its inventors, Belgian cryptographers Vincent Rijmen and Joan Daemen. AES originally came in five combinations of 128-bit or 256-bit blocks with 128-bit, 192-bit or 256-bit keys. However, the National Institute of Standards and Technology (NIST) settled on the 128-bit block size for the standard. The number of rounds depends on the key size: 10 rounds for 128-bit keys, 12 rounds for 192-bit keys and 14 rounds for 256-bit keys.

Each round uses a round key consisting of 128 bits chosen from the full key according to a *key schedule*. Before the first round, the preliminary operation AddRoundKey is performed, which is simply exclusive-ORing the block with the round key. Each of the next 9, 11 or 13 rounds consists of 4 operations, SubBytes, ShiftRows, MixColumns and AddRoundKey. The final round does not have the MixColumns step.

The 128-bit block is treated as a 4×4 matrix of bytes in what is called *column-major order*, which simply means the bytes are written into the matrix down the columns rather than across the rows, like this:

$$\begin{pmatrix} b_1 & b_5 & b_9 & b_{13} \\ b_2 & b_6 & b_{10} & b_{14} \\ b_3 & b_7 & b_{11} & b_{15} \\ b_4 & b_8 & b_{12} & b_{16} \end{pmatrix}$$

The first step in each round is SubBytes. This is a fixed simple substitution performed on each byte individually. The substitution was designed to be highly non-linear. The linearity property is discussed at length in section 12.3.1.

The next step is ShiftRows. This is a transposition in which the rows of the matrix are cycled left by 0, 1, 2 and 3 positions, respectively, like this:

$$\begin{pmatrix} b_1 & b_5 & b_9 & b_{13} \\ b_6 & b_{10} & b_{14} & b_2 \\ b_{11} & b_{15} & b_3 & b_7 \\ b_{16} & b_4 & b_8 & b_{12} \end{pmatrix}$$

The third step in each round, MixColumns, is the matrix multiplication. This is not ordinary integer matrix multiplication as described in section 11.3. The elements in the matrix are treated as coefficients of a polynomial. The scalar addition and multiplication operations are polynomial operations done modulo another polynomial. This has all been carefully designed so the operations can be performed rapidly in hardware. MixColumns is omitted in the last round.

The final step in each round is AddRoundKey. This is just a bitwise exclusive-OR of the block with a part of the key determined by the key schedule.

I find this exclusive-OR at the end to be highly suspicious. I have been told by several electrical engineers that the waveforms produced by the exclusive-OR of 00 and 11 are distinct from the waveforms produced by the exclusive-OR of 01 and 10, so an eavesdropper could discern what both bits were. This potentially reveals to the eavesdropper 128 bits of the key. When doing high-security cryptography I avoid using exclusive-OR whenever possible.

When I am forced to use exclusive-OR at the end of an encipherment, for example when I am implementing a standardized algorithm, I make sure to invert each bit of the ciphertext an even number of times. I keep two random bit strings R1 and R2, the same size as the block, and their exclusive-OR $R3 = R1 \oplus R2$. Then I exclusive-OR the ciphertext first with R1, then with R2, and finally with R3. This gets the bit string back to its original value, hopefully with the telltale waveforms obliterated.

Alternatively, you can use a substitution, rather than an exclusive-OR, to invert all the bits of the block. You do this twice, so you use two substitution steps in place of the three exclusive-ORs. If you are using AES, I highly recommend adding this extra final step.

11.6   *Fixed vs. keyed substitution*

Early in this book all of the substitutions used alphabets that were mixed using keywords or numeric keys. The ciphers in this chapter, DES and AES, use fixed substitutions that can be embedded in hardware S-boxes. Which is better? Which is stronger?

When you use a fixed substitution, you can use sophisticated mathematics to design a substitution that can resist a variety of attacks. For example, if some of the output bits have a strong correlation to some of the input bits, that lets Emily use a statistical attack on the cipher, such as the attack I used on the Jefferson Wheel Cypher in section 8.2.

Unfortunately, a fixed substitution is a sitting target for Emily. She can study the substitution for months or years, and possibly find a weakness that the designer missed. Carefully crafted substitutions tend to have a mathematical regularity. The substitute is expressed as a specific mathematical function. This, in itself, can be a weakness because it gives Emily a shortcut for simulating your cipher.

My preference is to use a substitution that is determined by a key that can be changed for every message. Each instance of a keyed substitution may be weaker than the fixed substitution, but Emily cannot exploit such a weakness because she does not have the substitution table for study. If Emily manages to obtain the plaintext, perhaps by espionage, she may be able recover the substitution and learn its weakness, but by then it's too late. The only value of knowing the weakness is to decrypt the message and obtain the plaintext. If Emily already has the plaintext, then the key no longer has value. Such a weakness would not help her decipher the next message, because that message would have a different key, hence a different weakness, if any.

Any other instance of the substitution, when the alphabet is mixed by the same method but using a different key, may not have the same weakness. It may have the same type of weakness, such as a correlation between some bits of the block and/or bits of the key and some bits of the output, but these are different bits for each instance.

One argument for using fixed S-boxes is that it allows for synchronous operation of the encryption hardware where one message follows another with no gap between. Using mixed alphabets could involve pausing while the alphabets get mixed. Using a mixed alphabet requires a setup. The pause can be eliminated or at least reduced if mixing the alphabet can be done in parallel. That is, the alphabet for the next message can be mixed while the current message is being enciphered or deciphered. Or, let the user mix the alphabets and include the mixed alphabets as part of a long key.

If synchronous operation is required, and mixing the alphabets in parallel is not feasible, then the fallback technique is to exclusive-OR the block with keys the same size as the block, both before and after the DES or AES step. I call this method *XDESX* or *XAESX*, as appropriate. These exclusive-ORs are extremely fast, and offer a significant boost in security. The total key size is 184 bits, 16 bits larger than 3DES. I suggest that the final output be inverted twice to mask the waveforms.

11.7 Involutory ciphers

Involutory cipher is a fancy-pants way of saying "a cipher that is its own inverse." In other words, enciphering is identical to deciphering. If you encipher twice using an involutory cipher (using the same key), you get back the original plaintext. This is also called *self-inverse* or *self-reciprocal*. We have already seen a few involutory ciphers. Exclusive-ORing the plaintext with a binary key is involutory (section 3.3). The piecewise reversal transposition in the Bazeries type 4 cipher (section 4.6.1) is involutory. Flipping a square matrix, that is, writing the characters into a square grid left-to-right and reading them out top-to-bottom is involutory. Here is a 3×3 example of flipping a matrix:

```
Before    After
1 2 3     1 4 7     Flipping a 3×3 matrix
4 5 6     2 5 8     Rows become columns and columns become rows
7 8 9     3 6 9
```

Mathematicians call this operation *transposing* the matrix. Since transposition has a different meaning in cryptography, I will call this *flipping* the matrix. A fast method for flipping a matrix was described in section 11.2.3.

If you are building your cipher in hardware, using involutory ciphers can reduce the cost and simplify the operation. Your cipher machine does not need to have separate encipher and decipher modes.

Let's look at how to construct some types of involutory ciphers.

11.7.1   Involutory substitution

In an involutory substitution, if a letter X changes to a Y, then Y must change to X. This means that the letters have to pair off. To construct an involutory substitution, first list all of the letters or characters. Choose any letter and then choose its mate. Cross these off the list. Then choose another letter and its mate. Cross those off the list. Continue this way until most of the letters have been paired. Any remaining letters are their own inverses. Selecting the successive letters can be done using a numeric key the same way that SkipMix does (section 5.2).

An involutory substitution can conveniently be represented in two rows. The letters in the top row get the substitute directly below, and the letters in the bottom row get the substitute directly above. Here is an example formed using the keywords WORDGAME and TULIP. In this example, R would become L and L would become R.

```
WORDGAMEBCFHJ
TULIPKNQSVXYZ
```

In other words, the key for this involutory substitution is this 2-row array.

It is not necessary that every letter is paired with a different letter. A few letters could remain unchanged by the substitution. These are called *invariants* or *fixed points*.

An involutory bigram substitution can be constructed by the same method.

11.7.2   Involutory polyalphabetic substitution

To construct a polyalphabetic cipher that is involutory, simply make every row of the tableau an involutory substitution.

11.7.3   Involutory transposition

Involutory transpositions are easiest to construct if the message is broken into blocks of a fixed size. Let's assume that. Call the fixed block size B. The transposition is involutory if for every letter that moves from position X to position Y, the letter in position Y moves to position X. In other words, the transposition will consist of pairwise swaps of letters.

To construct an involutory transposition, first write the numbers from 1 to B in a list. Select any 2 numbers from the list. They are the first pair of positions that interchange. Delete those 2 numbers from the list and select another pair of numbers from the list. These are the second pair. Delete them from the list. Continue doing this until the list has at most 1 number left. If you choose to have some fixed points in your transposition, just stop the pairing sooner. Another way to create fixed points is to select 2 numbers at a time randomly from the list. If those two numbers are the same, that becomes a fixed point.

One way to represent a general transposition cipher is to list all of the positions in the block, and below them show their new positions. For example,

```
 1  2  3  4  5  6  7  8  9 10 11 12 13 14 15 16 17 18 19 20
13  7 17  8 20 15  2  4 11 18  9 16  1 19  6 12  3 10 14  5
```

This is the best format for computer use. When a person is doing the transposition, it may be more convenient to collapse this down to half-width like this:

```
 1  2  3  4  5  6  9 10 12 14
13  7 17  8 20 15 11 18 16 19
```

This is the same transposition, but in half the space. Either form may be used as the key for the transposition. In both cases, the letter in the first position moves to 13th place, while the letter in 13th position moves to first place, the letter in second position moves to 7th place, while the letter in 7th place moves to second position, and so forth.

*11.7.4 Involutory block cipher

Now that we have seen how to construct involutory substitutions and transpositions, we are ready to pull those elements together to make an involutory block cipher.

It will help, at this point, to introduce some more notation. Let M be any message, either a plaintext or a ciphertext. We will denote applying a cipher C to that message as CM. If D is another cipher, then applying D to the text CM would be denoted DCM. This notation looks a little strange because DCM means applying C first and then D, but it works well. You can think of DCM as a shorthand for $D(C(M))$.

DC is then the cipher formed by enciphering with C and then with D. This new cipher is called the *composition* of D and C. Composition is an operation that combines two ciphers and forms a new cipher. (Some authors call this the *product* of the ciphers C and D, and denote it $C \circ D$.)

For example, Bazeries type 4 (section 4.6.1) combines a substitution with a transposition. Composition has one mathematical property that is important for forming an involutory cipher: composition is associative. This means that if A, B and C are ciphers, then $(AB)C = A(BC)$. Because of this property, compositions of multiple ciphers can be written without parentheses, like ABC or even ABCDEFGH. Parentheses can be inserted in such a composition without changing the result. For instance, ABCDEFGH could be written as $A((BC)(DE))F(GH)$.

Let I represent the *identity cipher,* the cipher that transforms every plaintext into itself. That is, IM = M for any message M. Let C be any cipher whatsoever. Denote its inverse by C'. (C must have an inverse, otherwise messages could not be read.) Then CC' = C'C = I. The cipher C is involutory when C = C'.

Suppose that T is an involutory cipher and C is any cipher. Then the cipher CTC' is an involutory cipher. This is because

$$(CTC')(CTC') = CTC'CTC' = CT(C'C)TC' = CTTC' = C(TT)C' = CC' = I.$$

Similarly, if A and B are any ciphers, then BCTC'B' and ABCTC'B'A' are involutory ciphers, and so forth.

11.7.5 *Example, poly triple flip*

Let's look at an example of an involutory block cipher that I call *Poly Triple Flip.* This cipher operates on 64-bit blocks, and has the form ABCTC'B'A', where A and C are general polyalphabetic ciphers, B is a columnar transposition operating on the 64 bits, and T is flipping the 64-bit square matrix.

Ciphers A and C are polyalphabetic ciphers of period 8. That is, there is a separate alphabet for enciphering each row of the block. The tableau for each cipher will have 8 rows, which are used in order. There are no keys for selecting the rows of the tableau. Instead, the 8 keys are used for mixing the 8 alphabets. Together, A and C require 16 different keys, each of which might be a sequence of numbers to use with the SkipMix algorithm (section 5.2). I recommend that these 16 keys each contain 3 to 8 numbers, each in the range 0 to 255.

Cipher B is a columnar transposition that treats the 64-bit block as a 4×16 grid, so there are 16! possible permutations of the columns. The 64 bits are written into the grid left to right across the rows and read out top to bottom down the columns. The order of the columns is determined by a keyword or keyphrase, or an equivalent string of 16 numbers.

Poly triple flip is rated Ten.**

11.8   *Variable-length substitutions*

Block ciphers can be built using either fixed-length or variable-length substitutions. *VLA* and *VLB* are examples of block ciphers that use variable-length substitution. Both the VLA and VLB block ciphers use 128-bit blocks viewed as 4 rows of 32 bits each. The idea is to use a variable-length substitution in the rows, and then mix the block by performing 4-bit substitutions in the columns. The keys for each cipher are the keys used to mix the sets of tags and the 4-bit substitution.

VLA and VLB use same-length Post tag substitution, as described in section 10.5.1. Thus a 4-bit tag is replaced by a 4-bit substitute, a 5-bit tag is replaced by a 5-bit substitute, and so forth. That way, each row in the block remains a constant 32 bits long. After each substitution the new tag is moved to the end of its row, and the row is shifted left to keep it on a 4-byte boundary. The tags should have an average length of at least 6 bits.

VLA is the simpler version. In each round, you first do the 4-bit substitution on the leftmost (high-order) bit of the row. Then you perform one Post tag substitution on each row, with the shift. This is repeated for 32 rounds. The entire encipherment uses 128 variable-length substitutions and 32 fixed-length 4-bit substitutions. This cipher is rated Eight.

When the average tag length is 6 bits, I suggest that VLB should have 4 rounds, each round having 6 substitution steps in row 1, 7 substitution steps in row 2, 8 substitutions in row 3, and 9 in row 4.

The vertical substitutions in the columns should be done after rounds 1, 2 and 3. For speed, it is not necessary to perform the column substitutions in every column on every round. One reasonable choice would be to substitute in every 3rd column, for example, in columns 1,4,7, ... ,31 after round 1, in columns 2,5,8, ... ,32 after round 2, and in columns 3,6,9, ... ,30 after round 3.

VLB is rated Ten, and is perhaps the fastest cipher with this rating. It requires 120 variable-length substitutions, with shifts, and 32 vertical 4-bit substitutions, so it is slightly faster than VLA.

11.9 Ripple ciphers

Ripple ciphers, also called *wraparound* ciphers or *end-around* ciphers, are block ciphers based on a principle entirely different from the ciphers earlier in this chapter. The basic idea is that each 8-bit character in the block is used as a key to encipher the next character to its right. This in turn is used to encipher the next character, and so forth, rippling down the length of the block and wrapping around at the end. That is, the last character in the block is used as a key to encipher the first character. Ripple ciphers are best suited for software implementations since they offer little opportunity for parallel operation.

There are a wide variety of ripple ciphers. They may have any block length from 2 up, and the block lengths may vary periodically or randomly. I suggest a minimum block length of 5 characters, but you might prefer to start at 8. For example, you could use the chained digit generator to choose the block lengths. When the generator produces the digit D, you could make the length of the next block D+5, or perhaps D+8 or even 20-D.

Blocks may overlap. For example, you could use a fixed block length of 8, with blocks starting at positions 1, 6, 11, 16, ... every 5 characters. The last block could wrap around to the start of the message. When the message length is 20, the last block could consist of characters 16, 17, 18, 19, 20, 1, 2, 3.

Ripple ciphers are purely substitution ciphers; they involve no transposition at all. The simplest form of a ripple cipher is to exclusive-OR each successive character to the next one, so x_n gets replaced by $x_{n-1} \oplus x_n$. Then x_{n+1} is replaced by $x_n \oplus x_{n+1}$, and so forth, rippling through the block.

There are many ways to use the preceding character to encipher the next character. A partial list follows. Here A, B and C are simple substitution ciphers and P is a general polyalphabetic cipher. A(x), B(x) and C(x) represent the character x enciphered with A, B and C, respectively, and P(k,x) represents the character x enciphered with P using the key k to select the row in the tableau.

xor	Exclusive-OR	x_n is replaced by $x_{n-1} \oplus x_n$.
sxor	Substitute and exclusive-OR	There are three variations, x_n may be replaced by $A(x_{n-1}) \oplus x_n$, or $x_{n-1} \oplus B(x_n)$ or $A(x_{n-1}) \oplus B(x_n)$.
xors	Exclusive-OR and substitute	x_n is replaced by $A(x_{n-1} \oplus x_n)$.
add	Add	x_n is replaced by $x_{n-1} + x_n$. As always, addition is modulo 256.
madd	Multiply and add, also called *linear replacement*	x_n is replaced by $px_{n-1} + x_n$, or $x_{n-1} + qx_n$, or $px_{n-1} + qx_n$, where p may be any integer and q may be any odd integer. (If you are using an alphabet whose size is different from 256, q must be coprime to the alphabet size.)
sadd	Substitute and add	x_n is replaced by $A(x_{n-1}) + x_n$, or $x_{n-1} + B(x_n)$ or $A(x_{n-1}) + B(x_n)$.
adds	Add and substitute	x_n is replaced by $A(x_{n-1} + x_n)$.
poly	General polyalphabetic substitution	x_n is replaced by $P(x_{n-1}, x_n)$.

Since **xor** or **sxor** may leak information about its operands, I recommend using **xors** instead, so that the simple substitution is done after the exclusive-OR to mask the waveforms, namely $A(x_{n-1} \oplus x_n)$.

Notice that **madd** is simply a special case of **sadd**. That is, px_{n-1} is just a particular choice for $A(x_{n-1})$. The advantage of **madd** is that it does not require a preliminary setup phase to mix the substitution alphabet. In the same vein, note that $P(A(x_{n-1}), B(x_n))$ simply permutes the rows and columns of the tableau, so it is equivalent to $P(x_{n-1}, x_n)$, just using a different tableau.

The strongest of these ripple methods is **poly**, where the preceding character x_{n-1} is used as the key to select the row in the tableau used to encipher x_n. I call this method a *Key Ripple*. This would require a tableau of 256×256 bytes. If this is too large, x_{n-1} can be reduced to a smaller range by applying a *reduction substitution* to x_{n-1} before using it as a key. For example, x could be reduced to x mod 16, or to (13x+5) mod 32. Suitable reduced ranges are 0 to 15, 0 to 31, and 0 to 63. If R is the reduction substitution, and P is the polyalphabetic substitution, then x_n will get replaced by $Q(R(x_{n-1}), x_n)$, where Q is a polyalphabetic cipher with a reduced tableau consisting of the top 16, 32 or 64 rows of P's tableau.

If you cannot use a polyalphabetic cipher, perhaps because even the reduced tableau uses too much space, or because the setup time is too long, the next-best choice is to use 3 simple substitutions. Replace x_n by either $A(B(x_{n-1}) + C(x_n))$ or $A(B(x_{n-1}) \oplus C(x_n))$. This is called a *space-time tradeoff*. The 3 simple substitutions may take a little longer than the single polyalphabetic substitution, but they reduce the space needed from 65,536 bytes to 768 bytes, a 98.8% reduction.

Ripple ciphers are not restricted to using only the preceding character to encipher the current character. You can go back several characters if you wish, for example replacing x_n by $A(x_{n-i} \oplus x_n)$, where i can be any value less than the block size. It is also possible to use more than one previous character, for example $x_{n-2} + x_{n-1} + x_n$ or, more generally, $x_{n-j} + x_{n-k} + x_n$. Using general polyalphabetic substitutions, x_n could be replaced by $P(x_{n-4} \oplus x_{n-2}, x_n)$, or $P(x_{n-5}, P(x_{n-1}, x_n))$ or endless other combinations.

As I mentioned, any block size can be used. The substitutions can begin at any character in the block, and end at any character in the block, provided that every character gets substituted at least once. You may go several times around the block if you desire, wrapping from the last character to the first where needed. It is even possible to overlap more than 2 blocks, or to have a block lie entirely within another block or set of blocks. The block sizes, the starting positions within the block, the number of characters to be substituted, and the overlap with the preceding and/or following block can be fixed, can be varied periodically, or can be generated randomly.

Ripple ciphers can be taken even further. A message could be enciphered using several rounds of a ripple cipher. In each round the message could be divided into blocks of different sizes so that the block boundaries line up infrequently or never, and encipherment begins and ends at different points in the blocks. This gives a mosaic or even kaleidoscopic effect.

There are too many variations of ripple ciphers to enumerate. The ratings for these ciphers can range from Four to Ten. Here are a few examples. The simple **xor** ripple using fixed-size blocks with 2 rounds of substitution starting at the first byte of the block and ending at the last byte, and using only the preceding byte as substitution key, is rated Four. A **sadd** ripple cipher using varying-sized blocks, starting at a variable position in the block, going for at least 3 rounds of substitutions, ending at a variable position, and using the preceding byte as the substitution key is rated Seven. A **poly** ripple cipher using varying-sized blocks, starting at a variable position in the block, going for at least 3 rounds of substitutions, ending at a variable position, and using the preceding byte plus one other byte that varies from block to block as the substitution key is rated Ten. Mosaic methods are stronger than single-layer methods.

11.10 Block chaining

Block chaining is a valuable tool that strengthens any block cipher. Block chaining means using each block to help encipher the next block. In effect, chaining is a ripple cipher operating on blocks rather than on individual characters. The group of bytes carried forward from block N to block N+1 is called the *chain vector*. Since the first block in a message does not have a predecessor, most chaining schemes use an *initialization vector* (IV) for enciphering the first block as though it were the chain vector from some imaginary predecessor block. The initialization vector can be derived from the encryption key, or may be treated as an additional key for the encipherment.

ASIDE The block chaining used for Bitcoin and other cryptocurrencies is a specialized form of the block chaining used in cryptography. Here is where they got the idea.

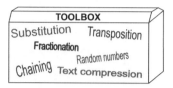

The most common form of chaining is combining the chain vector with the next block character by character. The most common method of combining characters is exclusive-OR. However, any of the combining methods described in section 11.8 can be used. This is normally done in one of four modes.

Mode	Description
PP	The plaintext of block N is combined with the plaintext of block N+1 before enciphering block N+1.
PC	The plaintext of block N is combined with the ciphertext of block N+1 after enciphering block N+1.
CP	The ciphertext of block N is combined with the plaintext of block N+1 before enciphering block N+1.
CC	The ciphertext of block N is combined with the ciphertext of block N+1 after enciphering block N+1.

For the greatest strength, the chaining operation should be cumulative. First the chain vector from block N–1 is combined with block N. This result becomes the new chain vector, which is combined with block N+1. Chaining mode **PP** is the strongest, and chaining mode **PC** is second-best. Modes **CP** and **CC** are far weaker because Emily can see the chain vector. I recommend that modes **CP** and **CC** be used only with the combining functions **xors**, **adds** and **poly**.

Although modes **CC** and **CP** are weaker, there is an advantage to using them. In modes **CC** and **CP** it is not necessary to have a separate initialization vector. Sandra can use the last block of the plaintext message as the initialization vector. Riva can simply decipher the last block first. In fact, Riva can decipher any block without needing to decipher the block before. This can be valuable if the cipher uses indicators (section 14.3). Riva would decipher the indicator block first.

Let's look at some stronger ways of chaining blocks.

11.10.1 Polyalphabetic chaining

Exclusive-OR is a weak way of combining block N with block N+1. A better way is **xors**, namely using exclusive-OR first, then using a simple substitution on the resulting characters. Far better than that is to use **poly**, a general polyalphabetic cipher. Use each character in the chain vector as a key to select the row in the tableau for enciphering the corresponding character in block N+1. Any of the 4 chaining modes can be used. Mode PP is strongest.

11.10.2 Enciphered chaining

The standard modes for chaining use either the plaintext or the ciphertext of block N as the chain vector as is, with no modification. It is far stronger to apply some encipherment to the chain vector. This can be rudimentary, such as a simple substitution or a piecewise reversal (section 4.6). Such simple methods can be effective if the substitution or transposition is different for each block. A key ripple is well-suited for this purpose (section 11.8). The encipherment used for the chain vector should have its own independent key. If the chain vector is more strongly enciphered, modes **CC** and **CP** will no longer be weak.

11.10.3 Lagged chaining

Chaining is not restricted to the preceding block. Chaining may also utilize earlier block(s). Block N may be combined with block N–i, or with multiple previous blocks, say block N–i and block N–j. If i > j, this requires an initialization vector of i blocks.

   Similarly, the chain vector can straddle several previous blocks. For example, the chain vector can come from the last half of block N–2 and the first half of block N–1.

11.10.4 Interior taps

One weakness of using either the plaintext or the ciphertext as the chain vector is that these are, or may become, known to Emily. One solution is to encipher the chain vector, as in section 11.10.2. A second solution is to take the chain vector from some intermediate round of the block encipherment. This is called a *tap*. For example, if the block cipher has 10 rounds, you could use the output of the 5th round as the chain vector. Combine this chain vector with the plaintext of the next block before starting to encipher the next block. This is mode **IP**.

   This can be taken a step further. You can use multiple taps, and they can be combined with the following block in multiple places, either with the plaintext, with the ciphertext or between rounds of the encipherment. Each tap produces a separate chain vector, so for N taps you must have N initialization vectors. Any or all of these chain vectors can be enciphered. The chain vectors can be enciphered using the same key, or each one can have its own independent key. A ripple cipher (section 11.8) is well-suited for enciphering the chain vectors.

11.10.5 Key chaining

Normally, chaining is done on the text of each block. However, it is also possible to use chaining with the keys. Suppose that you have a block cipher where the same key, K, is used for every block. That cipher could be greatly strengthened by using a different key for each block. One way to accomplish this is by chaining. You encipher the first block using K as the key. (An initialization vector is optional for key chaining.) Then you can encipher the second block using $K \bullet P_1$, $K \bullet C_1$ or $K \bullet I_1$ for the key, where $\bullet$ represents one of the combining functions, such as **xors** or **adds** performed byte by byte. Likewise, you encipher the third block using $K \bullet P_2$, $K \bullet C_2$ or $K \bullet I_2$ for the key, and so forth. This gives you three new chaining modes, **PK**, **CK** and **IK**. It is possible to use both key chaining and block chaining at the same time, say **PK** with **IP**. This is an extremely powerful combination.

11.10.6 Chaining mode summary

Together there are 12 possible modes for chaining. The chaining vector may be taken from any of three sources: the plaintext, an internal stage or the ciphertext of the current block. The chaining vector may be combined with any of four targets: the key, the plaintext, an internal stage or the ciphertext of the following block.

Beyond these choices, the chain vector may be taken fresh each time, or it may be combined with the chain vector from the previous block. The chain vector may be used as is, or it may be enciphered before combining it with the target. The chaining may operate on consecutive blocks, or it may be lagged. Lots and lots of options.

11.10.7 Chaining short blocks

When the last block in the message is short, and you use the overlap method (section 11.2.4) for handling short blocks, it is not clear how to chain the overlapped block. The solution is to chain from 2 blocks back. If there are N blocks, the chain vectors from block N–2 are used for both block N–1 and block N.

11.10.8 Chaining variable-length blocks

One last issue needs to be covered before we leave the topic of block chaining, namely variable block sizes. I suggest that the chain vector be kept at a fixed length. If the length L of the message block is less than the length of the chain vector, combine the first L bytes of the chain vector with the message block. Replace those L bytes of the chain vector, leaving the remainder unchanged. For example, if the chain vector is **1234567890** and the block is **SAMPLE**, combine **123456** with **SAMPLE**. If this yields **ZQm"w+** then the block becomes **ZQm"w+** and the chain vector becomes **ZQm"w+7890**.

1234567890	Chain vector from the previous block
SAMPLE	Plaintext block
ZQm"w+	Ciphertext block
ZQm"w+7890	New chain vector

If the chain vector is shorter than the message block, extend the chain vector for this block with as many copies of itself as needed. For example, if the chain vector is `123456` and the block is `CONVENTION`, combine `1234561234` with `CONVENTION`. If this yields `qA&Vm!7^oS` the block becomes `qA&Vm!7^oS` and the chain vector becomes `qA&Vm!`.

`123456`	Chain vector from the previous block
`CONVENTION`	Plaintext block
`qA&Vm!7^oS`	Ciphertext block
`qA&Vm!`	New chain vector

In both cases, the block remains the same length after chaining, and the chain vector remains the same length.

11.11 Strengthening a block cipher

Once you have a strong block cipher, it can be strengthened further with very little extra effort. All that is needed is to encipher the plaintext lightly before applying the block cipher, and to encipher the ciphertext lightly after completing the block cipher. I call this the *sandwich* technique, and the extra steps are called the *precipher* and *postcipher* steps. If you are feeling impish, you might call this the *Rubin sandwich*. By "lightly" I mean using a simple one-round one-step cipher such as simple substitution or key transposition (section 7.6). For example, you could use simple substitution before the block cipher and key transposition after, or vice versa. A stronger, but faster option is to treat the first 8 bytes of the block as two 32-bit integers, and multiply each integer by an odd multiplier in the range 3 to $2^{32}-1$ modulo 2^{32}.

Since the block cipher is already strong, the main purpose of these extra steps is to increase the total key size in order to foil brute-force attacks and meet-in-the-middle attacks. This works best when the precipher and postcipher steps have long keys that are independent of the block cipher key. For example, if the precipher or postcipher is simple substitution, it could have a long SkipMix key.

As a practical example, DES used a small 56-bit key. If you added simple substitution precipher and postcipher steps, each with an independent 64-bit mixing key, that would bring the total key size to 184 bits. This is stronger than 3DES, and nearly 3 times as fast.

DES, however, was designed without any setup phase. The precipher can easily be done with no setup. Simply exclusive-OR a 64-bit precipher key with the plaintext. This increases the total key size from 56 bits to 120 bits. This, alone, is stronger than 2DES and more resistant to a meet-in-the-middle attack. The postcipher step is a little trickier. We want to avoid using exclusive-OR as the final step, for reasons discussed earlier, and we also want no setup. This can be accomplished by using a fixed poly-alphabetic cipher. That is, the tableau is chosen beforehand and built into the device or software.

One possibility is to use a 16×16 tableau of 4-bit groups. The 64-bit block is treated as sixteen 4-bit groups. Each 4-bit group is enciphered using 4 bits of the 64-bit postcipher key. Thus the total key size is again 184 bits. This is also stronger than 3DES, and nearly 3 times as fast.

The reason this works is that DES is itself strong enough so that the only practical attack is brute force. Adding an extra 128 bits to the key makes brute force infeasible.

12

Principles for secure encryption

This chapter covers
- Five principles for secure encryption
- Large blocks and long keys
- Confusion, or non-linearity
- Diffusion and saturation

Let's pull together everything we learned in chapter 11. In sections 12.1 to 12.5 we will distill the 5 underlying principles that make a block cipher secure. One hallmark of a secure block cipher is that changing any bit in the key or any bit in the plaintext will cause about 50% of the bits in the ciphertext block to change, preferably in a random-looking pattern. Changing any other bit also will cause about 50% of the bits in the ciphertext block to change, but in a different pattern. Let's call this the *Fifty-Fifty* property. This chapter will describe how to make that happen.

12.1 Large blocks

We have seen that a bigram cipher can be solved just like a simple substitution cipher by compiling bigram frequencies and contact frequencies. This can also be done for trigrams and tetragrams, although a very large amount of ciphertext is needed. For block ciphers done by hand, the smallest block size that should be considered is 5 characters. For computer ciphers the minimum block size is 8 bytes. One purpose of a large block size is to prevent Emily from solving the cipher like a code. That is, Emily would find repeated ciphertext blocks and deduce their meaning from their frequency and their positions in the message. To take an extreme case, if the block size is 1 character, then no matter how large the key is, and how many encryption steps are used, the cipher is still just a simple substitution.

There are numerous 8-character sequences in English that are common enough to appear repeatedly in a long message. Here are a dozen examples, using an ellipsis ... to represent a blank space.

```
...AND...THE     THAT...ARE     WHICH...IS
FOR...THE...     THERE...IS     WHO...WERE
FROM...THE       THEY...ARE     ...WILL...BE
IT...WILL...     ...OF...THE... WITH...THE
```

Today's standard block size is 16 bytes. There is no high-frequency English phrase that long. There could be some long contextual phrases such as UNITED STATES GOVERNMENT, EXECUTIVE COMMITTEE, INTERNATIONAL WATERS, and so forth. However, to produce repeated ciphertext blocks, these plaintext repeats must align the same way with the block boundaries. For example, 16-byte plaintext blocks UNITED...STATES...GO and NITED...STATES...GOV would not produce recognizable ciphertext repeats when you are using a strong block cipher.

The problem of repeated ciphertext blocks disappears when you use block chaining (section 11.9). With block chaining, any block size 8 bytes or longer, can be used.

12.2 *Long keys*

We know that a secure cipher must have a large key to prevent a brute-force attack. The current standard is a 128-bit key. If you need your messages to remain secret for 20 years or longer, I recommend a minimum of 160 bits. That is equivalent to about 48 decimal digits, 40 hexadecimal digits or 34 single-case letters.

If you are typing the key by hand, I suggest that you structure your keys in a uniform way. Divide the key into blocks of equal size with a consistent format. Here are two styles of uniformly structured keys. In the first style, all of the characters in each block are the same type, uppercase letters, lowercase letters or digits. In the second style, the blocks have the same format, 2 uppercase letters and 3 digits.

```
18682 dcmpr KVOWZ 96583 pucmx 70584 GDNLS gsbif ZNEJR
BF242 KG679 UX591 WB485 DT649 MH537 PS506 CK841 HI458
```

The first of these two keys is equivalent to about 191 bits, and the second is equivalent to about 174 bits. For long keys like these you must be able to see the characters while you are typing, so that you can review them and make corrections when needed.

When the key is complete, the application should display a checksum so you can verify that the key is correct.

One advantage of this regularity is that it prevents mistaking a letter O for a digit 0, or a letter I for a digit 1. I do not recommend random mixing of characters, like `$v94H;t}=Nd^8`, because it leads to mistakes. If you have a data file encrypted using the key `$v94H;t}=Nd^8` and you decrypted it using the key `$V94H;t}=Nd^8`, that data file could now be unrecoverable. You may never figure out what went wrong and how to fix it. Using uniform blocks in your keys helps prevent such disasters.

Another form of key that helps to prevent typing errors is artificial words. Make up your own pronounceable letter combinations, like this:

```
obel ipsag lokitar malabak zendug foritut glapmar
```

Try to avoid patterns, such as using the same vowel combinations, **palek mafner vadel glabet**, and the like, where all of the words use the A–E vowel pattern.

These alphanumeric keys can be converted into binary form by software. The **madd** ripple cipher (section 11.8) is well-suited for this task.

An alternative to typing the keyword for each message or data file that gets encrypted is to use a *keyword manager* that generates the keywords and associates them with the messages or files. The keyword manager could be installed on a website accessible to both Sandra and Riva. This topic will not be covered in this book. Note that a keyword manager is different from a password manager because Sandra and Riva, working on different computers, must use the same keyword for each file.

12.2.1 Redundant keys

In some cases it may be possible for Emily to devise equations that relate the ciphertext to the plaintext and the key. If Emily knows, or can guess, some of the plaintext, these equations may make it possible for her to determine the key. For example, she may know that some of the messages begin with ATTENTION in all-cap letters. This might be sufficient for her to solve a 64-bit key when an 8-byte block size is used.

One way to defeat this potential attack is to enlarge the key. For example, if the block size is 64 bits, but the key is 32 bits larger, namely 96 bits, then you would expect, on average, that there would be about 2^{32} possible keys that transform the known plaintext into the ciphertext. Emily would need to sift through these 2^{32} solutions to find the correct one. This could be a difficult task because many of the more than 4,000,000,000 possibilities could look like plausible text.

Enlarging the key will make Emily's task much harder, but not necessarily impossible. If she has twice as much known plaintext, then the equations for two cipher blocks might be used to solve for the key. However, it is much rarer to have that much known plaintext, and solving twice as many equations may take far longer than merely twice as long. Depending on the type of equations Emily is using, it may be feasible to solve a set of 64 equations, but not a set of 128 equations.

If Emily does not have solvable equations, then redundant keys serve to make a brute-force attack far more difficult and costly. Either way, redundant keys make Emily work harder.

12.3 *Confusion*

In 1945 Claude Shannon, the founder of information theory, described two properties that a strong cipher must possess. He called these *confusion* and *diffusion*. By *confusion*, Shannon meant that there should not be a strong correlation between the plaintext and the ciphertext. Likewise, there should not be a strong correlation between the key and the ciphertext. By *diffusion*, Shannon meant that every part of the ciphertext should depend on every part of the plaintext and every part of the key.

There is a third property that I will add to Shannon's two. I call this property *saturation*. The idea is to measure how strongly each bit or byte of the ciphertext depends on each bit or byte of the plaintext and the key. The greater the saturation, the stronger the cipher. This section, and the following two sections, will discuss these three properties, confusion, diffusion and saturation, in detail.

There are two types of substitutions that are used in block ciphers, fixed and keyed. Keyed substitutions are variable, and can be changed for each message, or even each block. There is a discussion of the pros and cons of these methods in section 11.6. If you decide to use a keyed substitution, or if you find the math in this section difficult, then you can skip ahead to section 12.4. You can construct your mixed alphabet or tableau using the SkipMix algorithm described in sections 5.2 and 12.3.7 and choose the sequence of skips using a pseudorandom number generator.

Confusion, in Shannon's sense, is basically an issue of linearity versus non-linearity. If your block cipher uses a fixed alphabet or tableau, linearity is of paramount importance. The entire field of linear algebra is based on the concept of linearity. The term *linearity* comes from analytic geometry. The equation for a straight line is $ax+by=c$, where a, b and c are constants and the variables x and y represent the Cartesian coordinates of a point on a line. If the line is not parallel to the y-axis, the equation can be expressed as $y=ax+b$. Both $ax+by=c$ and $y=ax+b$ are examples of linear equations, or linear relationships.

The Caesar cipher (section 4.2) is an example of a linear cipher. The Caesar cipher may be regarded as adding the key to the plaintext to get the ciphertext, $c=p+k$. Here c is the ciphertext letter, p is the plaintext letter and k is the key. The key is the amount that the alphabet has been shifted. Julius Caesar used a shift of 3 positions, meaning that each letter of the alphabet was replaced by the letter 3 positions later, $c=p+3$, with letters near the end of the alphabet wrapping around to the front.

By the way, Caesar's method is not nearly as weak as it sounds because Caesar wrote his messages in Greek using the Greek alphabet. In Caesar's time well-educated upper-class Romans, like Caesar and his generals, knew Greek, just as in the 19th century the upper-class English studied Latin and aristocratic Russians spoke French.

In a block cipher involving both substitution steps and transposition steps, the cipher as a whole is non-linear if the individual substitutions are non-linear. In fact, if the block cipher has multiple rounds of substitution, the cipher as a whole is non-linear if just one early round is non-linear, provided that round involves all of the units in the block. Once linearity has been lost it cannot be regained in a later round. It would be much stronger to have every round be non-linear, but having even a single non-linear round is stronger than having none, especially if it comes near the start.

There are degrees of linearity and non-linearity. A substitution may be highly linear, weakly linear, weakly non-linear or highly non-linear. One example of each kind should get the point across. I have drawn a line between the position of each letter in the plaintext alphabet and its position in the ciphertext alphabet. You can see right away how much better the mixing of the alphabet becomes as the substitution becomes more non-linear.

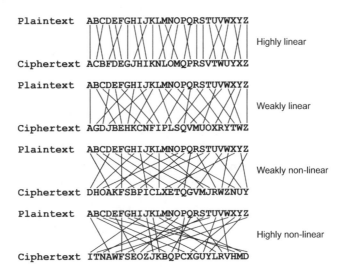

In the discussions that follow, I refer to the S-box inputs as the plaintext and the key, and to the output as the ciphertext. These terms mean the plaintext and ciphertext for that individual S-box, and not necessarily the plaintext and ciphertext for the entire multi-round block cipher. In some block ciphers the S-boxes do not have keys, they merely perform a simple substitution. In that case you can imagine that the S-box has a key that has the constant value 0, or that the S-box key is 0 bits long.

It is assumed here that Emily is able to test the S-box(es) for linearity because the cipher has been published, or she has obtained a copy of the device. If all that Emily has available is the input to the first round and the output from the last round, then linearity testing might not be feasible.

12.3.1 *Correlation coefficient*

There is a well-established statistical method for testing the correlation between two numerical variables. For example, you could test the correlation between daily temperature, measured in degrees Celsius, and sunlight, measured in hours. Temperature and hours are the numerical variables. You could make multiple trials taking the temperature at some fixed time of day, and recording the hours of sunlight that day. This would give you two lists of numbers, one list for the temperature and a corresponding list for the sunlight hours. The statistic measures the correlation between these two lists of numbers.

In our case the two variables are the plaintext letters and the ciphertext letters. The "trials" are the positions in the alphabet. For example, the first trial could be "A" and the last trial could be "Z". The letters of the alphabet need to be numbered in some manner. The numbering will depend on the size of the alphabet. For example, a 27-letter alphabet could be numbered using 3 ternary (base-3) digits as we did for the trifid cipher in section 9.9. The correlation could be between any ternary digit of the plaintext letters and any ternary digit of the ciphertext letters. In the following two sections I will discuss this in detail for the 26-letter alphabet and the 256-character alphabet.

Linearity is measured by calculating the correlation between the two variables. By far the most widely used measure of correlation is the Pearson product-moment correlation coefficient developed by English mathematician Karl Pearson, the founder of biometrics, and published in 1895, although the formula itself had been published in 1844 by French physicist Auguste Bravais, who was known for his work in crystallography. The purpose of the correlation coefficient is to have a single number that tells how well two variables are correlated, a number that has the same meaning regardless of the units of measurement or the sizes of the numbers involved.

If the two variables have a linear relationship the correlation is 1. If the variables have no correlation whatsoever the correlation is 0. If the two have an inverse relationship the correlation is –1. For example, the number of heads in 20 flips of a coin will have an inverse relationship to the number of tails. A correlation of .8 indicates a strong linear relationship, while a correlation of .2 indicates the relationship is highly non-linear.

Instead of merely presenting the formula, as most textbooks do, I am going to explain how and why it works. Understanding how it works will help you to use it appropriately and correctly.

The goal here is to compare two variables. This is done by comparing the sequence of values over the set of trials. For example, we might want to compare the price of magic carpets sold at the Qeisarieh bazaar in Isfahan, Persia, with their size. There are many factors affecting the price of magic carpets, including the type of yarn, the density of the knots, the complexity of the design and, of course, airspeed.

CENTERING

The first step in comparing the variables is to put them side by side, just as you would do if you were comparing them by sight. To put that a different way, you want to eliminate the +x term in the linear relationship P = mA+x, where P is price and A is area. It might seem like you could take the differences $P_i–A_i$ and then subtract the mean difference from P. However, this does not make sense because P and A are in different units. Carpet area A is measured in square *arsani* (roughly one meter), while carpet prices P in the bazaar are denominated in *toman* (Persian currency).

You need to adjust the area figures and the price figures separately because they are in different units. The trick is to take the mean price and subtract that from all the price figures to get new, adjusted price figures P'. You calculate the mean price μ_P by adding up the carpet prices and dividing by the number of carpets. For example, if the prices were 1000, 1200 and 1700 toman you would add up the 3 prices 1000+1200+1700 and divide by 3 to get the mean price of 1300. You would subtract 1300 from each of the prices to get the adjusted prices -300, –100 and 400. As you can see, the adjusted prices P' add up to 0. In a sense, the adjusted prices are centered around 0.

The area figures are centered in the same way. You add up the areas and divide by the number of carpets to get the mean area. For example, if the areas were 10, 12 and 17 square arsani you would add up the 3 areas 10+12+17 and divide by 3 to get the mean area of 13. You would then subtract 13 from each of the areas to get the adjusted areas –3, –1 and 4. The adjusted areas A' also add up to 0. The adjusted areas and adjusted prices are now both centered around 0. They are side by side and ready for the comparison.

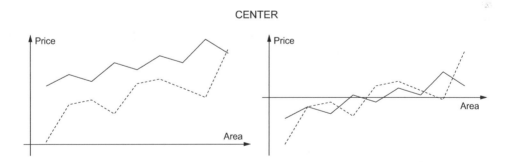

SCALING

The next step is to get the prices and the areas on the same scale. The prices are in toman, the areas are in square arsani, and there is no such thing as a conversion from toman to square arsani. That would be like a conversion from bushels to Celsius. Pearson, or rather Bravais, used an idea from linear algebra called *normalization*.

Suppose that you have a vector (a,b) and you want to find a vector pointing in the same direction, but whose length is 1. Any multiple of the vector (a,b), such as (ma,mb), will point in the same direction. Multiplying a vector changes its length, but not its direction. If you divide the vector by its length, the new vector (a/L,b/L) will have a length of 1 and the same direction as the original. This also clears the units. Imagine that the length of the vector is measured in feet. If you divide the vector by its length, then you have feet divided by feet. The result is just a number, with no units. It is dimensionless. The same is true when the vector is measured in toman or square arsani.

The length of the vector can easily be found by using the Pythagorean Theorem, $L = \sqrt{a^2 + b^2}$. This can be extended to any number of dimensions, $L = \sqrt{a^2 + b^2 + c^2 + ...}$. Let's try an example to see if this works. Try the vector (3,4). The length of this vector is $\sqrt{3^2 + 4^2} = \sqrt{9 + 16} = \sqrt{25} = 5$. The normalized vector is (3/5,4/5). Therefore $\sqrt{(3/5)^2 + (4/5)^2} = \sqrt{9/25 + 16/25} = \sqrt{25/25} = 1$ is the length of the normalized vector, as expected. It worked.

P, A, P' and A' are all lists of numbers, so they are vectors. They have lengths just like any vector, and they can be normalized like any vector. In geometry, a vector is normalized by dividing it by its length. The length of any normalized vector is always 1.

To normalize P' you just square all of the adjusted prices, add those squares and take the square root of the sum. That gives you the length of P'. Divide the adjusted prices P' by the length to get the normalized prices P''. To normalize A' you square all of the adjusted areas, add those squares and take the square root of the sum. That gives you the length of A'. Divide all of the adjusted areas A' by the length to get the normalized areas A''.

SCALE

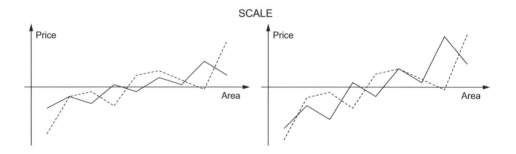

To recap, (1) center the prices and areas by subtracting the mean, then (2) normalize the prices and areas by dividing by the length. The result is a standardized list of prices and a standardized list of areas where the sum of the terms in each list is 0, and the sum of the squares of the terms in each list is 1.

Now we are all set up for the formula. Multiply each term in the normalized list of prices by the corresponding term in the normalized list of areas, so $P''_i \times A''_i$. Add up those products. That's the correlation coefficient. (In linear algebra this is called the *inner product*, or *dot product*, of the normalized price vector and the normalized area vector.)

Let's give this a reality check. Imagine we are testing the correlation between Celsius temperature and Fahrenheit temperature. We know these are related by the linear formula F = 1.8C+32, so the correlation coefficient ought to be 1. Suppose we measure the temperature at 11AM, 3PM, 7PM and 11PM, and find that the Celsius temperatures are (14, 24, 6, 0) and the Fahrenheit temperatures are (57.2, 75.2, 42.8, 32). The mean Celsius temperature is (14+24+6+0)/4 = 11, so the adjusted Celsius temperatures C' are (3, 13, –5, –11), and the corresponding adjusted Fahrenheit temperatures F' are (5.4, 23.4, –9, –19.8). The length of the Celsius C' vector is 18. Divide C' by 18 to get C", the normalized Celsius temperatures (3/18, 13/18, -5/18, –11/18). The length of the adjusted Fahrenheit vector F' is 32.4 and the normalized Fahrenheit vector F" is (3/18, 13/18, –5/18, –11/18).

We multiply C" by F" element by element and add the 4 products to get the correlation coefficient. This sum is $(3/18)^2+(13/18)^2+(-5/18)^2+(-11/18)^2$. It all adds up to 1. This supports the claim that the procedure described previously, centering by subtracting the mean, normalizing by dividing by the length, and then multiplying term by term and summing, does indeed produce a valid correlation coefficient.

To recap: you test for linearity by calculating the correlation coefficient. This section has shown you how to calculate the correlation coefficient. The calculation yields a number between –1 and +1. Here is a chart for interpreting the correlation coefficient.

```
Highly linear      .75 to 1.00   or   -.75 to -1.00
Weakly linear      .50 to  .74   or   -.50 to  -.74
Weakly non-linear  .25 to  .49   or   -.25 to  -.49
Highly non-linear  .00 to  .24   or   -.00 to  -.24
```

12.3.2 Base-26 linearity

Let's start the investigation of linearity with substitutions based on a 26-character alphabet. This might be valuable if you are designing a mechanical or electromechanical cipher device, or if you are simulating one. Each rotor in such a machine performs a substitution on a 26-character alphabet. Begin by considering an S-box that has no key. There are multiple forms of linearity that can occur with a 26-letter alphabet, depending on how the letters are numbered. There are 3 ways to view the alphabet: treating the alphabet as a single sequence of 26 letters, treating it as a 2×13 array of letters, or treating it as a 13×2 array of letters. These lead to 3 different ways of numbering the characters: N1, N2 and N3, as shown. The discussion of these 3 numbering schemes uses modular arithmetic. If you would like to review modular arithmetic at this time, see section 3.6.

	A	B	C	D	E	F	G	H	I	J	K	L	M	N	O	P	Q	R	S	T	U	V	W	X	Y	Z
N1	0	1	2	3	4	5	6	7	8	9	10	11	12	13	14	15	16	17	18	19	20	21	22	23	24	25
N2	00	01	02	03	04	05	06	07	08	09	0A	0B	0C	10	11	12	13	14	15	16	17	18	19	1A	1B	1C
N3	00	01	10	11	20	21	30	31	40	41	50	51	60	61	70	71	80	81	90	91	A0	A1	B0	B1	C0	C1

Numbering schemes N2 and N3 follow the usual convention of using the letters A, B and C to represent digits beyond 9. That is, they use the first 13 of the 16 hexadecimal digits. In the simplest linear encipherment (the Belaso cipher) the key is just added to the plaintext. When the key is added to the plaintext character, in the N1 numbering scheme it uses conventional addition modulo 26. When the key is added to the plaintext character in the N2 numbering scheme, the first digit is added modulo 2 and the second digit is added modulo 13. Conversely, when the key is added to the plaintext character in the N3 numbering scheme, the first digit is added modulo 13 and the second digit is added modulo 2. Here are examples showing how the word THE is enciphered by adding the key J in each of the 3 schemes.

N1			N2			N3			
T	H	E	T	H	E	T	H	E	Plaintext
19	7	4	16	07	04	91	31	20	Plaintext in numerical form
+ 9	9	9	+09	09	09	+41	41	41	Key letter J
2	16	13	12	03	00	00	70	61	Ciphertext
C	Q	N	P	D	A	A	O	N	Ciphertext in character form

If the plaintext, the key and the ciphertext alphabets are all numbered using the N1 scheme, then a linear substitution, or linear transformation, would take the plaintext character p and transform it using the key k into the ciphertext character $c = mp+f(k)$, where m is a multiplier which must be coprime to 26, $f(k)$ is any integer-valued function, and the arithmetic is done modulo 26. For example, if $m = 5$, $p = 10$, $k = 3$ and $f(k) = k^2+6$, then $c = 13$ because $5 \times 10+3^2+6 = 65 \equiv 13$ (mod 26). The constant m and the function $f(k)$ can be built into the substitution table.

If the plaintext, the key and the ciphertext alphabets are all numbered using the N2, or 2×13 numbering scheme, either the first digit or the second digit or both digits can be linear. Suppose that both digits are linear. Then a plaintext character p = a,b is transformed using the key k into the ciphertext character $c = ma+f(k),nb+g(k)$, where m must be coprime to 2, meaning $m = 1$, n must be coprime to 13, and $f(k)$ and $g(k)$ may be any integer-valued functions. The arithmetic is done modulo 2 and modulo 13, respectively. The constants m and n, and the functions $f(k)$ and $g(k)$ can be built into the substitution table.

If the plaintext, the key and the ciphertext alphabets are all numbered using the N3, or 13×2 numbering scheme, either the first digit or the second digit or both digits can be linear. Suppose that both digits are linear. Then a plaintext character p = a,b is transformed using the key k into the ciphertext character $c = ma+f(k),nb+g(k)$, where m must be coprime to 13, n must be coprime to 2, meaning $n = 1$, and $f(k)$ and $g(k)$ may be any integer-valued functions. The arithmetic is done modulo 13 and modulo 2, respectively. The constants m and n, and the functions $f(k)$ and $g(k)$, can be built into the substitution table.

There is no requirement that the plaintext and the ciphertext are numbered the same way. There can be a correlation between any digit of the plaintext and any digit of the ciphertext in any numbering. Emily might test any or all of these combinations, looking for an exploitable weakness. Consequently the designer of the cipher must test all of the possible numberings and correlations to verify that no such weakness exists, or to learn where countermeasures must be taken to prevent Emily from exploiting such a weakness. For example, you can use substitutions that have different weaknesses in alternating rounds of a block cipher. In most cases each substitution will diminish the weakness of the other. Of course, you should test this by hunting for linear relationships between the plaintext and the final ciphertext produced by the last round.

If you wish to test the linearity of a substitution, you cannot apply the correlation coefficient directly. This is because all of these substitutions are done using modular arithmetic. Consider this substitution using the N1 numbering scheme:

```
p= 0  1  2  3  4  5  6  7  8  9 10 11 12 13 14 15 16 17 18 19 20 21 22 23 24 25
c= 0  2  4  6  8 10 12 14 16 18 20 22 24  1  3  5  7  9 11 13 15 17 19 21 23 25
```

This is almost exactly $c = 2p$, so it is highly linear. However, the correlation coefficient between the plaintext and the ciphertext alphabets using this numbering scheme is .55556, indicating that the substitution is only weakly linear. The correlation coefficient should have been calculated using the following distribution, which is equivalent modulo 26.

```
p= 0  1  2  3  4  5  6  7  8  9 10 11 12 13 14 15 16 17 18 19 20 21 22 23 24 25
c= 0  2  4  6  8 10 12 14 16 18 20 22 24 27 29 31 33 35 37 39 41 43 45 47 49 51
```

The correlation coefficient using this numbering is .99987, correctly showing very strong linearity.

This illustrates a difficulty of using the correlation coefficient in cryptography. You are always working modulo the size of the alphabet. To find the correct correlation you need to add 26, then 52, 78 and so forth for the N1 numbering, or 13, 26, 39, ... for the N2 and N3 numberings. In the previous example the place where you needed to start adding 26 was obvious. It was where the ciphertext numbering went **22 24 1 3**. That drop from 24 down to 1 made it apparent.

When the ciphertext alphabet is less linear, when it jumps around a bit, it may be harder to spot. For example, this substitution has a correlation of .3265, moderately non-linear.

```
p= 0  1  2  3  4  5  6  7  8  9 10 11 12 13 14 15 16 17 18 19 20 21 22 23 24 25
c= 0  5  8 11 16  2 21 25  4  9 13 17 12 19  1 24  3  7 14 18 20 23  6 10 15 22
```

When it is adjusted by adding multiples of 26 like this

```
p= 0  1  2  3  4  5  6  7  8  9 10 11 12 13 14 15 16 17 18 19 20 21 22 23 24 25
c= 0  5  8 11 16 28 21 25 30 35 39 43 38 45 53 50 55 59 66 70 72 75 78 82 87 94
```

the correlation becomes .9944, highly linear. I have used <u>single</u>, <u><u>double</u></u> and **<u>bold</u>** underlining to show where <u>26</u>, <u><u>52</u></u> and **<u>78</u>**, respectively, have been added to the cipher-text characters. An important feature to notice here is that 26 was added to the ciphertext character 2, corresponding to plaintext 5, but not to the following cipher-text characters, 21 and 25. Likewise, 52 was added to the ciphertext character 1, corresponding to plaintext 14, but not to the following ciphertext character, 24.

It is fairly easy to determine which multiple of 26 to add when the ciphertext alphabet is close to linear. When the ciphertext alphabet is badly behaved it becomes much harder. But ... that doesn't matter. When the substitution is non-linear, that is all you need to know. It makes no difference if the correlation coefficient is .01 or .35. In either case there is not enough correlation for Emily to exploit. Don't waste time calculating the exact value.

That handles the case with no key. Now suppose there is a key. If the substitution is linear, then it will have the form $d(p)+f(k)$, where p is the plaintext, k is the key and d and f are integer-valued functions. The addition can be done in any of the 3 numbering schemes, N1, N2 or N3. In this case the key plays no role in testing the linearity. $f(k)$ is just a constant added to the ciphertext. Adding a constant has no effect on the correlation coefficient because it just gets subtracted back out when you subtract the mean value from each list of values (the centering operation). It is easy to test whether the substitution $S(k,p)$ takes the form $d(p)+f(k)$. Just choose two keys k_1 and k_2 and take the differences $S(k_1,0)-S(k_2,0)$, $S(k_1,1)-S(k_2,1)$, $S(k_1,2)-S(k_2,2)$, ... If the S-box has the form $d(p)+f(k)$, then all of these differences will be equal. If you repeat that for all possible keys, then you are certain $S(k,p)$ has the desired form, and you can test for linearity without considering the key.

12.3.3 *Base-256 linearity*

This analysis of linearity in base 26 is just a warmup for base-256 linearity because there are two distinct forms of linearity that can occur in base 256. Let's call them *serial* and *condensed*. In serial linearity each group of bits represents an integer. For example, the 3-bit groups 000, 001, 010, ... , 111 represent the numbers 0, 1, 2, ... , 7. The two forms of linearity can be combined to make a hybrid form of linearity. This is discussed later in section 12.3.6.

Serial linearity is what we saw with base 26. In base 26, there could be correlations between the N1, N2 and N3 numberings in any combination and in any order, so there were many pairings that had to be tested for linearity. In base 256 there are more possibilities. Serial linearity may exist between any group of bits in the plaintext alphabet and/or the key versus any group of bits in the ciphertext alphabet. These bit groups need not be the same size. A 4-bit group taken from the plaintext, covering the range from 0 to 15, may be highly correlated with a 3-bit ciphertext group covering the range 0 to 7, so the number of possible pairings is much greater.

To make matters worse, the 4 bits in that 4-bit group could be any bits from the plaintext byte. Bits 7,2,5,1 in that order are just as valid as bits 1,2,3,4. The linear substitution might add these 4 bits to 4 different bits of the key byte modulo 16. The number of possible combinations becomes enormous. To recap, any group of bits in any order in the plaintext character plus key character can be linearly correlated with any group of bits in any order in the ciphertext character. That's a boatload of correlations to test.

Before you reach for the Excedrin, or the tequila, here is some good news. You probably don't need to test for any of them. Unless the cipher is specifically designed to pass these values intact from round to round, these correlations won't matter. They will get so weakened with each successive round that they won't be detectable from the initial plaintext through the last round of the block cipher.

12.3.4   *Adding a backdoor*

You may have noticed that I said "probably." The exception is when you suspect that a cipher may have a backdoor, that is, it has been deliberately designed so that people who know the secret can read messages without knowing the key. For example, a national espionage agency might supply its agents with a cipher that has a backdoor so that the agency can monitor their messages and detect traitors.

At this point, let's change hats. Suppose that you are Z, the spymaster who has been tasked with designing this cipher. You need to build a cipher that looks and acts like a strong block cipher, so the users will not suspect a thing. For example, you would want your cipher to have the Fifty-Fifty property, where changing just one bit in the key or the plaintext would cause about half of the ciphertext bits to change in a random-looking pattern. If the substitutions in your block cipher were not all linear, this would be a sure sign of a strong block cipher. You want your fake cipher to mimic that property.

Here is one method you can use to hide a backdoor in a cipher. It is based on serial linearity, so let's call it the *Backdoor Serial* method for constructing a cipher, and let's call ciphers constructed by this method *Backdoor Serial* ciphers. Z can read messages that are sent using backdoor serial ciphers without needing to know the key, but for anyone who does not know how the backdoor works, they look like strong, secure block ciphers. The method has three parts: *disguise, concealment* and *camouflage.*

DISGUISE

The backdoor serial ciphers will use linear substitutions on hex digits. Each block of the plaintext and the key is treated as a sequence of 4-bit hexadecimal digits. The enciphering operation is addition modulo 16 on the hex digits of the message block and the key. Suppose the two hex digits in a byte are p_1 and p_2, and the hex digits of the key that is used to encipher them are k_1 and k_2. The linear substitution will replace p_1 and p_2 by

$$q_1 = ap_1 + bp_2 + ck_1 + dk_2 + e, \quad \text{and}$$
$$q_2 = fp_1 + gp_2 + hk_1 + ik_2 + j.$$

The coefficients a, b, c, d, e, f, g, h, i and j may be any integers from 0 to 15, and ag–fb must be odd. If your cipher has multiple rounds, these 10 values may be different for every round.

This type of linear substitution is easy for Emily to detect. In particular, the low-order bit of each hex digit is purely linear, so a simple bit-to-bit test for linearity will find it. To avoid detection, we can disguise the hex digits. First, list the hex digits in some scrambled order, like this:

0	1	2	3	4	5	6	7	8	9	A	B	C	D	E	F	Position
5	C	3	B	0	F	8	4	D	1	9	E	6	A	7	2	Scrambled (disguised) digits

To add two disguised hex digits, you add their positions in the scrambled list to get the position of the sum in the scrambled list. For example, to add **1+2**, you find that the digit **1** is in position 9 and the digit **2** is in position F, so you add 9+F mod 16 to get 8. The sum is in position 8 in the list. The digit in position 8 is **D**, so **1+2 = D**.

Likewise, to multiply two disguised hex digits, you multiply their positions in the scrambled list to get the position of the product in the scrambled list. For example, to multiply **2×3** you note that the digit **2** is in position F and the digit **3** is in position 2, so you multiply F×2 mod 16 to get E. The product is in position E in the list. The digit in position E is **7**, so **2×3 = 7**.

Essentially the disguise is a simple substitution done on the hex digits. If the substitution is non-linear, then none of the bits will have a linear relationship between the plaintext and the ciphertext. This type of disguised linearity is much harder for Emily to detect, but to really confound Emily you can conceal the disguised hex digits.

CONCEALMENT

If the hex digits are always bits 1–4 and bits 5–8 of each byte of the block and key, then Emily still stands a chance of discovering the linearity. To really make Emily's task seriously hard, you can conceal the bits within each byte. Instead of using bits (1,2,3,4) of the plaintext, and bits (1,2,3,4) of the key, and putting the resulting sum in bits (1,2,3,4) of the ciphertext, you could take the hex digits from bits (2,7,4,1) of the plaintext, in that order, and bits (4,8,3,5) of the key, and put the resulting sum into bits (8,6,1,7) of the ciphertext byte. You can use any combination of 4 bits that you choose, in any order, as long as the 2 hex digits in each byte use all 8 bits once each.

Just to be clear, we are not saying that Sandra extracts these bits from each byte, deciphers the disguised linear substitution, performs the arithmetic, then repacks the resulting bits in a different order. That would be far too slow, and Emily would know exactly what was afoot. Instead, Sandra does this when she builds the substitution tableau. To encipher, she simply uses the key byte to select a row in the tableau and then performs the substitution on the plaintext byte. All of the disguise and concealment are built into the substitution tableau.

CAMOUFLAGE

The cipher, as described so far, is merely a very complicated polyalphabetic cipher. Emily could solve messages using the techniques of section 5.8.3. To make a backdoor serial cipher look like a strong block cipher, you need some camouflage to hide the polyalphabetic cipher that is at its core.

One method is to use a bit transposition that is applied to the block after each round. This will make the cipher look like a substitution-permutation network (section 11.1). To preserve the hidden linearity, the 4 bits that make up each hex digit must end up in a single byte. They need not be in the same bit positions in that byte, and they need not be contiguous, but they must be in one byte together. In other words, each byte of the input gets split into two hex digits that are fed into two other bytes at the next round in some transposed order. Unfortunately, if Emily has access to the published specifications for the backdoor serial cipher, she might well discover this type of camouflage.

Let's look at a second form of camouflage that is much harder for Emily to uncover. This method borrows an idea from the Data Encryption Standard (DES) (section 11.2). Each cipher block is divided into two halves. In each round, first the left half is used as the keys to encipher the right half, then the right half is used as the keys to encipher the left half. We have already seen how the linearity can be disguised and concealed within the substitution tableau, so let's take advantage of that to create the illusion of a strong block cipher.

Each round of the cipher will consist of four steps. (1) Each byte in the left half is enciphered using one byte of the key. (2) Each byte of the right half is enciphered using one byte of the left half as the key. (3) Each byte in the right half is enciphered using one byte of the key. (4) Each byte of the left half is enciphered using one byte of the right half as the key.

To make this look ultrastrong, each byte of the block should be enciphered using a different byte of the key in each round, and each byte of one half of the block should be enciphered using a different byte from the opposite half in each round. You can fancy this up by shuffling the bytes in the block and the bytes in the key for every round. You can make the key larger than the block to present an even greater impression of strength. The cipher remains linear, however, because the linearity has been preserved in every step of every round.

STORAGE

Let's look at the mechanics of the backdoor serial cipher. In each byte of the key, the plaintext and the ciphertext there are two hex digits. Each of these could occupy any 4 bits of the byte, in any order. Let's call that ordered set of 4 bits the *bit configuration* of the hex digit, and the combination of 2 hex digits in a byte the *byte configuration*. The key does not normally change configuration, but the byte configuration of the plaintext and ciphertext can change at any stage of the encipherment.

For each substitution there are 6 bit configurations, 2 for the key, 2 for the plaintext and 2 for the ciphertext. For each hex digit, the permutation (scrambled order) of the 16 hex values also can be different, so there are also 6 permutations of the hex values for each substitution, 2 for the key, 2 for the plaintext and 2 for the ciphertext. This combination of 6 configurations and 6 permutations determines the substitution tableau. For each distinct combination of bit configurations and permutations a separate substitution tableau is needed.

Each tableau uses 65,536 bytes, so storage might be a problem. If this is an issue, I suggest using at most 2 byte configurations, and for each bit configuration using at most 2 different permutations, perhaps alternating from one round to the next. To further reduce the amount of storage required, you could consider using the same permutation each time you use any given bit configuration.

12.3.5 *Condensed linearity*

In most cases, you will not be building a backdoor into your cipher, and you will not be concerned with serial linearity. Let's turn our attention to the second type of linearity, condensed linearity. In this form of linearity, a group of bits is condensed down to a single bit by exclusive-ORing them together. Thus 000, 011, 101 or 110 would be condensed to 0, while 001, 010, 100 or 111 would be condensed to 1. Any group of bits from the plaintext and/or the key could potentially be correlated with any group of bits from the ciphertext for each S-box. If a block cipher uses exclusive-OR to combine the outputs of the S-boxes with the rest of the block, then this linearity can be passed from round to round, and there will be a linear relationship between the original first-round plaintext and the final last-round ciphertext. The designer of the cipher must either avoid using exclusive-OR this way, or must make a thorough check to be certain that the S-boxes do not contain any such linearities.

Suppose the S-box takes an 8-bit plaintext and produces an 8-bit ciphertext. There are 255 different ways a group of bits can be selected from the plaintext and likewise 255 ways a bit group can be selected from the ciphertext. (The order of the bits does not matter since $a \oplus b = b \oplus a$.) That makes $255^2 = 65,025$ different pairings of groups to test. Each test is a correlation between the 256 plaintext values and the 256 ciphertext values. This is easily feasible, even on a personal computer.

If the S-box takes an 8-bit plaintext plus an 8-bit key and produces an 8-bit cipher-text, then there are 65,535 different ways a group of bits can be selected from the plaintext plus key, and again 255 ways a bit group can be selected from the ciphertext. That makes $65,535 \times 255 = 16,711,425$ different pairings to test. This takes a good while on a PC because each correlation involves all 65,536 plaintext and key combinations. That's over 10^{12} values that need to be centered, scaled and summed.

This is the ideal time to talk about how to do these tests efficiently. There are a few tricks that greatly speed up the process. (1) To select a combination of bits, use a mask that selects those bits from each byte. For example, if you want bits 2, 4, and 7, use the mask 01010010, which has ones in bit positions 2, 4 and 7. AND this mask with each plaintext byte to select the desired bits. (2) To try all of the possible bit combinations, don't construct the masks one at a time, just step the mask through all of the values

1 through 255. (3) To condense the bits, don't use shift and XOR every time. Do that once and build a table of the condensed values. Then a bit combination can be condensed by a table lookup. If there is a combination of key bits and plaintext bits, these can be exclusive-ORed together and the result can be condensed using the table, so you will need one table lookup instead of two.

12.3.6 *Hybrid linearity*

For the sake of completeness, I will mention that it is possible to have a hybrid form of linearity that combines serial and condensed linearity. Suppose that you divide each 8-bit byte into four 2-bit groups. These 2-bit groups could be serially linear under addition modulo 4. You could condense two or more of these groups by adding them modulo 4. The same could be done with 3-bit groups modulo 8 or 4-bit groups modulo 16.

Let's stick with 2-bit groups. Each group could consist of 2 bits taken from anywhere in the byte. For example, a byte could be decomposed into 4 groups, bits (6,1), (4,8), (2,5) and (7,3). You can condense several 2-bit groups into a single 2-bit group by adding them modulo 4, or by taking any linear combination modulo 4. For instance, if the 2-bit groups are A, B, C and D you could combine them into a new 2-bit group pA+qB+rC+sD+t (mod 4), where p, q, r, s and t are fixed integers in the range 0 to 3, with at least one of p, q, r and s being odd.

These types of condensed groups could be correlated with similar hybrid groups of bits in the ciphertext, or with regular bit groups or condensed bit groups from the ciphertext. If you want to be absolutely thorough, then all of the possible pairings of linear groups, condensed groups and hybrid groups need to be tested for correlation.

12.3.7 *Constructing an S-box*

Here are three methods for constructing an S-box with good non-linearity properties: the *Clock Method*, *SkipMix* and the *Meld8 Method.*

CLOCK METHOD

On a sheet of paper, arrange the letters of the alphabet evenly spaced clockwise around a large circle like the numerals on a clock face. Choose a starting letter and a second letter and draw a straight line from the first to the second. Then choose a third letter and draw a straight line from the second letter to the third letter, and so forth. Define the *span* of each line to be the number of letter positions you move forward in a clockwise direction from each letter to the next. For example, using the 26-letter alphabet, the span from C to D is 1, and the span from D to C is 25. To make the substitution as non-linear as possible, make each span a different length.

Here is how it can be done. For each letter of the alphabet, make a list of all the letters that can possibly follow it. When you begin, the list for each letter will contain every other letter, so you would have 26 lists of 25 letters apiece. Each time you choose a letter and add it to the mixed alphabet, delete that letter from all of the lists. If the span from the previous letter to that letter is s, then also delete any other letter whose span is s from all of the lists. For example, suppose you have added P and then R to the alphabet. The span from P to R is 2 positions, PQR. Therefore, in the A list you would delete C, in the B list you would delete D, in the C list you would delete E, and so forth.

Eventually some lists become empty. If there is only one letter whose list is empty, then that letter will have to be the last letter in your mixed alphabet. If there are two lists that are empty, then you have hit a dead end. Start over, or backtrack and try again. Each time you choose the next letter to add to the alphabet, choose a letter that has a short list, but not one with an empty list, unless that's the last letter left.

Historic aside

This heuristic is called Warnsdorff's Rule for H. C. von Warnsdorff, who used it in 1823 for constructing knight's tours on a chessboard. An improved version that looked 2 moves ahead was given by Ira Pohl of UC Santa Cruz circa 1965.

Here is an example of an alphabet constructed by the clock method:

```
CHBOYEQFXGJZAVSDWUIMLTKRNP
```

There are 5 different numberings that need to be tested to check the linearity of this alphabet: the N1 numbering, the first and second digits of the N2 numbering, and the first and second digits of the N3 numbering. Each of these must be correlated with the same 5 numberings for the standard Latin alphabet, making 25 correlations in total. You want all of the correlations to be between −.5 and +.5. Even better would be to have them all between −.333 and +.333.

Here are the results of those tests, the 25 correlation coefficients.

```
  0.26632   0.14935   0.23985   0.26830  -0.05641
  0.24891   0.16129   0.18143   0.26075  -0.20365
  0.04386  -0.01814   0.12363   0.02451   0.28782
  0.27645   0.15286   0.25324   0.27935  -0.07132
 -0.17949  -0.06788  -0.22614  -0.19359   0.23077
```

As you can see, all of the correlations are between −.226 and +.288, with 6 of them falling between −.1 and +.1, so the clock method is an excellent method for constructing non-linear substitutions.

There is no guarantee that you will get such good results every time. You still need to test for linearity.

SkipMix

Earlier in this section (12.3) I mentioned that an alphabet could be constructed using the SkipMix algorithm (section 5.2) with a pseudorandom number generator. In general, choosing an alphabet at random does not lead to good non-linearity properties, so let me describe the best way to use SkipMix in more detail. This time I will illustrate with a 256-character alphabet.

As always, you begin by listing the 256 available characters. Generate a random number in the range 1 to 256 to select the first character. Suppose that is position 54 in the alphabet. Take that character and then delete it from the list. Now there are 255 characters left. Generate a random number in the range 1 to 255. Suppose that number is 231. The next position would be 54+231 = 285. Since that is greater than 255, you subtract 255 to get 30. Take the next character from position 30, and delete it from the list. You have now taken 2 characters, and there are 254 characters left, so you generate a random number in the range 1 to 254. And so forth.

The resulting alphabet has good non-linearity properties because you generate the random number in a different range each time. This is loosely analogous to making all of the spans different in the clock method. Here is an example of a 26-letter alphabet generated by this version of SkipMix.

DRWBMEFHNJCQZXTOILVAGUYPSK

This can be tested the same way as the clock alphabet. The results are

0.26838	0.33037	-0.11239	0.25608	0.15897
0.11314	0.16129	-0.09071	0.09891	0.20365
0.31523	0.34471	-0.04670	0.31860	-0.08223
0.24521	0.31470	-0.12798	0.23347	0.15283
0.32308	0.20365	0.24670	0.31585	0.07692

These results are good. All of the correlations lie between −.127 and +.344, with 5 of them falling between −.1 and +.1, however, they are not as good as the clock method results.

MELD8 METHOD

This method is basically a special-purpose pseudorandom number generator. I will assume that the computer language you are using is able to operate with 64-bit integers. Depending on the way large integers are represented, you may be able to handle integers up to 2^{62} or 2^{63}. To be cautious, I will assume 2^{62}. The first step is to choose two numbers, a multiplier m of 24 to 26 bits, and a modulus N of 35 to 37 bits. The modulus must be a prime. It is best if m is a primitive root of N, however, since I have not explained what that is yet, just make both m and N prime.

Test your choices of m and N by multiplying them together. If the result is greater than 2^{62}, or about 4.611×10^{18}, then make either m or N smaller.

To generate the random numbers, start with any integer s between 2 and N−1 as the seed. Multiply the seed by m and reduce it modulo N to get the first pseudorandom number. Multiply the first random number by m and reduce it modulo N to get the second random number, and so forth. That gives you a sequence of random numbers in the range 1 to N−1. You will use those random numbers to generate the alphabet.

Suppose N has 36 bits. Number the bits of N from 1 to 36 starting at the high-order end. Take the first 8 bits of each random number, bits 1 to 8. Delete them from the high-order end, and exclusive-OR them with the next 8 bits, bits 9 to 16. This is the Meld8 operation. Its purpose is to make the sequence of characters non-linear. Here is an example:

```
1       8 9     16                        36    Bit positions
10100111 01101000 00101001 11010011 0001       36-bit random number
         10100111                              Meld8 operation
         11001111 00101001 11010011 0001       28-bit result
```

The next step is to use the 28-bit random number to generate a character. This depends on whether you are building a 26-character or a 256-character alphabet. For a 26-character alphabet, multiply this number by 26 and divide by 2^{28} (or shift right 28 places) to get the next character. For a 256-character alphabet, just divide by 2^{20}, or shift right 20 places to get the next character.

Start with an empty alphabet and add one character at a time. If this is a new character, you append it to the alphabet. If this is a duplicate, you discard it. Since you are not taking consecutive random numbers, this also works to make the alphabet non-linear. Here is an example of such an alphabet generated with the modulus $N = 90392754973$, the multiplier $m = 23165801$ and the seed $s = 217934$:

ZEJBIRAFHGPYLVQWUTXOKSCNMD

The resulting correlation coefficients are

```
 0.13983   0.17650  -0.06716   0.14196  -0.04615
 0.16745   0.16129   0.01814   0.17084  -0.06788
-0.04934   0.03629  -0.17033  -0.05174   0.04112
 0.12566   0.17084  -0.08441   0.12821  -0.05094
 0.20000   0.06788   0.26726   0.19359   0.07692
```

The correlations range from −.170 to +.267 with 11 of them falling between −.1 and +.1. This is the best of the three examples, however, it would be folly to conclude that Meld8 was the best method based on a single example of each technique. Always test.

12.3.8 *S-box with a key*

In section 12.3.7 we dealt with S-boxes that had no key. They performed a simple substitution. When a key is used, the S-box performs a general polyalphabetic substitution (section 5.8.3). The S-box can be considered a tableau, with each row being one mixed alphabet. The S-box can be generated by constructing each of these mixed alphabets using the clock method, SkipMix or Meld8, or by any combination of methods.

If you use the clock method or SkipMix, use a different random seed each time. If you use Meld8, it is acceptable to use the same modulus each time, but use a different seed and a different multiplier. As always, test, test, test. Your objective is to avoid any linear relationship between the combination of the key and the plaintext with the ciphertext. If the results are subpar, meaning that a lot of the correlation coefficients are outside the range −.35 to +.35, it might take no more than replacing one row or swapping two rows of the tableau to fix the problem.

12.4 *Diffusion*

Shannon's second property is *diffusion*. The idea is that every bit or byte of the ciphertext should depend on every bit or byte of both the plaintext and the key.

To illustrate this, let's go back to Delastelle's bifid cipher, described in section 9.6. To refresh your memory, the bifid is a block cipher based on a Polybius square. If the block size is S, then each letter of the message is replaced by two base-5 digits and the digits are written vertically into a 2×S grid and read out horizontally. Then the pairs of digits are turned back into letters using the same or a different Polybius square.

Let the block size be 7, and call the letters in the plaintext block A,B,C,D,E,F,G. Let the digits representing these letters be aa,bb,cc,dd,ee,ff,gg. I have left off the subscripts because it does not matter here which digit is first and which digit is second. The block will then be

```
abcdefg    abcdefg    Write in vertically
abcdefg    abcdefg    Read out horizontally
```

When the letters are read out of the block horizontally you get ab,cd,ef,ga,bc,de,fg. Notice that each letter of the ciphertext depends on two letters of the plaintext. The first ciphertext letter depends on A and B, the second letter depends on C and D, and so forth.

At this point I need to introduce a special notation to show which plaintext letters each ciphertext letter depends on. If a ciphertext letter depends on plaintext letters P, Q and R it gets designated pqr. Using this notation, if you enciphered the letters A,B,C,D,E,F,G a second time, the block would look like this:

```
ab cd ef ga bc de fg
ab cd ef ga bc de fg
```

Reading these letters out horizontally you get abcd, efga, bcde, fgab, cdef, gabc, defg. Since the order of the digits is irrelevant, this could also be given as abcd, aefg, bcde, abfg, cdef, abcg, defg. After two encipherments, each ciphertext letter depends on four plaintext letters.

If you encipher this block a third time using the bifid cipher, every ciphertext letter will depend on all 7 of the plaintext characters. For the bifid cipher with block size 7, three rounds of encipherment are required to get full diffusion. If the block size were 9, 11, 13 or 15, four rounds of encipherment would be needed. (Recall that the block size in a bifid cipher should always be odd.)

In general, to test diffusion you begin with each plaintext character or bit depending on just itself. If the cipher operates on whole bytes or characters, you trace diffusion on the basis of bytes. If it operates on hexadecimal digits, digits in some other base, or individual bits, you trace the diffusion on the basis of those units. For the bifid cipher, the units are the Polybius square coordinates, or base-5 digits.

To track the diffusion, you need a way to represent the set of plaintext units and key units as they trickle through the rounds of the block cipher. When there are just a few plaintext units, as there were for the bifid example, it works well just to list them. When the number of plaintext, key and ciphertext units is larger, a more compact representation may be necessary. A good strategy is to make a binary vector for each ciphertext unit. Let's call this a *dependency vector*. Each element of the dependency vector will correspond to one input, either a plaintext or key unit. The dependency element will have the value 1 if the ciphertext unit depends on that input unit, and 0 otherwise.

When two or more input units are combined to form an output unit, their dependency vectors are ORed together to form the dependency vector for the output unit. To illustrate how this works, let's go through the bifid example again using this notation. Initially each character depends only on itself. This is represented by the vectors

        1000000 0100000 0010000 0001000 0000100 0000010 0000001

After the first application of the bifid cipher, each resulting letter depends on two of the plaintext letters. The first round 1 output byte depends on the first two round 1 input bytes, so you OR their dependency vectors together **1000000V0100000** to get **1100000**. The second output letter depends on the third and fourth plaintext letters, so you OR their dependency vectors together **0010000V0001000** to get **0011000**, and so forth. The output of the first round is represented by the vectors

        1100000 0011000 0000110 1000001 0110000 0001100 0000011

After the second round of bifid, the first output letter depends on the first and second outputs from the first round, so you OR their dependency vectors together **1100000V0011000** to get **1111000**. The second output letter depends on the third and fourth outputs from the first round, so you OR their dependency vectors together **0000110V1000001** to get **1000111**, and so on. After two rounds of bifid each letter depends on four plaintext letters, represented as

        1111000 1000111 0111100 1100011 0011110 1110001 0001111

After the third round of bifid, each output letter depends on all 7 of the round 1 plaintext letters, for example, `1111000V1000111` is `1111111`. The output of the third round is represented as

`1111111  1111111  1111111  1111111  1111111  1111111  1111111`

Any time an S-box is encountered, the dependency vectors for the output units are formed by ORing together the vectors for each input that contributes to that output. Let's look at some other situations that may occur in a block cipher.

If two units are exclusive-ORed together, the dependency vector for the output unit is formed by ORing together the vectors for each input. The same is done when several units are combined using any combining function, such as **sxor** or **madd**.

When the units of a block are transposed using a key, each output unit is then dependent on all of the units of that key, so the vectors for the key are ORed with the vector for each output unit.

Suppose an S-box is created by mixing its alphabet using a key. If the S-box is fixed or static, say by embedding it in hardware, then the mixing key is no longer involved. If the S-box is variable, perhaps mixed using a different key for each encryption, then the output units of that S-box are dependent on all of the units of that key. The vectors for the key are ORed with the vector for each output unit.

It is possible to express diffusion as a single number. Form a matrix from the dependency vectors for all of the output units. Each row in the matrix will represent one output unit from the final round of the block cipher. Each column in the matrix will represent one input unit, either key or plaintext. The measure of diffusion, or *diffusion index*, is the portion of these elements in this matrix that are 1. If the matrix elements are all 1, then there is complete diffusion and the diffusion index is 1. If the S-boxes are non-linear and the key is long, this is an indication that the block cipher is strong.

Diffusion is not the full story. There are valid cipher designs where the diffusion index may be less than 1, yet the cipher is strong. One example is a block cipher where there is a separate key for each round. The keys from the early rounds may achieve full diffusion, but the keys from the late rounds, and particularly from the final round, may not. However, if the keys that are fully diffused contain your target number of bits, then the cipher may well be secure, and the partly diffused keys are just insurance.

Here is an example that may help illustrate how the cipher can be strong even when there is less than full diffusion. Consider a cipher with 12 rounds, where each round has an independent 24-bit key. In this cipher it takes 6 rounds to achieve full diffusion, so after 6 rounds the plaintext and the first-round key are fully diffused. After 7 rounds the plaintext and the first- and second-round keys are fully diffused. And so forth. After 12 rounds, the plaintext and the keys for the first 7 rounds are fully diffused. With 24-bit round keys, that is 168 bits of fully diffused keys. If your target strength is 128 key bits, then you have already surpassed your goal. The partially diffused keys from rounds 8 through 12 are a bonus.

12.5   *Saturation*

Confusion and diffusion are two pillars of the security framework. To make certain that the block cipher is on a firm foundation I propose adding a third pillar, which I call *saturation*. Diffusion only indicates whether or not a given output unit depends on a given input unit. Saturation measures how much a given output unit depends on a given input unit. I show how to calculate a *saturation index* analogous to the diffusion index of the preceding section. Saturation is essentially a more refined version of diffusion. With diffusion, the dependency can have a value of only 0 or 1, but with saturation, the dependency can have any non-negative value.

Here is the quick explanation of saturation. Suppose block cipher X consists of several rounds of substitution. In each round, each byte of the message is exclusive-ORed with one byte of the key, and then a simple substitution is done on the result. Suppose that a different byte of the key is used in each round, so that every byte of the key gets used one time for each byte of the block. Cipher X would have little saturation because each byte of the ciphertext depends on each byte of the key only once. To get higher saturation, each output byte would need to depend on each input byte multiple times.

Another example might help make this clearer. Imagine a cipher that operates on a 48-bit block, viewed as six 8-bit bytes. Each round of this cipher consists of two steps: (1) the block is cycled left one bit position, so the leftmost bit moves to the rightmost position, then (2) a simple substitution S is performed on each of the 8 bytes. After the first round, the first output byte C1 depends on the last 7 bits of the first plaintext byte and the first bit of the second plaintext byte, like this:

P1	P2	P3	P4	P5	P6	Plaintext, 6 bytes
aaaaaaaa	bbbbbbbb	cccccccc	dddddddd	eeeeeeee	ffffffff	Plaintext, 48 bits
<u>aaaaaaab</u>	bbbbbbbc	<u>cccccccd</u>	ddddddde	<u>eeeeeeef</u>	fffffffa	Cycle left 1 bit
C1	C2	C3	C4	C5	C6	After substitution

Ciphertext character C1 depends on 7 bits from plaintext byte P1 and 1 bit from plaintext byte P2. It makes sense to say that C1 depends 7/8 on P1 and 1/8 on P2.

Let's look at the second round. Call the second-round outputs D1 ... D6.

C1	C2	C3	C4	C5	C6	Round 2 inputs
gggggggg	hhhhhhhh	iiiiiiii	jjjjjjjj	kkkkkkkk	llllllll	48 bits
<u>ggggggggh</u>	hhhhhhhi	<u>iiiiiiij</u>	jjjjjjjk	<u>kkkkkkkl</u>	llllllllg	Cycle left 1 bit
D1	D2	D3	D4	D5	D6	After substitution

Ciphertext character D1 depends 7/8 on C1 and 1/8 on C2. Here C1 depends 7/8 on P1 and 1/8 on P2, while C2 depends 7/8 on P2 and 1/8 on P3. The only contribution that P1 makes to D1 is from C1. Since D1 depends 7/8 on C1 and C1 depends 7/8 on

P1, it is reasonable to say **D1** depends 49/64 on **P1**. For the same reason **D1** depends 1/64 on **P3**. Let's call these figures *saturation coefficients*, and call this calculation, when there is a single dependency, the *S1 calculation*.

A diagram might make the configuration clearer.

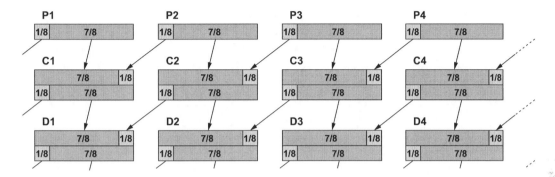

What about **P2**? **D1** gets contributions from **P2** via both **C1** and **C2**. It might seem reasonable to say that **D1** is 7/8 dependent on **C1**, which is 1/8 dependent on **P2**, and 1/8 dependent on **C2**, which is 7/8 dependent on **P2**, and conclude that **D1** is $(7/8)(1/8)+(1/8)(7/8) = 14/64$ dependent on **P2**. That is a reasonable calculation, and it leads to a more sophisticated version of diffusion. However, using that calculation, the total contributions to any given unit will always total 1. The total never grows. If this calculation is repeated many times, all these diffusion figures will converge to 1/48. That is not what the concept of saturation is trying to capture. Saturation should increase whenever a unit receives contributions from several different sources.

When a unit gets multiple contributions, a different calculation is used to determine the saturation coefficient. Suppose the two sources have saturation coefficients a and b, with $a \geq b$. Then the combined saturation coefficient is a+b/2. If there are three contributing saturation coefficients a, b and c, with $a \geq b \geq c$, the combined saturation coefficient is a+b/2+c/4. In each case the component saturation coefficients are sorted in descending order, $a \geq b \geq c \geq d \geq e....$ To recap, when multiple saturation coefficients are combined, the results are as follows:

> 2 coefficients: a + b/2,
>
> 3 coefficients: a + b/2 + c/4,
>
> 4 coefficients: a + b/2 + c/4 + d/8,
>
> 5 coefficients: a + b/2 + c/4 + d/8 + e/16,
>
> · · ·
>
> 8 coefficients: a + b/2 + c/4 + d/8 + e/16 + f/32 + g/64 + h/128.
>
> · · ·

Let's call this calculation, when there are multiple dependencies, the *S2 calculation*. Use the S1 calculation for a single source, and use the S2 calculation for multiple sources.

The S2 calculation may seem ad hoc, perhaps even eccentric, but it has just the right properties for a saturation computation. First, it always increases when a unit depends on more than 1 predecessor. This is because $a+b/2$ is always greater than a. Second, it does not increase too fast. At most, the saturation coefficients can double from one round to the next. This is because $a+a/2+a/4+...+a/2^n < 2a$ for any n. For example, $1+1/2+1/4+1/8 = 15/8 = 1.875$.

In the present case, **D1** depending on **P2**, the contributing coefficients are 7/8 and 1/8, so the combined coefficient is $7/8+(1/8)/2 = 15/16$. The saturation coefficients for an output unit can be formed into a vector, just as the diffusion numbers were. The resulting saturation vector for **D1** is thus (49/64, 15/16, 1/64, 0, 0, 0). These vectors can then be formed into a saturation matrix. The saturation index is the smallest coefficient in the saturation matrix.

Let's look at a more realistic cipher, one that has been proposed in the literature and has probably been used in practice. I will call it *SFlip*, short for *Substitute and Flip*. It is a cousin of poly triple flip in section 11.7.5. If you don't remember what flipping a matrix means, look at section 11.7. The SFlip cipher works on a block of 8 bytes and consists of several rounds plus a finishing step. Each round has two steps. (1) A simple substitution is applied to the eight 8-bit bytes. (2) The 8×8 matrix of bits is flipped. The finishing step is, again, substituting for each of the 8-bit bytes.

The 8×8 matrix of bits requires a 64×64 dependency matrix. This is too large to display legibly, so I will show the cipher in miniature. Let's use a 3×3 matrix of bits, which has a 9×9 dependency matrix. This cipher will be analyzed twice, once using diffusion, and once using saturation. Diffusion first. Let's start by labeling the bits in the text block and in the dependency matrix, like so:

```
abc       abcdefghi
def
ghi
```

Before the first round each bit depends only on itself, so the dependency matrix looks like (1). After the first-round substitution, each bit is dependent on all 3 bits in its character, so the dependency matrix looks like (2). After the first-round flip, the dependency matrix looks like (3). After the second-round substitution, the dependency matrix looks like (4).

```
     (1)          (2)          (3)          (4)
 a00000000    abc000000    abc000000    abcdefghi
 0b0000000    abc000000    000def000    abcdefghi
 00c000000    abc000000    000000ghi    abcdefghi
 000d00000    000def000    abc000000    abcdefghi
 0000e0000    000def000    000def000    abcdefghi
 00000f000    000def000    000000ghi    abcdefghi
 000000g00    000000ghi    abc000000    abcdefghi
 0000000h0    000000ghi    000def000    abcdefghi
 000000000i   000000ghi    000000ghi    abcdefghi
```

In other words, at this point every bit of the ciphertext depends on every bit of the plaintext. This will remain true after the second-round flip and again after the final substitution. So, if we relied only on the dependency calculation, we would conclude that this cipher would be secure after only two rounds. This is untrue. Adi Shamir has shown that two rounds are insufficient.

Now let's analyze the SFlip cipher using the saturation index. After the first-round substitution, each bit of the ciphertext depends 1/3 on each of the 3 corresponding plaintext bits. The saturation matrix will look like (5). After the first-round flip, the saturation matrix will look like (6).

(5)	(6)
⅓⅓⅓000000	⅓⅓⅓000000
⅓⅓⅓000000	000⅓⅓⅓000
⅓⅓⅓000000	000000⅓⅓⅓
000⅓⅓⅓000	⅓⅓⅓000000
000⅓⅓⅓000	000⅓⅓⅓000
000⅓⅓⅓000	000000⅓⅓⅓
000000⅓⅓⅓	⅓⅓⅓000000
000000⅓⅓⅓	000⅓⅓⅓000
000000⅓⅓⅓	000000⅓⅓⅓

The second-round substitution makes each bit of the output dependent on all 9 bits of the first-round plaintext. The saturation coefficient is $1/3 + (1/3)/2 + (1/3)/4 = 1/3 + 1/6 + 1/12 = 7/12$, about .583. Every element in the saturation matrix will have this value, so the saturation index will be $7/12$. The target value for the saturation index is 1, although you could set it higher if you wanted greater certainty. Here is what the saturation index will be after several rounds.

Round	3×3	8×8
1	.333	.125
2	.583	.249
3	1.021	.496
4	1.786	.988
5	3.126	1.969

So 3 rounds are sufficient for the 3×3 cipher, but 5 rounds are necessary for the 8×8 cipher.

Let's now turn to some of the other situations where an output unit depends on one or more input units.

When an S-box has both plaintext and key inputs, say p plaintext units and k key units, the dependency for each of its output units will be $1/(p+k)$. For example, if the inputs are 6 key bits and 4 plaintext bits, the dependency will be $1/10$ for each output bit. If the inputs to the S-box are themselves dependent on earlier inputs, then either the S1 or the S2 calculation should be used, as appropriate, to compute the saturation index.

Similarly, if two or more units are combined using exclusive-OR or some other combining function, the dependency is $1/n$ for n total inputs. The calculation of the saturation index is the same as for an S-box with the same inputs.

When a key of k bits is used for a transposition, each output unit of the transposition has a dependency of $1/k$ on each of the key bits, and a dependency of 1 on the plaintext input. Suppose that a plaintext character p is moved from position a to position b by the transposition. The saturation vector for p after the transposition will be the same as the saturation vector for p before the transposition, except in those columns corresponding to the bits of the transposition key. In those columns the saturation coefficient will be determined by either the S1 or S2 calculation.

Here is an example. Suppose that t is one of the bits of the transposition key. If p had no dependency on t before the transposition, that is, there was a 0 in column t of its saturation vector, then after the transposition the value in column t will be $1/k$. On the other hand, if p were already dependent on the key bit t, then the saturation coefficient would be determined by the S2 calculation. If the coefficient in column t were x, then after the transposition the saturation coefficient in column t would be $x+1/2k$ if $x \geq 1/k$, or $1/k+x/2$ if $x < 1/k$.

When a key of k bits has been used to mix the alphabet or tableau for a substitution step, the mixed alphabet or tableau has a dependency of $1/k$ on each bit of that key. Each time a character is substituted using that alphabet, the output character gets an additional dependency of $1/k$ on each bit of the key. This is combined with the dependencies of the input character (and substitution key, if any) using either the S1 or S2 calculation to get the saturation coefficient for the output character.

Summary

A block cipher will be unbreakable in practice if it adheres to *all* of these rules:

1 It has a sufficiently large block size. The current standard is 16 characters or 128 bits.

2 It has a sufficiently large key. The current standard is 128 to 256 bits. The key must be at least as large as the block, and preferably larger.

3 Either it uses fixed S-boxes that are strongly non-linear, or it uses variable substitution tables that are well-mixed using a large key.

4 The saturation index is at least 1.

As always, be conservative. Build yourself a safe margin of error. Make the key longer and use more rounds than required because computers get faster and new attacks get discovered continually. In particular, you could set your target for the saturation index higher than 1, perhaps 2, 3 or even 5.

13
Stream ciphers

This chapter covers
- Pseudorandom number generators
- Functions for combining the random numbers with the message
- Generating true random numbers
- Hash functions

Stream ciphers are the opposite of block ciphers. Characters in stream ciphers are enciphered as they are encountered, usually one at a time. The basic concept is to take a stream of message characters and combine them with a stream of key characters to produce a stream of ciphertext characters. This paradigm is well suited for continuous operation where messages are continuously enciphered and transmitted at one end, and continuously received and deciphered at the other end, with no pauses, or only momentary pauses to change keys.

We have already seen a few stream ciphers. The autokey and running key ciphers in section 5.9, the rotor machines of section 5.10, Huffman substitution in section 10.4, and the ciphers based on text compression in section 10.7 are all examples of stream ciphers.

13.1   *Combining functions*

The most common types of stream ciphers use one key unit to encipher one plaintext unit. The units are usually letters or bytes, but hex digits or even bits can also be used. The key unit is combined with the plaintext unit using essentially the same combining functions that were used with the ripple ciphers in section 11.8, but using a key unit in place of the preceding unit. Here are the analogous methods, with x_n being the nth unit of the message, k_n being the nth unit of the key, A and B being simple substitutions and P being a general polyalphabetic substitution. The substitutions A, B and P should be mixed using keys, not fixed or built in.

xor	Exclusive-OR	x_n is replaced by $k_n{\oplus}x_n$.
sxor	Substitute and exclusive-OR	There are three variations: x_n may be replaced by $A(k_n){\oplus}x_n$, or $k_n{\oplus}B(x_n)$ or $A(k_n){\oplus}B(x_n)$. That is, you may substitute for either k_n or x_n or both. (The use of $A(k_n)$ instead of k_n can serve to prevent Emily from recovering the pseudorandom sequence when there is known plaintext.)
xors	Exclusive-OR and substitute	x_n is replaced by $A(k_n{\oplus}x_n)$.
add	Add	x_n is replaced by k_n+x_n. As always, addition is modulo the size of the alphabet.
madd	Multiply and add	Also called *linear replacement*. x_n is replaced by pk_n+x_n, or k_n+qx_n, or pk_n+qx_n, where p may be any integer and q may be any odd integer. (If you are using an alphabet whose size is different from 256, q must be coprime to that size.)
sadd	Substitute and add	x_n is replaced by $A(k_n)+x_n$, or $k_n+B(x_n)$ or $A(k_n)+B(x_n)$.
adds	Add and substitute	x_n is replaced by $A(k_n+x_n)$.
poly	General polyalphabetic substitution	x_n is replaced by $P(k_n, x_n)$.

Since **xor** or **sxor** may leak information about its operands, I recommend using **xors** instead, so that the simple substitution is done after the exclusive-OR to mask the waveforms, namely $A(k_n{\oplus}x_n)$.

A stream cipher may also use one or more previous characters to encipher the current character. There are many combinations. One example is $P(k_n{\oplus}x_{n-i}, x_n)$ for some small integer i. This cipher requires an initialization vector to encipher the first i characters. A stream cipher can also be strengthened by switching among several combining functions, for example periodically switching among the 3 forms of **sadd**, or of **madd**, or by periodically varying the multipliers p and q in **madd**.

13.2 *Random numbers*

The long keys used in the stream ciphers listed in the previous table can come from several sources:

- They may be a list of numbers repeated as many times as needed. This was the standard method from the 16th through the 19th centuries.

- They may be generated by a mathematical process. Such numbers are called *pseudorandom* because they eventually repeat, as opposed to true random numbers, which never repeat. The process that generates these numbers is called a *pseudorandom number generator* (PRNG).

- They may be true random numbers that might be generated by some physical process such as gamma rays from an exploding star. Such processes are usually too slow for cryptographic needs, so these random numbers are usually collected over time and stored in the computer for later use. That is, they may be collected continuously and used only when you need to send a message.

Books and articles about cryptography often state that you need true random numbers for a secure cipher. They point out that it has been mathematically proven that a one-time pad using a true random key cannot be broken. This is certainly true, provided that for every plaintext unit p and every ciphertext unit c there is a key unit k that transforms p into c, that is, $S(k,p) = c$. A true random key is sufficient to make the one-time pad unbreakable. However, as everyone who has studied logic knows, a condition can be sufficient without being necessary, and vice versa.

For example, for an integer to be a prime it is necessary for it to be greater than 1. That is necessary but not sufficient, since 4 is an integer greater than 1 but is not a prime. For an integer to be composite it is sufficient for it to be a square greater than 1. That is sufficient but not necessary, since 6 is composite but not a square.

Requiring that the key for a one-time pad must be true random is overkill. To make the one-time pad unbreakable the key must be *unpredictable*, also called *cryptographically secure*. With a true random key, no matter how many key units Emily may know, it is impossible for her to determine any other units. With an unpredictable key it only needs to be computationally infeasible for Emily to determine any other units. Specifically, the amount of work Emily needs to do to determine another key unit must be greater than 2^k, where k is your chosen key size in bits. It is true that when the key stream is only pseudorandom you can no longer prove that the cipher is unbreakable, but this has no practical significance.

Later in this chapter I will describe several schemes to make pseudorandom number generators cryptographically secure, and point out one secure-looking scheme that is insecure, namely CG5, described in section 13.13.

All of the stream ciphers listed earlier can utilize pseudorandom number generators to produce the key stream, so let's look at a variety of PRNGs, starting with some classical methods from the 1950s. These generators use a small initial value, called the *seed* or the *initial state*, and some simple mathematical function that generates the next state from the current state, called the *state vector*. Common generating functions are addition, multiplication and exclusive-OR. These generators are still in wide use today because of their great speed and easy implementation.

Each generator produces a sequence of integers that eventually repeats after a period that depends on the seed. It is possible to have a repeating sequence of numbers that never repeats the seed, like 1,2,3,4,5,4,5,4,5,4,5, ... , but none of the generators in this book have that behavior. The period is limited by the size of the state vector. For example, a generator whose state vector is three 31-bit integers cannot have a period longer than 2^{93}.

13.3 *Multiplicative congruential generator*

A *multiplicative congruential PRNG* uses two parameters, a multiplier m and a modulus p. Starting from the seed s, the sequence of pseudorandom numbers x_n is generated by the recurrence

$$x_0 = s,$$
$$x_n = mx_{n-1} \bmod p \text{ for } n = 1, 2, 3, \ldots$$

In other words, to get the next pseudorandom number you multiply the previous number by m and then take the residue modulo p. The seed may be any integer 1,2,3,...,p−1. The modulus p is almost always chosen to be a prime because primes produce the longest periods. The choice of p often depends on the size of the registers in the computer you are using. For 32-bit registers, the prime 2^{31}−1, which is 2,147,483,647, is a common choice. The first PRNG in this class was published by Berkeley number theorist Derrick H. Lehmer (not to be confused with Berkeley number theorist Derrick N. Lehmer, his father) in 1949.

The multiplier m must be chosen carefully. The period of a multiplicative congruential generator can be any integer that evenly divides p−1. Since p is a prime, and presumably far greater than 2, p−1 will be even, so a very poor choice of m, such as p−1, could give a period of 2. A multiplier that has the maximum possible period, namely p−1, is called a *primitive root* of p. That means m, m^2, m^3, ... , m^{p-1} all have different residues modulo p. For a multiplicative congruential generator, it is best to make m a primitive root in order to get the longest possible period.

Fortunately, this is easy to do. On average just slightly less than 3/8 of the numbers in the range 2 to p−2 are primitive roots of p. The exact ratio is called *Artin's constant*, for Emil Artin, an Austrian mathematician who escaped from Nazi Germany in 1937 and finished his career at Princeton. Its value is about .373956. If you can factor p−1, then it is easy to test whether a given multiplier m is a primitive root of p. We know that the period of m must divide p−1, so begin by factoring p−1. Suppose the distinct prime factors of p−1 are a, b, c and d. Then you only need to test $m^{(p-1)/a}$ (mod p), $m^{(p-1)/b}$ (mod p), $m^{(p-1)/c}$ (mod p) and $m^{(p-1)/d}$ (mod p). If none of these are 1, then m is a primitive root. For example, if p = 13, the distinct prime factors of p–1 = 12 are 2 and 3, so you only need to test exponents 12/2 and 12/3, that is, m^6 and m^4. For example, 5 is not a primitive root of 13 because $5^4 = 625 \equiv 1 \bmod 13$.

There are efficient ways to compute m^x by taking successive squares. For example, to compute m^{21} you could successively compute m^2, m^4, m^8, m^{16}, m^{20}, m^{21} using just 6 multiplications. You can get further efficiencies by using these products to compute the next power. For example, if the next value to test were m^{37}, you could compute m^{32}, m^{36}, m^{37} using just 3 multiplications. It is more efficient to calculate the residue modulo p after each multiplication than to compute the huge number m^{21} and take the residue at the end. There are more sophisticated schemes that use somewhat fewer multiplications, perhaps 10% to 15% fewer, but if you are doing this only a few times the extra effort is not worthwhile.

If you are using a multiplicative congruential PRNG it is important to know that it is the magnitude of each number that shows random properties. To convert an output R of the generator to an integer in the range 0 to N–1, the correct calculation is ⌊RN/p⌋, where ⌊x⌋, read "floor of x," means x rounded down to the next lower integer. For example, ⌊27⌋ is 27, and ⌊27.999⌋ is 27. The expression ⌊RN/p⌋ is slightly biased toward smaller values, that is, it will yield lower numbers slightly more frequently than higher numbers. However, when p is much larger than N, say p > 1000N, this will not matter for cryptographic purposes.

Historical aside

Incidentally, the notation ⌊x⌋ and the corresponding ⌈x⌉ (read "ceil of x," which means x rounded up to the next higher integer, so ⌈27.001⌉ is 28) were both invented by Kenneth Iverson, the creator of the APL programming language, in 1962. APL was the first interactive programming language. Computer users today take interactivity for granted. You press a key or click the mouse, and the computer does something. They do not realize that this concept had to be invented. Before then, the standard model for computing was that you ran a card deck through a card reader, the computer printed the results, and a few hours later you got a sheaf of paper.

WARNING   Do not use (R mod N) as your random number. R mod N can be severely biased toward low values. For example, if the modulus p = 11 and N = 7, then the 11 possible values of (R mod 7) are 0, 1, 2, 3, 4, 5, 6, 0, 1, 2, 3, so that 0, 1, 2 and 3 are generated twice as often as 4, 5 or 6.

A multiplicative congruential generator will have decent random properties as long as $m > \sqrt{p}$. It is best if the multiplicative inverse $m' > \sqrt{p}$ as well. This means that the number of bits in m needs to be at least half the number of bits in p. You want p to be as large as possible so the generator will have a long period, and you want m to be large so the generator is random. How big can you go? The sizes of m and p are limited by the size of the registers in the computer. If you go bigger than one register, you will pay a penalty in speed.

Each pseudorandom number x_n is generated by multiplying the previous number x_{n-1} by m. The number x_{n-1} can have as many bits as p, so if p has b bits, x_{n-1} can also have b bits. Since m must have at least b/2 bits, the product mx_{n-1} can have 3b/2 bits. If the register size is 63 bits, then b can be at most 2/3 of 63, namely 42, which means m could have at most 21 bits. It is better to make m larger than $\sqrt{p}$. A reasonable trade-off is for m to be 25 bits and for p to be 38 bits. That lets the period be up to 2^{38}.

The property that is required to make the generator unpredictable is that the generated units have equal or uniform frequencies, pairs of units have equal frequencies, triples and quadruples have equal frequencies, and so forth. As a practical matter, you need not go beyond octuples or at most dectuples of bytes. If you want to be absolutely dead sure, take your desired key size and divide by the size of the generated units. For example, if your key size is 128 bits and the PRNG generates 4-bit hex digits, then you might require the n-tuples to have equal frequencies for all values of n up through 32. (Anyone who does that is clearly obsessive-compulsive and should seek treatment.) Even for 4-bit random numbers it is neither necessary nor useful to go beyond 16-tuples or at most 20-tuples (sexdectuples or vigintuples), that is, 64 or 80 bits.

Emily would need more than 2^{64} or 2^{80} bytes, respectively, of known plaintext to exploit these uneven frequencies. Even if Sandra never changed her key, it is implausible that Emily could ever accumulate that much material. To put this in perspective, suppose there were a satellite that beamed down telemetry at the rate of 1 MB per second. Suppose, further, that it beams this data down using two different key streams simultaneously, and that Emily has the key for one of them. Even though she is getting plaintext/ciphertext pairs at the rate of 1 MB per second, it would still take about 585,000 years for her to collect 2^{64} bytes. Even with 1000 satellites all using the same keys, it would take 585 years.

If the frequencies of the n-tuples are equal for every value of n, then your generator is true random. You have found a mathematical algorithm for generating true random numbers. Congratulations. Go collect your Fields Medal.

In order to have the tuple frequencies equal up through n-tuples it is generally necessary for the generator to have seeds that are themselves at least n-tuples. For multiplicative congruential generators the single-unit and pair frequencies are uniform, but the triples frequencies are never uniform, and the n-tuple frequencies for $n > 3$ are very far from uniform; most of these frequencies are 0.

Cracking a multiplicative congruential cipher is straightforward if you have a few characters of known plaintext, and if the cipher makes it easy to determine the random output from a plaintext/ciphertext pair, that is, if the combining function is **xor**, **add** or **madd**. For example, if the cipher exclusive-ORs the key byte to the plaintext byte to get the ciphertext byte, then all Emily needs to do is exclusive-OR the plaintext byte with the ciphertext byte to get the key byte.

If the generator has a 31-bit or 32-bit modulus, it is feasible for Emily to try all 2^{31} or 2^{32} values for the seed, even on a PC. The known plaintext characters would be used merely for verification. If the modulus is larger, say 48 or 64 bits, then the first 2 or 4 known plaintext characters are used to limit the search range. The first random output limits the current state of the generator to a narrow range, 1/256 of the total range. A second known plaintext character gives a second output that limits the state to 1/256 of that range, and so forth.

Thus a single multiplicative congruential generator is not cryptographically secure. It is possible to use a much larger modulus, using big-integer multiplication techniques like Karatsuba or Toom-Cook, but that would sacrifice the high speed of this class of generator. There are faster ways to produce cryptographically secure generators, so this book will not cover big-integer multiplication methods.

13.4 Linear congruential generator

Linear congruential generators are an extension of the multiplicative congruential generators. They add a linear constant term c to the recurrence formula. Starting from the seed s, the sequence of pseudorandom numbers x_n is generated by the recurrence

$$x_0 = s,$$
$$x_n = (mx_{n-1}+c) \bmod P \text{ for } n = 1,2,3, \dots$$

In other words, to get the next pseudorandom number you multiply the previous number by m, add c and then take the residue of that sum modulo P. The seed may be any integer 1, 2, 3, ... , P–1. The generator will have the longest possible period when these three conditions are met:

1 c is relatively prime to P,
2 For every prime p that is a factor of P, m has the form pk+1, and
3 If P is a multiple of 4, then m has the form 4k+1,

where k may be any integer. These are called the *Hull-Dobell conditions* for T. E. Hull and A. R. Dobell of the University of British Columbia, who published them in 1962.

For example, suppose P = 30, which is 2×3×5. Then m–1 must be a multiple of 2, of 3 and of 5. In other words, m must be 1. So, if s = 1 and c = 7, the pseudorandom sequence would be 1, 8, 15, 22, 29, ... This is an arithmetic progression, and not at all random. For this reason, the modulus P is usually chosen to be a power of a prime, most commonly 2. It is difficult to find values for m, c and P that produce good random properties.

There is, however, one good use for linear congruential generators. If you want to produce a generator that has an extremely long period, you can add the outputs of two or more linear congruential generators whose moduli are powers of different primes to get a generator with good random properties and a period equal to the product of those moduli. For example, suppose you added the outputs of the following three PRNGs. I chose the 3 moduli to be as large as possible, yet still fit in a 32-bit machine word, and I chose the multipliers and constants to satisfy the Hull-Dobell conditions. Other than that, I chose them arbitrarily.

$$x_{n+1} = (10000001x_n + 1234567) \bmod 2^{31},$$

$$y_{n+1} = (1212121y_n + 7654321) \bmod 3^{19},$$

$$z_{n+1} = (43214321z_n + 777777) \bmod 5^{13}.$$

Let $w_n = (x_n + y_n + z_n) \bmod 2^{31}$. Select the high-order byte of w_n by shifting it right 23 places, namely $v_n = w_n / 2^{23}$. The v_n sequence will have good random properties provided that (1) at least one of the three multipliers, and its multiplicative inverse, are greater than the square root of its corresponding modulus, and (2) neither of the other two multipliers is 1 or P–1. The period of the v_n sequence is $2^{31} 3^{19} 5^{13} = 3.0468 \times 10^{27}$.

13.5 *Chained exclusive-OR generator*

The simplest *chained exclusive-OR generator* operates on a string of bits, like 10111. The basic idea is to exclusive-OR the first bit to the last bit, delete the first bit, and append the new bit to the end of the string, that is, $x_i = x_{i-1} \oplus x_{i-n}$. Since there are 2^n possible values for an n-bit string, and since the all-zero string produces a sequence of all zeros, the longest possible period for a chained exclusive-OR generator is $2^n - 1$. Let's look at a small example using 3-bit strings.

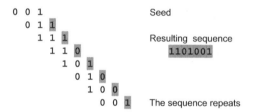

After 7 steps the initial string 001 repeats, so the period of this generator is 7. This is called a *full period* generator. The chained exclusive-OR generator has a full period when n is 2, 3, 4, 6, 7, 15 or 22. For $n = 37$ the generator comes within .00057% of being full period. That is, 99.99943% of all 37-bit values form one large cycle, and the rest belong to shorter cycles. For some purposes $n = 37$ may be a good choice. For most values of n there are several repeating sequences of bits, some short and some long. Their combined lengths total $2^n - 1$. You can talk about *the* period only for full period generators. Otherwise there will be multiple cycles that may have differing lengths.

Suppose that you need a generator with a period longer than 2^{22}, and you are unwilling to take a .00057% chance of getting a short cycle. What can you do? One option is to try other generating functions. Instead of $x_i = x_{i-1} \oplus x_{i-n}$, try the recurrence relation $x_i = x_{i-1} \oplus x_{i-j} \oplus x_{i-k} \oplus x_{i-n}$ for values of j and k such that $1 < j < k < n$. There is a good chance that some of these generators will have a full period. Note, however, that $x_i = x_{i-1} \oplus x_{i-j} \oplus x_{i-n}$, which has 3 terms, can never produce a full period generator. There must be an even number of terms.

Whichever generator you choose, the result is a sequence of bits. To get a pseudorandom sequence of bytes, take the bits in groups of 8, that is, bits 1 to 8, bits 9 to 16, bits 17 to 24, and so forth. That requires generating 8 bits for every byte. There is a faster way. Instead of exclusive-ORing single bits, exclusive-OR a byte at a time. In effect, you are running 8 separate single-bit generators in parallel. That way, you get a whole byte in one operation each time. If your programming language supports it, you could use full 32-bit words and get 4 bytes at a time.

Any of the combining functions listed in section 13.1 can be used to combine the pseudorandom stream with the plaintext to form a cipher. If Sandra chooses the combining function **xor**, **add** or **madd**, then the cipher will be easy for Emily to solve, provided she has enough known plaintext. She can easily determine the random outputs corresponding to the plaintext characters. This lets her reconstruct a section of the key stream. This section can be extended both ahead and back to reconstruct the entire key stream merely by exclusive-ORing.

There is a trick that Sandra can use to confound Emily. Suppose that the generator produces a sequence of 32-bit words, which Sandra carves up into four separate bytes. Instead of always starting with the high-order bit, Sandra could start from a different position each time. Equivalently, Sandra could shift the 32-bit word cyclically, either left or right, by a varying number of bit positions. For example, ABCDEF cyclically shifted left 2 positions gives CDEFAB. The lengths of the shifts could be a repeating sequence of numbers in the range 0 to 31. This way, Emily cannot match up successive outputs of the generator to reconstruct the key stream.

13.6 Chained addition generator

Chained addition generators, also called *lagged Fibonacci* generators, are similar to chained exclusive-OR generators, except that they use addition instead of exclusive-OR. The addition is understood to be modulo 2^w, where w is the word size in bits, $x_i = (x_{i-1} + x_{i-n}) \bmod 2^w$. Typical values for w are 15, 31 and 63 using signed addition, or 16, 32 and 64 using unsigned addition. Another way of looking at the mod 2^w operation is that the carry out of the high-order bit is ignored.

Because addition produces carries from one bit position to the next-higher bit position, the period of the higher bit is twice the period of the lower bit. The period of the low-order bit in each word is the same as the period of an exclusive-OR generator with the same seeds. That is because addition is the same as exclusive-OR with a carry. If the period of the low-order bit in a chained addition generator is P, then the period of the high-order bit is $2^{w-1}P$.

Chained additive generators are an easy way to get a longer period for little additional effort. Just find a chained exclusive-OR generator with a long period, preferably a full period, and then expand it from single-bit width to full word width.

Like the multiplicative congruential generators, the most random part of the sequence of outputs is the high-order end. For a sequence of pseudorandom bytes, use only the high-order 8 bits of each word.

Once again, you may use any of the combining functions from section 13.1 to combine the pseudorandom stream with the plaintext to form a cipher.

13.7 *Shift and XOR generator*

Another class of PRNGs is the shift and exclusive-OR generators invented by George Marsaglia of Florida State University. Marsaglia is best known for developing the Diehard suite of random number tests. These generators use two operators that work on integers.

- << *Shift left.* For example, 80<<2 shifts the integer 80 left 2 bit positions to give the value 320.
- >> *Shift right.* For example, 80>>2 shifts the integer 80 right 2 bit positions to give the value 20.

Bits that are shifted out of the high- or low-order end of the computer word are lost. For example, 25>>1 is 12, not 12.5. These operations contrast with the cyclic shifts <<< and >>>, where the bits that are shifted out of one end of the computer word are placed at the opposite end. For example, if the hex digits in a 32-bit computer word are 12345678, then 12345678<<<4 gives 23456781, and 12345678>>>12 gives 67812345, because each hex digit has 4 bits. If the word is contained within a larger computer register, the unused bits need to be zeroed out.

There are several different generators in this class. The lengths and directions of the shifts must be carefully chosen so that the generator will have a long period. Following are two examples of the *Xorshift* generator devised by Marsaglia. They have long periods, and strong random properties, although they fail some of the more sensitive randomness tests. Each generator uses 3 shift and exclusive-OR steps in a left-right-left pattern to produce the next number in the sequence. The variable y is used to hold intermediate values. Any positive integer is a qualified seed.

32-bit generator. Period $2^{32}-1$.
$$y = x_n \oplus (x_n << 13)$$
$$y = y \oplus (y >> 17)$$
$$x_{n+1} = y \oplus (y << 5)$$

64-bit generator. Period $2^{64}-1$.
$$y = x_n \oplus (x_n << 13)$$
$$y = y \oplus (y >> 7)$$
$$x_{n+1} = y \oplus (y << 17)$$

13.8   *FRand*

FRand, for Fast Random generator, is my own creation. FRand uses an array of S binary words of width W, that is, it uses the low-order W bits of each word in the array to hold an unsigned integer value. The period depends on the values of S and W. I have found that W = 29 works best, and that S = 40 and S = 64 give extremely long periods. The array of seeds can be viewed as a 40×29 matrix of bits. Each row is one seed, and each column represents one bit position within each seed word.

For S = 40 the period is $2^{1160}-2^{40}$, about 1.566×10^{349}, for qualified seeds. A seed is *qualified* if at least one of the 40 seed words is neither all-zeros nor all-ones. This generator has a weakness. If the seed array contains almost entirely zeros, then the generator may produce dozens or even hundreds of successive outputs that are mostly zero. In the extreme case, when the seed array contains 1159 zeros and only 1 one, it will take at least 1120 cycles before there is at least one 1 in every column.

It is best if the initial seeds contain plenty of ones and zeros in a random-looking pattern. One way to get a suitable seed array is to take a mnemonic or numerical key expressed in UTF-8 code, and hash it into an 1160-bit value. A suitable hash function is

$$x_1 = x_1 + 19x_{40} \bmod 2^{29},$$
$$x_n = x_n + 19x_{n-1} \bmod 2^{29} \text{ for } n = 2, 3, 4, \ldots, 40, \text{ (Initial full pass)}$$
$$x_1 = x_1 + 19x_{40} \bmod 2^{29},$$
$$x_n = x_n + 19x_{n-1} \bmod 2^{29} \text{ for } n = 2, 3, 4, \ldots, 10. \text{ (Partial second pass)}$$

Once the generator has been seeded, the pseudorandom sequence can be generated by the recurrence formula. The recurrence formula for this generator uses an index or placemarker, n.

$$n = n + 1$$
$$x_n = x_n \oplus x_{n-1}$$

At the end of each pass through the seed array, when n = 40, the index is reset to 1, and the next pseudorandom number is generated by $x_1 = (x_1 \oplus x_{40}) \ggg 1$. That is, the first 29-bit word x_1 is cyclically shifted right one bit position.

This pseudorandom sequence passes many of the randomness tests, but it falls far short of being cryptographically secure. To produce a secure sequence, the trick is to take each successive output byte from a different part of the 29-bit word. The pseudorandom sequence itself can be used to select these locations. Suppose the next 3 pseudorandom outputs are a, b and c. Take s = a mod 25. If s is in the range 0 to 21, then shift b right by s positions and take the low-order 8 bits. In this case only a and b are generated. c will be generated for the next pseudorandom number. If s > 21, then shifting s positions right would leave fewer than 8 bits. In this case discard a and take s = b mod 22. Shift c right by s positions and take the low-order 8 bits as the random output. To put this algebraically,

$$s = x_{n+1} \bmod 25$$
$$\text{if } s \leq 21 \text{ then}$$
$$\qquad r = (x_{n+2} >> s) \text{ and FF} \quad \text{(the low-order 8 bits of r)}$$
$$\text{else}$$
$$\qquad s = x_{n+2} \bmod 22$$
$$\qquad r = (x_{n+3} >> s) \text{ and FF} \quad \text{(the low-order 8 bits of r)}$$

This process uses an average of 2.12 pseudorandom outputs to produce each secure key byte. That way, the key byte comes from the even-numbered outputs about half the time, and from the odd-numbered outputs half the time. The generator switches back and forth from odd to even and back about once every 8 cycles in an irregular pattern.

13.9 *Mersenne Twister*

Mersenne Twister has the longest period of any class of PRNG. It was developed in 1997 by Makoto Matsumoto and Takuji Nishimura of Hiroshima University. It is named for French theologian Marin Mersenne, 1588–1648, widely known for his work on primes of the form 2^n-1, and important for disseminating the works of Galileo, Descartes, Pascal and Fermat, among others.

The twister has decent random properties, although it fails some randomness tests. It is far slower than the other random number generators described in this chapter. Its main importance is its humongous period, the Mersenne prime $2^{19937}-1$, which was discovered in 1971 by Bryant Tuckerman of IBM Research, Yorktown, NY. IBM Research was so proud of this discovery that it put "$2^{19937}-1$ is prime" on its stationery and its postage meter imprint.

Like FRand, Mersenne Twister suffers from the drawback that if the initial state is mostly zero, it could take many cycles to become random-looking. With the Mersenne Twister it is common to require 10,000 or even 50,000 startup cycles before beginning to use the outputs. By contrast, the FRand package has a function that initializes the generator without needing any startup cycles.

13.10 *Linear feedback shift registers*

The *linear feedback shift register* (LFSR) is the darling of electrical engineers, because it is so simple to implement as a digital circuit. The LFSR uses an array of bits $x_1, x_2, \ldots, x_n$. The next bit is generated by exclusive-ORing several of the preceding bits, for example

$$x_{n+1} = x_n \oplus x_{n-i} \oplus x_{n-j} \oplus x_{n-k}$$

using 3 feedbacks. The number of feedbacks, of course, need not be 3, but an odd number of feedbacks will typically give a much longer period than an even number of feedbacks.

This LFSR would have k+1 bit positions, assuming i < j < k. After each new bit is generated the low-order bit is shifted out, and the new bit is placed in the high-order position, so the register always contains the most recent k+1 bits of the pseudorandom sequence.

An obvious disadvantage of using an LFSR is that they are slow because they require 8 cycles to produce each pseudorandom output byte. LFSRs are also the weakest of the pseudorandom generating functions because they are entirely linear. If Emily has some known plaintext, and if she can determine the corresponding key bits, then she can reconstruct the entire pseudorandom sequence just by solving a set of linear equations, which is easy. Emily can determine the key bits if Sandra has used **xor**, **add** or **madd** for the combining function.

For this reason, the pseudorandom outputs are usually run through a non-linear substitution before combining them with the plaintext. This can be done two ways, bitwise or bytewise. Non-linear bitwise substitutions are possible because at every cycle there are k+1 bits accessible in the register. The bits that are used as inputs to the non-linear function are called *taps*, and may be taken from anywhere in the register. Using these non-linear functions makes it harder for Emily to determine the key bits.

One suitable non-linear function is the *majority function*. This function has the value 1 if the majority of its input bits are 1, and the value 0 otherwise. For the case with 3 input bits A, B and C the majority function is ABVBCVCA, where V is the Boolean OR function. The majority function is defined for any odd number of inputs, 3, 5, 7, ... One elaboration of this idea is to use 9 taps and three 3-bit majority function circuits. Three of the 9 bits go into each circuit. Then the 3 output bits are run through a fourth majority circuit.

Bytewise substitutions are inherent if the combining function is **sxor**, **sadd** or **poly**. Construction of these non-linear substitutions is discussed at length in section 12.3. It is possible to combine bitwise and bytewise substitutions. Each of the 8 bits in an output byte is generated using the taps and a non-linear bit function, then the 8 single-bit outputs of those circuits are fed into the bytewise substitution.

Let's look at what Emily must do to break an LFSR cipher. Suppose that Sandra is using a 40-bit hardware LFSR with taps at bit positions 3, 6 and 9 feeding into a majority function circuit, M, and that she has naively used **xor** as the combining function. Suppose further that Emily has a few characters of known plaintext, and therefore knows a sequence of the output bits. For each known bit, the 3 LFSR tap positions that feed into M are narrowed to only 4 of the 8 possible values. If the bit is 0, then the 3 taps must be 000, 001, 010 or 100. If the bit is 1, the 3 taps must be 011, 101, 110 or 111.

After 4 cycles, 12 bits have fed into the 3 taps, so there are $4^4 = 256$ possible combinations for the 12 bits. This is a great reduction from $2^{12} = 4096$ combinations. Even better, from Emily's standpoint, the bit that was originally at position 3 is now at position 6, and the bit that was originally at position 6 has now moved to position 9. This means that some of the 12-bit combinations can be eliminated. The number of combinations that can be removed depends on the sequence of output bits. If the first and fourth output bits are the same, fewer combinations are eliminated. If they are different, more combinations are eliminated. Each additional known output bit gives a further reduction in the number of possible combinations for the bits in the shift register.

An example may help. Suppose Sandra is using a 40-bit LFSR with 3 taps that feed into the majority function to produce each output bit. Also suppose Emily knows all the details of the device and knows that the message came from General Headquarters, where all the messages begin *GHQ*. That gives her 24 bits of known plaintext. If she exclusive-ORs these 24 bits with the corresponding bits of the ciphertext, she gets 24 output bits from the device. For each of these output bits there are 4 possible 3-bit input combinations that produce the known value. That makes 72 bits of possible bit values at the 3 tap positions. Since the bits in the LFSR shift one position every cycle, these bit combinations will overlap, so the total number of combinations can be continually reduced.

What should Sandra learn from this brief analysis? (1) Make the shift register big, preferably at least 128 bits. (2) Space the taps far apart. (3) Do not space the taps evenly. Here 3, 6, 9 was an exceptionally poor choice. (4) Use a combining function that makes it hard for the opponent to determine the key bits. Do not use **xor**, **add** or **madd** for the combining function. Better choices are **xors** and **adds**, but the best choice is **poly**.

13.11 *Estimating the period*

If you are a crypto hobbyist, you may want to try designing your own pseudorandom generator. This book will not cover how to test a PRNG, which is a big subject, but let's look at how you can estimate the period of your generator. The method depends on the size of the state vector (section 13.2).

If the state vector is small, say 31 bits, you can just run your generator for 2^{31} cycles and see when it repeats. Unfortunately, it is possible that the initial seed will never repeat. There is a trick to handle that possibility. Make 2 copies of your PRNG and initialize them with the same seed, S. Then run the first copy 1 step at a time, and run the second copy 2 steps at a time. Suppose you find after 3000 cycles that the 2 copies produce the same state vector. That means $R_{3000} = R_{6000}$, so the period of your generator is 3000, at least with the seed S.

If the state vector is larger, say 64 bits, it is not feasible to run your generator for potentially 2^{64} cycles. You can still estimate the period by using sampling. Make a table of, say, $T = 1,000,000$ entries. Entry N in this table will hold the number of the cycle when your generator produces the value N. Initially, set all of the entries in this table to zero, since no values have been produced yet. Choose a seed in the range 1 to T–1 and run your generator for, perhaps, G = 1,000,000,000 cycles. On each cycle, if the value N that is produced is less than T, you record the cycle number in table entry N. If the entry is not zero, then you have a repeat, and that tells you the period. For example, if the value 12795 was produced on cycle 33,000 and again on cycle 73,500, then the period of your generator for that seed is 73500–33000 = 40500.

If you do not find any repeats, then you can estimate the period by seeing how many of the T values were produced. If E entries in the table are nonzero, then the portion of entries that are produced is E/T. Since you ran the generator for G cycles, the estimated period is G/(E/T) = GT/E.

As we saw with the chained digit generator (section 4.5.1), a generator may have several different cycles, some long and some short. You should make several estimates for the period of your generator, using different seeds. One good strategy is first to use the seed 1. For the second seed, use the lowest value that was not generated by the first seed. For the third seed, use the lowest value that was not generated by the first or second seed. You can do this by making the table cumulative. Do not reset it to zero between estimation runs. If the estimates for the period are consistent over, say, 20 to 100 such runs, then you can have confidence that your generator has a long period for most seeds.

13.12 Strengthening a generator

One method for strengthening a PRNG is using a *selection generator* that separates the operation of generating the numbers from the operation of selecting the numbers. This can be done by keeping N numbers in an array, say 32, 64 or 256 numbers. Each number in the array should be the size of the desired random outputs. For example, if you want to generate random bytes, the array should contain 8-bit numbers. The PRNG is first run for N cycles to produce the initial numbers, which are put into the array in the order that they are generated. Then the PRNG is restarted with a new seed. The generator is then used to produce a sequence of pseudorandom numbers in the range 1 to N. Each of these numbers is used to select an element of the array. This element becomes the next pseudorandom output. The selected array element then gets replaced by a new pseudorandom number using the PRNG.

This means that the first, third, fifth, ... random numbers are used for selection, while the second, fourth, sixth, ... numbers are used to replace the numbers in the array. It may be convenient to use two separate copies of the PRNG with different seeds, however, this will not increase the period. A better strategy is to use two different generators whose periods are coprime. Then the period of the combined generator is the product of their periods. For example, if the numbers are generated by a multiplicative congruential generator with period $2^{31}-1$, and the numbers are selected by a linear congruential generator with period 2^{31}, then the period of the combined generator is $2^{62}-2^{31}$, or 4.612×10^{18}.

The period of 4.612×10^{18} is long enough for cryptographic work, but the selection generator is still not cryptographically secure. That is because Emily can brute-force the selector sequence and try all 2^{31} possible seeds. With enough known plaintext this could give her a sequence of outputs from the first generator, which would be enough to solve it.

There are several possible remedies. (1) Use a combining function like **xors**, **adds** or **poly,** which makes it hard for Emily to determine the random outputs. (2) Make the selector generator bigger, say 63 bits instead of 31 bits. (3) Make the seed for the selector generator bigger, for example by making the multiplier and/or the additive constant part of the seed, namely m and c in the generating function $x_{n+1} = (mx_n+c)$ mod P. (4) Use the techniques in the following section to construct a selector with a longer period.

13.13 *Combining generators*

Pseudorandom number generators can be combined in a variety of ways to get longer periods or better randomness properties, or to become cryptographically secure. These improvements usually go hand in hand. You do not trade one off to achieve the other. If you increase the period, you will normally improve the randomness at the same time. There are two classes of combined generators, fixed combinations and variable combinations.

FIXED COMBINATIONS

In fixed combinations, there are several PRNGs, preferably with periods that are coprime. These could be multiplicative congruential, linear congruential or Xorshift generators. The outputs of these generators can be combined bitwise or bytewise. One bitwise method is to take a fixed set of bits from each generator and input them into some combining function. For example, the high-order bit could be taken from each of 8 generators, or the two high-order bits could be taken from each of 4 generators. These 8 bits would then be input into a highly non-linear substitution. The substitution step prevents Emily from separating the outputs from each of the generators and solving them individually.

One bytewise method is to take the high-order byte from each generator and combine them by adding them modulo 256, or by exclusive-ORing them. Two generators may be combined by multiplying their outputs and taking the middle 8 bits of the product. Another technique is to take a linear combination such as $(a_1x_1+a_2x_2+a_3x_3+a_4x_4)$ mod 256, where x_1, x_2, x_3 and x_4 are the 8-bit outputs taken from four PRNGs, and the four coefficients a_1, a_2, a_3 and a_4 may be any odd integers from 1 to 255. These coefficients may be different for each message.

For example, the four PRNGs could be multiplicative congruential generators using the prime modulus $2^{31}-1$ with 4 different, but fixed, multipliers. The four 31-bit seeds plus the four 7-bit coefficients make a combined seed of 152 bits.

Three PRNGs can be combined by using the >>> cyclic shift operation (section 13.7). With a 32-bit unsigned generator, the 32-bit outputs can be combined using $x_1 + (x_2 >>> 11) + (x_3 >>> 21)$ mod 2^{32}. The optimal shift amounts are 1/3 and 2/3 of the 32-bit register size. If you wish to use more than 3 generators, make the shift amounts as uniform as possible. For example, with 5 generators the shift amounts should be 1/5, 2/5, 3/5 and 4/5 of the word size, rounded to the nearest integer.

Another fixed generator, *CyGen*, combines two generators, C and G, by cyclic shifting. C may be any size, but G should be either 32 bits or 64 bits. On each cycle 5 or 6 bits, respectively, are taken from C to get the shift amount. The output from G is then cycled left that number of positions to get the output from CyGen. This makes it infeasible for Emily to reconstruct G from a sequence of its outputs.

You are not restricted to linear combinations. For example, 3 generators can be combined using $x_n + y_n z_n$, or $x_n + y_n^2 + z_n z_{n-1} z_{n-3}$, or ... At least one term in the sum should be linear. The possibilities are endless, and, of course, you can switch around among multiple methods.

VARIABLE COMBINATIONS

One example of a variable combination is the selection generator shown in section 13.11. However, let me start this section with a cautionary tale. Here is a combined generator, *CG5*, that seems to be surefire secure, but is not.

The combined generator CG5 uses 5 multiplicative congruential generators, each with a different multiplier and different 31-bit prime modulus. Call these generators G0, G1, G2, G3 and SEL. (Alternatively, SEL could be a linear congruential or Xorshift generator with a 2^{31} period.) The production generators G0 through G3 are used to produce pseudorandom numbers, and the selection generator SEL is used to select which of G0–G3 to use to produce the next pseudorandom output. Specifically, the high-order 2 bits of SEL determine which among G0–G3 to use. Suppose SEL generates 10, which selects G2. Then the G2 generator is run for 1 cycle, and its output becomes the next output for CG5. The combined generator will have a period of about 2^{155} and will have good random properties ... but will not be cryptographically secure. Here's why:

Assume that Emily has sufficient known plaintext, and consider the first 17 outputs from CG5. At least 5 of these 17 outputs must have been produced by the same generator. (If 4 generators produced at most 4 outputs each, then there could be at most 16 outputs, not 17.) There are only 6188 ways that 5 items can be chosen out of 17. Emily can try all of them. This gives about 1.33×10^{13} combinations of placement plus seed to test, however, this can be reduced substantially. Emily knows the high-order 8 bits of each of the 5 chosen outputs. Instead of starting with the first of the 17 outputs, she should start with the first of the 5 chosen outputs. Then she needs to try only 2^{23} values instead of 2^{31} values. That cuts her work down to a manageable 5.19×10^{10} combinations. The CG5 combined generator is not safe.

Let's look at a safer generator. I will call it *Gen5*. Once more, the combined generator uses 5 multiplicative congruential generators, each with a different multiplier and different 31-bit prime modulus. The moduli and multipliers are fixed, and chosen to have good random properties. This time let's call the generators G1, G2, G4, G8 and SEL. Only the 4 high-order bits of the selector SEL are used. In this 4-bit number, a 1 in the first bit means select G1, a 1 in the second bit selects G2, a 1 in the third bit will select G4 and a 1 in the fourth bit selects G8. Whenever fewer than two generators are selected, SEL is run for another cycle to generate a new selection. Only 11 out of the 16 possible 4-bit output values from SEL are used, so SEL is run for an additional cycle $5/16$ of the time, two additional cycles $25/256$ of the time, and so forth.

When two or more generators are selected, they are each run for 1 cycle, and their outputs are added together modulo 2^{31} to produce the Gen5 pseudorandom output. The generators that were not selected are not run, so that the 4 generators run asynchronously. This output is slightly biased toward lower numbers, but not nearly enough for Emily to exploit. If you are concerned about this bias, either (1) discard the high-order bit and use high-order bits 2 through 9 of the sum as the output byte, or (2) use the Meld8 operation (section 12.3.7). That is, form the output byte from the Gen5 generator by exclusive-ORing the high-order 8 bits of the sum with the second 8 bits of the sum, namely exclusive-OR bits 1 to 8 with bits 9 to 16.

*Emily can no longer isolate any of the four generators. It might appear feasible for Emily to separate out one of the 6 pairs Gi+Gj, where i and j can be 1, 2, 4 or 8. Such a pair could be treated like a single generator, and then Gi could be separated from Gj later. Let's look at that approach first. In order to solve for the seeds of both Gi and Gj, at least 9 random outputs from Gen5 are needed. Since each of these pairings occurs only $1/11$ of the time, Emily may have to look at 89 or more message characters. This is because, simply by chance, the 5 combinations of 3 or 4 generators may occur more frequently than the 6 combinations of 2 generators.

There are about 6.356×10^{11} possible placements for 9 items out of 89, so it is more efficient for Emily simply to try all of the approximately $2^{31} = 2.147 \times 10^9$ seeds for the SEL generator. This lets Emily find the next 10 positions for all 6 of the Gi+Gj pairs. It also lets her count how many times Gi and Gj have been used up to each of those occurrences. For example, suppose that G2+G4 occurs at the 14th cycle of Gen5. It may happen that among those 14 cycles, G2 was used in 6 of those cycles and G4 was used in 9 of those cycles. So now Emily knows the value of the 6th output of G2 plus the 9th output of G4.

If Emily can put together 10 such output values for, say, G2+G4 then she can determine the seeds of those two generators in about $2^{31+31-8} = 2^{54} = 1.801 \times 10^{16}$ trials. This must be done for each of the approximately 2^{31} seeds of SEL, so the total work is about $2^{85} = 3.869 \times 10^{25}$. This is a huge improvement over the 2^{155} trials that a brute-force solution to Gen5 would require, but it falls far short of the goal of 2^{128} trials. This generator is rated Nine.**

Now we are ready for the coup de grâce. This is a souped-up version of Gen5, which I will call *GenX*. There are two parts to GenX, a pseudorandom number generator and a cipher. The GenX PRNG will generate a sequence of 10-bit pseudorandom outputs, and the cipher will combine the key bytes k_n with the message bytes x_n to produce the ciphertext. This will push the cipher beyond the 128-bit key size.

The GenX generator is just an extended version of the Gen5 generator. It uses four production generators, G1, G2, G4 and G8, and a selection generator, SEL. The high-order 4 bits of SEL are used to select some combination of 2 to 4 production generators. The selected production generators are run for one cycle, and their outputs are added modulo 2^{31} to produce a sum, G. The high-order 10 bits of G are exclusive-ORed with the next 10 bits of G to produce the 10-bit output. The 10-bit output is divided into an 8-bit key byte k_n and a 2-bit control c_n.

The GenX cipher combines the key byte k_n with the message byte x_n according to the control c_n using a well-mixed keyed substitution, S. The control bits c_n determine which combining function is used for each plaintext byte. One possible way to interpret the 2 control bits is

00 x_n is replaced by $S(k_n)+x_n$,
01 x_n is replaced by $k_n+S(x_n)$,
10 x_n is replaced by $S(k_n)+S(x_n)$,
11 x_n is replaced by $S(k_n+x_n)$.

All sums are modulo 256. Cipher GenX is rated Ten. The keys for this cipher are the five 31-bit seeds for G1, G2, G4, G8 and SEL plus the key for mixing the substitution S, for example a SkipMix key.

13.14 *True random numbers*

All of the techniques for generating random numbers that have been discussed so far in this chapter produce pseudorandom numbers. Every book I have ever seen that discusses random numbers repeats the belief that it is impossible to produce true random numbers using software. This is because they are limiting themselves to a too-narrow range of possible methods. In this section I will present a workable method for producing true random numbers in bulk using software.

All the methods in the literature for producing true random numbers depend on physical phenomena like cosmic rays, thermal noise, vibration, nuclear decay, and so forth. These methods are much too slow for cryptographic purposes.

Instead, you can produce true random numbers by a 3-step process. (1) Build up a large body of true random numbers taken from nature. (2) Make their probability distribution uniform. (3) Generate the random numbers by selecting and combining numbers from this corpus. The next few sections will detail how these steps can be done.

Nature is full of randomness. The shape, coloration and position of every leaf on every plant and tree on earth is random. They are the result of winds and breezes, sunlight filtering through the foliage, nutrients flowing up from the roots, raindrops and hailstones that have struck the foliage, insects that have chewed it, birds, squirrels, ground tremors, and many other factors. Every wave on every ocean, every plant and rock in every desert, every ripple on every river, every cloud, every shell on every beach is random in size, shape, colors, location, orientation and sometimes velocity.

Some of this randomness can be captured simply by photographing these locales. You don't even need to leave home. Just take a handful of popcorn and drop it on a patterned surface. You can also use your own photos of people you know and places you have been. There are photos you have downloaded from websites and emails. There are hundreds more that have been placed on your computer by the operating system and by apps you have. There are billions more photos you can find using a web browser. As an experiment, I invented a pseudo-word, ZRMWKNV, and searched for images. I got over 6,000 search results with pictures related to ZRMWKNV, and some of those sites contained hundreds of images.

13.14.1 Lagged linear addition

Each such image file contains lots of randomness, particularly if the resolution is high, but the distribution of byte values is far from uniform, and far from independent. The distribution can be flattened out by using *lagged linear addition*, treating the whole image file, including the headers, as one long byte string of length L. Here is an example:

$$x_n = (7x_n + 31x_{n-40} + 73x_{n-1581}) \bmod 256 \text{ for } n = 1, 2, 3, \ldots, L.$$
$$x_n = (27x_n + 231x_{n-137} + 109x_{n-10051}) \bmod 256 \text{ for } n = 1, 2, 3, \ldots, L.$$
$$x_n = (241x_n + 19x_{n-64} + 165x_{n-2517}) \bmod 256 \text{ for } n = 1, 2, 3, \ldots, L.$$

The subscripts wrap around, as always. Three passes, as shown, are sufficient, but feel free to use more. You don't want the frequencies too uniform, because that would no longer be random. If you want to use a streamlined version, like $x_n = (x_n + x_{n-179}) \bmod 256$, note that five passes are needed. Be sure to use a different lag on each pass.

There is nothing special about these coefficients, 7, 31, et al. I picked them arbitrarily. They may be any odd integers from 1 to 255. For each pass the lags 40, 1581, etc. should be chosen so that one lag is considerably larger than the other. Small step, big step. One idea is to make the smaller lag about $\sqrt[3]{L}$ and the larger lag around about $\sqrt[3]{L^2}$. For example, if the image file is 1,000,000 bytes, you might make the lags about 100 and about 10,000, respectively. The smaller lag could be chosen between 50 and 200, and the larger lag could be between 5000 and 20,000. Following the lagged linear addition with a keyed simple substitution makes it harder for Emily to reconstruct the image file.

13.14.2 Layering images

Another way to construct a true random sequence is to take two images and layer them one over the other using some combining function such as **xor** or **add** (see section 13.1). A good method would be to perform one pass of lagged linear addition on each image before combining, and a final pass after they have been combined.

Three images can be combined bit by bit using the non-linear majority function (section 13.10). Again, I suggest one pass of lagged linear addition on each image before combining, and a final pass after they have been combined. This method can be used even when none of the three images are the same size. Align one short image to begin at the same point as the largest image, and the other short image to end at the same point as the longest image, like this:

Where only two of the images overlap, add them bytewise modulo 256. Where all three images overlap, combine them bitwise using the majority function, or use a linear combination modulo 256, such as $c_n = (113x_n + 57y_n + 225z_n) \bmod 256$. The coefficients may be any odd integers from 1 to 255.

An alternative approach to aligning the images is to extend the short images by repeating them. In the example, the x image has 22 bytes and the y image has 33 bytes. The x image can be extended to 33 bytes by repeating the first 11 bytes of x. This way, the majority function can be used in all 33 byte positions. In practice these images would have millions of bytes.

13.15 Refreshing the random bytes

Good. Now we have a table, T, of several million true random bytes. They are true random because, if Emily had all but one of the bytes in T, that would not enable her to determine the one missing byte. Both Sandra and Riva have a copy. What then? Surely we cannot repeat this process every time we want to send a message.

One way to utilize T is to partition it into keys for use with a block cipher. One million random bytes can make 62,500 keys of 128 bits each. Eventually the million bytes will get used up. If Sandra is using a strong block cipher, perhaps that does not matter. She can use keys repeatedly, as long as Emily cannot tell which messages have been enciphered with the same key. Of course, Sandra cannot reuse keys with a stream cipher.

Suppose Sandra does not wish to take the risk of reusing keys. One solution is for her to refresh the list of random numbers. Sandra could layer on another image, but that means Riva also must have a copy of the same image. That could be managed if the image comes from a website to which both Sandra and Riva have access. This could be a good strategy if there is a high risk that transmitted keys could be intercepted.

A different method is to refresh T using lagged linear addition (section 13.14.1). Call the refreshed table T_1. Now Sandra needs to transmit only the 9 coefficients and the 6 lags, and she has another 62,500 keys to use. Assuming 1 byte for each coefficient and 2 bytes for each lag, Sandra needs to transmit only 21 bytes to generate T_1. Then to select a key for a message, only the position of this message key within T_1 is needed. Two bytes are sufficient for this because all of the positions are multiples of

16. When T_1 is exhausted, a new set of coefficients and lags can be used to construct T_2, and so forth.

In sections 13.5 and 13.6, linear functions were used to assure a long period for the generator. Here there is no period, so there is no such constraint. Some non-linear functions that can be used are

$$x_n = (ax_n + bx_{n-i} + S(x_{n-j})) \bmod 256 \text{ for } n = 1, 2, 3, \ldots, L,$$
$$x_n = (ax_n + bx_{n-i} + E(x_{n-j}x_{n-k})) \bmod 256 \text{ for } n = 1, 2, 3, \ldots, L.$$

Here the subscripts wrap around, a and b are odd integers from 1 to 255, and i, j and k are integers between 1 and L–1. S can be either a fixed non-linear substitution or a variable key-mixed substitution. The function $E(x)$ is defined as

$$E(x) = x + (x >> 8) + (x >> 16) + (x >> 24) + \ldots = \lfloor 256x/255 \rfloor.$$

When you take $E(x_{n-j}x_{n-k}) \bmod 256$ you are essentially adding the individual bytes of $x_{n-j}x_{n-k}$. This is stronger than just using $x_{n-j}x_{n-k}$ because $x_{n-j}x_{n-k}$ is even 3/4 of the time.

Alternatively, Sandra could obtain keys from T by taking 1 byte, skipping 3, taking the next byte, skipping 2, taking 2 bytes, skipping 4, and so forth in some periodic sequence. The skips can be small, so 2 or 3 skips could be coded in one key byte. It is possible that if Emily obtained the random source T she could determine the sequence of small skips. To prevent this, skipping could be combined with adding a sequence of numbers to the selected bytes modulo 256, also periodically. It is safest if the number of skips and the number of additives are coprime, say 12 skips and 11 additives. Using this method, each message key would use 2 bytes for the starting point, 6 bytes to encode the 12 skips, plus the 11 additives, for a total of 20 bytes, or 160 bits. This method could be called *Skip & Add*.

It is essential in this type of system that it is infeasible for Emily to reconstruct T. For example, Emily might, over time, acquire the plaintexts for numerous messages and recover their keys. If she also knows the placement of these keys within T, perhaps because Sandra transmits the location to Riva with each message, then she may be able to reconstruct portions of T. For this reason, T itself should never be used for keys. T should be retained to construct T_1, T_2, ... which then may be carved up into message keys. Retaining T protects Sandra and Riva in case any of the T_i are lost or garbled. T could be called the *base* key and T_1, T_2, ... the *derived* keys.

Even if Emily could somehow reconstruct T_1 or T_2, she cannot go backward to recover T, because T is true random. If Emily tried all possible combinations of coefficients and lags, there is nothing that would indicate which among those quintillions of strings is the correct random string, T.

13.16 Synchronized key streams

In Secret Key cryptography Sandra and Riva must use the same key. Usually that means either (1) the key is enciphered and transmitted with the message, or (2) they have a list of keys, and choose each key from the list based on the date, time of day, or some other external factor. There is a third method that is unique to stream ciphers.

Sandra and Riva could use synchronized key streams. This means that Sandra and Riva both continuously generate the same key streams. When Sandra enciphers a message, she begins with the next key byte in her key stream, which must also be the next key byte in Riva's key stream. When Riva receives the message, she must begin from the same point in the key stream. Sandra and Riva must begin generating from the same initial seed at precisely the same time. The synchronized method is most useful when there is a direct cable from Sandra to Riva, or a line-of-sight tower-to-tower connection, or when both receive over-the-air broadcasts from the same transmitter. It is well-suited for transmitting digitized speech in close quarters.

If the messages are being sent over a network that has significant delays at the nodes or relay points, particularly packet-switched networks where portions of a message may arrive by different paths and must be reassembled at the receiving end, it is necessary for the sender to provide a time stamp for the start of transmission, say in a message header.

Since it takes time for Sandra to encipher the message and time for the message to travel from Sandra to Riva, it might seem that Riva would have to generate the random keys a few microseconds later than Sandra. By the same token, when Riva sends a message to Sandra, Sandra would have to generate the keys a few microseconds later than Riva.

There are several ways out of this impasse. One method would be for Sandra to begin messages only at specific cycles in the pseudorandom stream. For example, Sandra might begin a message only at every 100,000th cycle. Then when Riva receives a message at, say, cycle 123,456,789,123, she knows that the key started at cycle 123,456,700,000. If the message were received closer to an even multiple of 100,000, say cycle 123,456,701,234, Riva could try 123,456,700,000 and 123,456,600,000. Riva would need to store the last two sets of 100,000 pseudorandom numbers. The figure 100,000 cycles can be adjusted up or down according to the speed of the PRNG and the transmission time between the two parties.

There is one issue left to tackle, namely how Riva can detect the start and end of each enciphered message. If the communications channel has an idle state where neither zeros nor ones are being transmitted, then there is no problem. Let the channel idle between messages. Otherwise, let's assume that the channel emits a steady stream of zeros whenever it is idle. In this case, you add an extra 1 bit before and after the message, like enclosing the message in quotation marks, and you require that a minimum of 64 zeros must be transmitted before the next message can begin. The odds of 64 zeros happening by chance within a legitimate message are negligible. (Also, note that the average time between messages will actually be more than 50,000 cycles; 64 cycles is just the worst case.) So, when Riva detects a 1 bit after at least 64 zeros, she can be confident that is the start of the next message, and when she finds a 1 followed by 64 or more zeros, that marks the end of the message.

13.17 *Hash functions*

Hash functions are not ciphers, but they are closely related to ciphers and often used together with cryptography. In this section I will discuss two uses for hash functions, and present one hash function suited for each use.

Hash functions are often used for searching. Suppose you have a list of people such as customers, patients or students, and you need to search this list frequently for information about those people. Hashing provides a quick way of searching by converting the person's name into a number that can be found directly in a table. For example, the name "John Smith" could get turned into the number 2307, where entry 2307 in the table contains the information about John Smith.

Here is a hash designed for this purpose. For each letter L of the alphabet, randomly choose a binary value R(L) of some fixed size, say 32 bits. To hash the name, simply exclusive-OR the 32-bit numbers for each letter in the name. A weakness of this hash is that names that are anagrams will have the same hash value. For example, ARNOLD, ROLAND and RONALD all hash to the same value. To avoid this problem, after adding each letter, cycle the hash value left 1 bit position. That is,

$$H_n = (H_{n-1} \oplus R(M_n)) <<< 1.$$

Call the final hash value H. H can be converted to an index I into a name table of size T by scaling it, $I = \lfloor HT/2^{32} \rfloor$. For example, if the name hashes to 917354668 and the table has 5000 entries, the index is $\lfloor 917354668 \times 5000/4294967296 \rfloor = \lfloor 1067.94 \rfloor = 1067$. Let's call this hashing method *Hash32*.

There can be several names that produce the same index. Various methods are used for handling these index crashes, such as having a separate table to hold the duplicates, hashing the name a second time to choose a different slot in the table, or chaining the duplicate names together.

Hash functions are also used for message authentication. In this case the entire message is hashed to produce a long hash value. Let's suppose 16 bytes. This hash value must be sent to Riva in a tamper-proof way, such as sending it via a trusted third party that records and timestamps the hash value. Riva will then hash the message and compare the hash values. If they are different, then the message may have been altered. The hash function used for this purpose must make it infeasible for Emily to modify the message without changing the hash value. That is, Emily cannot find a different message that produces the same hash value. Likewise, Sandra cannot change the message and claim that she had sent the changed message, because the hash value will no longer match.

For this hash we will use 4 highly non-linear substitutions, A, B, C and D. These may be publicly known fixed substitutions. It is worthwhile putting some effort into making the four substitutions highly non-linear and minimally correlated with one another. The basic operation is to combine each byte of the message with 4 previous bytes using the **xors** combining function, that is, to perform an exclusive-OR and then to make a simple substitution on the result. Let H be a copy of the message M, so that the message is not destroyed by the hashing process. Each character H_n in the copy is hashed by

$$H_n = A(B(C(D(H_n) \oplus H_{n-1}) \oplus H_{n-4}) \oplus H_{n-16}).$$

This way, every byte of the hash depends on every byte that came before, and every byte that comes after depends on it.

The hash requires an initialization vector (section 11.10) in order to hash the first 16 bytes of the message. A copy of the first 16 bytes of the message can be used for this purpose. That is, initially bytes H_{-15} through H_0 are the same as bytes H_1 through H_{16}, which are the same as bytes M_1 through M_{16} of the message. With the initialization vector it is possible to propagate the hash from H_1 to H_L, where L is the length of the message.

This leaves the last few bytes rather weakly hashed. It may be possible for Emily to change the last few bytes of the message without much effort. The solution is to continue the hashing process beyond the end of the message. To do this, when we hash the first 16 bytes of the message, we save these hash values for later use. When we reach the end of the message, we append those 16 bytes and continue the hashing until the end of the extended message. Those last 16 bytes become the hash value for the message. Call this hash method *Hash128*.

For some machines it may be faster to hash a message 4 bytes at a time using the machine's 32-bit arithmetic functions. The message and hash values are treated as lists of L 32-bit words rather than 4L bytes. The hash array H is initially a copy of the message. If the message length is not an even multiple of 4 bytes, up to 3 bytes are appended to fill out the last word. Copies of the first two words of H are appended to the front, namely $H_{-1} = H_1$ and $H_0 = H_2$. After the first 4 words of the message have been hashed, these 4 words are appended to the end of the message.

This hash, called *HashPQ*, uses two primes which are $P = 2^{32}-5 = 4294967291$ and $Q = 2^{32}-17 = 4294967279$, and the magic multiplier $R = 77788888$, which is a primitive root of both P and Q. The hashing operation is

$$H_n = H_n + (RH_{n-1} \bmod P) + (RH_{n-2} \bmod Q) \text{ for } n = 1, 2, 3, \ldots, L+4.$$

If the sum exceeds $2^{32}-1$, the value is truncated to 32 bits simply by ignoring the extra high-order bit(s). That is, we get the modulo 2^{32} operation free. The last 4 words of the H array are the 16-byte hash value. HashPQ uses less storage than Hash128 since it does not need the 4 simple substitutions.

Hash32, Hash128 and HashPQ all have the ideal property required for a good hash function, namely that a change to any bit or combination of bits in the input causes about half of the bits in the output to change. All three hashes are fast, and can be done in a single left-to-right pass.

14

One-time pad

This chapter covers

- One-time pad ciphers
- The Vernam cipher, which approximates a one-time pad
- Diffie-Hellman key exchange
- Constructing the large primes needed for Diffie-Hellman and Public Key cryptography

The best-known stream cipher is the *One-Time Pad.* Many writers restrict this term to mean only a cipher where the plaintext and the key stream are exclusive-ORed byte by byte. This is historically inaccurate. The first one-time pad cipher was published in 1882 by Frank Miller, a Sacramento, CA banker, for the purpose of saving money by shortening telegraph messages. Miller's telegraph code used 5-digit code groups to represent words and phrases that were common in commercial telegrams. To obtain secrecy, Miller proposed a cipher that consisted of adding a 3-digit number to each 5-digit group. His code values were small enough that the sum could never exceed 99999. That is, the codes were all less than 99000. So the one-time pad was originally a decimal system, not a binary system.

The system that gives the one-time pad its name was devised by cryptographer Werner Kunze of the German Pers Z S (Signal Intelligence Agency) around 1922. Kunze's system was based on a standard diplomatic code of 5-digit groups. Like Miller's cipher, Kunze's cipher added the key groups to the code groups. Kunze used 5-digit key groups that were added to the code groups digit by digit, without carrying. Thus 33333+56789 would result in 89012, not 90122. Kunze distributed the keys in pads of 50 sheets, with each sheet containing 8 rows of 6 key groups each. The pages of these pads were used one time for enciphering one message and then discarded. Hence the name one-time pad. Later developments included the use of water-soluble inks and water-soluble paper for rapid disposal.

Another version of the one-time pad was invented by Leo (Leopold Samuel) Marks, a British author and screenwriter (*Peeping Tom*), about 1940. It was widely used by British spies. Marks's version used letters instead of numbers. The sender would add the key letter to the plaintext letter modulo 26 to get the ciphertext letter. In other words, Marks's one-time pad was a Belaso cipher with a random key. MIT professor Claude Shannon invented the same cipher sometime between 1940 and 1945, and Soviet information theorist Vladimir Kotelnikov invented a version in or before 1941, but its details remain classified. Both Shannon and Kotelnikov produced mathematical proofs that the one-time pad cannot be broken. It remains the only cipher method that has been proved unbreakable.

Since Miller's 1882 one-time pad and Kunze's 1922 one-time pad both used decimal addition for their combining functions, and since Marks's 1940 one-time pad used addition modulo 26, it is hardly reasonable for anyone to assert that the one-time pad is restricted to combining the key and the plaintext with exclusive-OR. The defining features of the one-time pad are

1　The key is at least as long as the message,
2　The key is indistinguishable from true random,
3　Each character or block of the key is combined with one character or equal-sized block of the plaintext, and
4　The key is used only one time.

Any cipher that meets these 4 criteria is a one-time pad. To prove that the one-time pad cannot be broken, however, requires another, stronger condition:

5　There is an equal probability that any given plaintext character is transformed into any given ciphertext character.

With that much said, let's look at a historical cipher, based on the exclusive-OR, that is closely related to the one-time pad system.

14.1　*The Vernam cipher*

By 1918 many diplomatic missions had moved away from having human telegraph operators send and receive messages that then needed to be hand-typed. Instead, messages were punched into reels of paper tape in a 5-column Baudot code, invented by French telegraph engineer Émile Baudot in 1870, or Baudot-Murray code, invented by Donald Murray, a New Zealand journalist, in 1901. (I won't cover the details of these codes, since they changed several times between 1870 and the 1950s, when Western Union ceased using them. Baudot-style codes were abandoned entirely after 1963 when ASCII code supplanted them.) The important feature is that a human typist keyed the message onto a 5-column paper tape from which it could be directly transmitted and printed out at the receiving end without any further human involvement.

Like Morse code, neither Baudot code nor Baudot-Murray code offered any secrecy. Anyone could read the message directly from the tape. Up to 1918, if secrecy were required, the message would have to be enciphered by hand by a human cipher clerk before being typed onto the tape, and then printed out and deciphered by hand by another clerk at the receiving end. A method was needed to speed up that process. Enter Vernam.

The *Vernam* cipher was developed by Gilbert Sandford Vernam of AT&T Bell Labs in 1918 at the request of Joseph O. Mauborgne of the Army Signal Corps. The idea was simple and ingenious. A human typist would key the message onto a tape as before, but what got transmitted was the exclusive-OR of the character code with a key code. The key codes were supplied from a separate paper tape that had a seeming random sequence of characters punched into it. At the receiving end the transmitted characters would be exclusive-ORed with a copy of that tape, which deciphered them. Each tape had 1000 random-ish characters so that long messages would repeat the key every 1000 characters.

This diagram shows two tapes containing the plaintext and the key, pickups for reading the tapes, circuits for exclusive-ORing the key with the plaintext, and a hole punch at the receiving end, which may be at a distant location. The hole punch could be replaced by a printer or a transmitter, depending on the setup.

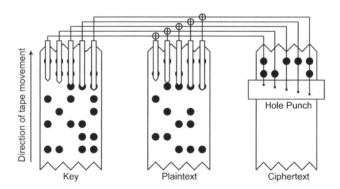

This my own diagram, since I could find no picture of the Vernam machine itself, presumably because it had been classified.

I called the key tapes "random-ish" because they were produced by a person tapping away at a typewriter-style keyboard, a forerunner of the Friden Flexowriter.

The result is that the characters near the center of the keyboard were used more often than the characters near the corners. Humans are poor at producing random numbers or characters. But for 1918, this was a very strong cipher.

Many sources mistakenly refer to the Vernam cipher as a one-time pad, probably because it was the first cipher to exclusive-OR a message expressed in binary with a binary key. However, the Vernam cipher was not a one-time pad because it repeated. It had a fixed period of 1000 characters. Besides, the one-time pad had been invented by Miller 36 years earlier, and was originally a decimal-based system.

For a busy embassy, there could be 100 or more cipher messages per day. If the embassy corresponded with several other embassies, multiple sets of tapes were needed. The tapes for Washington-to-Berlin would be separate from the tapes for Berlin-to-Washington traffic. The tapes were all marked with 6-digit serial numbers. Before each message was sent, the tape number would be transmitted in *clear*, that is, unenciphered. The clerks would need to keep straight which tapes were for which embassy, and which tapes had already been used and needed to be destroyed. New tapes had to be supplied continually to each embassy.

Vernam soon devised a second version that used two tapes, both of which were exclusive-ORed with the plaintext. One tape had 1000 characters and the other tape had 999 characters, making an effective period of 999,000 characters. The same two tapes could be used for an entire day, just by starting each message at a different point on each tape. If an embassy had, say, 100 tapes, different combinations of tapes could be used on different days for as long as the paper tapes held up.

It is easy to see how Vernam's 2-tape machines could be extended to 3 or 4 tapes. So far as I know, this never happened because these tape-based machines were soon supplanted by rotor machines (see section 5.10).

14.2   *Key supply*

The big problem with the one-time pad is supplying enough keys. The paper tape method may be adequate for 10 stations, each sending 100 messages a day, but it is unworkable for 100 stations, each sending 1000 messages a day.

Many books and papers on cryptography describe the following conundrum: Sandra and Riva decide to exchange messages using a one-time pad. They each have a copy of a long random key. They use this key section by section until they use it up. Now they need another random key. Sandra can choose it and send it to Riva, but it needs to be encrypted so that Emily cannot get it. The safest way is to encrypt it using a one-time pad, so they need another key of the same length to encrypt the new key. Again, Sandra can choose it and send it to Riva, but that key also needs to be encrypted. So they need yet another key, ad infinitum.

The solution to this dilemma is two-pronged. First, the random key stream can be refreshed using the techniques of section 13.15, such as lagged addition. For example, once per day, or whenever the parties decide, a new key can be derived from the base key. Second, these derived daily keys need not be used directly as message keys.

Instead, message keys can be constructed from the daily keys. This way, even if Emily recovers any of the message keys, she will be two layers away from recovering the base key. The next few sections will describe some methods for producing message keys.

Each method is designed to meet two goals: Either (1a) the method must be able to generate enough message key material each day that no two message keys overlap, or (1b) it must not be feasible for Emily to detect overlapping sections of the message keys, and (2) it must not be feasible for Emily to reconstruct sections of the derived keys or of the base key.

14.2.1 Circulating key

The daily key is derived using the technique of section 13.14. Consecutive sections of the daily key are used to generate the message keys, for example by lightly encrypting them. A keyed simple substitution is sufficient. I recommend leaving a gap of random width, perhaps 1 to 32 bytes, between successive keys. When the end of the daily key is reached, it wraps around using a single pass of lagged linear addition (section 13.14.1) to extend it for use on days with heavy message volume. You can visualize this by imagining that each time a message is sent, its key, plus any gap, is moved from the front of the daily key to the end of the daily key, and then refreshed using lagged linear addition. Sandra and Riva must do this in sync.

This works well for low message volumes when there is little chance that Sandra and Riva will send messages to each other at the same time. For higher message volumes, it is better to use two base keys and two daily keys, one for Sandra-to-Riva messages and the other for Riva-to-Sandra.

14.2.2 Combined key

For each message of length L, three segments of length L are taken from the daily key. Call these segments x, y and z, and call their starting positions in the daily key p_x, p_y and p_z. If any of these positions is near the end of the daily key, that segment may wrap back to the beginning. Each byte of the message key is formed by taking a linear combination of the corresponding bytes in x, y and z. That is,

$$k_n = (ax_n + by_n + cz_n) \bmod 256,$$

where the coefficients a, b, and c may be any odd integers from 1 to 255. The values of the three coefficients a, b and c and the three starting positions p_x, p_y and p_z must be different for each message. These may be agreed upon beforehand, or enciphered and sent with each message.

14.2.3 Selection key

For each message of length L, two non-overlapping segments are taken from randomly chosen locations in the daily key. The first segment is the *selector*, s, which has length L. The second segment is the *stock*, x, which has length 256. To encipher the nth character m_n in the message we first take the corresponding byte $p = s_n$ from the selector. This p selects the position in the stock where the key byte is taken, namely $k_n = x_p$. The key byte k_n is combined with the message byte m_n using any of the combining functions such as **xors** or **adds**.

After the key byte k_n is used, x_p is replaced in the stock by $(ax_p + b)$ mod 256. The coefficients a and b must satisfy the Hull-Dobell conditions (section 13.4), namely $a \equiv 1 \pmod 4$ and $b \equiv 1 \pmod 2$. In effect, each of the 256 positions in the stock, x, becomes a separate linear congruential pseudorandom number generator (PRNG). The coefficients a and b may be the same for all 256 positions in the stock, or they may vary. One option is to use two different pairs of values for a and b, and choose either the first or second pair according to some fixed pattern. Regardless of how many pairs of values are used, they should be different for different messages.

Another scheme for updating the stock is to replace x_p by $(ax_p + bx_{p-1})$ mod 256, where a and b are any odd integers from 1 to 255. You might also choose to replace x_p by $(ax_p + bx_{p-i})$ mod 256 where i is any integer from 2 to 255.

Since there are only 8192 possible values for a and b, and since the value $a = 1$ should be avoided, duplication is inevitable. This is not a problem, however, as long as Emily cannot tell which pair of values is used for each message. The important point is that Emily cannot accumulate multiple messages that she knows have the same values of a and b. One downside of using indicators is that opponents may collect several messages with the same indicator, so they know those messages have the same key.

14.3   *Indicators*

In classical cryptography, the same key was often used for a long time, sometimes for months or years. In modern times, keys are usually used for a single message. With the one-time pad, message keys must be used only once. Otherwise, Emily could slide one message against another and use the index of coincidence (section 5.7) to detect the overlap.

For moderate 2-way message traffic Sandra and Riva could use a small book that would list the keys to be used according to, say, the time of day and the day of the week. A common practice before computers was to number each message. The message number could be enciphered and sent with the message. Sandra and Riva would use the message number to look up the key in the book.

The key book becomes unworkable when the message traffic becomes higher, or when there are many parties exchanging messages. This stays true even when the book is replaced by a computer file. One solution to this problem is to use indicators. An *indicator* is a piece of information that is sent along with the message that the recipient can use to determine the key.

In the early days, the indicator was just the key itself, hidden inside the message. For example, the third group of the message was the key, or the first characters of the first 8 groups formed the key. A slightly more sophisticated version might be that the middle digit of the second group told you which group was the key. The obvious problem with these types of indicators is that once Emily learned the system, she could read all of the messages. Even if Emily does not know the system, she can simply try all of the groups in the message to see if one of them is the key. If she finds a few of these keys, then she may be able to deduce the pattern.

A safer approach is to encrypt the key and use that as the indicator. That is what the Germans did during World War II with their Enigma machines. They had a special setting, which they changed each day, for encrypting the message key. They would first set the Enigma to the daily setting and encrypt the message key twice with that setting. Then they would reset the machine to the message key, which the individual operator would choose at random, and encrypt the message. The Polish *Bomba* exploited this double encryption of the message key to deduce those keys. (The *bomba kryptologiczna* was an electromechanical device devised by Polish chief cryptographer Marian Rejewski in 1938 for cracking German Enigma messages.) When the Germans realized this, they stopped the practice, and the Poles were blacked out; they could no longer read Enigma messages. Alan Turing anticipated this problem and designed his *Bombe* to work with cribs, or probable plaintext, instead. The French Enigma-cracking machine was also called a bombe, supposedly named for *bombe glacée*, a frozen dessert with a similar dome shape, like Baked Alaska.

Section 14.2 described several methods for generating message keys from the daily key. Each of these methods used a small set of parameters to generate each message key, such as the coefficients for lagged linear addition, or a location within the daily key. These sets of parameters are ideal for use as indicators.

14.4 Diffie-Hellman key exchange

So much for classical methods. Let's talk about a more modern method. *Diffie-Hellman key exchange* was invented in 1976 by Martin Hellman, a professor at Stanford University, and Bailey Whitfield Diffie, his research assistant, later of Sun Microsystems. The underlying concept of Public-Key cryptography was invented in 1974 by Ralph Merkle, then an undergrad at UC Berkeley.

The essential feature of Diffie-Hellman key exchange is that Sandra and Riva can establish a secure encryption key even if Emily intercepts all of the messages they exchange. To set up the exchange, Sandra and Riva must agree on a large prime, P, and a primitive root, w, of that prime. Or, Sandra can simply choose P and w and send them to Riva. P and w can be sent in clear. Recall from section 13.3 that it is easy to find primitive roots. For most primes at least one of 2, 3, 5 or 7 is a primitive root.

Sandra chooses a secret exponent s and computes $x = w^s \bmod P$. She sends the value x to Riva, but keeps the value of s to herself. Riva chooses a secret exponent r and computes $y = w^r \bmod P$. She sends the value y to Sandra, but keeps the value of r to herself. Now Sandra can compute $y^s \bmod P$, which is $w^{rs} \bmod P$, and Riva can compute $x^r \bmod P$, which is $w^{sr} \bmod P$. Since $w^{rs} = w^{sr}$, Sandra and Riva have computed the same value, which they can use as an encryption key, or which they can split into several encryption keys. An efficient way of performing the exponentiations is described in section 13.3.

Some authors (and Wikipedia) describe Diffie-Hellman key exchange as a public key method. They talk about combining Sandra's and Riva's public keys and their private keys. This is not true. There are no public keys involved in Diffie-Hellman. Even if you consider the exponents r and s to be keys, they are both secret keys.

Suppose Emily has intercepted all of the messages between Sandra and Riva. Then Emily knows P, w, x and y, that is, $w^s \bmod P$ and $w^r \bmod P$, but she does not know s, r or $w^{rs} \bmod P$. Determining $w^{rs} \bmod P$ is called the *Diffie-Hellman problem*. It is not known if this is the same as determining r and s, but they are believed to be equally difficult problems. Determining s and r, given P, w, and either x or y is known as the *discrete logarithm problem*. It is known to be a very difficult problem. When P, r and s are sufficiently large, the problem is believed to be computationally infeasible. Experts disagree on how large P must be, but common recommendations are 300 and 600 decimal digits. Some implementations allow for P to be up to 1234 decimal digits, which is 4096 bits. The exponents r and s can be much smaller. Expert recommendations range from 40 decimal digits up to 150 decimal digits.

An algorithm called the *Silver-Pohlig-Hellman* algorithm, for Roland Silver, Stephen Pohlig and Martin Hellman, makes it easy to solve the discrete logarithm problem when P–1 has only small factors. The algorithm lets you solve for each of the small factors separately. Therefore, Sandra must make certain that P is a *safe* prime, meaning that P–1 has at least one large factor, say $q > 10^{35}$. Ideally, Sandra should choose P to be a prime of the form 2Q+1 where Q is also prime. The corresponding prime Q is called a Sophie Germain prime, named for French number theorist Marie-Sophie Germain, who also studied acoustics and elasticity. It is even stronger if Q–1 and Q+1 both have large prime factors. In the next section we will explicitly construct Q so that Q–1 has a large prime factor. It is highly likely that Q+1 also has a large prime factor, simply by chance, just because Q is so large. Numbers that have only small factors are called *smooth numbers*. They become very rare as the numbers get large.

*14.4.1 Constructing large primes, old

The conventional method for constructing large primes, which you can find on many websites, begins by randomly choosing an odd number N of the desired size, and then testing whether N is prime. First you try a few hundred small primes. If N is divisible by any of these, then it's not prime. Choose again. This preliminary test is worthwhile because it is so fast. Next, you test whether N is prime by applying a probabilistic primality test. The most common test is the *Miller-Rabin* test invented by Gary L. Miller and Michael O. Rabin. Let $N-1 = 2^h d$, where d is odd. That is, 2^h is the largest power of 2 that evenly divides N-1. The first step is to choose a base b in the range 2 to N–2, and test whether $b^d \equiv 1 \pmod{N}$. If this is true, then N passes. If not, then see whether $b^{2d} \equiv -1 \pmod{N}$, or $b^{4d} \equiv -1 \pmod{N}$, etc. Keep going as long as the exponent $2^g d$ remains less than $2^h d$. If you find such a value g, then N passes the test, and b is called a *witness* for the primality of N. If no such g is found, then you know for certain that N is not prime, so you must start again with a new value for N.

If N passes, there is still a 1/4 probability that N is composite. If you want to push the probability that N is not prime down to 1 in 2^{128}, you will need 64 Miller-Rabin tests, each with a different base, b. Unfortunately, this is still no guarantee. The Miller-Rabin test falsely identifies the Carmichael numbers as prime. These are numbers that are not prime, but for which every b is a witness. They were discovered by Robert Carmichael of the University of Illinois in 1910. The first few Carmichael numbers are 561, 1105, 1729, 2465, 2821, 6601, 8911, 10585, 15841, 29341 and 41041. Carmichael numbers tend to have small prime divisors, so passing 64 Miller-Rabin tests, and also finding that N is not divisible by any of the first few hundred primes, makes it overwhelmingly probable that N is a prime.

This is a good method for finding primes of a particular size, but it does not guarantee that N is a safe prime, and it is much slower than the method of this section. If S is the size of the primes you need, the number of trials you need to find a prime is about ln(S). So, for a 500-digit prime you need about $\ln(10^{500})$ or about 1151 trials, each requiring 64 Miller-Rabin tests and hundreds of trial divisions. Using the method I present in this section can save you hours or even weeks of computer time, depending on what kind of computer you are using and how large the primes need to be.

14.4.2 Constructing large primes, new

One way you could attempt to find a large prime is to start with any large integer N, then try 2N+1, 2N+3, 2N+5, ... testing each one until you hit a prime. A small improvement on this is to test 6N+1, 6N+5, 6N+7, 6N+11, 6N+13, ... That eliminates all the multiples of 2 and 3 from the testing. You can also try 30N+1, 30N+7, 30N+11, 30N+13, ... to eliminate the multiples of 2, 3 and 5, and similarly for $2 \times 3 \times 5 \times 7 = 210$, and so forth.

There are a variety of ways to test whether a given integer N is a prime. The simplest method is trial division. To test if N is a prime, try dividing N by each of the primes up to $\sqrt{N}$. If any of these primes evenly divides N, then N is composite, otherwise N is prime. Trial division is useful up to about $N = 10^{12}$, possibly 10^{14}, but for larger N, trial division is too time-consuming. Most other prime tests are merely probabilistic tests that can tell you that the number is *probably* a prime.

There is one test that tells you with certainty that a number is prime: an integer N > 1 is prime if it has a primitive root. Recall from section 13.3 that r is a primitive root of N if $r^{N-1} \bmod N = 1$, and $r^{(N-1)/p} \bmod N \neq 1$ for any prime p that divides N−1. To test N for primality you only need to evaluate $r^x \bmod N$ for the values x = N−1 and x = (N−1)/p for each distinct prime factor p of N−1. Let's call this method the *primitive root primality test*, or *root test* for short. It was invented by French mathematician Edouard Lucas in 1876, the same Edouard Lucas who coined the term *Fibonacci number* (section 3.4). Lucas died in 1891 from a tragic soup accident.

It is sufficient to try 2, 3, 5, 7, 11 and 13 as possible primitive roots. If N has any primitive roots, it is very probable that at least one of these 6 values will be a primitive root. If none of these values is a primitive root, don't waste time trying other values. It is more efficient to move on to the next candidate for a prime.

The problem with Lucas's root test is that you need to factor N–1, and if N has 300 or more digits, then factoring N–1 is effectively impossible, at least without a quantum computer. That's why you don't see this test mentioned in many books or websites that discuss prime testing.

There is a way around this hurdle. Remember that your goal is not to find a general way to test for primes. Your goal is to obtain just one large prime to use as the modulus for Diffie-Hellman key exchange. So, instead of *finding* that prime, you can *construct* the prime.

The trick is to choose N–1 with known factors. For example, you could choose N–1 to have the form 2^n so N would have the form 2^n+1. The only prime factor of N–1 would be 2. To find primes of the form 2^n+1 you only need to find a number b such that $b^{N-1} \mod N = 1$ and $b^{(N-1)/2} \mod N \neq 1$. I suggest that you try b = 2, 3, 5, 7, 11 and 13. If none of these is a primitive root, then skip $N = 2^n+1$ and see if $N = 2^{n+1}+1$ is a prime. That search will net you the primes 3, 5, 17, 257 and 65537. It is not known whether there are others, although people have spent thousands of hours of computer time searching. These 5 primes are called Fermat primes for French mathematician Pierre de Fermat, famed for his margin note about the equation $a^n+b^n = c^n$.

OUTLINE

Before I get into the details, let me outline the general method for constructing a large prime, P. The method must accomplish three things:

1 P–1 must have a large prime factor so that P is safe,
2 Each candidate P should have a high probability of being prime so that you need to do as few prime tests as possible, and
3 P–1 should have few distinct prime factors so that each prime test is as fast as possible.

Any search for a large prime will involve testing hundreds or even thousands of candidates. Let's call the expected number of tests E. The approach here will be to make each candidate for P–1 the product cK of two numbers. The coefficient c will be stepped through a sequence of relatively small numbers, typically comparable to E. The kernel K will be either a large prime, the product of two large primes, or the product of powers of at most 2 primes, $p^a q^b$, where at least one of p and q is a large prime. Let's look at how to choose the coefficients first, and then at how to choose the kernel.

COEFFICIENTS

The simplest way to choose the coefficients is to step through the primes, one at a time. Since the coefficients must be even, you use twice each prime, 2×2, 2×3, 2×5, 2×7, ... Let's call this method *PickPrimes*. PickPrimes minimizes the number of distinct prime factors in cK. There are at most 2 distinct prime factors in c, and at most 2 distinct prime factors in K. However, PickPrimes does little to reduce the number of tests needed.

A second way to choose the coefficients is to make them of the form $p^a q^b$, or $p^a q^b r^c$, or similar. Here p, q and r are small primes such as 2, 3 and 5, or 2, 5 and 7. (Later in this section we will see a case where 3 must be omitted.) This way, P can never be a multiple of 2, 3 or 5, which significantly increases the chance that P will be prime. If you use this method, you may want to precompute and sort the list of coefficients.

KERNEL

The kernel, K, must have at least one large prime factor, R. I suggest that R be at least 2^{128}, about 3.4×10^{38}. If your opponent has a quantum computer, make R at least $2^{256} = 1.16 \times 10^{77}$. So, where do you get these primes? If you are willing to settle for 30-digit primes, you can get some online from bigprimes.org.

If you expect to generate many large primes, or very large primes, you can grow your own. Prepare ahead of time by building up a table of primes of various sizes. Call this table PrimeTab. Be sure to save PrimeTab so whenever you need more primes you don't have to repeat this process. You can start your prime table with the 25 primes under 100. You probably know these by heart, so just type them into your program. Next, if you like, you could generate some primes of 3 to 12 digits, say 2 or 3 primes of each size, using trial division. I suggest that you do this randomly so that you don't construct the same primes every time you use this method (and so that every reader who uses this method doesn't generate the same primes). At this stage PrimeTab might have about 50 primes.

CONSTRUCTING R (SMALL STEP METHOD)

Now let's start trying to construct R, the large prime factor of Q–1. You can build up to R in small steps by finding primes that are each a little bigger than the last prime, or you can jump there in one leap. If you expect to generate many large primes, build in small steps so that PrimeTab will have lots of entries for use later. To illustrate both techniques, let's construct R in small steps, and construct Q in a giant leap.

Suppose that PrimeTab contains k primes, $p_1 < p_2 < p_3 < ... < p_k$. To construct the next prime, start by choosing any two primes from the table, say p_i and p_j. Let r be the product $p_i p_j$. If $r < p_k$, you might want to use a larger i or j so that you don't generate too many small primes. Of course you need some small primes, so I suggest choosing a larger i or j when $p_i p_j < p_k^{2/3}$. First, use the Lucas test to see whether R = 2r+1 is a prime. This is easy since you know the only prime factors of R-1 are 2, p_i and p_j. If 2r+1 is not a prime, try 4r+1, 6r+1, 10r+1, ... using the PickPrimes method to choose the coefficients. When the numbers start to get over 20 digits, finding a prime may take 50 or more trials per prime.

REDUCING THE NUMBER OF TESTS

When the numbers get very large, you can save time by checking whether each candidate nr+1 is divisible by many small primes before you search for a primitive root. For example, you could verify that nr+1 is not divisible by any of the first 100 primes. You can make this test much faster by calculating $x_i = r \bmod p_i$ ahead of time for each of the first 100 primes. Then, instead of computing $(nr+1) \bmod p_i$, where r may have several hundred digits, you compute $(nx_i+1) \bmod p_i$, where x_i has only 1 to 3 digits. That is, you do the trial divisions $(r \bmod p_i)$ only once instead of once for each value of n. Let's call this method *PrimeCheck*.

PrimeCheck works because the candidate primes are chosen in sequence. You cannot do this with the conventional method for finding large primes, because the candidate primes are chosen at random. That makes the trial division by small primes much faster for this method, and since it is faster you can use more small primes, say 300 instead of 100, and thereby reduce the number of trials needed.

As before, if none among 2, 3, 5, 7, 11 or 13 is a primitive root of $nr+1$, skip that candidate and try the next value of n, until you find the next prime. Since this method uses only 6 tests per candidate, and the conventional method uses 64 tests, this method is more than 10 times as fast. Add each prime you find to PrimeTab.

CONSTRUCTING P AND Q (GIANT LEAP METHOD)

Suppose your goal is to find a 300-digit Sophie Germain prime. Continue growing PrimeTab until it has at least one large prime, say $R > 2^{128}$. Now you are ready to generate your 300-digit prime using a giant leap. Start by choosing a target T of the desired size, say $T = 10^{300}$. It is possible to make P arbitrarily close to the target value, but that is not needed for Diffie-Hellman key exchange. T will simply be a desired minimum size.

The next step is to find Q. Recall that Q must meet three requirements: Q must be prime, Q-1 must be a multiple of the large prime R, and $P = 2Q+1$ must also be prime. The strategy to find Q is to start with some seed number t whose prime divisors are all known and try 2t+1, 4t+1, 6t+1, 10t+1, ... using PickPrimes.

> **WARNING**   If you make t a multiple of 3, then Q will have the form 3x+1. That makes $P = 2Q+1 = 6x+3$ a multiple of 3. Making t a multiple of 3 means P can never be prime.

Since T is the minimum value for P, and Q is about P/2, then t should be about T/2. To construct t, begin with the largest prime in PrimeTab, namely R. Take the largest power of R that is less than T/2, say R^r. For example, if T is 10^{300}, and R is about 10^{40}, then T/2 is about 5×10^{299}, so r is 7. This means R^r is about 10^{280}. Getting from 10^{40} directly to 10^{280} is the giant leap. This R^r is well short of 5×10^{299}, so set $t = R^7 S$, where S is about 5×10^{19}. When $S < 10^{12}$, you can use trial division to find the next prime greater than S. If this is S', then t is $R^7 S'$. When $S > 10^{12}$, you can make S' the product of a prime from PrimeTab and a prime less than 10^{12} that you must choose, or you can make S' the square or cube of a prime. Suppose the latter. In this example S is about 5×10^{19}. The square root of this is about 7,071,067,812. The next higher prime is $U = 7,071,067,851$. So t will be $R^7 U^2$.

Now that you have constructed t, and you know all of its prime factors, you can begin the search for Q, by testing 2t+1, 4t+1, 6t+1, 10t+1, ... using the root test. A number N chosen at random has a probability of about $1/\ln(N)$ of being prime. When N is on the order of 10^{300}, $\ln(N)$ is about 690. This means it will take about 690 tries to find a prime of the form $nt+1$. It is also necessary for P to be prime, which also has a probability of about $1/690$. This means it will take about $690^2 = 476100$ tries to find $Q = nt+1$ and $P = 2Q+1$, which are both prime. That's a lot of tests.

These tests are time-consuming, so any technique to cut down on the number of tests is valuable. In this case we can use a natural extension of PrimeCheck. For each prime p_i, calculate $x_i = t \bmod p_i$ as before. For each value of n, check whether nx_i+1 is divisible by p_i to verify that Q is not a multiple of p_i, and also check whether $2(nx_i+1)+1$, which is $2nx_i+3$, is divisible by p_i to verify that P is not a multiple of p_i. This way you get double value from the x_i list.

SECRET PRIMES

For some ciphers you may need to use a secret prime, known only to yourself and your legitimate correspondents. You can still use the methods of this section to construct your prime, however, you need to make certain that any opponent cannot follow the same steps and discover your prime. I recommend two precautions. (1) When you initialize PrimeTab, instead of 2 or 3 primes each of sizes 3 to 12 digits, randomly choose 5 to 10 primes each of sizes 3 to 14 digits. Aim for at least 100 initial primes in PrimeTab. (2) Use the small step method for constructing P, Q and R, preferably using at least 100 additional steps beyond the initial primes.

EXACT SIZE

The giant leap method for constructing primes can easily be modified to find primes of a precise size. Here is an example. Suppose you need a prime between 10^{300} and 1.1×10^{300}. Choose r slightly larger than $10^{300}/2000000$, that is, 5×10^{294}. Use PickPrimes, but start your primes at 1000000, that is, 1000003, 1000033, 1000037, 1000039, ... Use PrimeCheck to reduce the number of tests.

There are about 6700 primes between 1,000,000 and 1,100,000, and about 1 out of every 690 numbers between 10^{300} and 1.1×10^{300} is prime, so it is a near certainty that you will find a prime of the required size. The probability can be easily calculated. The odds that any given number in the desired range is not prime is 689/690. The odds that all 6700 chosen numbers are not prime is $(689/690)^{6700}$, or .00006. So the chance of success is 99.994%.**

Matrix methods 15

This chapter covers

- Ciphers using multiplication by a matrix of integers, or a matrix of ring elements
- Ciphers using multiplication by large and small integers
- Solving linear congruences
- Constructing rings and invertible matrices

Matrices are a tool well-suited for cryptography because they can encipher arbitrarily large blocks of text in one operation. Typically, each block in the message is treated as a vector of bytes, meaning integers modulo 256.

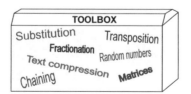

When Sandra uses a matrix to encipher a message, Riva must use the inverse of that matrix to decipher the message. Let's begin the discussion of matrix methods with a technique for inverting a matrix.

15.1 *Inverting a matrix*

There are several ways of solving a matrix equation such as $C = AP$ when there is known plaintext. Since Emily knows P and C, but does not know A, she can solve the equation for A by right-multiplying it by P' to get $CP' = APP' = A$. So Emily needs to invert P. Riva does the opposite. She knows A, but does not know P, so she needs to invert A. Left-multiplying the equation by A', she gets $A'C = A'AP = P$.

The method illustrated here has the advantage of obtaining the inverse matrix directly, without the intermediate step of back-substitution, which is required for other methods. The method is to place the given matrix side by side with the identity matrix in an n×2n double-wide matrix. The left size is reduced to an identity matrix using only *elementary row operations*. These row operations are applied across each row of the double matrix, so as the left half changes from the original matrix to an identity matrix, the right half changes from an identity matrix to the inverse of the original.

The elementary row operations are (1) multiplying a row by an invertible constant, (2) swapping two rows, and (3) subtracting a multiple of one row from another row.

The algorithm turns the elements of the original matrix into the elements of the identity matrix one by one starting in the upper-left corner, then working down the left column. Then it does the same for the second column, and so forth. If at any time the algorithm gets stuck, meaning that all of the elements in the active column are multiples of 2, or all of them are multiples of 13, then the matrix is not invertible. If this happens to Sandra, she needs to try a different matrix A. It is often sufficient to add 1 to some element on the bottom row. If this happens to Emily, she will need n more characters of known plaintext. This will give her an (n+1)×n matrix. When she applies this algorithm, the inverse matrix is in the upper-right n×n portion of the double-wide matrix.

Here is a 3×3 example. This matrix works on the 26-letter English alphabet, so the matrix elements are integers modulo 26. There are no fractions and no negative numbers involved. Since this is done modulo 26, each element that is not a multiple of 2 and not a multiple of 13 has a multiplicative inverse. This lets us turn the first nonzero element in each row into a 1, which makes it easy to decide which multiple of a row to subtract from any other row. The original matrix is

$$\begin{pmatrix} 13 & 4 & 11 \\ 6 & 15 & 1 \\ 10 & 9 & 22 \end{pmatrix}$$

This gets expanded to double-wide format by appending a 3×3 identity matrix on the right.

$$\begin{pmatrix} 13 & 4 & 11 & 1 & 0 & 0 \\ 6 & 15 & 1 & 0 & 1 & 0 \\ 10 & 9 & 22 & 0 & 0 & 1 \end{pmatrix}$$

You are immediately in trouble because none of the first elements in any row is invertible. I did this deliberately in order to show a very useful trick. The first element in row 1 is a multiple of 13, but not a multiple of 2. The first element in row 2 is a multiple of 2, but not a multiple of 13. If you simply add row 2 to row 1, then the first element becomes 19, which is a multiple of neither 2 nor 13, hence it is invertible. Problem solved.

$$\begin{pmatrix} 19 & 19 & 12 & 1 & 1 & 0 \\ 6 & 15 & 1 & 0 & 1 & 0 \\ 10 & 9 & 22 & 0 & 0 & 1 \end{pmatrix}$$

The multiplicative inverse of 19 is 11 modulo 26 because $19 \times 11 = 209 \equiv 1 \pmod{26}$. You multiply row 1 by 11 to turn the first element in the matrix into a 1.

$$\begin{pmatrix} 1 & 1 & 2 & 11 & 11 & 0 \\ 6 & 15 & 1 & 0 & 1 & 0 \\ 10 & 9 & 22 & 0 & 0 & 1 \end{pmatrix}$$

Now you can finish column 1 by subtracting 6 times the top row from row 2, and subtracting 10 times the top row from row 3. This will set the first element in rows 2 and 3 to zero.

$$\begin{pmatrix} 1 & 1 & 2 & 11 & 11 & 0 \\ 0 & 9 & 15 & 12 & 13 & 0 \\ 0 & 25 & 2 & 20 & 20 & 1 \end{pmatrix}$$

Time to work on the second row. The first nonzero element on row 2 is 9. The multiplicative inverse of 9 is 3 because $9 \times 3 = 27 \equiv 1 \pmod{26}$. You multiply row 2 by 3 to turn the first element in the row to a 1.

$$\begin{pmatrix} 1 & 1 & 2 & 11 & 11 & 0 \\ 0 & 1 & 19 & 10 & 13 & 0 \\ 0 & 25 & 2 & 20 & 20 & 1 \end{pmatrix}$$

This lets you finish column 2 by subtracting row 2 from row 1, and subtracting 25 times row 2 from row 3. Notice how the left side of the double-wide matrix is gradually turning into the identity matrix.

$$\begin{pmatrix} 1 & 0 & 9 & 1 & 24 & 0 \\ 0 & 1 & 19 & 10 & 13 & 0 \\ 0 & 0 & 21 & 4 & 7 & 1 \end{pmatrix}$$

Almost done. The first nonzero on row 3 is 21. The multiplicative inverse of 21 is 5, so you multiply the bottom row of the matrix by 5.

$$\begin{pmatrix} 1 & 0 & 9 & 1 & 24 & 0 \\ 0 & 1 & 19 & 10 & 13 & 0 \\ 0 & 0 & 1 & 20 & 9 & 5 \end{pmatrix}$$

Now you can finish the third column by subtracting 9 times row 3 from row 1, and subtracting 19 times row 3 from row 2.

$$\begin{pmatrix} 1 & 0 & 0 & 3 & 21 & 7 \\ 0 & 1 & 0 & 20 & 24 & 9 \\ 0 & 0 & 1 & 20 & 9 & 5 \end{pmatrix}$$

Done. The left half of the double-wide matrix now holds the identity matrix, and the right half is the inverse of the original matrix. You can check this by multiplying the original matrix by the inverse. The result should be the identity matrix — and it is.

$$\begin{pmatrix} 13 & 4 & 11 \\ 6 & 15 & 1 \\ 10 & 9 & 22 \end{pmatrix} \begin{pmatrix} 3 & 21 & 7 \\ 20 & 24 & 9 \\ 20 & 9 & 5 \end{pmatrix} = \begin{pmatrix} 1 & 0 & 0 \\ 0 & 1 & 0 \\ 0 & 0 & 1 \end{pmatrix}$$

15.2   *Transposition matrix*

Let's begin with a very simple matrix method, namely the *transposition matrix*, which is equivalent to the *permutation matrix* in mathematics. This is a square matrix that has exactly one 1 in each row and each column. All the other matrix elements are 0. If you wish to transpose a block of 10 letters, you can do this by treating the block as a row matrix of size 1×10 and multiplying it on the right by a transposition matrix of size 10×10. The result will be a 1×10 matrix with the letters transposed.

To move a letter from position 2 in the block to position 5, you would set the element on row 2 in column 5 to 1. Here is an example of a 4×4 transposition matrix that changes the message block ABCD to BADC.

$$\begin{pmatrix} 0 & 1 & 0 & 0 \\ 1 & 0 & 0 & 0 \\ 0 & 0 & 0 & 1 \\ 0 & 0 & 1 & 0 \end{pmatrix}$$

Transposition matrices by themselves are not particularly practical, but if you have a matrix M that performs a substitution on a block, and a transposition matrix T, you can combine them into a single step by using the matrix MT in place of M. That way, you get both the substitution and the transposition in a single operation.

15.3   *The Hill cipher*

The earliest cipher based on matrices is the *Hill cipher*, invented in 1929 by Lester S. Hill of Hunter College and published in the *American Mathematical Monthly*. A similar cipher had been invented in 1924 by then-teenaged Jack Levine, later of North Carolina State College, and published in 1926 in *Flynn's Weekly*, a pulp detective magazine. The crypto column in *Flynn's* was run by M. E. Ohaver, who invented fractionated Morse (section 4.4). Coincidentally, *Flynn's Weekly* is where Kendell Foster Crossen, also mentioned in section 4.4, published many of his stories. Levine spent his entire career trying to knock down Hill's cipher and promote his own.

Hill's cipher operates on the 26-letter alphabet, with the letters numbered from 0 to 25 in some scrambled order. That is, you perform a simple substitution before the matrix operation. You take the plaintext letters in blocks of 3. These form a column vector, that is, a 3×1 matrix, P. You multiply this column vector on the left by a 3×3 matrix, A, and then add a column vector, B, to get the ciphertext vector, C. In matrix notation this is written as C=AP + B, using addition and multiplication modulo 26. Finally, you convert the numbers back into letters using the same letter-to-number correspondence.

Unfortunately, many authors restrict the term *Hill cipher* to mean a weak, watered-down version of this cipher. To avoid ambiguity, let's number the several versions of the Hill cipher. Hill-0 is the weakest version. You use the standard English alphabet, without mixing, and omit the B vector, so that C=AP. Hill-1 is somewhat stronger. You still use the unmixed alphabet, but the B vector is nonzero. Hill-2 is the version that Hill originally proposed. You use a mixed alphabet and nonzero B vector. Hill3 is an even stronger version where you use one mixed alphabet to convert the letters to numbers, but you use a different mixed alphabet to convert the numbers back to letters. This is comparable to the conjugated matrix bifid cipher in section 9.6.1.

Hill's cipher, Hill-2, as originally published, was basically a secret method cipher. The conversion of letters to numbers and both matrices A and B were fixed. There was no key. Anyone who knew the method could read the messages as easily as the intended receiver. Most recent books and websites that discuss the Hill cipher ignore the mixed alphabet and concentrate solely on the matrix operations. This would be legitimate if a fixed conversion from letters to numbers were used, because the known mixing of the alphabet could be stripped off.

Let's first look at case Hill-0, where A is an unknown n×n matrix, and the vector B is 0, so C=AP. This is plain old matrix multiplication, which we saw in section 11.3. Riva can decipher the message by multiplying the ciphertext by the *inverse matrix* A' of A. The inverse matrix has the property that A'A=AA'=I, where I is the *identity matrix*. In the matrix I, every diagonal element is 1, and every other element is 0. The identity matrix is akin to the number 1 in ordinary multiplication, that is, 1×N=N×1=N for every number N. With matrices, this translates to IA=AI=A for every square matrix A. Emily can also decipher the message if she can determine A'.

This B=0 version of the Hill cipher is vulnerable to a known-plaintext attack. If Emily has n^2 characters of known plaintext, she can form them into an n×n matrix.

Call this matrix P, and call the corresponding ciphertext matrix C. Then C = AP, where C, A and P are all n×n matrices of integers modulo 26. There are several ways to solve this matrix equation. One way is shown in section 15.1.1.

If the additive vector B is not all-zero, then Emily just needs n more characters of known plaintext, and she can eliminate B from the equation. The extra known plaintext characters can form a column vector P_2, and the corresponding ciphertext characters can form a column vector C_2. These vectors can be subtracted from the equation like this: $(C–C_2) = A(P–P_2)$. This has the same form as C = AP, and is solved the same way, namely by inverting the matrix $P–P_2$. You subtract an n×1 column vector from an n×n matrix by subtracting the first element of the vector from each of the elements on the top row of the matrix, subtracting the second element of the vector from each of the elements on the second row of the matrix, and so forth.

$$\begin{pmatrix} a & b & c \\ d & e & f \\ g & h & i \end{pmatrix} - \begin{pmatrix} x \\ y \\ z \end{pmatrix} = \begin{pmatrix} a-x & b-x & c-x \\ d-y & e-y & f-y \\ g-z & h-z & i-z \end{pmatrix}$$

Suppose that you have no known plaintext. It is still possible to solve the Hill-0 variation. Let's continue assuming a secret 3×3 multiplicative matrix, C = AP. Multiplying by A', the inverse of A, gives P = A'C. In each block of the message, the first plaintext character of the block depends only on the top row of A. That is only $26^3 = 17,576$ possibilities, so it's easy to try them all. Each combination for the top row will determine the letters in positions 1, 4, 7, . . . in the plaintext. For each such combination, count the letter frequencies.

You can compare those letter frequencies to standard English letter frequencies using the tall peaks method described in section 5.9.1. Take those combinations that have the best match, say the top 1%, or top 175 combinations. Do the same for the second and third plaintext letters of each block by using the second and third rows of the inverse matrix A'. This gives you 175 plausible combinations for each of the 3 rows. You can now try combinations of these combinations to get possible reconstructions for the entire message. There are only $175^3 = 5.36×10^6$ combinations to try. The combination for row 1 gives you the first letter in each block, the combination for row 2 gives you the second letter in each block, and the combination for row 3 gives you the third letter in each block, so you have every letter.

You can now use trigram frequencies to determine the most plausible plaintext. Use all of the trigrams, not just the 3-letter blocks, but the trigrams spanning blocks as well. This is the same process we used in section 5.10 and section 8.2, so I won't repeat all of the details here. If this fails to produce a satisfactory result, go back to the start and take the top 2%, or top 350 combinations for each letter.

The Hill cipher Hill-1 with a secret 3×3 multiplicative matrix and a secret 3×1 additive matrix, but with an unmixed alphabet, is rated Three. With a key-mixed substitution both before and after the matrix operations it is rated Five. It can be solved as a general trigram substitution cipher. The rating increases for larger matrices. In order to reach a rating of Ten, the matrix must be at least 8×8, and the Hill-3 matrix operation must be applied twice. Here are the steps. (1) Convert the message to numeric form using a keyed non-linear substitution. (2) Multiply each block by the matrix and add the column vector. (3) Perform a second non-linear substitution on the numbers. (4) Multiply each block by a second matrix and add a second column vector. (5) Convert the result back to letters using a third keyed non-linear substitution. The two multiplier matrices may be fixed, but the 3 keys for mixing the alphabets and the 2 additive column vectors should be changed for every message. Call this cipher *DoubleHill.*

15.4   *Hill cipher, computer versions*

Hill's cipher was too complex for cipher clerks to do by hand. Hill also created a mechanical device for performing the encryption and decryption. This was done to satisfy the patent laws of the time, which allowed patenting a machine but not a mathematical algorithm. Still, the cipher saw very little use in practice.

Today, in the computer age, the Hill cipher has become practical again. Matrix multiplication is child's play for a computer. Instead of 3×3 matrices it is easy to use 10×10 matrices. Instead of 9 characters of known plaintext, Emily needs 100 characters for a known-plaintext attack. That is pretty much impossible, other than by espionage or capturing a message on the battlefield. The Hill cipher using a secret 10×10 matrix using the standard alphabet is rated Six. The Hill cipher using a secret 10×10 matrix, with key-mixed substitutions both before and after the matrix multiplication, is rated Eight.

You can further strengthen the Hill cipher by having several matrices and choosing the matrix for each block either periodically or randomly. The matrices and plaintext blocks may vary in size. Since matrix multiplication is not commutative, you almost always get a different result when you multiply by a matrix on the left or on the right. Each plaintext block must be taken as a column vector when you multiply on the left but a row vector when you multiply on the right. This suggests that you can get a more secure cipher by alternating sides, either periodically or randomly. Variable matrices, variable block sizes and variable sides. You can take your pick or mix 'em up.

You can also combine transposition with the Hill cipher, however, not every transposition will improve the security. Suppose that you are using the Hill-0 or Hill-1 variant, and after the matrix multiplication you transpose the letters in each block. This the same as using the Hill cipher with a different matrix multiplier. Let T represent the transposition. Applying T after a Hill-1 encipherment gives you $C = T(AP+B) = (TA)P+(TB)$. All that you have accomplished is to use the matrix TA in place of A, and TB in place of B. Emily can solve the cipher using known plaintext, and she will never know that there was a transposition. If you wish to use transposition with Hill-0 or Hill-1, you must swap letters among different blocks, or you must swap different letters in different blocks.

Surprisingly, the situation is exactly the same when you use Hill-2 or Hill-3. This is because simple substitution and transposition commute. If S is any simple substitution, T is any transposition, and M is any message, then $S(T(M)) = T(S(M))$, and hence $ST = TS$. Therefore, regardless of which Hill cipher variant you use, if you are going to add a transposition step, you must swap letters among different blocks, or you must swap different letters in different blocks, either periodically or pseudorandomly.

Another idea is to multiply the message by matrices on both sides. As mentioned earlier, a block of text must be treated as a column vector when you multiply it on the left by a matrix, but as a row vector when you multiply it on the right. Suppose that you are using 3×3 matrices, with the additive matrix $B = 0$. With single-sided matrix multiplication, the expression for each ciphertext character has 3 terms, each involving one plaintext letter and one matrix element. With two-sided matrix multiplication, the expression for each ciphertext letter has 9 terms, each involving one plaintext letter and the product of 2 matrix elements. So the coefficients of the plaintext letters are quadratic. Of the 81 possible quadratic coefficients, 27 appear in these expressions.

For the Hill-0 and Hill-1 cases Emily can still use known plaintext to solve these equations. There is an easy way and a hard way. The hard way is to use 18 characters of known plaintext to solve the 18 quadratic equations for the 18 unknown elements in the two 3×3 matrices. Good luck with that!

The easy way is to treat each of the 27 quadratic coefficients as a separate variable. This changes the equations from quadratic in 18 variables to linear in 27 variables. Ignore how the 27 variables are formed from the 18 matrix elements, just treat them as indivisible units. Since there are now 27 unknowns Emily will need 27 known letters rather than 18. Unlikely, but possible, especially if she has intercepted multiple messages that she knows used the same key. For example, suppose that Emily knows that every message sent from Sweden ends with the word STOCKHOLM. Since the occurrences of STOCKHOLM likely begin in different positions in the 3-letter blocks, 3 different messages can give her 27 known letter placements. She can easily solve the 27 linear equations to get the 27 coefficients.

From there it is easy to solve the 27 single-term quadratic equations to find the 18 matrix elements — but why bother? The relationships between the plaintext letters and the ciphertext letters are all in terms of the 27 quadratic coefficients. There is no benefit for Emily to know how those coefficients were produced.

The case for Hill-1 is essentially the same as Hill-0. There are 36 unknowns, so Emily will need 36 characters of known plaintext. Otherwise, the solution process is the same. There is no comparable process for Hill-2 and Hill-3. These are best solved as trigram substitution ciphers.

You can get even greater strength from two-sided matrix multiplication by using different-sized matrices on each side, and by aligning the matrices differently on each side. Here are two examples of these techniques. In the first example, the left-side multiplications are by 3×3 matrices, while the right-side multiplications are by 4×4 matrices. Since the 3×3 matrices butt heads with the 4×4 matrices, as shown, let's call this the *Butthead configuration.*

3×3	3×3	3×3	3×3
4×4		4×4	4×4

This gives you an effective block size of 12 characters. Since each right-side 4×4 matrix spans two left-side 3×3 matrices, each ciphertext character depends on 6 plaintext characters, rather than 4. With this configuration, producing each ciphertext character takes only 7 multiplications, so this method is very fast. When the mixed alphabets are secret, but the matrices are known, the Butthead cipher is rated Six. If the mixed alphabets and the matrices are both secret, it is rated Eight. The rating increases to Ten if the matrices are 6×6 and 7×7 or larger. Of course, whatever matrix sizes Sandra uses should be mutually prime.

The *Brick Wall* is another recommended configuration for 2-sided matrix multiplication. Here the matrices are all of the same size, but they are offset by half their width, just like the bricks in a wall. This diagram illustrates the method.

4×4	4×4	4×4	4×4
2×2	4×4	4×4	4×4	2×2

Notice that the boundaries of the matrices never line up. This configuration has no block structure, or, equivalently, you could say that the entire message is a single block. Since each of the 4×4 right-side matrices spans two left-side 4×4 matrices, each ciphertext letter depends on 8 plaintext letters. This is sufficient for high-security work.

If you actually used 2×2 matrices for the first and last blocks, that would leave those blocks weak and vulnerable. It also requires you to have 1×1 and 3×3 matrices to handle uneven message lengths. It is better to use 4×4 matrices throughout. The next two diagrams show how this can be done for a message of length 13. The first diagram shows the placement of the left-side matrices, with the last 4×4 matrix flush with the right end of the message.

A	B	C	D	E	F	G	H	I	J	K	L	M
A	B	C	D									
				E	F	G	H					
								I	J	K	L	
									J	K	L	M

The next diagram shows the placement of the right-side matrices, offset by 2 characters. The first and last 4×4 right-side matrices are flush with the ends of the message.

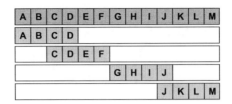

This method of positioning the last matrix makes the last left-side matrix and the last right-side matrix align. This can be avoided by wrapping around to the start of the message, like this.

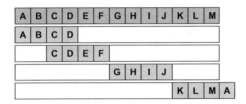

When you have a key-mixed simple substitution before the left-side matrix multiplication, with another after the right-side matrix multiplication, and you use secret matrices of size 6×6 or larger, the brick wall cipher is rated Ten.

Since it takes some effort to invert the matrices, it may be preferable to use fixed matrices for both left- and right-side multiplication. Using fixed matrices weakens the cipher, but you can compensate by adding a third simple substitution between the two matrix multiplication steps. The matrices may be of any even size, 6×6 or larger. By comparison to the Hill cipher, let's call this the *Everest cipher*. The Everest cipher is rated Ten.

15.5 Large integer multiplication

Large integer multiplication is similar to matrix multiplication in one important sense: in matrix multiplication each element of the product is the sum of products of two elements, one from each matrix. In large integer multiplication each digit of the product is the sum of products of two digits, one from each large integer. Anyway, that's my rationale for putting this topic in the matrix chapter.

A 128-bit block can be viewed as 16 bytes, or as 16 base-256 digits of a 128-bit integer. If you multiply two such base-256 integers, that involves 256 products and 256 additions (including the carries). It's a lot faster if the language you use allows you to multiply two 32-bit unsigned integers to get a 64-bit unsigned product. Then you need only 16 multiplications and 16 additions. If the language allows multiplication of 64-bit integers with 128-bit products, it's even simpler.

There are faster methods for multiplying very large numbers, such as Karatsuba and Toom-Cook, but the benefits of these methods for multiplying 128-bit numbers, or even 256-bit numbers, are too small to make these worthwhile for present purposes, so I will not get into the mechanics of large integer multiplication. Some computer languages handle the mechanics automatically, so the user need never become involved.

That said, consider a cipher, *Mult128*, where the message is taken in 128-bit blocks, and each block is multiplied by a secret 128-bit integer M modulo 2^{128}. In other words, only the low-order half of the 256-bit product is used, and the high-order half is discarded. This means that some of the intermediate products in the multiplication need not be calculated because they contribute only to the high-order end of the product.

Riva can read the message by multiplying the ciphertext by the multiplicative inverse M' of M modulo 2^{128}. This inverse exists whenever M is odd. Let's see how to find a multiplicative inverse.

15.5.1 *Multiplying and dividing congruences*

I promised early in this book that I would present all the necessary math as it was needed. This is one of those sections. The method for calculating multiplicative inverses involves multiplying linear congruences. Before I show how that is done, let's look at an example to see why this is an issue. (I used part of this example in section 3.6. You might wish to reread that section before proceeding.)

Not all congruences have the same strength. Some congruences are strong, and have a unique solution. Some congruences are weak, and have many solutions. The stronger the congruence, the more information it gives. Consider these congruences, listed from strongest to weakest:

$$5x \equiv 1 \pmod{12}. \quad \text{Unique solution } x \equiv 5 \pmod{12}.$$
$$10x \equiv 8 \pmod{12}. \quad \text{Two solutions } x \equiv 2, 8 \pmod{12}.$$
$$9x \equiv 3 \pmod{12}. \quad \text{Three solutions } x \equiv 3, 7, 11 \pmod{12}.$$
$$8x \equiv 4 \pmod{12}. \quad \text{Four solutions } x \equiv 2, 5, 8, 11 \pmod{12}.$$
$$6x \equiv 6 \pmod{12}. \quad \text{Six solutions } x \equiv 1, 3, 5, 7, 9, 11 \pmod{12}.$$

The reason for this disparity is that in all but the first of these congruences, ax≡b (mod n), the parameters a, b and n have a common factor. In 10x≡8 (mod 12), the parameters 10, 8 and 12 have the common factor 2, and the congruence has 2 solutions. In 9x≡3 (mod 12), the parameters 9, 3 and 12 have the common factor 3, and the congruence has 3 solutions. And so forth. The larger the common factor, the more solutions, and the weaker the congruence.

When a, b and n have a common divisor d, you can divide the congruence through by d. For example, 9x≡3 (mod 12) has a common factor of 3. Dividing through by 3 gives 3x≡1 (mod 4). You can solve that by sight. The solution is x≡3 (mod 4). That checks out, since 3×3 = 9≡1 (mod 4). To translate this result back to (mod 12), the first solution is 3 (mod 12), and you get the other two solutions by adding $12/3 = 4$ and then adding 4 again, namely 7 (mod 12) and 11 (mod 12).

To recap, if a, b and n have a common divisor d, then there are d distinct solutions. The first solution is the solution to $a/d \equiv b/d$ (mod n/d), and the other solutions are spaced apart by n/d.

Let's look at two other situations. Suppose, again, that $ax \equiv b$ (mod n) and that a and n have a common divisor that does not divide b, for example $3x \equiv 7$ (mod 30). Then the congruence has no solution. Suppose, instead, that a and b have a common divisor d that does not divide n. Then you can divide a and b by d. For example, if $10x \equiv 25$ (mod 37), then $2x \equiv 5$ (mod 37). This can be solved in your head by adding 37 to 5, making $2x \equiv 42$ (mod 37). Dividing by 2 gives $x \equiv 21$ (mod 37).

Just as you can divide a and b by a constant, you can also multiply a and b by a constant, m. That m must not have a common factor with n. In other words, m must be invertible modulo n. Otherwise you will make the congruence weaker and lose information. For example, suppose you are given $9x \equiv 3$ (mod 12). This is a weak congruence with 3 solutions. If you multiply a and b by 2, the congruence becomes $18x \equiv 6$ (mod 12), which is equivalent to $6x \equiv 6$ (mod 12), which has 6 solutions. The weak congruence has become even weaker.

You can also add and subtract congruences that have the same modulus. Suppose $ax \equiv b$ (mod n) and $cx \equiv d$ (mod n). These can be added to get $(a+c)x \equiv b+d$ (mod n), or subtracted to get $(a-c)x \equiv b-d$ (mod n). This can be used to strengthen a set of weak congruences. For example, suppose you have $9x \equiv 3$ (mod 12) and $8x \equiv 4$ (mod 12). The first congruence has 3 solutions and the second has 4 solutions. If you add them, you get $17x \equiv 7$ (mod 12), which reduces to $5x \equiv 7$ (mod 12), which has the unique solution $x \equiv 11$ (mod 12). Even smarter, if you subtract the two congruences, that gives $(9-8)x \equiv (3-4)$ (mod 12), which gets you directly to $x \equiv 11$ (mod 12).

*15.6 Solving a linear congruence

Now that you know how to safely manipulate congruences without losing strength, we can tackle the problem of how to solve a linear congruence $ax \equiv b$ (mod m), where a, b and m are given constants, and x is the unknown value we are trying to find. In the special case when $b = 1$, x is the multiplicative inverse of a modulo m. Most textbooks mention only one technique called the *Extended Euclidean Algorithm*. (The Euclidean algorithm is commonly attributed to Theaetetus of Athens, who lived about a century before Euclid.) That is a perfectly good method. It may be the right method to use when the modulus is small, or when the modulus has several different small prime factors. It is definitely the right method when the factorization is unknown and there is a likelihood of small factors.

In cryptography, however, there are only two common cases where we need to calculate the multiplicative inverse, when the modulus is a prime, and when the modulus is a power of 2. This section will describe a simpler, more direct method.

15.6.1 *Reducing a congruence*

The basic method for solving a congruence ax≡b (mod m) is to repeatedly reduce the coefficient of x. The simplest method is *ResM*. It multiplies the congruence by an integer n that is just large enough to make the coefficient of x at least as large as the modulus. That is a(n–1)<m≤an. You can determine the value of n just by dividing m/a and rounding up, so 2.0000 stays as 2, but 2.0001 would become 3. When the coefficient is reduced modulo m, the result is a smaller coefficient.

Let's begin with a simple example of ResM just to get the basic idea, and to make it easier to follow the discussion later, when things start getting complicated. Take the congruence 38x≡55 (mod 101). We know 101/38 = 2.658, so we multiply the congruence by 3 and then reduce it modulo 101, like this:

$$3{\times}38x \equiv 3{\times}55 \text{ (mod 101) is } 114x \equiv 165 \text{ (mod 101),}$$
$$\text{which reduces to } 13x \equiv 64 \text{ (mod 101).}$$

Notice that the coefficient of x was reduced from 38 to 13. This can be reduced again. We have 101/13 = 7.769, so we multiply the congruence by 8, like this:

$$8{\times}13x \equiv 8{\times}64 \text{ (mod 101) is } 104x \equiv 512 \text{ (mod 101),}$$
$$\text{which reduces to } 3x \equiv 7 \text{ (mod 101).}$$

We're almost there. 101/3 = 33.667, so multiply that last congruence by 34, and the coefficient of x is reduced to 1:

$$34{\times}3x \equiv 34{\times}7 \text{ (mod 101) is } 102x \equiv 238 \text{ (mod 101),}$$
$$\text{which reduces to } x \equiv 36 \text{ (mod 101).}$$

We can check this result by plugging x = 36 back into the original congruence, 38x≡55 (mod 101). Replacing x by 36 gives 38×36≡55 (mod 101), which is 1368≡55 (mod 101), which is true. The correct answer is x≡36 (mod 101).

15.6.2 *Half-and-Half Rule*

Let's look at a small improvement. We can call it the *Half-and-Half Rule*. About half the time, the fractional part of m/a is less than 1/2, and half the time it is more than 1/2. Let q = m/a. Then half the time qa is closer to m, and half the time (q+1)a is closer to m.

A numeric example may help to make this clearer. Let m be 101, and let a be 40. Then q = 101/40 = 2.525. The fraction .525 is more than 1/2. If you take 40×2 the result is 80, which is 21 less than 101. If you take 40×3 the result is 120, which is 19 more than 101. So 40×3 is closer to 101 than 40×2. Thus n = 3 is the best multiplier.

Suppose, instead, a is 41. Then m/a = 101/41 = 2.463. This time the fraction .463 is less than 1/2. If you take 41×2 the result is 82, which is 19 less than 101. If you take 41×3 the result is 123, which is 22 more than 101. So 41×2 is closer to 101 than 41×3. Thus n = 2 is the best multiplier.

To recap, when the fractional part of $q = m/a$ is less than $1/2$, na is closer to m if we round q down, but when the fractional part of m/a is more than $1/2$, na is closer to m if we round q up. Using the floor and ceil notation (section 13.3), if $frac(q) < 1/2$, choose $n = \lfloor q \rfloor$, but if $frac(q) > 1/2$, choose $n = \lceil q \rceil$. That sounds easy enough, but there is a complication. When $n = \lceil q \rceil$, na is larger than m, so you reduce the congruence by subtracting multiples of m, as we did at the beginning of this section. When $n = \lfloor q \rfloor$, na is smaller than m, so you reduce the congruence by subtracting it from multiples of m.

Start with

$$41x \equiv 90 \pmod{101}.$$

Since $101/41 = 2.463$, multiply the congruence by 2, giving

$$82x \equiv 180 \pmod{101}.$$

Subtract this from multiples of 101, namely

$$101x \equiv 202 \pmod{101}.$$

Since $101 - 82 = 19$ and $202 - 180 = 22$, you get

$$19x \equiv 22 \pmod{101}.$$

To illustrate how much of an improvement this makes, let's solve a congruence with and without the Half-and-Half Rule, side by side.

Without Half & Half	With Half & Half
$135x \equiv 77 \pmod{1009}$	$135x \equiv 77 \pmod{1009}$
$71x \equiv 616 \pmod{1009}$	$64x \equiv 470 \pmod{1009}$
$56x \equiv 159 \pmod{1009}$	$15x \equiv 457 \pmod{1009}$
$55x \equiv 1003 \pmod{1009}$	$4x \equiv 660 \pmod{1009}$
$36x \equiv 895 \pmod{1009}$	$x \equiv 165 \pmod{1009}$
$35x \equiv 730 \pmod{1009}$	
$6x \equiv 990 \pmod{1009}$	
$5x \equiv 825 \pmod{1009}$	
$x \equiv 165 \pmod{1009}$	

Without the Half-and-Half Rule the reduction takes 8 steps. With the Half-and-Half Rule the reduction takes 4 steps. The ratio varies for different coefficients and moduli, but 8:4 is reasonably typical. ResM using the Half-and-Half Rule can be called *ResMH*.

15.6.3 *Laddering*

When the integers are very large, this is still a bit slow, because we are multiplying and dividing large numbers. The *laddering technique* can be used to avoid this. It uses two congruences for each step. Instead of multiplying the coefficient of x by ever-increasing numbers to make the value close to the modulus, the laddering technique is to multiply the coefficient in each congruence by a small number to make it close in value to the preceding coefficient. This requires an extra congruence to get the process started. For this purpose we use the congruence mx≡m (mod m), which is equivalent to 0x≡0 (mod m).

Let's look at an example using larger numbers:

$$28338689x \equiv 28338689 \ (\text{mod} \ 28338689) \qquad \text{Artificial initial congruence}$$
$$6114257x \equiv 90926 \ (\text{mod} \ 28338689) \qquad \text{The congruence we wish to solve}$$

Since 28338689/6114257 is about 4.635, multiply by 5 and subtract to get

$$6114257x \equiv 90926 \ (\text{mod} \ 28338689),$$
$$2232596x \equiv 454630 \ (\text{mod} \ 28338689).$$

Here 6114257/2232596 is about 2.739, so multiply by 3 and subtract to get

$$2232596x \equiv 454630 \ (\text{mod} \ 28338689),$$
$$583531x \equiv 1272964 \ (\text{mod} \ 28338689).$$

Continue this way to get, successively,

$$101528x \equiv 4637226 \ (\text{mod} \ 28338689),$$
$$25637x \equiv 26550392 \ (\text{mod} \ 28338689),$$
$$1020x \equiv 16548275 \ (\text{mod} \ 28338689),$$
$$137x \equiv 9585163 \ (\text{mod} \ 28338689),$$
$$61x \equiv 6129512 \ (\text{mod} \ 28338689),$$
$$15x \equiv 25664828 \ (\text{mod} \ 28338689),$$
$$x \equiv 16824956 \ (\text{mod} \ 28338689).$$

Each of these examples used a prime modulus. The situation gets more complicated when the modulus is composite. I will not cover all of these complexities here. The case that is of most importance for cryptography is when the modulus is a power of 2, such as 2^{32} or 2^{128}. In this case, the multiplier that you choose at each stage must be odd. So, instead of rounding the multiplier to the nearest integer, you always round toward the odd integer. For example, 3.14 would be rounded to 3, and 3.99 would also be rounded to 3. ResMH using laddering can be called *ResMHL*.

15.6.4   *Continued fractions*

Once you have two or more linear congruences, you can reduce the coefficient of x far more quickly by using a technique called *continued fractions*. A continued fraction is a way of closely approximating a decimal number by a fraction. Consider the decimal number R = .13579. R is somewhere between 1/7 and 1/8. More precisely, R is about 1/7.3643. This can also be written as $\frac{1}{7+}$.3643. Notice that the plus sign + is in the denominator of the fraction. This indicates that the addition is done in the denominator, as opposed to adding the two fractions $\frac{1}{7}$+.3643.

The fraction .3643 can be approximated as $1/2.745$, or $\frac{1}{2+}.745$, so R is now $\frac{1}{7+}\frac{1}{2+}.745$. Here .745 is very close to $3/4$, so the approximation can be $\frac{1}{7+}\frac{1}{2+}\frac{3}{4}$. To get that back to an ordinary fraction, just work backward:

$$\frac{1}{7+}\frac{1}{2+}\frac{3}{4} = \frac{1}{7+}\frac{1}{2\,3/4} = \frac{1}{7+}\frac{1}{11/4} = \frac{1}{7+}\frac{4}{11} = \frac{1}{7\,4/11} = \frac{1}{81/11} = \frac{11}{81}$$

The fraction $11/81$ is .13580, which differs from .13579 by only .00001. As you can see, this method gives excellent approximations.

Let's try that example from section 15.4.3 again,

$$6114257x \equiv 90926 \ (\text{mod } 28338689).$$

For the second congruence, we use the $0 = 0$ trick,

$$28338689x \equiv 28338689 \ (\text{mod } 28338689).$$

Here $6114257/28338689$ is

$$\frac{1}{4+}\frac{1}{1+}\frac{1}{1+}\frac{1}{1+}\frac{1}{2+}\frac{1}{1+}\frac{1}{4+}\frac{1}{1+}\frac{1}{2+}\frac{1}{1+}\frac{1}{24+}\frac{1}{7+}\frac{1}{2+}\frac{1}{4+}\frac{1}{15}$$

A good rule of thumb to get a close approximation is to stop just before a large denominator, in this case 24. Truncating the continued fraction before 24 gives

$$\frac{1}{4+}\frac{1}{1+}\frac{1}{1+}\frac{1}{1+}\frac{1}{2+}\frac{1}{1+}\frac{1}{4+}\frac{1}{1+}\frac{1}{2+}\frac{1}{1}$$

which works out to $241/1117$.

Multiplying the 6114257 congruence by 1117 and the 28338689 congruence by 241 and subtracting gives

$$
\begin{aligned}
6829625069x &\equiv 101564342 \ (\text{mod } 28338689) \\
6829624049x &\equiv 0 \ (\text{mod } 28338689) \\
\hline
1020x &\equiv 101564342 \ (\text{mod } 28338689) \\
1020x &\equiv 16548275 \ (\text{mod } 28338689)
\end{aligned}
$$

This reduces the coefficient of x from 6114257 to 1020, a factor of 5994. So the continued fraction method uses far fewer steps than other methods. However, it is tricky to use because the coefficient from one step may be much larger than the next coefficient, for example 6829625069 vs 1020. You can balance the coefficients by alternating between continued fraction steps and half-and-half steps.**

15.7 Large integer ciphers

There are many ciphers that can be constructed using large integer multiplication. Section 15.3 describes the Mult128 cipher, where the message is taken in 128-bit blocks. Each block is treated as a 128-bit integer and multiplied by a secret 128-bit integer M modulo 2^{128}. To get good mixing, every byte of the multiplier should be nonzero. This is still weak because the low-order n bits of each ciphertext block depend only on the low-order n bits of the plaintext and the low-order n bits of the key M. This makes the encipherment of the low-order byte a simple substitution. Performing a simple substitution before and after the multiplication does not fix this weakness. Similarly, the low-order 2 bytes undergo bigram substitution, and the low-order 3 bytes undergo trigram substitution. Mult128 is rated Three.

A superfast way of fixing the low-order byte problem is to combine the high-order byte with the low-order byte, for example by using the **xors** or **adds** combining function. That would boost the rating to Five. A better solution would be to combine the high-order 8 bytes with the low-order 8 bytes using **xors** or **adds**. That boosts the rating to Seven. Here's an example.

`ABCDEFGH`	First 8 letters used as keys
`ABCDEFGHIJKLMNOP`	Plaintext block
`ABCDEFGH;8i=W?6}`	After combining, before multiplication

One way to strengthen the cipher would be to permute the 16 bytes, however, with sufficient ciphertext Emily could detect which byte position has the least variability and therefore must be the permuted low-order byte. *Permuted Mult128* is rated Four.

A much stronger approach would be to multiply, permute, and multiply again. The permutation needs to move the weak low-order bytes into the high-order half of the block. Suitable permutations are (1) reversing the order of the bytes, (2) swapping the low-order and high-order halves of the block, or (3) interleaving the low-order and high-order bytes in reverse order. If the bytes are numbered from high to low order using the hex digits 0 through F, then these 3 permutations can be represented by

Reversed	Halves swapped	Interleaved
`FEDCBA9876543210`	`89ABCDEF01234567`	`F7E6D5C4B3A29180`

If your programming language lets you manipulate the block as both 32-bit words and single bytes, it may be faster to reverse the order of the 4 words, resulting in this permutation:

`CDEF89AB45670123`

This cipher, designated *MPM128*, is rated Seven.

When you add substitution steps to this process, the strength shoots up. Let S_1, S_2, S_3 and S_4 be 4 independent well-mixed keyed substitutions, let P be the fixed permutation 5BF4AE39D28C1706, and let M_1, M_2 and M_3 be multiplication by 3 secret 128-bit integers. Then the cipher $S_1M_1PS_2M_2S_3PM_3S_4$, called *Tiger*, is rated Ten.

15.8 Small integer multiplication

A miniature version of Mult128 can be done using ordinary unsigned 32-bit multiplication. The 128-bit block is treated as four 32-bit integers. Each of these integers is multiplied by a secret 32-bit integer modulo 2^{32}. The 4 multipliers must be odd to allow for deciphering later. This produces a 32-bit cipher. To get to a 128-bit cipher, the 4 separate 4-byte products can be treated as a 16-byte block, and mixed using this fixed 16-byte key transposition (section 7.6):

3E9472D8B61CFA50

This transposition is followed by a second multiplication step, again treating the 16-byte block as four 32-bit integers. You may use the same multipliers or new multipliers. This is followed by a second transposition, and another round of multiplication, so that there are 3 rounds of multiplication and two rounds of transposition. This cipher is called Mult32, and is rated Seven. It is much faster than any of the Mult128 cipher variants.

Let's view the 16 bytes of a 128-bit block as a 4×4 matrix of bytes. The 4 bytes in any row of this matrix can be treated as a 32-bit integer. Normally the 4 bytes of the integer are taken from left to right, with the leftmost byte being the high-order byte. However, they may also be taken in the opposite order, with the leftmost byte being the low-order byte. Consider the hexadecimal number 01020304. If we multiply this by the hexadecimal number 01010101 modulo 2^{32} in the normal way, the result is hexadecimal 0A090704. If we multiply this in the reverse order 04030201 by the hexadecimal number 01010101 modulo 2^{32} the result is hexadecimal 0A060301.

In a similar way, we can treat the 4 bytes in any column as a 32-bit integer, both in the top-to-bottom order and in the bottom-to-top order. Call the two horizontal directions East and West, and the two vertical directions North and South. If we multiply the rows and columns by odd 32-bit integers modulo 2^{32} in the order East, North, West, South, this provides thorough mixing. This requires 16 separate 32-bit multipliers. The total key size is 16×31 = 496 bits, not 16×32 = 512, because the multipliers must be odd. This cipher, which could be called *Compass*, is rated Eight.

To push the rating up to Ten, add one or more rounds of substitution, for example, East, North, Substitute, West, South. Better yet, add multiple substitutions, like East, Substitute, North, West, Substitute, South. Call this *CompassS*. Even if you use fixed substitutions, if they are highly non-linear, CompassS is rated Ten.

A different way to use small integer multiplication is to do *Cyclic Multiplication*. Let the bytes in each 32-bit row of the block be numbered 1, 2, 3, 4 from left to right, that is, from the high-order byte to the low-order byte. Multiply this by an odd integer modulo 2^{32}. Move byte 1 to the low-order end so the order is now 2, 3, 4, 1. Multiply again by an odd integer modulo 2^{32}. Repeat this two more times, so every byte occupies every position once. That is, the bytes are taken in order 1234, then 2341, 3412, and finally 4123. This should be done for each of the 4 rows of the 4×4 matrix of bytes, for a total of 16 multiplications and 12 cyclic shifts.

Then the same operations are done on the columns. Altogether there are 32 multiplications and 24 cyclic shifts. This cyclic multiplication cipher is rated Eight. It can have up to 32 different 32-bit multipliers for keys.

The methods of this section can be combined with the methods of section 15.4 in a variety of ways. Here is just one example, which I will call *Mat36*. Take the message in blocks of 36 characters that are treated as nine 32-bit integers. These form a 3×3 matrix of integers modulo 2^{32}. This matrix will be multiplied by a secret 3×3 invertible matrix of integers. If you simply multiplied on the right by another 3×3 matrix, the low-order bytes of the 9 integers would be weakly enciphered. Instead, cycle the entire 36-byte block left by 16 bit positions, and then multiply the block on the right by a second secret 3×3 invertible matrix of integers. Mat36 is rated Eight.

15.9   *Multiplication modulo P*

When the multiplication is done modulo 2^n, the low-order bytes are weakly enciphered, and we need to jump through hoops to fix that weakness. This problem does not occur when the multiplication is done modulo a prime, P. With a large multiplier, each bit of the product depends on every bit of the plaintext. There is a different problem. Let's assume you have chosen a prime $P < 2^n$, and a multiplier M, with $1 < M < P$. This lets you safely multiply the values from 0 through P–1 by M modulo P, so Riva can decipher these values by multiplying by M', the multiplicative inverse of M.

However, the plaintext value 0 would be left unchanged, and the plaintext values from P through $2^n - 1$ cannot be multiplied safely because the result would be ambiguous. For example, 3 and P+3 would give the same result when multiplied by M modulo P, since $3M \equiv PM + 3M \pmod{P}$, so Riva could not tell whether the message was 3 or P+3. This means that values from P through $2^n - 1$ would have to be left unchanged. To do this, define the function modp as follows:

$$\text{modp}(x) = \text{Mx mod P} \quad \text{if } x < P,$$
$$\text{modp}(x) = x \quad \text{if } x \geq P.$$

One solution for this problem is for Sandra to exclusive-OR a secret value to the plaintext. This suggests a family of *Modulo P ciphers*. Let's settle on the values n = 64, meaning a block size of 8 bytes, the prime modulus $P = 2^{64} - 59 = 18446744073709551557$ and the multiplier $M = 39958679596607489$, which is also prime.

Sandra enciphers a 64-bit plaintext block B by choosing a secret 64-bit constant C_1 as the key, and computing $x = \text{modp}(C_1 \oplus B) + C_1$. This is the first cipher in the family. Call it *PMod1*. It is rated Five. The second cipher in the family, *PMod2*, is two iterations of PMod1, using a second 64-bit constant, C_2:

$$x_1 = \text{modp}(C_1 \oplus B) + C_1,$$
$$x_2 = \text{modp}(C_2 \oplus x_1) + C_2.$$

PMod2 is rated Seven. The third cipher in the family, *PMod3*, has 3 iterations, and is rated Nine:

$$x_1 = \text{modp}(C_1 \oplus B) + C_1,$$
$$x_2 = \text{modp}(C_2 \oplus x_1) + C_2,$$
$$x_3 = \text{modp}(C_3 \oplus x_2) + C_3.$$

The fourth member, *PMod4*, is rated Ten. It has a total key size of 256 bits, 4 times the block size:

$$x_1 = \text{modp}(C_1 \oplus B) + C_1,$$
$$x_2 = \text{modp}(C_2 \oplus x_1) + C_2,$$
$$x_3 = \text{modp}(C_3 \oplus x_2) + C_3,$$
$$x_4 = \text{modp}(C_4 \oplus x_3) + C_4.$$

Each of the additions is done modulo 2^n, not modulo P.

The four PModX ciphers are all extremely fast because 64-bit addition, multiplication and modulo division are all directly supported by most programming languages. In some computers they are a single machine instruction. This lets the PModX ciphers operate on 4 or 8 bytes as a unit, instead of handing each 4-bit chunk separately, as DES does. This class of ciphers is ideally suited for software encryption. PMod2 is more secure than DES because of the much larger key size, and PMod4 is more secure than 3DES.

There is a second approach to multiplication modulo P that eliminates the unchanged values. The idea is to divide the range of integers from 0 to $2^{64}-1$ into two separate ranges, with a different prime modulus and a different multiplier for each range. Choose two primes P and Q such that $P+Q = 2^{64}+2$. There are about 10^{16} such pairs, so they are easy to find, for example $P = 9228410438352162389$ and $Q = 9218333635357389229$, and two large multipliers $M < P$ and $N < Q$. The tricky part is that you have to shift each range so that you are only multiplying the numbers in the range 1 to P–1 or 1 to Q-1. You do this by redefining the modp function.

$$\text{modp}(x) = ((x+1)M \bmod P) - 1 \qquad \text{if } x \le P-2,$$
$$\text{modp}(x) = ((x-P+2)N \bmod Q) + P - 2 \quad \text{if } x > P-2.$$

With this redefined modp function, the PMod1 through PMod4 ciphers work the same as before, and have the same ratings. This diagram shows how the range 0 to $2^{64}-1$ is divided.

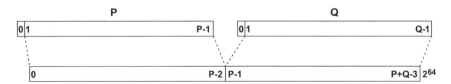

15.10 *Change of base*

Changing the number base is closely related to multiplication by a large integer. Changing number bases is a slow operation when the number is very large, so the best strategy is to divide the message into blocks and convert each block separately. Changing the base blurs the separations between message bytes.

There are two methods for converting numbers from one base to another. You can work from the low-order end or from the high-order end. Many people learn these techniques in school, but often forget them over time. To refresh everyone's memories, both methods are illustrated here. We will convert the number 1A87 from base 11 to base 7 using the low-end technique, and then back to base 11 using the high-end method.

With the low-end technique you repeatedly divide the number by the new base. Each remainder becomes the next digit of the converted number. Here are the steps to convert 1A87:

1A87/7 is 312 with remainder **4**.

312/7 is 49 with remainder **5**.

49/7 is 7 with remainder **4**.

7/7 is **1** with remainder **0**.

So 1A87 in base 11 becomes 10454 in base 7.

With the high-end technique you repeatedly multiply the high-end digits by the old base and add the next digit. Here are the steps to convert 10454:

1×7+**0** is 7.

7×7+**4** is 49.

49×7+**5** is 312.

312×7+**4** is 1A87.

If those numbers don't look quite right to you, remember that the numbers 7, 49, 312 and 1A87 are all in base 11.

There are lots of neat ciphers you can make, based on changing bases. For example, a 16-byte block is also a 16-digit number expressed in base 256. Convert that number to another base, say 263. Now you can transpose the base-263 digits, or perform a substitution, or both. Then you could convert that to base 277, and do the same thing. Finally, you convert back to base 256. This requires a 17-byte number to hold the result. You can use any number base from 256 through 362. Remember that if any result has a leading digit 0, that digit is required so that Riva can decipher the ciphertext.

If each successive base is a little larger than the previous, the same number of digits are required at each stage. The number of digits will increase only at the last step when the number is converted back to base 256. There is no reason that the bases need to be prime.

Here is a concept for a block cipher based on base changes. Begin with a secret well-mixed keyed simple substitution S. S operates on bytes, that is, on integers from 0 to 255. S can be extended to bases larger than 256 by leaving any digit greater than 255 unchanged. This eliminates the need to have a separate substitution table for every possible base. Choose 3 number bases B_1, B_2 and B_3 satisfying $256 < B_1 < B_2 < B_3 < 363$. You will also need 3 keyed transpositions T_1, T_2 and T_3 on 16 elements. The elements are integers that can be as large as B_3-1, so they will need more than 1 byte each.

Block cipher *3Base* consists of the following steps: (1) Substitute S. (2) Convert to base B_1. (3) Substitute S. (4) Transpose T_1. (5) Convert to base B_2. (6) Substitute S. (7) Transpose T_2. (8) Convert to base B_3. (9) Substitute S. (10) Transpose T_3. (11) Convert to base 256. (12) Substitute S. The cipher block consists of 16 elements up through step 11. Step 12 expands the block to 17 bytes. Cipher 3Base is rated Ten.

*15.11 Rings

A *ring* is an abstract version of the integers. That is, a ring is a set of elements that can be added and multiplied analogously to the way integers are added and multiplied. You are already familiar with several rings: the integers, the rational numbers, the real numbers, the integers modulo some fixed number, and perhaps the complex numbers and algebraic numbers. Some less-familiar rings are polynomials whose coefficients are members of a ring, matrices whose entries are elements of a ring, numbers of the form $a+b\sqrt{13}$, numbers of the form $a+b\sqrt[3]{7}+c\sqrt[3]{49}$, and numbers of the form $a+b\sqrt{2}+c\sqrt{3}+d\sqrt{6}$, where a, b, c and d can be integers, rationals, or integers modulo some fixed integer.

Before we discuss how to use rings in cryptography, let's lay out the formal rules for a ring. Ring addition is denoted by the + sign, a+b, and ring multiplication is denoted by juxtaposition, ab.

- For all ring elements a and b, a+b and ab are elements of the ring. (Closure)
- For all ring elements a, b and c, a+(b+c) = (a+b)+c. (Associative rule for addition)
- For all ring elements a and b, a+b = b+a. (Commutative rule for addition)
- There is a ring element 0 such that 0+a = a+0 = a for all ring elements a. (Additive identity)
- For every ring element a there is an element −a such that a+(−a) = (−a)+a = 0. (Additive inverse)
- For all ring elements a, b and c, a(bc) = (ab)c. (Associative rule for multiplication)
- For all ring elements a, b and c, a(b+c) = ab+ac, and (a+b)c = ac+bc. (Distributive rule)
- There is a ring element 1 such that 1a = a1 = a for every element a. (Multiplicative identity)

The parentheses are usually dropped when adding an additive inverse, so (−a)+b becomes −a+b, and a+(−b) becomes a−b.

Notice that ring multiplication need not be commutative. If the ring multiplication is commutative, then the ring is called *commutative*. All the previous examples are commutative rings. For the time being, let's assume that all of the rings under discussion are commutative. If a ring element a has a multiplicative inverse a', so that aa' = 1, then a is called *invertible*. When working with finite rings, it is advisable to try multiplying all possible pairs of elements to determine which elements are invertible, and keep a table of the inverses for quick reference.

A simple way to use ring arithmetic for encryption is to combine the ripple cipher of section 11.8 with the lagged linear addition of section 13.14.1. Let's choose the ring *R13*, whose elements take the form $a+b\sqrt{13}$, where a and b are hexadecimal digits, that is, integers modulo 16. The two hex digits a and b form a byte that represents a character. For example, the letter X is represented in ASCII code as hexadecimal 58, corresponding to the *R13* ring element $5+8\sqrt{13}$.

Two *R13* ring elements $a+b\sqrt{13}$ and $c+d\sqrt{13}$ are added as $(a+c)+(b+d)\sqrt{13}$, and multiplied together as $(ac+13bd)+(ad+bc)\sqrt{13}$, with all addition done modulo 16. For example, if $x = 2+3\sqrt{13}$ and $y = 4+5\sqrt{13}$, then $x+y$ is $6+8\sqrt{13}$ and xy is $11+6\sqrt{13}$.

For the combined ripple + lagged linear addition cipher, which could be called *Lag Ripple*, you replace x_n with $ax_n+bx_{n-i}+cx_{n-j}$, where the coefficients a, b and c are elements of the ring, in this case *R13*, and the lags *i* and *j* are small integers such as 2 and 5. The plaintext could be divided into blocks of, say, 16 bytes, but for short messages the cipher could be applied to the entire message. Let's suppose the latter. The encipherment would then be

$$x_n = ax_n + bx_{n-2} + cx_{n-5} \text{ for n = 1,2,3, ...,L.}$$

Here a is an invertible element of *R13*, b and c are any elements of *R13*, and L is the length of the message. The arithmetic is carried out in the ring. You may recognize this as a variant of the **madd** combining function from section 11.8. The usual wraparound would be used for enciphering the first few bytes.

For a single pass using known fixed lags, lag ripple is rated Two, since there are only 256^3 combinations of coefficients possible. With a simple substitution before and after the lagged ripple phase, the rating increases to Five. Using 3 passes, with different coefficients and different lags for each pass, the rating goes to Six.

Triple Ripple uses 3 passes with a secret keyed simple substitution before each ripple pass and after the last ripple pass. Each pass has different secret coefficients and lags. Optionally, you can start the ripple from a different position in the message for each pass and wrap around. Triple Ripple is rated Ten.

15.12 *Matrices over a ring*

In sections 15.1 and 15.2 we looked at the Hill cipher, which consisted of treating each block of the message as a vector of integers, and multiplying that vector by a matrix of integers modulo 26 or 256. There is nothing magical about integers modulo 26 or 256. You can represent the characters of a message using elements of any ring. If there are more characters than ring elements, you can use pairs or triplets of ring elements, much as pairs of integers 1 to 5 are used in the Polybius square (section 9.1) to represent a 25-letter alphabet.

Suppose that you used a matrix over **R13**, the ring whose elements have the form $a+b\sqrt{13}$. If you view a plaintext block as a vector of 32 hex digits instead of 16 bytes, and you write out the expression for every digit of the matrix product, you will see that every hex digit in the ciphertext is a linear combination of the plaintext digits. So using a 16×16 matrix over the **R13** ring is equivalent to using a 32×32 matrix over the hex digits, that is, the integers modulo 16. Therefore such a cipher would still be vulnerable to a known plaintext attack. The attack would require at least 256 bytes of plaintext. Probably 16×17 = 272 bytes would be sufficient.

You, the sender, can easily defeat such an attack by using a keyed simple substitution before and after the matrix multiplication. Or, you could construct your own ring, a ring unknown to anyone except your legitimate correspondents. As long as you can keep your ring secret, nobody can mount any attack against your matrix cipher.

15.13 Constructing a ring

A ring of N elements, called a ring of *order* N, is represented by two N×N tables, its addition table and its multiplication table. Constructing a ring can be done in stages. Let's construct a ring of 8 elements as a demonstration. Begin by constructing the addition table. You know from the outset that the ring must have two elements, 0 the additive identity, and 1 the multiplicative identity. The sums 0+a and a+0 are known for all a. This gives us the top row and left column of the addition table.

+	0	1	2	3	4	5	6	7
0	0	1	2	3	4	5	6	7
1	1	-	-	-	-	-	-	-
2	2	-	-	-	-	-	-	-
3	3	-	-	-	-	-	-	-
4	4	-	-	-	-	-	-	-
5	5	-	-	-	-	-	-	-
6	6	-	-	-	-	-	-	-
7	7	-	-	-	-	-	-	-

Next, start on the second row. The strategy is to take the first sum whose value is not yet assigned, assign that sum a value, and then make all possible deductions about other sums by using the associative rule. Suppose you wanted 1+1 = 2, 2+1 = 3, 3+1 = 4 and 4+1 = 0. Using the associative rule, you can now fill in the upper-left section of the table. For example, you can determine 2+2 because 2+2 = (1+1)+2 = 1+(1+2) = 1+3 = 4.

+	0	1	2	3	4	5	6	7
0	0	1	2	3	4	5	6	7
1	1	2	3	4	0	-	-	-
2	2	3	4	0	1	-	-	-
3	3	4	0	1	2	-	-	-
4	4	0	1	2	3	-	-	-
5	5	-	-	-	-	-	-	-
6	6	-	-	-	-	-	-	-
7	7	-	-	-	-	-	-	-

Since 4+1 = 0, it follows that the additive inverse of 1 is 4 and the additive inverse of 4 is 1. Likewise, 2 is the additive inverse of 3, and 3 is the additive inverse of 2. So, what value should we assign to 5+1? It can't be 0, because 4 and 5 cannot both be the additive inverse of 1. It can't be 1 because then 5 would be 0. It can't be 2 because 5+1 = 1+1 means 5 = 1. Likewise, 5+1 can't be 3 or 4. It also can't be 5 because 5+5 = 5 means 5 = 0. That leaves 5+1 = 6 or 5+1 = 7. These are equivalent, so assume 5+1 = 6. This forces 6+1 = 7 and 7+1 = 5. That means 5+1+1+1 = 5. That makes 1+1+1 = 0. Since we already know 1+1+1 = 3, that means 3 = 0. Impossible. This is a dead end. Setting 4+1 = 0 does not work.

What went wrong? The cycle 1+1+1+1+1 = 0 has 5 terms. The length of any such cycle in a ring of order N must evenly divide N. Since 5 does not evenly divide 8 it was impossible to complete the addition table. That leaves you with 3 choices, to make the length of the cycle 2, 4 or 8. If you choose cycle length 8, then the ring is the integers modulo 8. If you choose cycle length 2, then addition is the same as exclusive-OR. Since the goal was to develop a new ring, that leaves cycle length 4. The addition table must be

+	0	1	2	3	4	5	6	7
0	0	1	2	3	4	5	6	7
1	1	2	3	0	7	4	5	6
2	2	3	0	1	6	7	4	5
3	3	0	1	2	5	6	7	4
4	4	7	6	5	2	1	0	3
5	5	4	7	6	1	0	3	2
6	6	5	4	7	0	3	2	1
7	7	6	5	4	3	2	1	0

The multiplication table can now be worked out by using the distributive rule. For example, $2 \times 2 = 2 \times (1+1) = 2+2 = 0$.

×	0	1	2	3	4	5	6	7
0	0	0	0	0	0	0	0	0
1	0	1	2	3	4	5	6	7
2	0	2	0	2	2	0	2	0
3	0	3	2	1	6	5	4	7
4	0	4	2	6	4	0	6	2
5	0	5	0	5	0	5	0	5
6	0	6	2	4	6	0	4	2
7	0	7	0	7	2	5	2	5

Let's call this ring **R8**. It is a commutative ring, since ab = ba for all ring elements a and b. Notice that 1 and 3 are the only elements in ring **R8** that have multiplicative inverses, and that each is its own inverse.

There are two rings that deserve special mention, Gaussian integers and quaternions.

15.13.1 *Gaussian integers*

Gaussian integers are numbers of the form a+bi, where a and b are integers, and i is the imaginary number $\sqrt{-1}$. In other words, Gaussian integers are complex numbers where the real and imaginary parts are both integers. For cryptographic use, a and b may be integers modulo 16. The Gaussian number a+bi can thus be used to represent the hexadecimal number ab. For example, the letter X, which is 58 in hexadecimal ASCII code, would be represented by the Gaussian integer 5+8i.

Gaussian integers are added and multiplied like this:

$$(a+bi) + (c+di) = (a+c) + (b+d)i,$$
$$(a+bi) \times (c+di) = (ac-bd) + (ad+bc)i.$$

where the addition and multiplication are done modulo 16 for cryptographic use.

15.13.2 *Quaternions*

Quaternions were invented by Irish mathematician William Rowan Hamilton of Trinity College Dublin, the Royal Astronomer of Ireland, in 1843 to describe the motions of a rotating body. They are numbers of the form a+bi+cj+dk, where a, b, c and d are ordinary numbers, and i, j and k are abstract units. The defining relationship for quaternions is $i^2 = j^2 = k^2 = ijk = -1$. From this relationship, you can derive these rules for multiplication:

```
ij = k      ji = -k
jk = i      kj = -i
ki = j      ik = -j
```

Quaternion multiplication is not commutative. Quaternions are often used as *the* example of a non-commutative ring.

Quaternions are widely used in physics for representing such things as points on a spherical surface, and the rotations of solid bodies. They can be adapted for cryptographic use by letting a, b, c and d be integers modulo 16 or modulo 256. That will let each quaternion represent 2 or 4 characters of a message.

Another way to use quaternions is to let the coefficients a, b, c and d be integers modulo 2^{32}. You can use a secret well-mixed set of 5-bit, 6-bit or 8-bit character codes so that each coefficient can represent 6, 5 or 4 characters, respectively. The entire quaternion will therefore represent 24, 20 or 16 characters of the message. You can encipher the message quaternion M by either left-multiplying or right-multiplying M by a secret quaternion multiplier. Since quaternion multiplication is not commutative, it is much stronger to both left-multiply and right-multiply it, say AMB. As with ordinary multiplication, the low-order byte in each component is weakest, so it is a good idea to cyclically shift the entire 16-byte block left by 16 bit positions after the first multiplication. The same set of character codes can be used to convert the product back to standard ASCII characters, but it is stronger to use a different set of codes, preferably different-sized codes.

Let's call this method *Qmult*. Qmult is rated Ten. To decipher this message, Riva must left-multiply by the inverse quaternion A', and right-multiply by the inverse quaternion B'. The inverse of the quaternion a+bi+cj+dk is given by $(a–bi–cj–dk)/(a^2+b^2+c^2+d^2)$. Since we are working modulo 2^{32}, $a^2+b^2+c^2+d^2$ will have a multiplicative inverse whenever it is odd, that is, whenever either one or three of the coefficients are odd.

15.14 *Finding an invertible matrix*

To use a matrix for a Hill-style cipher, that matrix must be invertible. Invertible matrices are often difficult to find. If the number of invertible elements in the ring is i, and the total number of elements is r, then the probability that a random n×n matrix over that ring is invertible is $(i/r)^n$. For the *R8* ring, i/r is $2/8 = 1/4$. (This is in sharp contrast to matrices over the rational numbers or the real numbers where every element except 0 has a multiplicative inverse, and therefore almost every matrix is invertible.) If the matrices are small, you can usually find an invertible matrix by choosing the elements at random, and then trying all possible values for the last element, or, at worst, the last two elements. By using the last 1 or 2 elements you can reduce the matrix to the bottom two rows and not have to do a full reduction for each trial.

I have chosen not to cover determinants in this book, since I don't know of any use for them in cryptography, however, for readers who are familiar with determinants, a matrix is invertible if the value of its determinant is an invertible element in the ring. In particular, a matrix over the integers is invertible only if its determinant is +1 or –1.

When the desired matrix is larger, it may not be feasible to *find* an invertible matrix. Instead, you need to *construct* an invertible matrix. You begin by constructing a set of matrices of the desired size in one of two specific forms: triangular and block diagonal. Here are 4×4 examples of the four types of triangular matrices.

Upper triangular	Lower triangular	Upper anti-triangular	Lower anti-triangular
$\begin{pmatrix} a & b & c & d \\ 0 & e & f & g \\ 0 & 0 & h & i \\ 0 & 0 & 0 & j \end{pmatrix}$	$\begin{pmatrix} a & 0 & 0 & 0 \\ b & c & 0 & 0 \\ d & e & f & 0 \\ g & h & i & j \end{pmatrix}$	$\begin{pmatrix} a & b & c & d \\ e & f & g & 0 \\ h & i & 0 & 0 \\ j & 0 & 0 & 0 \end{pmatrix}$	$\begin{pmatrix} 0 & 0 & 0 & a \\ 0 & 0 & b & c \\ 0 & d & e & f \\ g & h & i & j \end{pmatrix}$

An upper triangular matrix has nonzero entries only on or above the main diagonal (upper left to lower right). All other entries are zero. A lower triangular matrix has nonzero entries only on or below the main diagonal. All other entries are zero. An upper anti-triangular matrix has nonzero entries only on or above the anti-diagonal (lower left to upper right). All other entries are zero. A lower anti-triangular matrix has nonzero entries only on or below the anti-diagonal. All other entries are zero.

A triangular matrix is invertible if all of the entries on the diagonal are invertible. An anti-triangular matrix is invertible if all of the entries on the anti-diagonal are invertible. The inverses of these matrices may be found easily using the techniques of section 15.1.1. For upper triangular and lower anti-triangular matrices, the reduction process of section 15.1.1 should be carried out from right to left.

A general invertible matrix can be constructed from these triangular forms by multiplying them. This must be done prudently. The product of two upper triangular matrices will still be upper triangular, and the product of two lower triangular matrices will still be lower triangular. Anti-triangular matrices do not have this property. A sound course would be to construct one matrix of each of the four triangular types, and then form their product. If the triangular matrices are A, B, C and D, and their inverses are A', B', C' and D', then the inverse of the product ABCD is D'C'B'A'.

In addition to triangular matrices, block diagonal matrices can be used to construct invertible matrices. Here is a 5×5 example of a block diagonal matrix. This matrix may be called type 2,3 because it consists of a 2×2 matrix and a 3×3 matrix arranged along the diagonal of the 5×5 matrix.

$$\begin{pmatrix} a & b & 0 & 0 & 0 \\ c & d & 0 & 0 & 0 \\ 0 & 0 & e & f & g \\ 0 & 0 & h & i & j \\ 0 & 0 & k & l & m \end{pmatrix}$$

When two block diagonal matrices of the same type are multiplied, the result is a block diagonal matrix of the same type.

The advantage of using a block diagonal matrix is that you can find the inverses of each of the blocks separately. If you string these inverses along the diagonal, the result is the inverse of the entire matrix. It may not be feasible to find an invertible 16×16 matrix, but it is not too challenging to find four 4×4 invertible matrices. You can expand your invertible block diagonal matrix to a full matrix by multiplying by block diagonal matrices of other types, or by some invertible triangular matrices.

Go all out. Construct your invertible block diagonal matrix using the largest blocks that you can, and use 4 triangular matrices, one of each kind. Your final invertible matrix is the product of all five of these matrices.**

Three pass protocol 16

This chapter covers
- Three pass protocol based on exponentiation
- Three pass protocol based on matrix multiplication
- Three pass protocol based on 2-sided matrix multiplication

Sections 2.2 and 2.3 describe how modern cryptography is divided into 3 branches, Secret Key, Public Key and Personal Key. Up to this point, this book has described only methods for Secret Key cryptography. Public Key cryptography is described in many books, so it will not be covered here. This chapter will discuss Personal Key cryptography, the lesser-known third branch of cryptography. Personal Key cryptography is sometimes called *keyless* cryptography, since the parties do not need to transmit or share any keys.

The basic concept of Personal Key cryptography is that each of the two correspondents, Sandra and Riva, has her own personal key. This key is never transmitted or shared with anyone else, not even with one another, so there is no possibility that Emily can learn any of the personal keys through wire-tapping, intercepting broadcasts, or any other form of eavesdropping. The great advantage of Personal

Key cryptography is that you don't need to set anything up in advance. There does not need to be any secret, secure channel for exchanging keys. The messages can be exchanged on public channels. No key servers or other infrastructure are required.

Personal Key cryptography is accomplished by means of the *three pass protocol*, which was invented by Adi Shamir of the Weizmann Institute in Israel, about 1975. To illustrate the method, I devised a little story:

> *There once was a King who loved the Queen of a neighboring country. To woo the Queen, the King wished to send her a precious gem. The King had an impervious strongbox and a pickproof lock. But how could he send the key? If the messenger had both the key and the strongbox, he could open the box and steal the gem. The King could send the key with a second messenger, but he feared the two messengers would arrange to meet up along the route and steal the gem together. The Queen proposed an ingenious solution.*

> *The King would put his lock on the strongbox and send it to the Queen. She would then add her own lock and send the strongbox back with both locks. The King would then remove his lock with his key, and send the strongbox back with only the Queen's lock. She could then unlock the box with her own key and get the gem.*

Here the two locks are stand-ins for two encryptions, and the two keys represent the corresponding decryptions. The message would be encrypted with the sender's encryption function, sent to the receiver, encrypted with the receiver's encryption function, sent back to the sender, decrypted with the sender's decryption function, sent back to the receiver and decrypted with the receiver's decryption function. This means the message is sent 3 times, hence the name *three pass protocol*.

*Let's break that down. Let the message be M, let Sandra's encryption and decryption functions be S and S', and let Riva's encryption and decryption functions be R and R'. On the first pass Sandra encrypts the message M with her encryption function S and sends SM to Riva. On the second pass, Riva encrypts that message SM with her own encryption function R and sends the doubly encrypted message RSM back to Sandra. On the third pass Sandra applies her decryption function S' to the message RSM to get S'RSM. This is intended to remove the S encryption. It will only do that if either R and S commute, or S' and R commute. That would mean S'RSM = RS'SM = RM. This lets Riva remove her encryption and read the message.

So, to get this three-pass scheme to work we need to find a commutative encryption function, or two encryption functions that commute with one another. I can think of 3 commutative encryption functions right off the top of my head: addition, multiplication and exclusive-OR. It is easy to imagine an encryption where there is a key the same length as the message, and encryption consists of adding the key byte by byte to the message, or multiplying the message bytes by the key bytes, or exclusive-ORing the message with the key. These are all simple forms of the one-time pad.

None of these is secure. If Emily manages to obtain all three encrypted messages, she can easily remove the encryptions. If the function is addition, the 3 messages are M+S, M+S+R and M+R. If Emily adds the first and third messages and subtracts the second message, she gets $(M+S)+(M+R)-(M+S+R) = M$. The result is exactly M. The same method works when the encryption function is multiplication. The 3 messages are $(M\times S)$, $(M\times R)$, and $(M\times S\times R)$. Taking $(M\times S)\times(M\times R)\div(M\times S\times R)$ again yields M. When the encryption function is exclusive-OR, finding M is even simpler, since exclusive-OR is its own inverse. Simply exclusive-OR the 3 encrypted messages together, and the result is the original message, $(M\oplus S)\oplus(M\oplus R)\oplus(M\oplus S\oplus R) = M$.

Two encryption functions that commute are substitution and transposition. These are also insecure. Since Emily will see the message both before and after the transposition, she can trivially determine the transposition.

What is required, then, is a pair of encryption functions S and R that commute, and such that Emily cannot determine M even if she has SM, RSM and RM.

16.1   Shamir's method

Shamir's solution to this problem was to use exponentiation. Let p be a large prime, say in the range of 300 to 600 decimal digits. Sandra will choose an encryption exponent s. The corresponding decryption exponent is s' such that $ss'\equiv 1 \pmod{p-1}$. This follows from Fermat's Little Theorem, if $0<a<p$, then $a^{p-1}\equiv 1 \pmod p$. Section 14.4.2 describes how to choose the prime p, and section 15.4 describes how to determine s'. In the same way, Riva chooses her encryption and decryption exponents, r and r'. The two encryptions commute because $(M^s)^r = M^{sr} = M^{rs} = (M^r)^s$.

Sandra computes $(M^s \bmod p)$ and sends it to Riva. Riva computes $(M^{sr} \bmod p)$ and sends that back to Sandra. Sandra computes $(M^{srs'} \bmod p) = (M^r \bmod p)$ and sends it back to Riva, who finally computes $(M^{rr'} \bmod p) = M$, which is the original message. The method is believed to be secure because determining s or r requires solving the discrete logarithm problem. As discussed in section 14.4, this problem is known to be computationally difficult. No computationally feasible algorithms are known.

This method is very slow. All these exponentiations and modulo reductions of large numbers take a great deal of computing. The next section describes one attempt at a solution.

16.2   Massey-Omura

The *Massey-Omura* method was invented by James Massey of ETH Zurich, and Jim K. Omura of UCLA in 1982. (His name is listed on the patent as Jimmy Omura. He was my classmate at MIT, although I do not remember him.) The Massey-Omura system is essentially the same as the Shamir system, except that the modulus is of the form 2^k. This means that the residue modulo 2^k can be computed simply by taking the low-order k bits of the number. This is much faster than computing the residue modulo p, which is done essentially by long division using these 300- to 600-digit numbers.

The question of which method is faster was hotly debated for several years in Association for Computing Machinery (ACM) and Institute of Electrical and Electronics Engineers (IEEE) publications.

16.3 Discrete logarithm

The security of Diffie-Hellman key exchange, the Shamir three pass protocol and the Massey-Omura method all depend on the difficulty of solving the discrete logarithm problem. Three popular algorithms for this problem are exhaustive enumeration, good up to 10^{12}, Daniel Shanks's baby-step giant-step algorithm, good up to 10^{18}, and John Pollard's rho algorithm, good up to 10^{22}. However, we need an algorithm suitable for 10^{300}. To give some feel for how difficult the discrete logarithm is, let's look at a composite method for solving it. This is not something you can do at home with a PC. It takes a mainframe with massive storage, or a network of many PCs working cooperatively. Or, you can skip this section and just accept that the discrete logarithm problem is hard.

16.3.1 Logarithms

Start by considering how people computed ordinary logarithms back before computers. One method was to take a number like $b = 1.000001$ and laboriously take successive powers of it. You would find that b^{693148} was the closest power to 2, and that $b^{2302586}$ was the nearest power to 10. Then you would know that $\log_{10}(2)$ was very nearly $693148/2302586$, which is .3010302. The correct value is .3010300, so this method gives an excellent approximation.

You can do the same thing in a ring such as integers modulo some prime p. Suppose Sandra sends the message 6 mod 13 and Riva returns the message 7 mod 13. Emily wishes to know what exponent Riva has used for her encipherment. Instead of powers of 1.000001 you would use a primitive root of the modulus 13, for example 2. With such a small modulus Emily can easily enumerate all the powers of 2 modulo 13.

1	2	3	4	5	6	7	8	9	10	11	12	N
2	4	8	3	6	12	11	9	5	10	7	1	2^N (mod 13)

Emily now knows that Sandra sent 2^5 and Riva sent back 2^{11}. So $(2^5)^r \equiv 2^{5r} \equiv 2^{11}$ (mod 13). This means $5r \equiv 11$ (mod 12). You can solve this in your head. Just think $11+12 = 23$, $23+12 = 35$. Since 35 is a multiple of 5, namely 5×7, that means r must be 7. You can check it with a hand calculator, $6^7 = 279936 \equiv 7$ (mod 13). Sandra sent 6, Riva sent back 7, so this checks out.

16.3.2 Powers of primes

Exhaustive enumeration gives Emily one way to search, but that's not going to work when p is large. Let's try an idea from John Pollard's *rho algorithm*. The first step is to generate multiple sequences of powers modulo p, and look for repeats. Emily can do that with several primitive roots simultaneously, one root per core. Now let's double that. If b is a primitive root modulo p she can compute b^2, b^3, b^4, b^5, ... (mod p) on one processor, and b^2, b^4, b^8, b^{16}, ... (mod p) on another processor. That gives Emily two separate sequences of powers for each primitive root she uses.

Besides the primitive roots, Emily can also check directly. Sandra sends SM and Riva sends back RSM. Emily can generate the sequences $(SM)^2$, $(SM)^3$, $(SM)^4$, $(SM)^5$, ... and $(SM)^2$, $(SM)^4$, $(SM)^8$, $(SM)^{16}$, ..., and likewise for RSM. This gives Emily four more sequences of powers.

In addition to these orderly sequences of powers, she can also generate some disorderly sequences. These are commonly called *random walks* or *drunk walks*. One way to do this is to square the last power that was generated, and then multiply that by one of the earlier powers. Emily can choose the early power at random, or she could use the middle element of the list. For example, suppose she already has the powers x, x^2, x^4, x^8 and x^{16}. For the next power she could square x^{16} to get x^{32}, then multiply by, say, x^2 to get x^{34}. For the following power she would square x^{34} to get x^{68} and multiply that by another list element, say x^8, to get x^{76}. And so forth.

Another form of random walk Emily can generate uses 2 or 3 base primes. Each base prime should be a primitive root. Begin with the product of these primes. To generate the next product, she would choose one of the primes at random and multiply by that. The more sequences Emily has going, the sooner she will start to get results.

16.3.3 *Crash*

Okay, now Emily has all of these sequences. Then what? She is looking for the same number to show up on two lists. This is called a *collision*, or *crash*. Say she finds $3^{172964} \equiv 103^{4298755} \pmod{p}$. This lets her express 103 as a power of 3 (mod p) by solving the congruence $172964r \equiv 4298755 \pmod{p-1}$. The method is described in section 15.4. Once she accumulates enough crashes she can establish a chain such as $RSM \equiv 19^a$, $19 \equiv 773^b$, $773 \equiv 131^c$, ..., $103^y \equiv (SM)^z$. Multiply all of the exponents modulo p–1 and she will get $RSM \equiv (SM)^r \pmod{p}$. That exponent r is Riva's encryption function. Emily has cracked the cipher!

That's not quite as easy as it sounds. When p is a 300-digit prime, she needs on the order of 10^{150} of these powers before she starts seeing any crashes. If Emily had 1,000,000 processors cranking out these powers at a rate of 1,000,000 per second, she could potentially generate 3×10^{19} per year. This would mean it would take about 10^{130} years before she started seeing any results, and far more than that until she could establish such a chain. Also, it would take some multiple of 10^{150} bytes of storage.

16.3.4 *Factoring*

Instead of searching for crashes, each time a new power is generated Emily could try to factor its residue modulo p. Suppose that she succeeds in factoring the residue of $97^a \pmod{p}$ and finds $97^a \equiv 11^b 29^c 83^d \pmod{p}$. She can solve this congruence for 97. Let the multiplicative inverse of a modulo p–1 be a'. Raise the congruence to the a' power. $97^{aa'} \equiv 97 \equiv (11^b 29^c 83^d)^{a'} \pmod{p}$. After multiplying all of the exponents and reducing them modulo p–1, the result is $97 \equiv 11^e 29^f 83^g \pmod{p}$ for some values e, f and g. (The actual values could be up to 300 digits each if p has 300 digits.) Once she has an expression for one of the base primes, in this case 97, she can substitute that value into all of the factored products, both the ones she already has and the ones she will find later.

Emily will not be able to factor the residue of every power. Factoring a 300-digit number is very difficult, meaning very time-consuming. The best strategy is to choose a fixed base set F(B) of primes, say all the primes up to $B = 10^6$, or perhaps up to $B = 10^7$. F(B) is called the *factor base*. Try to factor each power using only the primes in the factor base. Numbers that can be factored this way are called *B-smooth*. As the numbers get larger, the proportion that are B-smooth gets smaller and smaller. Among 300-digit numbers the B-smooth numbers are rare. As Emily finds each factor, the unfactored portion of the number shrinks. If she has tried all of the primes in the base set, and some unfactored portion of the number remains, she should not try to factor it any further. It is more efficient to discard this power and move on to the next power.

Here is what Emily must do: continue generating products and factoring their residues modulo p. Keep only the B-smooth numbers and discard the rest. Check for crashes among the B-smooth numbers. Each time a crash is found, solve the congruence for the largest prime in the product so that fewer and fewer base primes are needed to express each product. She may reserve one or more processors dedicated solely to this task.

Suppose that q^n is a power of a prime, and let its residue modulo p be x. Try to factor x using the primes in the base set B. If x is not B-smooth, try to factor the numbers $x+p$, $x+2p$, $x+3p$, ... It is not much harder to factor a 301-digit or 302-digit number than a 300-digit number. Set a fixed number of such trials, say 10 trials, for each residue.

When she generates these powers she needs to place special emphasis on SM and RSM. Remember, the goal of this exercise is to find the exponent r such that $(SM)^r \equiv RSM \pmod{p}$. She can't do that until she has expressed both SM and RSM in terms of powers of the base primes. To begin, she should develop numerous sequences of powers of SM and RSM. Once she has succeeded in finding such an expression, she looks for primes within the expression that have not yet been expressed in terms of powers of smaller primes. Place the emphasis on these primes next. Continue until both SM and RSM are expressed as powers of a single prime. She can now find r using the methods of section 15.3.2.

16.3.5 *Estimates*

Suppose that she uses 10^6 base primes, that is, primes up to $B = 15,485,863$. To express all of these in terms of a single prime will require 10^6 congruences. Storing these requires a $10^6 \times 10^6$ matrix of exponents. The matrix is initially sparse, but it grows dense as the solution progresses, so sparse-matrix techniques will not be beneficial. Each exponent is a 300-digit number. This requires on the order of 10^{15} bytes, or one *petabyte*, of storage. As of this writing (March 2022), the largest supercomputer in the world is the Summit computer at the Oak Ridge National Laboratory, which has 2.76 petabytes of addressable storage.

The running time obviously depends on how long it takes to find B-smooth numbers. The density of B-smooth numbers is given by the de Bruijn function $\Psi(p,B)$, which gives the number of B-smooth integers less than p. It was studied by Dutch mathematician Nicolaas Govert de Bruijn. The value of $\Psi(x,x^{1/u})$ is closely approximated by $x\rho(u)$, where $\rho(u)$ is the Dickman function invented by actuary Karl Dickman. The Dickman function $\rho(u)$ is approximated by u^{-u}. In this case $x = 10^{300}$ and $x^{1/u} = 15,485,863$, so $u = 41.725$. Thus it will take about $41.725^{41.725} = 4.08 \times 10^{67}$ tries to find each B-smooth number.

Altogether it will take more than 10^{73} trials to find 10^6 B-smooth powers. Factoring each number may take up to 10^6 trial divisions, so there are 10^{79} total trial divisions. Since the numbers are 300 digits, each trial division will take some multiple of 300 operations. Call it 10^{82} operations altogether. This is a huge improvement over 10^{150} for the crash method, but still well out of reach for current computers.

This shows that 300 digits are more than sufficient for the foreseeable future, perhaps for the next 20 to 30 years. This may change as quantum computers develop, but for now 300 digits is safe.

16.4   *Matrix three pass protocol*

The Shamir and Massey-Omura methods for the three pass algorithm both use exponentiation. A different approach to the three pass algorithm is to use matrices. We have seen this before with the Hill cipher, section 15.1. The message is divided into blocks. Each block is treated as a vector of integers modulo 256. This vector is multiplied by an invertible square matrix of integers modulo 256, either on the left or on the right. For the three pass version, Sandra will have a matrix S for encryption and its inverse S' for decryption, while Riva will have encryption matrix R and decryption matrix R'. These matrices are not over the integers modulo 256, but over a ring *R* of 256 elements, and the characters of the message are treated as elements of this ring. Let the message block be M, so Sandra sends SM to Riva, Riva sends RSM back to Sandra, and Sandra deciphers it with S' to get S'RSM = RM. Now Riva can decrypt it with R', namely R'RM = M.

The tricky part is making S'RSM = RM. Matrix multiplication is not commutative, so Sandra and Riva need to choose special matrices S and R that commute with each other. To be clear, S and R are not commutative matrices. If you choose a matrix X at random, it is nearly certain that $SX \neq XS$ and $RX \neq XR$. This is an essential point, so let me repeat it, S and R are not commutative matrices. They do not commute with most other matrices. They commute with each other.

16.4.1 *Commutative family of matrices*

Sandra and Riva will need a large supply of these matrices so that Emily cannot simply try them all. This means that they need a large commutative family **F** of matrices from which to select the matrix for each block of the message.

> **NOTE** **F** is a commutative family of matrices, not a family of commutative matrices. It is essential to understand that it is the family that is commutative, and not the matrices themselves. Nearly all matrices in **F** will *not* be commutative. They will commute with one another, but not with other matrices.

The easiest way to construct a commutative family is to begin with any invertible matrix, F, and take its powers, F^0, F^1, F^2, F^3, ... , where F^0 is the identity matrix I, and $F^1 = F$. Call F the *generating matrix* for the family **F**.

Sandra and Riva will each need to use a different matrix for each block of the message, otherwise Emily might solve the set of linear equations $R(SM_i) = RSM_i$ given a sufficient set of message blocks M_i with known plaintext.

16.4.2 *Multiplicative order*

To make the family **F** large, you need to find or to construct a generating matrix F of high multiplicative order. That is, the smallest integer $n > 0$ such that $F^n = I$ needs to be large, at least 10^{25}, but preferably larger. If the matrix F is invertible, such an n will always exist, and the multiplicative inverse F' of F is F^{n-1}. A method for finding invertible matrices was given in section 15.8. Determining the multiplicative order of F is a bit of an art. It is clearly not feasible to take successive powers F until $F^n = I$, certainly not when $n > 10^{25}$. But it can be done.

To find the multiplicative order, begin with 1×1 matrices, namely the ring elements. Look at the multiplicative order of these elements. These can easily be found by enumeration, since the highest possible value for n is 255. Likely values are 2, 3, 7, 15, 31, 63, 127 and 255. The multiplicative orders for larger matrices will tend to be multiples of these values.

Suppose that the multiplicative orders of the ring elements happen to be 2, 7 and 31. When you try 2×2 matrices, first raise each matrix A to some multiple of the single-element orders, say $2^4 7^2 31 = 24304$. Then enumerate the powers of $B = A^{24304}$. Suppose you find that $B^{52} = I$. You now know for certain that the multiplicative order m of A evenly divides $x = 24304 \times 52 = 2^6 7^2 13 \times 31$, and that it is a multiple of $2^6 13$. You should next try $A^{x/7}$ and $A^{x/31}$ to see if those are I. If $A^{x/7}$ is I, you then try $A^{x/49}$. In this case the highest multiplicative order might be $2^6 7 \times 13 \times 31$.

You next tackle the 3×3 matrices. If no other prime factors besides 2, 3, 7, 13 and 31 appeared in the multiplicative orders of the 2×2 matrices, then a good starting exponent might be $x = 2^8 7^2 13^2 31^2$. Enumerate successive powers of $B = A^x$ and repeat the process of narrowing down the exponent. As the matrices get larger, the multiplicative order may increase by a factor too large to find by enumeration. In this case you will need to guess at the new prime factors that will appear.

Watch for patterns that appear in the sequence of multiplicative orders. This requires some detective work. For example, suppose 2^3-1, 2^6-1, 2^9-1 and $2^{12}-1$ appear. You won't see these directly, because they are not all prime. $2^6-1=63=3^2 7$, $2^9-1=511=7\times73$ and $2^{12}-1=4095=3^2 5\times7\times13$. So finding a 13 among the prime factors is a clue that the "real" factor may be $2^{12}-1$, and finding a 73 is a strong indicator that 2^9-1 is a factor. If you see 2^3-1, 2^6-1, 2^9-1 and $2^{12}-1$ all appear, you should expect $2^{15}-1$ to appear soon. If all of these appear, they are each divisible by 7, so the multiplicative order will be divisible by 7^4.

16.4.3 *Maximum order*

Sandra's objective in all of this is to make the family **F** as large as possible so that she and Riva have lots of choices for their matrices S and R. A useful trick is to watch the multiplicative orders for differences in the sets of factors. For example, if the multiplicative order of A is 19m and the multiplicative order of B is 23m, then the multiplicative order of AB just might be $19\times23m=437m$. If that doesn't work, then A'B or AB' may have multiplicative order 437m.

If at all possible, Sandra should choose a generating matrix F whose multiplicative order has a large prime factor, say $m>10^{35}$, in order to prevent a Silver-Pohlig-Hellman attack (section 14.4). Sandra will need to factor 2^n-1 for various n to find the ones that have large prime factors, and then find a generating matrix whose multiplicative order is divisible by one of those 2^n-1 by trying successively larger matrices.

16.4.4 *Emily attacks*

Suppose that Sandra has chosen F and **F**, and that she has sent a message to Riva. Since Sandra and Riva are communicating over a public channel, such as the internet, assume that Emily knows F, **F**, SM, RSM and RM. Her goal is to find either R or S, so she gets two chances. Let's concentrate on how Emily might find R. Emily knows two things about R. First, she knows the values of SM and RSM, so that gives her a set of n linear equations in the n^2 unknown elements of R. Second, she knows that R is in the family **F**, so it must commute with F, namely RF=FR. If the ring **R** is commutative, then this gives her $n(n-1)$ additional linear equations in the n^2 elements of R.

This works because the left side of the matrix equation RF=FR produces sums of terms of the form rf, where r is an unknown element of R and f is a known element of F. The right side produces terms of the form fr. Since the ring is commutative, the left-side terms rf can be converted to the form fr and combined with the right-side terms to form linear equations.

With n^2 linear equations in n^2 unknowns it would seem like child's play to solve those linear equations and find R. It's not that easy. Recall from section 15.3.1 that there are strong congruences and weak congruences. The same is true for linear equations over any finite ring whose size is not a prime. The more prime factors the ring size has, the more potential for weak equations. In the present case, the ring size is 2^8, with 8 prime factors, so many of the linear equations are likely to be weak. A typical size for the matrices might be 30×30 if the ring **R** were well-chosen, or 128×128, or even 256×256 with a poor choice of ring. Even with a well-chosen ring, and even if half of the equations are strong, you would expect to have at least 2^{450} solutions to the set of 30×30 = 900 equations. In practice the number of solutions is much greater because there can be equations with 4, 8 or possibly 16 solutions.

There is good news for Emily. Emily can solve for R' instead of R, and whichever one of those 2^{450} or more solutions she gets will be a valid inverse of R, letting her obtain the message by R'RM = M.

16.4.5   *Non-commutative ring*

It looks like Sandra and Riva are sunk. Emily has won this battle.

One possible answer to this attack would be for Sandra and Riva to use a non-commutative ring. Two examples of non-commutative rings are matrices and quaternions (section 15.7.2). You can form matrices whose elements are themselves matrices or quaternions, or, conversely, quaternions whose coefficients are matrices or quaternions. None of these are good choices. You would need to make them very large to produce matrices of high multiplicative order.

A better route is to construct your own ring **N** using the techniques of section 15.7. You should choose a ring that has many elements that (1) are invertible, (2) have high multiplicative order, and (3) are non-commutative. It is a tricky balancing act to find a ring that has all of these features. For example, a ring that has elements of maximal multiplicative order (255 for a 256-element ring) could not have any non-commutative elements. If you could find a ring where half of the elements are invertible, half have multiplicative order equal to about half the ring size, and half are non-commutative, *dayenu* (it would be sufficient). You cannot achieve all 3 of these goals simultaneously, but you may exceed some while coming close on the others.

With a non-commutative ring, the matrix equation RF = FR can no longer be linearized, because it is no longer certain that rf = fr. Instead, the matrix equation leads to a set of *bilinear* equations. The general term in a bilinear equation takes the form axb, where a and b are elements of the ring, and x is a variable whose value you wish to determine. While linear equations can be solved using a simple systematic approach, namely Gaussian elimination, there is no such method for bilinear equations. There is not even a general method for solving such a simple equation as ax+xb = c with a single variable, x. So solving bilinear equations over a ring is "impossible."

16.4.6   *Solving bilinear equations*

That said, I will now show you how to solve bilinear equations. The trick is to change the representation of the elements in the ring **N**. We have already seen several examples of how this can be done. In the ring **R13**, elements are represented as $a + b\sqrt{13}$. Gaussian integers are represented as a+bi. Quaternions are represented as a+bi+cj+dk. Here, i, j and k are abstract units whose products determine the behavior of the ring, and a, b, c and d are commutative elements of the ring. Quaternions can be non-commutative because the multiplication of the units is not commutative, that is, $ij \neq ji$, $ik \neq ki$ and $jk \neq kj$. With only one unit, Gaussian integers are necessarily commutative.

The trick is to *linearize* the bilinear equations by finding a representation for the non-commutative ring *N*. This is easily done. Start by dividing the elements of *N* into two sets, A and B, where A contains the elements that have representations, and B contains the remaining elements. Initially A is empty and B contains all the elements of the ring. Begin by taking the commutative elements and moving them into set A. These ring elements will represent themselves. They are the "a" term in the representation. Choose any remaining invertible element as the unit i. Take all of the ring elements that can be represented as a+bi, where a and b are commutative elements of the ring, and move them from set B into set A. So far, all of the elements of A are still commutative.

Set B cannot be empty because *N* is not commutative. We already noted that a ring with only one unit, like the Gaussian integers, must be commutative. So take a second invertible element from set B and call that the second unit, j. This time you take all elements that can be represented as a+bi+cj and move them from set B to set A. There may still be ring elements remaining in set B. In that case you would repeat these steps, but for simplicity let's suppose that (1) only two units are needed; (2) all of the elements in the ring can be represented as a+bi+cj, where i and j are the abstract units; and (3) a, b and c are commutative elements of the ring *N*. In practice, the number of units you get may depend on your choice of i and j, so you should make multiple trials to get the fewest units. This is important because more units means you will have more equations when you linearize. Since the time needed to solve a set of linear equations is proportional to the cube of the number of equations, this has a large impact.

Let's go back to the matrix equation RF = FR, and put the ring elements into the form a+bi+cj. The unknown elements of *R* would have the form x+yi+zj, where x, y and z are unknown commutative ring elements. Now a term of the matrix product RF would have the form

$$(x{+}yi{+}zj)\,(a{+}bi{+}cj) \;=\; ax + bxi + cxj + ayi + byi^2 + cyij + azj + bzj\,i + czj^2$$

where i^2, j^2, ij and ji would be further expanded as linear combinations of 1, i and j, such as d+ei+fj. The actual expansions, of course, would depend on the choice of ring and which elements were chosen as i and j.

The same must be done with the terms in the matrix product FR. In the end, instead of 900 equations in 900 unknowns you get 2700 equations in 2700 unknowns. This boosts the number of false solutions from 2^{450} up to 2^{1350}. This is bad news for Emily. False solutions do not allow her to recover the message.

16.4.7 Weaklings

The family **F** will include some weaklings, such as diagonal matrices and triangular matrices, which Emily can easily invert. These weaklings should not be used as keys. When choosing a matrix from **F**, verify that there is at least one nonzero element both above and below the main diagonal. To make this test fast, just verify that at least one of X_{12}, X_{13} and X_{23} is nonzero, and at least one of X_{21}, X_{31} and X_{32} is nonzero. Otherwise reject X and choose again. The percentage of matrices that get rejected is negligible.

16.4.8 Making it fast

The advantage of using matrices instead of exponentiation may not be clear yet. Choosing a matrix S or R from the family **F** requires taking a large power of the generating matrix F. How is that any better or faster than taking a large integer to a large power? The difference is preparation. In the Shamir and Massey-Omura methods, Sandra and Riva must take the number each has received from the other party and raise that to a large power. Since they do not know that number in advance, they cannot make any preparations to speed up the exponentiation.

With the matrix method, however, the generating matrix F is known beforehand. Both Sandra and Riva can generate some powers of F in advance, then keep this base set of matrix powers on hand so that they can generate a new power of F by just 1 or 2 matrix multiplications. For starters, they could generate the set of 16 matrices F, F^2, F^4, F^8, ... , F^{32768} using just 15 matrix multiplications.

If they did only that much, then Emily could do the same. She would have the same base set of matrices as Sandra and Riva, so she could easily determine their encryption matrices, S and R. To prevent this, Sandra and Riva need to randomize their sets of matrices. They do this by choosing two of their matrices at random and multiplying them. This product will replace one of those two matrices in the base set. Sandra and Riva do this independently. Neither one knows which powers of F the other one has chosen.

This replacement operation should be repeated many times during setup, say 1000 times, so that each party's set of matrices is thoroughly random. If 1000 seems excessive, remember that in the Shamir method using a 300-digit prime, each exponentiation will require about 1000 multiplications and 1000 modulo reductions. Sandra and Riva also need to keep the inverses of their matrices. Each time they multiply two of the powers of F they need to multiply the corresponding powers of F' so that they never need to invert any of the powers.

This setup step, generating the base set, needs to be done only once, before the first message is sent. When you have this expanded set of generating matrices you can produce a matrix for sending a message using just one multiplication for the matrix, and one for its inverse. You randomly choose two different matrices F^a and F^b from your base set, multiply to get F^{a+b}, then replace F^a by F^{a+b} so you generate different matrices each time.

Using this technique, I have found that the matrix method is about 2100 times as fast as either the Shamir or Massey-Omura exponentiation method for a 30×30 matrix versus a 1024-bit modulus.

16.5   *Two-sided three pass protocol*

The matrix multiplication in the previous matrix method may be done on either the left side or the right side, meaning the message may be enciphered as SM or MS. It is also possible to multiply on both sides. In this case the message is split into blocks of n^2 characters, and there are two independent commutative families of n×n matrices, **F** and **G**, with generating matrices F and G. Sandra will encipher the message with matrices S from **F** and T from **G**, and Riva will superencipher with matrices R from **F** and Q from **G**.

Sandra sends Riva the enciphered message SMT. Riva superenciphers this and sends back RSMTQ. Sandra removes her encipherment by using the inverse matrices S' and T', sending S'RSMTQT' = RMQ back to Riva, who deciphers it using her inverse matrices R' and Q', as R'RMQQ' = M. The 2-sided method is not practical for short messages due to its large block size, but for long messages it is much faster than the 1-sided methods because you get n^2 characters in each block instead of n characters. For 30×30 matrices it can be 15 times as fast as the 1-sided method, hence about 30,000 times as fast as the Shamir or Massey-Omura method.

Emily must solve for two matrices simultaneously. Let the 3 matrices that Emily intercepts be called X, Y and Z, that is, X = SMT, Y = RSMTQ and Z = RMQ. Emily knows that Y = RXQ and Z = S'YT'. It looks like Emily will need to solve a large set of quadratic equations over the non-commutative ring **N**, which is much more difficult than solving linear or bilinear equations. However, if these equations are multiplied by R', Q', S and T, respectively, they become R'Y = XQ, YQ' = RX, SZ = YT' and ZT = S'Y. These matrix equations multiply out to yield bilinear equations. We saw how to solve bilinear equations in section 16.4.6.

Emily can recover M if she can find both R' and Q', or if she can find both S' and T'. She has the choice of solving either the first two or the last two of these four equations. Let's continue the example of 30×30 matrices, and concentrate on solving R'Y = XQ. There are 900 unknowns in R' and 900 more in Q. This matrix equation provides 900 bilinear equations in these 1800 unknowns. Emily also knows that R' is in **F**, and Q is in **G**, so R'F = FR' and QG = GQ. Each of these yields an additional 30×29 = 870 bilinear equations. This gives Emily a total of 2640 bilinear equations in 1800 unknowns. These equations can be linearized by changing the representation of the ring elements.

This results in 7920 linear equations in 5400 unknowns. When there are more equations than unknowns the system is called *overdetermined*. As Emily reduces the set of equations, the excess equations simply drop away. That is, many rows of the

7920×5400 matrix become all-zero. They may be shifted to the bottom of the matrix and ignored. In the end, the same difficulties appear as the 1-sided case, namely that there are a multitude of solutions. Since the 2-sided equations are overdetermined, they are stronger than the 1-sided equations. On the other hand, there are twice as many unknowns. It is not clear which method is ultimately stronger. You might simply opt for the 2-sided method because it is so much faster.**

Codes

17

This chapter covers

- Ideas for constructing a code

Over the centuries, despite advances in ciphers, then cipher machines, and now digital cryptography, the military has always relied on codes. Even today, we can assume that the military still has codes as a backup in case electronic devices fail or power is unavailable.

Most codes replace letters, syllables, words or phrases with groups of a fixed size, usually 3, 4 or 5 decimal digits, or groups of 3 or 4 letters. Variable-length codes are uncommon. Codes generally fall into two types, single codes and double codes. In a single code the words and phrases are listed alphabetically and the code groups are assigned in numeric order, although not consecutively, so words and code groups can be looked up using the same list. The weakness of this method is obvious. If your opponent has figured out that code 08452 means CANNON then they know that any codes close in value to 08452 must have meanings such as CAMOUFLAGE, CAMPAIGN, CANCEL, CANINE, CANVAS, CAPITAL, CAPITULATE, CAPSIZE, CAPTAIN, and so forth.

In a double code, the code groups are assigned in random order. The code book will contain two separate lists, one that lists the words and phrases in alphabetic order, and one that lists the code groups in numeric order. In the past, double codes took months to compile, and were very costly. A government might, therefore, use the same code for years, largely negating its effectiveness. Since the 1960s, the job of compiling a double code can be done by computer in seconds.

Compilers of codes had lots of tricks to make their codes more secure. For common words and phrases they would provide lots of equivalent code groups, or synonyms. Thus a naval code might have 10 to 20 code groups for "ship", while an army code might have that number of code groups for "artillery" and a diplomatic code might have as many groups for "treaty". Codes tend to have lots of null groups. Whole sections of a message may be entirely null. Some code groups may have multiple meanings depending on some indicator, such as the last digit of the preceding group.

Some code books are printed in two columns. The code is taken from either the left or the right column according to some indicator. For example, if the current code group begins with an even digit, take the next code group from the left column, otherwise take the next code group from the right column.

17.1   The Joker

The *Joker* is a style of code of my own invention. If any readers want to devise their own codes, the Joker may give them some useful ideas. The basic concept is that in each code group one letter or digit is distinct from the others. In a 5-character group, for example, 4 characters would carry the meaning, while the other character, called the Joker, is there to cause mayhem. Simply having one null character makes the opponent's job a good deal harder, but there is much more you can do with this special letter or digit.

Let's assume a code of 5-digit groups. Four of the digits are the code itself, and the other digit is the Joker. To get started, suppose the Joker is always in the middle position in the first code group in each message. Let's also assume that this is a 2-column code book, where the codes in the left column have entirely different meanings from the codes in the right column. For example, 0022 in the left column could mean "rescue," while 0022 in the right column means "engine."

Similarly, there could be two columns of meanings for the Joker, so the Joker can move to a different digit position, and also move to a different column.

Here is a list of possible meanings you could assign to the Joker. There are a lot more than 10. You can pick the 10 you want. Or, use 2 columns and have 20 meanings for the Joker. Or, use letters instead of digits and choose 26 meanings for the Joker.

- Starting with the next group, the Joker moves 1 position left.
- Starting with the next group, the Joker moves 1 position right.
- Starting with the next group, the Joker moves to position 1.
- Starting with the next group, the Joker moves to position 2, and so on.
- For the next group only, the Joker is in position 1.
- For the next group only, the Joker is in position 2, and so on.
- Switch to the left column of codes.

- Switch to the right column of codes.
- Switch to the opposite column of codes.
- For the next code only, use the opposite code column.
- For the next 2 codes, use the opposite code column, and so on.
- The next group is null.
- The group after next is null.
- The next 2 groups are null, and so on.
- In the next group, the code is null but the Joker is real.
- In the next group, the code is real but the Joker is null.
- Swap the order of the next 2 groups.
- Add 1111 to the code in the next group (non-carrying addition).
- Add 3030 to the code in the next group (non-carrying addition), and so on.
- If the next code is even, add 2222, otherwise subtract 2222 (non-carrying).
- Add 1 to the Joker in the next group (non-carrying).
- Add 2 to the Joker in the next group (non-carrying), and so on.
- Add this 4-digit code to the next 4-digit code. The Joker is excluded.
- Read the digits of the next code backward, for example 1075 really means 5701.
- Ignore the following codes until there is a code starting with 0.
- The next group is a special indicator.

For an example of non-carrying addition, see section 4.6.

Special indicators require a fuller explanation. In a special indicator, all 5 digits of the code group serve a special purpose, such as telling where the Joker will be, or which column to use. For example, a special indicator of 13152 could mean that in the following 5 groups the Joker will be in positions 1, 3, 1, 5 and 2 in that order. The special indicator could also tell which column the next 5 codes are taken from, an odd digit indicating the code is from the left column and an even digit indicating the code is from the right column. A special indicator of 10384 could mean that in the following 5 groups the codes are taken from the left, right, left, right and right columns successively.

Another use for a special indicator might be to specify numbers to add to the codes in the next 5 groups. For example, the special indicators might mean to add the following values to the 4-digit codes:

```
1 1000    5 1100    9 0111
2 0100    6 0110    0 1111
3 0010    7 0011
4 0001    8 1110
```

These values would be added using non-carrying addition, addition modulo 10.

The Joker always indicates an action to be taken in the following group or groups, never in the current or preceding group. For example, you should not use a Joker whose meaning is "cancel the previous Joker." When a Joker indicates an action covering several subsequent groups, make certain that the actions of two different Jokers do not conflict. For example, you should not have a Joker in group 20 saying, "the next 3 codes are taken from the left column" followed by a Joker in group 21 saying, "the next 3 codes are taken from the right column."

Another trick that can be used with the Joker code is to use a letter A through E instead of a Joker. This letter may appear in any position, and supersedes the expected position for the Joker. A letter A means the next Joker will be in position 1, a B indicates position 2, and so forth. You can also assign meanings to the letters F, G and H. For example, F could indicate that the code should be taken from the opposite column and the next Joker will be in position 1.

Do not use the letter I if there is any chance that it could be mistaken for the digit 1. I like to use the letter J as a super-Joker. It means that everything following is null. You can bang on for another 10, 20 or 100 code groups of gibberish and really send Emily into delirium. Or, you can use those nulls to send a misleading false message, say "Normandy landing postponed to June 10 at Utah beach."

Quantum computers 18

This chapter covers

- Properties of quantum computers
- Using quantum computers for communications
- Using quantum computers for key exchange
- Using quantum computers for solving optimization problems
- Using quantum computers for decrypting block ciphers
- Ultracomputers, a step beyond quantum computers

As I write this book, quantum computers are in their infancy. There are no more than 20 quantum computers in the entire world, none of which contain more than about 50 qubits, or quantum bits. I write this chapter knowing that much or all of it may be outdated, or proven wrong, even before the book gets released. Much of the mathematics used in quantum mechanics and quantum computing is well beyond the scope of this book, so parts of this chapter will simply mention quantum methods and algorithms without any explanation of how they work.

The basis for quantum computing is the *quantum bit*, or *qubit*. A qubit has two *basis states* that are denoted |0⟩ and |1⟩, corresponding to the 0 and 1 states of an ordinary bit in a conventional computer. The notation |1⟩ is called *bra-ket* notation. When the angled brace is on the left, like ⟨0| it is called *bra*, so ⟨0| is read "bra-0." When the angled brace is on the right it is called *ket*, so |1⟩ is read "ket-1." The notation was invented by Nobel Prize winner English physicist Paul Adrien Maurice Dirac.

An ordinary bit in a conventional computer has a definite value that may be 0 or 1. The value can be only 0 or 1, not some value between, not multiple values at once, and not sometimes 0 and sometimes 1. The physical device, such as a magnetic spot on a surface, may be switched from one value to the other by applying a current or a magnetic field. There can be a brief transition, but the device cannot stay in any type of intermediate or mixed state.

18.1   Superposition

By contrast, a qubit does not have a value until a measurement or observation is taken. At that point its value will be either 0 or 1. The basis state |0⟩ means that there is a 1.0 probability that its value will be 0, and the basis state |1⟩ means that there is a 1.0 probability that its value will be 1. In general, the qubit will be in a *superposition* of both basis states $\alpha|0\rangle+\beta|1\rangle$, where α and β are complex numbers such that $|\alpha|^2+|\beta|^2=1$. The probability that this qubit yields a 0 when it is measured is $|\alpha|^2$, and the probability that the qubit yields a 1 is $|\beta|^2$. The notation $|\alpha|$ means the *magnitude* of α. The magnitude of a complex number a+bi is $\sqrt{a^2+b^2}$. Since the result of the measurement is probabilistic, the measurement of two qubits in identical states can give different results. Any number of states may be superposed.

When a quantum state x consists of several qubits, say x_1, x_2, x_3, the state ⟨x| is represented as a row vector $(\bar{x}_1, \bar{x}_2, \bar{x}_3)$ where the bar over each component means the *complex conjugate*. If the complex number α is a+bi, then its complex conjugate $\bar{\alpha}$ is a−bi. The complex conjugate has the property that the product $\alpha\bar{\alpha}=a^2+b^2=|\alpha|^2$. Conversely, the state |y⟩ is represented by a column vector

$$\begin{pmatrix} y_1 \\ y_2 \\ y_3 \end{pmatrix}$$

Since the row vector in this example is a 1×3 matrix, and the column vector is a 3×1 matrix, they can be multiplied. The matrix product, denoted ⟨x|y⟩, is a 1×1 matrix whose single element is the inner product $\bar{x}\cdot y$. That is, ⟨x|y⟩ is a scalar. (If this is unfamiliar, you can review section 11.3.)

Since any two states can be superposed, and those states, in turn, can be superposed, any qubit may be in a superposition of arbitrarily many states.

Superposed states are fragile. Small perturbations, such as temperature fluctuations or mechanical vibrations, can cause the qubit to drop out of the superposed state and back into one of the basis states. This is called *decohering*. This fragility is a major obstacle in achieving large reliable quantum computers. In particular, when a measurement is taken, the qubit will *decohere* and drop into whichever basis state was observed. Similarly, a qubit cannot be copied because that would require an observation.

If it is hard to understand the concept of a coefficient that is a complex number, maybe this will help. Visualize the point (a,b) in Cartesian coordinates. The line segment from the origin (0,0) to the point (a,b) is a vector. It has both magnitude and direction. When two states are superposed, these vectors are added according to the rules of coordinate geometry, which is exactly how complex numbers are added. This is the reason why the probabilities are represented as complex numbers. After the vector addition, the coefficients must be rescaled to make $|\alpha|^2+|\beta|^2 = 1$ again. The rescaling can be eliminated if α and β are described in terms of angles, using the trigonometry formulas for sums and differences of angles.

Qubits can be manipulated using some elementary logic functions to form quantum circuits. One example is the conditional NOT function, CNOT, which operates on 2-bit qubits, $|xy\rangle$. CNOT is defined as $|xy\rangle$ if x = 0, and $|xy'\rangle$ if x = 1. In other words, the first bit is left unchanged, and the second bit is the exclusive-OR of the two bits.

18.2 Entanglement

Besides superposition, particles can display a second quantum-mechanical property called *entanglement*. A group of particles is called *entangled* if there is a correlation between some property of one particle and the same property of the others. For example, electrons have a property called *spin*. The spin about a specific axis, such as the x-axis, may be correlated among the group of particles. Or, the polarization among a group of photons may be entangled. This entanglement may exist even when the particles are far apart. This allows entanglement to be used for communications.

The process begins by creating an entangled pair of particles. One method is to pass a laser beam through a special type of crystal. This causes some high-energy photons to split into two low-energy photons. Some of those photon pairs will be entangled, although the yield is very low, like one in a billion. The next step is to carry these entangled photons to wherever Sandra and Riva will be transmitting and receiving. For long distances the usual way is by transmitting them over a fiber-optic cable, although they can be carried physically using cavities in a crystal lattice.

When Sandra is ready to send her message, she interacts her photon with some specially prepared ancillary photons called *ancillas*. This interaction causes her photon to take the desired state that she wishes to transmit. This causes Riva's entangled photon, which may be miles away, to take on a complementary state. It used to be imagined that this happened instantaneously, but the change is propagated at the speed of light. Information cannot be transmitted instantaneously, despite what generations of science fiction writers have fantasized.

Finally, Riva measures her entangled photon and determines the 1-bit message — or not, since this is a probabilistic process. This is sometimes called *quantum teleportation* by scientists who grew up reading way too much science fiction. This is supposedly secure against eavesdropping because if Emily measures the photon it will decohere, and this presumably is detectable by Sandra and Riva.

There are two flaws here. (1) Emily may not care if her eavesdropping is detected. As long as she knows the information, it may not matter if Sandra and Riva know that she knows. (2) Emily's goal might not be to gather information; her goal might be to disrupt communications. Emily might not learn the secret battle plans, but neither will Riva. In fact, if Sandra and Riva detect that Emily is eavesdropping, they might use the quantum link less often, which would also be to Emily's advantage.

18.3   Error correction

Since quantum events are probabilistic, quantum computers have a much higher error rate than conventional computers. There must be some means of detecting and correcting errors. In classical computers, there are error-detecting and error-correcting codes. These codes use extra bits to detect discrepancies, for example by adding a parity bit to each byte to detect errors. The parity bit is usually the exclusive-OR of the 8 data bits. That means the 9-bit byte with the error bit will always have even parity. If the parity is odd, that shows an error has occurred, but it does not tell what the error was.

The simplest form of an error-correcting code for conventional computers is the 2-out-of-3 code. There are 3 copies of each bit. If a single-bit error occurs, two of the copies will still have the correct value. If the chance of a single-bit error is, say, 1 in 10^7, then using that common value reduces the chance of an error to 3 in 10^{14}, a vast improvement. Using 3 bits to represent each data bit is expensive, but there are several types of codes, such as Hamming codes and convolutional codes that use fewer extra bits, some of which can detect and correct multibit errors. Error-free communication is absolutely essential in current cryptography where changing even a single bit could render a message unreadable.

 This type of error detection and error correction is impossible in a quantum computer. These codes rely on the ability to copy the value of a bit and check the parity of a code. These cannot be done with qubits, because measuring the value of a qubit causes it to decohere. Efforts to provide quantum error correction generally rely on using extra qubits. The error-detection and -correction qubits may be interspersed with the data qubits in a planar lattice arrangement known as a *surface code*.

So far, quantum error correction is just theoretical. Nobody has yet built a practical device. The need for extra error-correcting bits boosts the number of qubits required for a practical quantum computer. Since quantum error rates are high, practical quantum computers are probably still far in the future. Bear this in mind as you read the descriptions of the various quantum algorithms in the following sections.

18.4   Measurement

Measuring the polarization of a photon is a tricky business. Think for a moment about how you would measure the polarization of a beam of light. You pass the beam through a polarity filter and observe the brightness. Then you slowly rotate the filter until the filtered light reaches maximum brightness. At that point the filter is aligned with the polarization of the beam, and you can measure the angle.

Riva, however, has no such luxury. She is dealing with a single photon. It passes through her filter or crystal, and either she detects a flash or she doesn't. If her filter is not aligned the same way as Sandra's emitter, then her odds of getting the same state as Sandra depends on the relative angle. For instance, if her detector is at a 90° angle to Sandra's emitter, then she has exactly a 50% chance of getting the same value for the qubit.

The solution to this problem is for Sandra to send a burst of photons. Riva can sample these photons, sending them through a variety of filters. She can measure the brightness of each sample by using a light sensor and voltmeter, and calculate an accurate polarization angle. She then measures at that angle and gets the same basis state as Sandra with a very high probability. The ability to use quantum computers for cryptography may ultimately depend on the ability to distinguish tiny gradations in polarization.

18.5   *Quantum 3-stage protocol*

This sets the stage for the *Three-Stage Quantum Protocol* invented in 2006 by Subhash Kak of the University of Oklahoma Stillwater. Kak's 3-stage protocol uses the same 3-message framework as the other three-pass algorithms discussed in sections 16.1, 16.2 and 16.4. In the quantum version, the encipherment operation is rotating the polarization by a random angle around a chosen spatial axis. Sandra and Riva must agree on the axis, otherwise the rotations will not commute. (1) Sandra sends the photon rotated by her random angle φ, (2) Riva rotates the photon by her secret angle ψ and sends back the photon rotated by $\varphi+\psi$, and (3) Sandra applies the inverse rotation $-\varphi$ and sends back the photon rotated by Riva's angle ψ, which Riva removes to read the qubit. If Emily attempts to measure any of the rotated qubits, she has no way of knowing if her detector has the correct angle, and therefore no way to know the probability of getting the correct value.

With this method Sandra and Riva must change their angles frequently, preferably for every bit. Otherwise, Emily can just pick a random angle and attempt to read every message. If Emily's angle is close to the correct angle, then she will get the correct value for 80% or even 90% of the bits. This could be enough to enable her to read the message. With luck she will be able to read about 25% of the messages. Note that it is just as useful for Emily's angle to be close to 180° off, because that would give her the inverses of 80% to 90% of the bits.

18.6   *Quantum key exchange*

There are several algorithms for quantum key exchange, analogous to Diffie-Hellman key exchange. The best-known of these algorithms is *BB84*, named for its inventors Charles H. Bennett of IBM Research and Gilles Brassard of the Université de Montréal.

The algorithm uses 4 qubits to allow for the detection and correction of noise in the communications channel. Any perturbations caused by Emily are simply treated as additional noise in the channel, so they need no further detection or correction.

A corollary of this work is that several loosely entangled particles may be combined to produce a smaller number of tightly entangled particles.

18.7 Grover's algorithm

Grover's cryptographic algorithm is an algorithm for breaking secret key block ciphers such as DES and AES using quantum computers. It was developed in 1996 by Lov Kumar Grover of Bell Labs based on his quantum file-searching algorithm. It treats each evaluation of the encryption function as one read access of an unsorted database. The algorithm reduces the expected number of evaluations from K to $\sqrt{K}$, where K is the number of possible keys. In effect this reduces the key size from n bits to n/2 bits.

Grover's algorithm finds, with high probability, the key k for which $E(k,p)=c$, where E is the encryption function, p is the plaintext and c is the ciphertext. The algorithm requires one block of known plaintext for each such key. A quantum physicist, who may know little about cryptography, might conclude that defending against Grover's algorithm requires doubling the size of all cryptographic keys. That would be inefficient because it would require extra rounds of the block cipher. For example, AES with a 128-bit key uses 10 rounds, while AES with a 256-bit key uses 14 rounds.

A cheaper alternative is to inflate the key size by preceding and following the main encryption with a simple, fast cipher step such as simple substitution. The keys for mixing the two simple substitution alphabets can be up to 1684 bits each (section 5.2) since each alphabet can have 256! possible arrangements, which is close to 2^{1684}. A simple transposition can also help expand the key size, but in a more limited way since 16! is only around 2^{44}. If you choose to use transposition, you can transpose the blocks 2 at a time, since 32! is about 2^{118}, a significant increase in total key size.

Readers of this book will realize that Grover's algorithm also can be defeated by such elementary means as using nulls, using a different key for each block, chaining the blocks or compressing the message. This means that preceding the block encryption by a compression cipher like mixed Huffman (section 4.2.1) achieves both goals, larger key and compression, in a single step. The downside of mixed Huffman is that it changes the block size. It may be wiser to use Huffman substitution (section 10.4) or Post substitution (section 10.5) before and after the block cipher.

18.8 Equations

Before we can discuss the next topic, quantum simulated annealing, we need to discuss equations. Many ciphers can be expressed as systems of equations. The Belaso cipher can be expressed as $C = P+K$, where C is the ciphertext, P is the plaintext and K is the key, all expressed as integers modulo 26. The Hill cipher is a set of linear equations. Ciphers like the Playfair and Two-Square would be expressed as equations in base 5.

18.8.1 *Transpositions*

Transpositions are easily expressed as sets of equalities. For example, the columnar transposition

```
E  X  A      Plaintext:   EXAMPLE
M  P  L      Ciphertext:  EMEXPAL
E
```

can be expressed as $c_1 = m_1$, $c_2 = m_4$, $c_3 = m_7$, $c_4 = m_2$, $c_5 = m_5$, $c_6 = m_3$, $c_7 = m_6$, where the m_i are the plaintext message characters and the c_j are the ciphertext characters.

Logical functions can be converted to numerical equations like this:

not $x \rightarrow 1-x$
x **or** $y \rightarrow x+y-xy$
x **and** $y \rightarrow xy$
x **xor** $y \rightarrow x+y-2xy$

18.8.2 *Substitutions*

Substitutions can be converted to equation form by a 3-step process. First, express each ciphertext bit as a Boolean expression using the bits of the key and the plaintext. For example, consider this substitution that takes a 1-bit key K and a 2-bit plaintext AB to produce a 2-bit ciphertext XY.

K	AB	XY	Boolean inputs
0	00	01	$\bar{K}\bar{A}\bar{B}$
0	01	11	$\bar{K}\bar{A}B$
0	10	00	$\bar{K}A\bar{B}$
0	11	01	$\bar{K}AB$
1	00	10	$K\bar{A}\bar{B}$
1	01	00	$K\bar{A}B$
1	10	10	$KA\bar{B}$
1	11	11	KAB

Here $\bar{K}\bar{A}\bar{B}$ means that K = 0, A = 0 and B = 0, $\bar{K}\bar{A}B$ means that K = 0, A = 0 and B = 1, and so forth. The ciphertext bit X can now be written as $X = \bar{K}\bar{A}B + K\bar{A}\bar{B} + KA\bar{B} + KAB$. There is a similar expression for Y.

18.8.3   Karnaugh maps

Karnaugh maps are used to reduce or simplify these expressions. This is the second step. The concept was invented by Maurice Karnaugh of Bell Labs in 1953. The idea is to picture the set of all possible n-bit inputs as an n-dimensional space, $2\times2\times2\times...\times2$. Fill each cell where the output bit is 1. This is the space for the output bit X. There would be a similar map for Y.

	$\bar{A}\bar{B}$	$A\bar{B}$	AB	$\bar{A}B$
$\bar{K}$				
K				

Notice how the columns in this map are labeled. As you move from one cell to the next going left to right only one bit changes at each step, including the wraparound step from column 4 to column 1. This arrangement is called a *Gray code*. Gray codes were invented by Frank Gray of Bell Labs in 1947. It is easy to construct a Gray code by appending one bit at a time. For example, to extend this 2-bit Gray code to a 3-bit Gray code, first you list the 4 A,B pairs in the order $\bar{A}\bar{B}$, $A\bar{B}$, AB, $\bar{A}B$ with a $\bar{C}$ appended to each pair, then you list them in the reverse order with a C appended to each pair. The C-bit changes only twice, after the fourth code group and after the eighth code group wrapping around to the start.

The Karnaugh maps let you optimize the logic by eye up to about 6 bits, 3 horizontal and 3 vertical, which uses an 8-cell by 8-cell map. Above 6 bits it is best to do it by a program. At each step you add the largest rectangular block that fits within the filled region, and that covers at least one new cell that has not already been covered. Every dimension of the block must be a power of 2, so its volume will also be a power of 2. If there are several blocks of maximal size, choose the one that covers the most cells not yet covered. Continue until all filled cells are covered.

In the K,A,B example, there are two 1×2 blocks in the filled region, namely KA and $K\bar{B}$. Each one covers 2 cells. Since together they cover 3 cells, both are needed. That leaves only the cell $KA\bar{B}$ to be covered. So, the reduced expression for X is $KA+K\bar{B}+KA\bar{B}$.

The third step in expressing the substitution as a set of equations is to replace the **and, or** and **not** functions in these expressions by arithmetic expressions, following the earlier rules.

18.8.4   Intermediate variables

If you attempt to express each ciphertext bit in a complex block cipher like AES as a single expression, the size of that expression will grow exponentially with each round. This problem is sometimes cited as a reason why you cannot use equations to break block ciphers. Horse feathers. This problem can be eliminated by using intermediate variables. Let the outputs of each round be a separate set of variables.

The inputs to the first round, the key, the plaintext and the chain vector(s), are *independent* variables. Any one of these bits may change independently of the others. The outputs of each round, or each stage within a round, are *dependent* variables. This includes the chain vectors for the next block. Their values are completely determined by the values of the independent variables. It is impossible to change one of these bits without changing some of the other variables.

18.8.5 Known plaintext

Suppose Emily has a quantity of known plaintext. For simplicity, let's suppose this is an n-bit message block. Her goal is to use the known plaintext and the intercepted ciphertext to determine the key. Suppose Emily has found an expression for each ciphertext bit in terms of the plaintext, the key and possibly the chain vector. Let the expression for bit i be E_i, and let c_i be bit i of the ciphertext. For any given key K, Emily can measure the difference between the ciphertext that would result from enciphering the known plaintext using the key K, and the intercepted ciphertext by calculating

$$D(K) = (E_1\text{-}c_1)^2 + (E_2\text{-}c_2)^2 + (E_3\text{-}c_3)^2 + \ldots + (E_n\text{-}c_n)^2.$$

When the correct key has been found, D(K) will be 0. Here, D(K) is called the *objective function*, or simply the *score*.

18.9 *Minimization*

Introducing the objective function converts the problem of finding the correct key into a minimization problem. The purpose is to minimize the value of the function D(K). Quantum computers work because the quantum state of the system always tends to the lowest energy state. If the quantum computer can be configured so that qubits, or groups of qubits, represent the values of the variables, and the energy of the system corresponds to the value of the objective function, then the lowest energy state will correspond to the minimum value of the objective function. If this configuration can be accomplished, then quantum computers will be able to solve a wide range of real-world problems, including code-breaking.

To begin, replace the bits in the key with real numbers. Ultimately these numbers must be either 0 or 1, but it is advantageous to allow the variables to get outside the 0–1 range during the search. Start from some initial value such as setting all the bits to .5, or to random values in the 0–1 range, then tweak their values to reduce the value of D(K), trying to get it down to 0.

There are many optimization techniques now used with conventional computers, but let's look at just three. Using these algorithms to find cryptographic keys will require a large amount of known plaintext. At a minimum the known plaintext should be at least 3 times the size of the key.

18.9.1 *Hill climbing*

Hill Climbing, also called *Steepest Descent* or the *Gradient Method*, is the oldest of the optimization methods. The idea is to start at some point P_1 and look at several equidistant points in random directions. Among these points, choose the point P_2 with the greatest improvement, in this case with the lowest value of $D(K)$. Then refine the direction by looking at random points near P_2. The distance from P_2 to any of these points will be considerably smaller than from P_1 to P_2. Call this point P_3. The line from P_1 to P_3 defines the search direction. Finally, find the point P_4 on this line for which $D(K)$ is minimum. The search repeats using P_4 as the starting point. As the search progresses, the sizes of the steps from P_i to P_{i+1} are increased each time an improvement is found, and decreased if there is no improvement.

This form of search works well when the search space is shaped like a single mountain in n-dimensional space, or a large central mountain surrounded by much smaller foothills. It can fail badly in more complex topography with many local optima. In this picture, the darker the color, the better the score.

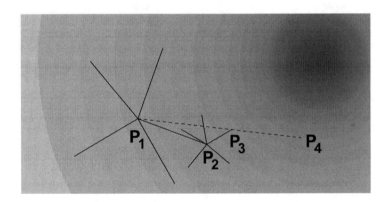

18.9.2 *Mille sommets*

Mille Sommets, or *Thousand Peaks*, is an idea I used for achieving winning scores in a variety of puzzle contests that I entered in the 1970s. I later started to write up this search method for some computer journals, but I got bogged down in trying to characterize the types of objective functions for which this search method was better than other search methods. The method was rediscovered in the 1990s under the name *particle swarm* optimization.

Picture the search space as a mountain range with many peaks, valleys and ridges. Now imagine a fleet of planes flying over the terrain and dropping hundreds of mountaineers by parachute. In other words, there are many simultaneous starting points. These climbers will look at nearby points to see if those spots are higher or lower. There are two variants. (1) You can take only the best one of these points and move the climber there. In this case, if none of the points is better, you reduce the step size and try again. If this fails, say, 3 times in a row, then you bring in a new climber who starts at a random location. (2) You keep several of the points that show improvement. You can think of this as the climbing team splitting up into several parties to try different paths. It is best not to take all of the improved solutions, because that quickly concentrates all of the climbers into just a few areas.

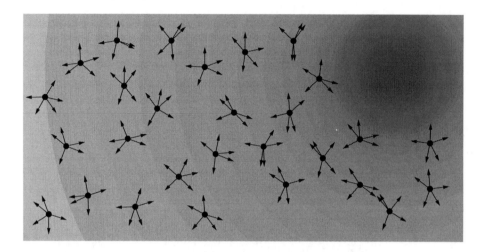

My original idea was to keep all of the solutions in a heap structure so that the top entry is always the worst solution. You take that worst entry and try to improve it. This proved to be inefficient because you spend a great deal of effort improving poor solutions that you eventually discard. Conversely, always choosing the best solution concentrates all the climbers on a single peak. The best strategy is to choose the next climber at random. In the same vein, when a solution yields several improved solutions, it is not always beneficial to choose the best among these. Sometimes it is better to choose randomly among the several improved solutions.

18.9.3 *Simulated annealing*

Simulated Annealing is a popular optimization technique, mainly because it is so easy to implement. You start from a random point in the search space, and look at a nearby point. If that solution is better, then you move to that point with probability B. If that solution is worse, then you move to that point with probability W.

The defining feature of simulated annealing is that you change the probabilities while you search. Initially you set the chance of rejecting a good solution or accepting a bad solution fairly high. Say you reject 40% of better solutions and accept 30% of worse solutions, that is B = .6 and W = .3. Then after a time, say after 1000 steps, you reduce the probability of rejecting a good solution. Perhaps in this second stage you reject 20% of better solutions and accept 15% of worse solutions. After another interval, say another 2000 steps, you might start rejecting only 10% of better solutions and accepting 7% of worse solutions.

This process is called simulated annealing because it resembles the heat annealing process in metallurgy, where the metal is first heated until glowing, and then very slowly cooled. This changes the crystalline structure of the metal to reduce its hardness and increase its ductility and malleability, so it can be worked more easily. In simulated annealing, the high initial probabilities of rejecting better solutions and accepting worse solutions are analogous to the initial high-temperature state of the metal, and the gradual reduction of these probabilities is analogous to the slow cooling of the metal. Descriptions of simulated annealing commonly refer to the several stages in which the probabilities are stepped as *reducing the temperature*.

Let me pass on a few tips from my own experience with simulated annealing:

- It doesn't pay to go too slowly. It is a waste of time to reject 40% of improved solutions, then 39%, then 38%, and so forth. At each stage the acceptance/rejection rate should be somewhere between 1/2 and 2/3 of the preceding rate. For example, 40% in the first stage, then 20%, 10%, 5% and 3%. Or, start at 40%, then 25%, 15%, 10%, 6%, 4%, and finally 2.5%.

- Five stages are usually enough.

- It is a waste of time to start with a 50% acceptance rate. Start between 60% and 75%.

- It does not pay to go to 0%. You will get greater improvement if the last stage accepts 2% to 3% of worse solutions.

- Quit when nothing is happening. You may have planned 1000 trials in each stage, but if you have made 100 tries with no changes, stop.

- Make the percentages depend on the size of the improvement. For example, in the first stage you might accept 60% of the changes that improve the score by 1%, 75% of the changes that improve the score by 2%, and 90% of the changes that improve the score by 3% or more.

- Experiment. Every optimization problem is different. Try varying the number of stages, the number of trials per stage, the rates of changing the probabilities, the step size and the relationship between the degree of improvement and the percentage of acceptance.

The hill climbing, mille sommets and simulated annealing techniques may be freely combined to produce a variety of hybrid methods.

18.10 Quantum simulated annealing

There are several proposed methods for using quantum computers to do simulated annealing. These methods use quantum phenomena such as superposition to perform many searches in parallel. However, every trial requires evaluating the objective function at the chosen point. Quantum computers are not made for evaluating expressions. There are, as yet, no methods for evaluating these functions in parallel by quantum means. The quantum computer can use a conventional computer to evaluate the expressions, but this loses the parallelism. So far, quantum searches have not shown any speed improvement over conventional computer searches.

18.11 Quantum factoring

The strength of the RSA public key cryptosystem rests on the difficulty of factoring large integers. Given two large integers A and B it is easy to multiply them to get the product AB, but it is very hard to reverse that process and determine the factors of a large integer. Factoring a large number has the same degree of difficulty as computing a discrete logarithm (section 16.3), and uses many of the same techniques.

This security may potentially be breached by Shor's algorithm for factoring large numbers. This was the first quantum algorithm ever developed, invented by Peter Shor of MIT in 1994. If the algorithm can be implemented successfully for large integers, either RSA must be abandoned, or the modulus must be made much larger, perhaps millions of bits. So far, using Shor's algorithm, the number 15 was factored into 3×5 in 2001, and the number 21 was factored into 3×7 in 2012. At this rate we may expect the number 35 to be factored into 5×7 some time around 2023.

Humor aside, it may be decades before Shor's algorithm becomes a real threat to the security of RSA.

18.12 Ultracomputers

Quantum computers are not made for evaluating expressions — today. But let's suppose that this is merely a technical problem. Suppose that in time there will be hybrid computers that combine the calculating power of supercomputers with the parallelism of quantum computers. Let's call these *ultracomputers.*

What can Sandra do today to prepare for the time when Emily has an ultracomputer? We can take a cue from the way we defeated Grover's algorithm (section 18.6). We expanded the size of the key to exceed the capability of the algorithm. This can also be done with ultracomputers. We can increase the number of unknowns that the computer needs to deal with beyond whatever capabilities you estimate the ultracomputer may possess. Let us look at two aspects of this, substitution and random number generation.

These algorithms will require extremely large encryption keys. Let's simply accept that in the future world where ultracomputers exist, such huge keys will be manageable.

18.12.1 Substitution

If a substitution is not defined by some mathematical rule, then it can be defined by a substitution table. Each entry in the table is a value known to Sandra, but unknown to Emily. Each table entry can be regarded as a variable in the mathematical sense. Initially, each variable can take on any value. If Emily learns some of these values, that narrows the choices for the other variables, but initially any character could substitute for any other.

Sandra's objective is to overwhelm the capabilities of the ultracomputer. A general polyalphabetic cipher has a 26×26 tableau for hand use, but a 256×256 tableau for computer use. That provides 2^{16}, or 65,536 unknown values. There is, however, no reason why you should limit yourself to 256 rows in the tableau. If Emily has an ultracomputer, it is reasonable that Sandra also would have a computer with high speed and large memory. Sandra could use a tableau of 1024 rows with 10-bit keys, or 4096 rows with 12-bit keys, or even 65,536 rows with 16-bit keys. That requires $2^{24} = 16,777,216$ bytes of internal storage for the substitution table, well within the capacity of current personal computers. Plus, having a 16-bit key for an 8-bit substitution provides a very desirable redundancy. Let's call the 2^{24}-element tableau *Tab24*. Each row of Tab24 has its own mixing key. If this mixing key has 256 bits, then the entire tableau has 256×65536 = 16,777,216 key bits.

It is also feasible for Sandra to use a full bigram table. A 256×256 bigram table using an 8-bit key to select a row (actually, a layer) would require $2^{25} = 33,554,432$ bytes of internal storage. Again, this is feasible today. It would require a much larger computer if the tableau had 65,536 layers and 16-bit keys.

Remember, however, these substitution tables must be kept secret, and they must be fully random. Even if they are generated by some algorithm, it must be absolutely beyond the capability of Emily's ultracomputer to determine the initial state and parameters of the generator. See section 13.13 for some relevant methods.

18.12.2 Random numbers

The methods of section 13.13 are a good start, but to produce a pseudorandom number generator that will stand up to an ultracomputer we combine the concept of a selection generator from section 13.11 with the techniques for refreshing the generator in section 13.15.

The *ultragenerator* UG (pronounced HUGE-ee) uses three arrays, A, B and C. Arrays A and B each contain 65,536 entries that are 24-bit integers. Array C contains 2^{24}, or 16,777,216 entries that are 8-bit integers. The 3 arrays can be initialized from nature photos, as described in section 13.14.2. Sandra and Riva must have identical arrays. The generator produces an 8-bit output in each cycle. Cycle n consists of these steps:

1   Calculate $x = (A_n + A_{n-103} + A_{n-1071})$ mod 16777216, and replace A_n by x.
2   Reduce $x = x$ mod 65536, and set $y = B_x$.
    The output of the UG generator on this cycle is C_y.
3   Replace B_x by $(B_x + B_{x-573} + B_{x-2604})$ mod 16777216.
4   Replace C_y by $(C_y + C_{y-249} + C_{y-16774})$ mod 256.

The subscripts wrap around modulo 65536, or modulo 16777216, as appropriate. There is nothing special about the lags 103, 1071, ..., 16774. I did not test to see whether these values produce especially long periods. With such huge seed arrays, even degenerate periods will be extremely long. You may use any of the combining functions of section 13.1, such as **madd**, or lagged linear addition from section 13.14.1.

When you refresh these random numbers, the two methods of section 13.14 are not sufficient when your opponent has an ultracomputer, but they can be combined to make a strong refresh function. Each time you refresh you will need a new random array R of 65,536 or more 24-bit integers. Let the lengths of A, B, C and R be L_A, L_B, L_C and L_R.

Step 1: Combine R with A, B and C.
Replace A_n by $(A_n + R_n)$ mod 16777216   for n = 1, 2, 3, . . . , L_A.
Replace B_n by $(B_n + R_n)$ mod 16777216   for n = 1, 2, 3, . . . , L_B.
Replace C_{an} by $(C_{an} + R_n)$ mod 256   for n = 1, 2, 3, . . . , L_R.

Here $a = \lfloor L_C/L_R \rfloor - 1$. The notation $\lfloor L_C/L_R \rfloor$, which is read "floor of L_C/L_R", means the greatest integer not exceeding L_C/L_R. For example, $\lfloor 8/3 \rfloor$ is 2 and $\lfloor 9/3 \rfloor$ is 3. The effect of using C_{an} instead of C_n is to spread the bytes of R evenly throughout the C array.

Step 2: Propagate the changes.
Replace A_n by $(A_n + A_{n-229} + A_{n-6141})$ mod 16777216   for n = 1, 2, 3, . . . , L_A.
Replace B_n by $(B_n + B_{n-503} + B_{n-3829})$ mod 16777216   for n = 1, 2, 3, . . . , L_B.
Replace C_n by $(C_n + C_{n-754} + C_{n-25887})$ mod 256   for n = 1, 2, 3, . . . , L_C.

These 2 steps should be repeated 3 or more times. As always, the subscripts wrap around.

By the way, there is no requirement that the size of the C array must be a power of 2. L_C could be, for example, 77,777,777 in which case the A, B and R arrays would need to contain integers modulo 77777777, and the modulus 16777216 would be replaced by 77777777 in the calculations above. The only limits on the size of L_C are the amount of storage you wish to use and the practicalities of distributing such a large key.

These two techniques, substitution and random number generation, can be combined to make any number of block and stream ciphers that will withstand ultra-computers. The next two sections illustrate one cipher of each type.

18.12.3 *Ultrasubstitution cipher US-A*

One great temptation in writing this section is to specify a gigantic block size such as 65,536 or even 16,777,216 bytes. However, simply because the cryptography must change in the era of ultracomputers does not mean that the types of messages will change. Messages of fewer than 100 characters will still be common, and it would be grossly inefficient to pad such messages to a block size of 65,536 bytes or larger.

Let's call the sample ultrasubstitution cipher *US-A*. The US-A cipher operates on blocks of 32 bytes, or 256 bits. The 32 bytes in each block are viewed alternately as 32 individual bytes, and as a 16×16 array of bits. The US-A cipher has 15 rounds, each consisting of 3 steps: a substitution, a row transposition, and flipping the array. The 15 rounds are followed by a final substitution step.

The 16 substitution steps use the Tab24 substitution table, which needs 16 key bits for each character for a total of $16 \times 32 = 512$ bits per round, or 8192 bits for the 15 rounds plus final substitution. The second stage in each of the 15 rounds is to transpose each row. This might be just a cyclic shift of the row, which would require only 4 bits per row, hence 64 bits per round or 960 bits altogether.

A stronger option for the bit transposition would be to have a table of transpositions, say 256 different transpositions, such as key transpositions (section 7.6). Each row of the 16×16 bit matrix would be transposed separately. Each row transposition would be specified by 16 hexadecimal digits, say **5A3F1E940B2D68C7**, meaning that the first bit would go to position 5, the second bit to position A, which is 10, and so forth. The transposition for each row would be chosen from the table by an 8-bit key, requiring $8 \times 16 = 128$ bits per round, or 1920 bits altogether for the 15 rounds.

The third stage in each round is flipping the array of bits, that is, swapping the bit at (i,j) with the bit at (j,i). This is described in section 11.7, and a fast method for flipping the array is given in section 11.2.3. This stage does not have a key.

Let's pull all 3 stages together. The US-A cipher requires 8192 bits for the substitution keys and, say, 1920 bits for the key transpositions, or 10,112 key bits altogether. This is far short of the 65,536 bits needed to resist an ultracomputer. Fear not. Don't forget that the substitution uses the Tab24 tableau, which used 16,777,216 key bits for mixing its 65,536 rows, not to mention however many bits were used to mix the transposition table.

For just that extra layer of strength, I recommend using plaintext-to-plaintext (mode **PP**) block chaining (section 11.10) with the US-A cipher.

18.12.4 Ultrastream cipher US-B

The Tab24 substitution of section 18.11.1 and the pseudorandom number generator of section 18.11.2 can be combined to make a stream cipher of enormous strength. Call it the *US-B* cipher. US-B uses a preliminary step before enciphering to give the plaintext a random look. Let the message be M and its length be L_M. The pre-encipherment step is

$$M_n \text{ is replaced by } (M_n + 19M_{n-1} + 7M_{n-16}) \bmod 256 \quad \text{ for } n = 1, 2, 3, \ldots, L_{M+16}.$$

The extra 16 wraparound iterations serve to doubly hash the first 16 characters of the message. This step adds no cryptographic strength, but it makes it difficult for Emily to recognize when she has found the correct key.

Each 16-bit character key K_n is generated by taking two consecutive output bytes from the random number generator, x and y, and combining them 256x+y. (Or, you could make the C array 16-bit integers, at the cost of doubling the storage needed.) The key K_n is used to encipher message character M_n in the Tab24 substitution table as Tab24(K_n,M_n). That is, the substitute for M_n is taken from row K_n of the tableau.

You may recognize this as a general polyalphabetic cipher using a large tableau and a random key. Recall that the French called the polyalphabetic cipher *Le Chiffre Indéchiffrable*. Using the UG ultragenerator, the US-B polyalphabetic cipher finally is indecipherable, even in the era of ultracomputers. We have achieved Unbreakable Cryptography.

Fun pages

There are four separate ciphers in this diagram, S1 to S4. Each cipher is a simple monoalphabetic substitution. Your job is to identify the type, such as Morse code, and then solve it. Each cipher is written in standard English, using uppercase letters without spaces or punctuation. Each cipher is between 75 and 90 letters long. All begin in the upper-left cell. The first 3 ciphers read left to right across the rows. The last cipher reads clockwise around the border.

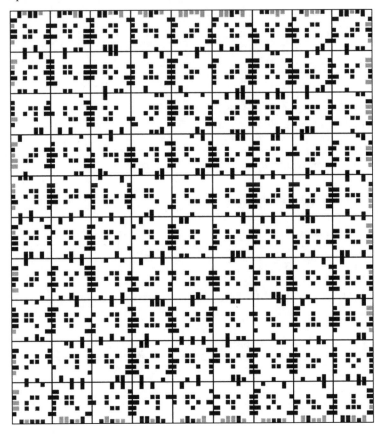

The methods are all described in this book. The only difference is the visual presentation. You need to determine which features are relevant in each cipher, such as height, width, position or color. You can submit your answers for credit by following the instructions hidden elsewhere in this book.

Here are some additional fun ciphers using some of the most popular hobbyist ciphers. These are in standard English, with a few proper names. By convention, the letters are grouped by fives, regardless of the period. If you want lots more ciphers like these, consider joining the American Cryptogram Association at cryptogram.org. You can submit your answers for credit by following the instructions hidden, in plain view, elsewhere in this book. You can find more cryptograms to solve at www.contestcen .com/crypt.htm.

F1: BELASO CIPHER (SECTION 5.8.1)

```
HZRRJ GHEEM ZZHXU AYNLJ GYXCV LRRDL UMIEE PHMET PIPWA ELZOC
BNPBK SHSLV GQVLP AIVBM LVFLB RLOHX BNZUH MATSM LHVTL ZRH
```

F2: VIGENÈRE CIPHER (SECTION 5.8.2)

```
MGGAP AGXCD IFDAZ GZFSH OODAZ HGYBS HZNEB KBQAZ BBCGF ADRDZ
KDVXZ LFTYZ ZGYVW JVXUH MBYBN TLRLZ HGWJZ IJAAI EGUOD ADWAQ
ADAGS ADA
```

F3: COLUMNAR TRANSPOSITION (SECTION 7.2)

```
DUSEL CQTNT ACNLH HLTME AEOEO RLRES TEHNT TAERW AEGLR EDAEE
TEYEH UBSHE OVAAE HRDCI INHWE SFTEA LYWIR TIIOT BITRD AEBRT
NATTT ENLRU HDHTE AE
```

F4: PLAYFAIR CIPHER (SECTION 9.2)

```
EIWDU WJHYL BHFBK NWVKY TKHDE WVBXF GKTDB XXHIY DHNZT ZHDAR
HAYEG SLHXB CIDPH YEIWP HYLYA TCAYE VHUWT XFRBN HWVFL YILEE
LYHYD HIOFB BKTEX D
```

F5: BIFID CIPHER (SECTION 9.6)
The block size is 7, and the subject is horticulture.

```
SZSAPNF RBHBKNV OAABCBI LFIOUUD IRFTPNZ SBLANBA GEPNEAX
ONNAMLB GFRMEUV LIMASUT BFUIEZM CBBRHTI LHROSVV ALSEOET
FHWBTXL UWRBIKL TUHTIEI IFIGOKP
```

F6: ONE-TIME PAD (CHAPTER 14)

For each letter in the message, a random number is generated. If this number is even, X is added modulo 26 to the letter, otherwise Y is added modulo 26.

```
UVTUQ JYRMV GJVSI FTZEL YFIJV JVAVI JZETV YMJKF IGFEA RIZVK
DNRXK ZIJKI TRJXY NHRKV URSFL YWNKK PWNAV YLEUI JIDVF WXFLF
```

The one-time pad, of course, is not a hobbyist cipher. I included this as a fun cipher to make the point that some one-time pad ciphers can be broken in practice. Can you see how to find the values of X and Y without trying all 676 combinations?

F7: GENERAL POLYALPHABETIC (SECTION 5.9.3)

For an extra level of fun there are characters from several languages, and more than 26 characters are used. Each alphabet, however, contains only 26 different characters, and the message is in standard English.

Challenge

These cryptograms are presented as a challenge to readers. The methods are not given. It is your task to determine the method and solve the cryptogram. Sufficient material is given so that a skilled amateur who has determined the method can solve it. In all cases the language is English. The text reads normally and grammatically. No special effort has been made to distort standard English letter frequencies or contact frequencies.

These are all single-step ciphers. There is no mixing of methods, such as combining a substitution with a transposition. These challenge ciphers are rated Three.

C1: CHALLENGE #1
This is a paper-and-pencil cipher. The plaintext consists of 250 uppercase letters without word spaces or punctuation.

```
LIUJE  IETOJ  TUUIL  PICLO  RNETH  SEVWP  GRHJS  OIMTO  ETEPI  CETBE
OOKIP  AHOSA  GRHJO  AHETB  AUTTI  RAHTV  NENAH  TTUTG  ICOSI  YHNFN
ENAAC  OGNET  JTGUA  FNMEE  EHITR  OAHET  SHHNW  TJTOE  EGRHJ  NETHT
GUTTO  HTTRP  HNCOH  OIEIO  AHETB  ALCOW  TJSEV  CMPIC  SIYOF  SPMHN
VNSWE  AOHES  TSSEV  OSAWY  ITDPI  CSLAU  UIYFS  PMHNI  OOSCA  RHTRR
```

C2: CHALLENGE #2
This cipher can be solved by hand, but it is easier with some computer assistance to manage the hexadecimal representation. The plaintext consists of 200 characters in mixed case with word spacing and punctuation.

```
4CB1BAB35A  68C7BAA966  6947C49FA6  F509C4B144  4F48864F03
F3C68DD25E  4F468653A6  F509C4B144  4F48864F04  8F6B537F01
F06829B286  8974E37F12  6F87BDA94F  8D3E24DCF1  F3F8E64D66
02F9C06553  8879B6CF1C  8969B9B286  F529BBAA46  F247B014FE
8975CACF1B  8968E32D41  8969B6D246  0147CDFF12  8D35C9A94D
4F55C4FCE4  6AEA864F0E  B24696D0ED  0E4691D0ED  6C99536B01
F110E33D5D  6C49BAAB42  6AF886495A  4F7424FCE1  8D2AE364ED
F0C7BF2955  8BEBC4CDC2  8954E3295B  4F4FBAB342  8879BAE64D
```

C3: CHALLENGE #3

This cipher can be encrypted and decrypted by hand. The plaintext consists of 180 letters in uppercase without word spacing or punctuation.

```
ZNQXI VAKSG UZONV ALQPR EMYNN WBXXS NPPYB DQPIP KSYEC RXKVE
CGQZI NHIRA NLTSD VGRXH NQVBU EBORK IWOPK SWZIJ EMJTA YNVWD
AUMLP VZIQM XZRMJ CXJKM OMONN UXIPL JWESX CRMJT QRKBL TQVBL
TACSA GUPKC QKIIU LTJFT QPZFB KVBUU V
```

Epilogue

This book has presented some 140 different ciphers, along with innumerable variations. This may bewilder some readers. They may want to know just one thing: "What is the best cipher for me?" That question is complicated, because the book is intended for such a wide range of readers. In this epilogue I hope to provide some useful answers.

Children: There are several ciphers here that children can understand and use. They can use simple substitution ciphers, especially the Caesar cipher. Children particularly like ciphers where the letters are replaced by pictures or symbols, such as ☺︎)♡◉⚓︎🗘🔗✿◆☆. Children also like route transpositions. Teens may like columnar transpositions and the Belaso cipher.

Hobbyists: Hobbyists may enjoy exchanging ciphers with friends, challenging one another to solve them. Ciphers that are best suited for this are simple substitution, polyalphabetic substitution, autokey, running key, Playfair, bifid, diagonal bifid, trifid, Two Square, route transposition, columnar transposition, Bazeries, and fractionated Morse.

I encourage hobbyists to join the American Cryptogram Association, www.cryptogram.org, where they can submit their ciphers for other members to solve, and solve the cryptograms that other members have submitted. Their webpage https://www.cryptogram.org/resource-area/cipher-types/ has a list of the cipher types they accept.

Developers: People who want to develop or invent their own ciphers will find scores of methods here, which can be combined in myriad ways. Letters can be replaced by other letters, or by fixed-length or variable-length groups of bits, Morse symbols, digits in any number base, or elements of a mathematical ring. All of these may be transposed and regrouped. Groups may be substituted again, compressed, multiplied by large integers or by matrices, converted into other number bases, or chained together. Parts of some groups may be used to encipher parts of other groups.

Crypto service providers: Companies that provide encrypted communication services typically use their own proprietary algorithms. They may use any of the techniques just listed for developers, but they must ensure that their cipher meets all of the criteria of chapter 12. The cipher should have large blocks and long keys. It should be highly non-linear, and have good diffusion and saturation.

If the service provider uses a standard algorithm such as 3DES or AES, then the standard cipher should be preceded and followed by a keyed secret substitution or a keyed secret transposition.

Banking: Banking and financial companies are required to use AES for all communications so that they can interchange information among themselves, as well as with the Federal Reserve, the SEC, the IRS and other government agencies. Banks also make wide use of public key cryptography to establish encryption keys and for authentication and verification.

Military and diplomatic: The US military and State Department are mandated by NSA regulations to use 256-bit AES. This has the force of law. This is done on PCs, laptops and even smartphones with an AES chip, or with AES software. However, the military and the intelligence services operate in places and conditions where computers and cell phones may not work, or where a phone equipped with AES would be suspicious or illegal. Possession of any form of cryptographic equipment, literature or work product is illegal in many countries. Additionally, foreign armies and diplomatic corps may distrust any AES hardware or software, all of which can come only from the NSA or suppliers regulated by the NSA.

For these reasons, armies and intelligence services have both codes and ciphers to back up their electronic cryptographic equipment. Hand ciphers suitable for use in combat conditions include diagonal bifid, TwoSquare+1, Two Square ripple, and Playfair TwoSquare. Another idea is to use bifid or Two Square followed by a piecewise transposition.

Large files: For very large files it is much faster to use a stream cipher rather than a block cipher. You generate a stream of pseudorandom numbers and combine this with the data file to simulate a one-time pad. You can use Xorshift, FRand or Gen5 for the PRNG, and you can use **xors**, **adds** or **poly** for the combining function. Or, you could use GenX for both generating and combining.

index